STRATEGIC ASIA 2013–14

STRATEGIC ASIA 2013–14

ASIA IN THE SECOND NUCLEAR AGE

Edited by

Ashley J. Tellis, Abraham M. Denmark, and Travis Tanner

With contributions from

Linton Brooks, Christopher Clary, Gaurav Kampani, Jacob W. Kipp, Jeffrey Lewis, John S. Park, Mira Rapp-Hooper, Robert Reardon, Richard J. Samuels, James L. Schoff, and Ashley J. Tellis

THE NATIONAL BUREAU *of* ASIAN RESEARCH
Seattle and Washington, D.C.

THE NATIONAL BUREAU *of* ASIAN RESEARCH

Published in the United States of America by
The National Bureau of Asian Research, Seattle, WA, and Washington, D.C.
www.nbr.org

ISBN (print): 978-1-939131-28-7
ISBN (electronic): 978-1-939131-29-4

NBR makes no warranties or representations regarding the accuracy of any map in this volume.
Depicted boundaries are meant as guidelines only and do not represent the views of NBR or
NBR's funders.

Design and publishing services by The National Bureau of Asian Research

Cover design by Stefanie Choi

Publisher's Cataloging-In-Publication Data
(Prepared by The Donohue Group, Inc.)

Asia in the second nuclear age / edited by Ashley J. Tellis, Abraham M.

  Denmark, and Travis Tanner ; with contributions from Linton Brooks ...

[et al.].

   p. : ill., maps ; cm. -- (Strategic Asia, 1933-6462 ; 2013-14)

  Issued also as an ebook.

  Includes bibliographical references and index.

  ISBN: 978-1-939131-28-7

  1. Nuclear weapons--Asia. 2. Asia--Military relations. 3. United States--Military relations-
-Asia. 4. World politics--1989- I. Tellis, Ashley J. II. Denmark, Abraham. III. Tanner, Travis.
IV. Brooks, Linton F. V. National Bureau of Asian Research (U.S.) VI. Series: Strategic Asia ;
2013-14.

UA830 .A85 2013

355.02/17/095

Printed in Canada

The paper used in this publication meets the minimum requirement of the American National
Standard for Information Sciences—Permanence of Paper for Printed Library Materials, ANSI
Z39.48-1992.

Contents

An overview of the contemporary nuclear developments in Asia
that are described in this volume and an analysis of the implications
for the United States and its ambitions regarding comprehensive
nuclear disarmament.

Established Nuclear Powers

An assessment of Russia's posture as a major nuclear weapons
state that examines the role of Russian nuclear forces within the
complex security environment of Eurasia.

A consideration of the evolution of China's nuclear posture and the
current status of its nuclear modernization programs that draws
implications for the Asia-Pacific region and the United States.

Latent Nuclear Powers

Special Study

Linton Brooks and Mira Rapp-Hooper
> An analysis of the complex relationships that exist around the
> extended deterrence of China and North Korea, the assurance of
> U.S. allies in Asia of the reliability of U.S. security guarantees, and
> the reassurance of China that the United States does not seek to
> thwart its peaceful rise.

Indicators

Preface

Richard J. Ellings

With six of the world's nine established nuclear powers and most of the near nuclear powers, the Asia-Pacific is the central stage on which the drama of the second nuclear age will be played out. A fundamental shift has taken place in world power, driven by the extraordinary economic growth in this region, of course, but also in part by the broadening distribution of deliverable nuclear weapons among multiple countries there. From the dominance of the U.S.-Soviet competition—the first nuclear age—the strategic environment has transformed into one that is concentrated in Asia rather than Europe and that is fundamentally multipolar rather than bipolar, with a major challenger to the strategic order at its geopolitical center.

Europe is no longer the core of great-power contention. Today, the most powerful nations on earth straddle Asia and the Pacific, and the schisms that divide them—over territory and seas, spheres of influence and buffer states, reunification of important nations, diplomatic issues, economic and trade policies, the nature of political systems and political values, and arms races—are the ones most likely to bring the greatest of the great powers into conflict. America's "rebalance" toward the Asia-Pacific, an objective of multiple administrations, reflects these long-developing realities.

The Asia-Pacific's evolving nuclear environment is a highly dynamic one that can be characterized as skewed or uneven multipolarity. The strategic forces of the members of the nuclear club range in number and quality, but those of the United States, Russia, and China have intercontinental reach, with the latter, for example, having deterrent or potentially "compellent" targets to the north and east, south, southeast, and west. India is developing long-range delivery systems to deter China but remains otherwise focused on Pakistan. Pakistan is consumed with its immediate neighbor but has played a critical role in proliferation with North Korea, which is itself seeking long-range capability. This array of actors—with China in the middle—complicates the strategic calculations of all the nations in the region and particularly two latent members of the nuclear club, Japan and South Korea.

Although the second nuclear age may have its roots in the mid-1960s, it did not begin in earnest until 1998. This was a memorable year, as India and Pakistan tested multiple nuclear devices within weeks of one another, and Iran and North Korea tested ballistic missiles, igniting regional and international fears over clandestine nuclear weapons programs in two rogue nations and sparking debate within non-nuclear neighbors over whether to pursue nuclear capability themselves.

The fears were not unwarranted. Nuclear proliferation has made Asia a more dangerous place. When Pakistan and India came to the nuclear brink by trading tests during their hostilities in 1998, we had a glimpse of the fragility of the second nuclear age. Several factors weaken stability. Regional considerations are preeminent for the nuclear powers of Asia, which have bitter, historical rivalries and often share contiguous borders. Relatively vulnerable nuclear facilities and delivery systems, as well as concerns about conventional military inferiority, may entice some antagonists to consider preemptive attacks. Short distances between potential antagonists put extraordinary pressure on crisis managers, as reaction times to imminent threats or attacks must be close to instantaneous. Misperception or poor intelligence could prove disastrous, producing failed deterrence or the launching of an unneeded counterattack. In most cases of rivalry between regional nuclear powers, global nuclear powers also perceive high stakes.

There are also domestic considerations, particularly in nuclear powers that are dictatorships or otherwise politically illegitimate or unstable. As a consequence of lagging political modernization in North Korea and Pakistan, for example, there seems to be a greater likelihood of "irrational" decision-making, less sophisticated nuclear doctrine, and ineffective safety procedures than in some other nuclear powers. Moreover, with the proliferation of actors, the odds of a nuclear accident or of a weapon falling into the hands of terrorists rise. In sum, politically unstable, deep-seated rivals armed with nuclear arsenals in various stages of technological development and deployment, possessing competing interests, and lacking experience in managing nuclear safety and diplomacy increase the potential for suspicion, misperception, accidents, terrorism, and conflict. In the second nuclear age, complexity does not seem to engender stability.

Not all proliferation is equal. Several democracies face very difficult strategic decisions in view of challenges to the liberal international order and security structure in the Asia-Pacific. At the core of these challenges are uncertainties about the sustainability of American power due to dysfunctions and vicissitudes in the U.S. political system, combined with a persistently weak economic recovery and the pending reduction of military power. Another factor is China's rise, which includes an intensification of Chinese nationalism, periods of domestic instability, the development of ever more capable conventional and nuclear military forces, ongoing assertiveness over disputed areas, and efforts to decouple South Korea and Japan from the U.S. alliance system.

One can see how these dynamics are likely to raise fundamental questions about the long-term viability of American military power in the Western Pacific in the minds of allied strategists and political leaders. Such concerns have surely catalyzed discussions in the halls of power of some American allies and partners about pursuing an indigenous nuclear capability. Geographically vulnerable allies and partners would potentially have a wide range of options available to them, beyond a latent nuclear capacity for the development of flexible nuclear weapons and warfighting strategies that maximize deterrence. While it is not clear that the pursuit of these options would destabilize the region—such proliferation among responsible democratic allies might in fact have a stabilizing effect—it remains incumbent on the United States to reassure its allies not only of its commitment to come to their defense but also of its capability to do so.

This is the thirteenth volume in the series of annual assessments produced by the Strategic Asia Program of The National Bureau of Asian Research (NBR). This year's volume analyzes the role of nuclear weapons in the grand strategies of key Asian states and the impact of nuclear weapons capabilities—both established and latent—in various Asian nations on regional and international relations.[1] By better understanding the contours of this new nuclear system, the United States and its allies can devise strategies to avoid or manage foreseeable crises.

The Strategic Asia Program

NBR developed the Strategic Asia Program to fulfill three objectives, which comport with undertaking analysis of the emerging nuclear dynamics in Asia: (1) to provide the best possible understanding of the current strategic environment in Asia, (2) to look forward five years, and in some cases beyond, to contemplate the region's future, and (3) to establish a record

---

[1] For the purposes of this volume, established nuclear powers are those nations that are in possession of operational nuclear devices. Latent nuclear powers include those nations that possess the technical, material, and financial resources to achieve a relatively rapid nuclear breakout should a decision to that effect be reached. The grouping of nations as established nuclear powers should not be misconstrued as recognition of the legality of their respective nuclear programs under the Nuclear Non-Proliferation Treaty (NPT) but rather as simply a reflection of these nations' possession of operable nuclear devices.

of data and assessments for those interested in understanding the changes taking place in Asia's strategic landscape.

In keeping with this tradition, *Strategic Asia 2013–14: Asia in the Second Nuclear Age* is designed to complement the series' existing work by providing U.S. decision-makers with authoritative analysis on the changing role of nuclear weapons in Asia and the implications for U.S. interests and stability in the region writ large. Through a collection of country-specific studies, divided into sections encompassing Asia's "established" and "latent" nuclear powers, and concluding with a special study analyzing the future of U.S. extended deterrence, this volume explores the complex and interlinking dynamics influencing Asia's current and future nuclear environment. Based on the findings of these chapters, the volume seeks to identify policy options for U.S. decision-makers that will facilitate and strengthen efforts to craft effective policy toward Asia.

Acknowledgments

Past volumes of *Strategic Asia* have examined nuclear issues, but this is the first time an entire volume has been devoted solely to them. Nuclear weapons are re-emerging as a topic of intense importance to the stability and security of Asia, and indeed the entire world. It is imperative that American policymakers, strategists, scholars, and the public understand how these dynamics will shape the international environment of the 21st century, and in particular its most important region—Asia.

Beyond contributing to the wealth of scholarly research in the *Strategic Asia* series, this year's volume also forms the intellectual foundation of NBR's multiyear project entitled *Approaching Critical Mass: Asia's Multipolar Nuclear Future*. This broader project—building on the research contained in these pages—will develop a new theoretical framework through which we can better understand the nature of a skewed multipolar nuclear system, predict the effects of interaction among nuclear powers within that system, and develop cogent strategies for managing the complexities of the second nuclear age.

The Strategic Asia Program encourages research by others. In recent years, the program has expanded its database, which now covers more than two decades of over 70 indicators of national power across 37 countries. The database also includes a cutting-edge geospatial mapping tool incorporating satellite imagery to display current and historical Asian military developments and exercises. Further, the Strategic Asia Program has grown to include a customized briefing series that provides leaders from the government, military, and corporate world with unique insights into current and future trends in Asia. This remarkable expansion is in large part due to the hard work of NBR senior vice president Karolos Karnikis and NBR executive director for strategy and development Enders Wimbush. The success of this program is also due to the tremendous work of Greg Chaffin, Alison Chang, Andrew Kaiser, Naomi McMillen, and many others who have kept NBR's Strategic Asia database updated and accurate.

This year's volume would not have been possible without the hard work and dedication of many individuals. The program's senior adviser—Aaron Friedberg, professor of politics at Princeton University and former deputy national security adviser to the vice president—provided invaluable guidance and support. Dr. Friedberg served as the first research director for the Strategic Asia Program. His scholarship and support are directly responsible for the success of many programs at NBR, including Strategic Asia.

This year marks Ashley Tellis's tenth anniversary as research director of the Strategic Asia Program. His intellectual leadership through this period is an extraordinary achievement and has been absolutely essential to every aspect of the program. As always, the volume's pertinent focus and the high quality of the authors are testaments to his guidance and expertise. Similarly, NBR vice president for political and security affairs Abraham Denmark has been instrumental in driving this and other programs forward.

I would like to express my personal gratitude to Travis Tanner, who after acting as director of the Strategic Asia Program for the past five years leaves us to begin a new chapter of his career with the 100,000 Strong Foundation. Throughout his many years of exemplary service with NBR, Travis embodied the values of leadership, dedication, and scholarship that we as an institution hold so dear. I, along with everyone at NBR, wish him and his family the very best as they embark on this new journey together.

Bridge Award Fellow Andrew Kaiser and project associate Greg Chaffin provided research and logistical support for the production of this year's book and the planning of launch events surrounding its release. NBR's editorial team—Joshua Ziemkowski, publications director; Jessica Keough, managing editor of *Asia Policy*; Jonathan Walton, project manager; and interns Josiah Byers, Rebekah Kennel, Kevin Lee, and Christopher Martin— was responsible for the technical editing, layout, and proofreading of the volume. The program is also grateful to NBR fellows, staff, and interns working behind the scenes to bring this volume to publication. Interns Zane Buckey, Alison Chang, Miriam D'Onofrio, Chris Huang, Christopher Martin, Isaac Medina, Kuni Shimoji, and Taylor Washburn provided research assistance to scholars and contributed in many essential ways, notably by helping produce the "Strategic Asia by the Numbers" section.

Since the inception of Strategic Asia in 2000, NBR senior vice president Michael Wills has worked to ensure its continued success. The Strategic Asia Program—and indeed, many of NBR's endeavors—has also benefitted from the advice and expertise of NBR senior adviser Roy Kamphausen.

This year's scholars have done a tremendous job in providing clear yet technical assessments of the capabilities of Asia's established and latent nuclear powers and the implications for the future of security, stability, and American interests in Asia. For our singular special study, Linton Brooks (former administrator of the National Nuclear Security Administration) and Mira Rapp-Hooper (Stanton Nuclear Security Fellow at the Council on Foreign Relations) wrote an exceptional chapter on the implications for U.S. extended-deterrence guarantees in the Asia-Pacific. We greatly appreciate the diligence of each of our authors in adhering to a very tight production schedule and yet producing such excellent work. These authors join a community of over 125 leading specialists who have written for the series. In addition, the anonymous reviewers, both scholars and government experts, also deserve acknowledgement. Their prompt and thorough evaluations of the draft chapters were essential to ensuring the high quality of the final product.

Finally, I would like to extend my deepest thanks to the Strategic Asia Program's core sponsor, the Lynde and Harry Bradley Foundation, whose support of the program is a testament to its value. The Bradley Foundation has supported the Strategic Asia Program since the beginning and continues to be a critical partner. In addition, the John D. and Catherine T. MacArthur Foundation has generously supported a two-year study of the implications of Asia's multipolar nuclear future for the United States, including several chapters in this year's Strategic Asia volume. I am grateful to our colleagues at these organizations for their commitment to NBR's values and mission in strengthening and informing policy toward the Asia-Pacific region.

Richard J. Ellings
President
The National Bureau of Asian Research

STRATEGIC ASIA 2013–14

OVERVIEW

EXECUTIVE SUMMARY

This chapter examines the logic of nuclear weapons abolitionism, surveys the contemporary nuclear developments in Asia that are described in this volume, and highlights implications for the U.S. and its ambitions regarding comprehensive nuclear disarmament.

MAIN ARGUMENT:

Although the emergence of new nuclear powers in the post–Cold War era has triggered fears of widespread nuclear proliferation and renewed calls for nuclear abolition, the pursuit and development of nuclear weapons in Asia are likely to only increase in the years ahead. Continuing interstate competition, along with the expectations of many states that nuclear weapons will enhance their security and offer deterrence value, ensures that regional arsenals will grow. The U.S., therefore, must prepare for a reality that is quite different from the vision offered by nuclear abolitionism: an Asia that hosts many nuclear powers whose arsenals vary in capacity, architecture, and doctrine.

POLICY IMPLICATIONS:

- Preserving stable deterrence even as the U.S. protects its primacy is the critical obligation facing Washington in the second nuclear age. The U.S. must maintain its deterrent capabilities, which function as the fundamental "backstop" on which the nation's security, the protection of U.S. allies, and the durability of the global order ultimately depend.

- Washington should carefully consider the quantitative requirements of nuclear sufficiency and extended deterrence. The process of nuclear reductions may be reaching—if it has not already reached—the limits of its success.

- The consequences of forfeiting U.S. nuclear superiority vis-à-vis China for the viability of extended deterrence in Asia require careful consideration.

- Despite budgetary challenges, the U.S. must ensure that its nuclear weaponry, force triad, and production complex, including the necessary human capital, do not diminish in capability.

No Escape: Managing the Enduring Reality of Nuclear Weapons

Ashley J. Tellis

The dream of a world without nuclear weapons has once again seduced Washington. To be sure, this quest dates back to the beginning of the nuclear age. But the threats posed by the Soviet Union during the Cold War, the value of extending deterrence for purposes of limiting proliferation, and the recognition that erasing the knowledge of nuclear weaponry was impossible all combined to compel policymakers to treat nuclear weapons as a permanent feature of international politics. The era of bipolar competition also demonstrated that whatever the anxieties produced by nuclear weapons, they contributed toward preserving the longest peace witnessed in modern European history. Consequently, although the horrific consequences of deterrence failure ensured that the search for alternatives to nuclear weaponry never quite disappeared throughout the Cold War, the absence of more durable antidotes to war essentially settled the issue. U.S. policymakers concluded that nuclear weapons were here to stay, and hence their principal task consisted of ensuring that these capabilities remained perpetually safe, secure, and effective enough to preclude any actual use.

The end of the Cold War drastically reduced the prominence that nuclear weapons had once enjoyed. Although all the established nuclear powers still maintained their strategic arsenals, the demise of the Soviet Union conclusively ended the previously intense nuclear competition. It also

Ashley J. Tellis is a Senior Associate at the Carnegie Endowment for International Peace and Research Director of the Strategic Asia Program at the National Bureau of Asian Research. He can be reached at <atellis@carnegieendowment.org>.

eroded, however, the tacit cooperation between the superpowers, which had helped constrain the rise of new nuclear weapons states. This collaboration had been driven largely by the superpowers' mutual interest in limiting the number of nuclear competitors in order to avoid both catalytic crises and any further diffusion of coercive power in the international system. With the decay of these disciplining benefits of bipolarity, the number of countries acquiring or demonstrating nuclear capabilities slowly increased. This evolution has renewed fears that the *arrivistes* will engender—through emulation or reaction—further proliferation in the years to come.

One influential scholar, Paul Bracken, has argued that these trends constitute nothing less than a "second nuclear age,"[1] an era defined by all the instabilities that theorists had long feared would attend nuclear multipolarity. In particular, Bracken notes that the principal achievement of the Cold War—the absence of nuclear weapons use despite intense geopolitical competition—is now at risk. The emergence of many new nuclear states magnifies the problems of stability that were once better contained because they were limited to mainly two states, or at most only a few. Moreover, many of the new nuclear powers are neither wealthy nor overly sophisticated, raising unsettling questions about whether they have the requisite resources to maintain the surety and safety of their strategic assets. Finally, as other scholars have argued, many of the new nuclear nations may lack the cold instrumental rationality that previously defined the nuclear competition between the United States and the Soviet Union, which, if true, could considerably magnify the challenges of achieving stable deterrence.[2]

Whatever the veracity of these conclusions, the emergence of new nuclear powers in the post–Cold War era has triggered fresh fears that the international system might be on the cusp of a cascade of proliferation. Because such a development would acutely stress the stability of deterrence worldwide, many individuals who might have otherwise focused on the challenges of managing stability have now shifted entirely to the pursuit of nuclear abolition. Among the most prominent of these has been the so-called Gang of Four—Henry Kissinger, George Shultz, William Perry, and Sam Nunn—erstwhile Cold Warriors, who in 2007 published the first of several articles highlighting the importance of "reversing reliance on nuclear weapons globally as a vital contribution to preventing their proliferation

---

[1] Paul Bracken, *The Second Nuclear Age: Strategy, Danger, and the New Power Politics* (New York: Times Books, 2012), 3.

[2] For a useful review of these arguments, see Peter R. Lavoy, "The Strategic Consequences of Nuclear Proliferation: A Review Essay," *Security Studies* 4, no. 4 (1995): 695–753.

into potentially dangerous hands, and ultimately ending them as a threat to the world."[3]

While this initiative evoked controversy for many understandable reasons, the vision it advanced received dramatic impetus when two years later President Barack Obama declared his support for the utopian objective of seeking "the peace and security of a world without nuclear weapons."[4] Although all previous U.S. presidents since Richard Nixon had declared fealty to the aspiration of pursuing comprehensive nuclear disarmament—the ambition memorialized in Article VI of the Treaty on the Non-Proliferation of Nuclear Weapons (NPT)—Obama for the first time committed the United States to an abolitionist agenda that seeks not simply to eliminate nuclear weaponry but rather to transform international politics itself in a way that causes these weapons to fundamentally lose their relevance.[5]

This chapter reviews the logic of abolitionism in the context of contemporary nuclear developments in Asia. Toward that end, it is divided into three sections. The first part examines the arguments for nuclear abolition and assesses whether this agenda, now pursued by the United States, might resolve various contemporary challenges in regard to nuclear proliferation. The second part surveys contemporary developments in Asia, as detailed in this volume of the *Strategic Asia* series, and concludes that the current nuclear effervescence in Asia ensures that nuclear weapons will be durably emplaced in the most important sub-system of global politics for a long time to come. Finally, the third part highlights what nuclear developments in Asia imply for the United States and its ambitions regarding comprehensive nuclear disarmament.

Is "Zero" the Solution to Nuclear Proliferation?

The current pursuit of nuclear abolition is driven largely by fears that continued proliferation will likely end up in a catastrophe of unprecedented magnitude. Kissinger, Shultz, Perry, and Nunn, for example, have repeatedly argued that "reliance on nuclear weapons for…[deterrence]…is becoming increasingly hazardous and decreasingly effective"; that "the likelihood that non-state terrorists will get their hands on nuclear weaponry is increasing"; and that "with the spread of nuclear weapons, technology, materials and

---

[3] George P. Shultz et al., "A World Free of Nuclear Weapons," *Wall Street Journal*, January 4, 2007.

[4] Barack Obama, "Remarks by President Barack Obama" (remarks at Hradčany Square, Prague, April 5, 2009).

[5] In addition to the Prague speech referenced above, see Barack Obama, "A Just and Lasting Peace" (Nobel Lecture, Oslo, December 10, 2009); and Barack Obama, "Remarks by President Obama at the Brandenburg Gate" (speech, Berlin, June 19, 2013).

know-how, there is an increasing risk that nuclear weapons will be used."[6] While these claims are debatable, they do not clarify how exactly abolition would produce a better peace beyond the assertion that if nuclear weapons cease to exist, then, by definition, the dangers arising from their presence would cease to exist as well.

To the degree that a positive logic obtains, it often has to be read into claims that are diffuse. The best argument that has been proffered for the benefits of abolition—which is not to say that it is necessarily a good argument—is that nuclear disarmament would reduce the incentives of currently non-nuclear states to acquire nuclear weapons themselves. This claim essentially hinges on the belief that if the existing nuclear powers were to give up their nuclear weaponry, they would eliminate a key source of threat that might be experienced by other states, thereby arresting the momentum toward further proliferation. The legal variant of this idea is anchored in the expectation that if the established nuclear states demonstrate credible progress toward denuclearization, ending ultimately with abolition, they will have fulfilled their Article VI commitments under the NPT. By doing so, established nuclear states will have denied the non-nuclear states any incentives to rethink their own obligations not to acquire nuclear weaponry.

While claims made on these expectations are plausible, they are ultimately not persuasive. The assertion that the current nuclear powers would reduce the intensity of the threats felt by non-nuclear states if they divested themselves of their nuclear arsenals is tenable only if all nations seeking nuclear weaponry did so because they were threatened by other states possessing nuclear weapons. The evidence in many cases, however, suggests otherwise. Because nuclear weapons are such splendid instruments of politics, the motivations for acquiring them are not surprisingly quite diverse: some nations may seek nuclear weapons as an antidote to conventional threats, not necessarily nuclear ones; other states could be moved to acquire nuclear capabilities to bolster the survival of their governing regimes versus various internal challengers or as instruments of strategic bargaining vis-à-vis the larger international system; and still others may seek nuclear weaponry in order to demonstrate technological sophistication or achieve national prestige, considerations that have little to do with external threats. The expectation that forgoing nuclear weaponry would thus inexorably stymie further proliferation therefore may be optimistic. This conclusion is corroborated by the fact that the world's largest nuclear arsenals have been

---

[6] Shultz et al., "A World Free of Nuclear Weapons"; and George P. Shultz et al., "Deterrence in the Age of Nuclear Proliferation," *Wall Street Journal*, March 7, 2011.

progressively contracting in size without much impact on the proliferation trends so feared by the advocates of abolition.[7]

In this context, the contention that an elimination of nuclear weapons is necessary for the P5 countries (the five permanent members of the UN Security Council) to authenticate their Article VI obligations under the NPT is both spurious and dangerous: it is spurious because, contrary to what non–nuclear weapon states may now insist, the NPT does not entail any bargain whereby the recognized nuclear powers would give up their arsenals as the price for non-nuclear states continuing to eschew the acquisition of nuclear weapons; and it is dangerous because the continued assertion of such a linkage not only obfuscates the negotiating record leading up to the NPT but also, and more importantly, entrenches false expectations about an untenable end state that cannot be realized without engendering perhaps even greater hazards to international peace.[8] The best that can be said about the political value of denuclearization, therefore, is that continued progress here may provide the established nuclear powers with greater legitimacy in the context of their crusades against nuclear proliferation. Progress toward denuclearization arguably strengthens the perception that the nuclear weapons states occupy "the moral high ground" if their campaigns against incipient proliferators unfold against the backdrop of compliance with their own undertaking to one day eliminate nuclear weaponry.[9]

If one version of the consequentialist argument for nuclear abolition—reducing the incentives of non-nuclear states to acquire nuclear weapons—fails on both logical and empirical grounds, a second version, which argues the imperative because of fears that nuclear use will be more likely in the future, unfortunately does not fare much better. To the degree that this claim entails more than the simple probabilistic expectation that the risks of nuclear use rise as the number of nuclear weapon states increases, it appears in the writings of the Gang of Four and others in three different versions. Sometimes it materializes in the following assertion:

> It is far from certain that we can successfully replicate the old Soviet-American "mutually assured destruction" with an increasing number of potential nuclear enemies world-wide without dramatically increasing the risk that nuclear weapons will be used. New nuclear states do not have the benefit of years of step-by-step safeguards put in effect during the Cold War to prevent nuclear accidents, misjudgments or unauthorized launches. The United States and the

---

[7] Robert S. Norris and Hans M. Kristensen, "Global Nuclear Weapons Inventories, 1945–2010," *Bulletin of the Atomic Scientists* 66, no. 4 (2010): 77–83.

[8] Christopher A. Ford, "Debating Disarmament: Interpreting Article VI of the Treaty on the Non-Proliferation of Nuclear Weapons," *Nonproliferation Review* 14, no. 3 (2007): 401–28.

[9] Michael E. O'Hanlon, *A Skeptic's Case for Nuclear Disarmament* (Washington, D.C.: Brookings Institution Press, 2010), 3.

Soviet Union learned from mistakes that were less than fatal. Both countries were diligent to ensure that no nuclear weapon was used during the Cold War by design or by accident. Will new nuclear nations and the world be as fortunate in the next 50 years as we were during the Cold War?[10]

At other times, the claim is manifested in fears that "in today's war waged on world order by terrorists, nuclear weapons are the ultimate means of mass devastation."[11] And finally, and most intriguingly, the fear of prospective deterrence failure is attributed to the rise of new warfighting phenomenologies, such as cyberwarfare, which "could have disastrous consequences if the command-and-control systems of any nuclear weapons state were compromised by mischievous or hostile hackers."[12]

The first argument in this group of claims essentially derives from the anxiety that the emerging nuclear powers will not be able to develop and maintain, for either financial or technological reasons, all the safeguards that the two superpowers slowly and assiduously put in place during their lengthy Cold War. This suspicion may well turn out to be true. But to infer from this the increased likelihood of inadvertent, mistaken, or accidental nuclear use is premature, because the argument fails to take into account the radically different nuclear postures maintained by emerging proliferators in contrast with the superpowers. Because the new nuclear states have as a rule not configured their arsenals either for nuclear warfighting or for the conduct of prompt operations, the dangers of unintentional nuclear use are quite different from the challenges the United States and the Soviet Union faced from each other.[13] Even if this were not the case, however, it is highly unlikely that the emerging nuclear powers would give up their arsenals simply because of the presence of such dangers—so long as nuclear weapons are perceived to be essential to either national security or regime survival. In the face of such necessities, no modern-day proliferant would sacrifice the benefits of nuclear possession merely to avoid its accompanying risks, no matter what any other nation did in regard to eliminating nuclear weaponry.

As arguments for abolition, threats of nuclear terrorism do not appear to be particularly persuasive either. Despite the empirical evidence for terrorist groups seeking nuclear weapons being unclear, the dangers pertaining to nuclear security must be addressed seriously. Any state that possesses nuclear weapons would recognize the need to protect these capabilities as being in

---

[10] Shultz et al., "A World Free of Nuclear Weapons."

[11] Ibid.

[12] George P. Shultz et al., "Toward a Nuclear-Free World," *Wall Street Journal*, January 15, 2008.

[13] Jordan Seng, "Less Is More: Command and Control Advantages of Minor Nuclear States," *Security Studies* 6, no. 4 (1997): 50–92.

its own self-interest.[14] If there are exceptions to this rule, these challenges must be addressed through diplomacy, technical and financial assistance, and even coercion if necessary. But, again, it is unlikely that the dangers of terrorist access to nuclear weapons can be extinguished by attempting to abolish these capabilities because none of the possessor states would accept such a solution as long as nuclear weapons continue to serve critical purposes of high politics.

A similar conclusion obtains regarding the dangers posed by new warfighting phenomenologies. The challenges of maintaining stable deterrence have undoubtedly become more complex over time, but the threats posed by cyberwarfare and the like are a continuation of the problems faced by the superpowers during the Cold War. The rise of cybertechnology today admittedly intensifies the hazard of "catalytic war"—a crisis between two powers caused by "the mischief-making of some third party"[15]—but all nuclear weapon states will respond to this threat by strengthening their command-and-control systems against external intrusion. No matter how effective these actions may be, nuclear weapons states are more likely to emphasize such investments, given the value of nuclear weapons to their national strategies, than they are to abandon these crown jewels merely because of uncertain dangers that lurk in the international system.

The critical problem with abolition as a solution to all these nuclear risks is not that the hazards highlighted by its advocates are unreal. Any failure of deterrence that results in mass casualties would undoubtedly be horrific. But the presence of such perils does not by itself inevitably produce these unnerving consequences. As the theorists and moralists of yesteryear understood all too well, the use of nuclear weapons in an interstate context has been avoided—no matter the number of nuclear powers or the infirmities of their arsenals—because, when all is said and done, the scary effects of any nuclear employment concentrate the mind in a way that few other instruments of war can. Nuclear dangers associated with nonstate actors are admittedly not susceptible to similar discipline. Yet precisely because their human and political consequences can be just as devastating as interstate nuclear war, state managers are likely to be extraordinarily careful where control of their nuclear assets is concerned, given that they (and their countries) could pay a high price for any negligence that produces nuclear devastation. This same calculus also helps limit the risks posed by different forms of nuclear accidents.

---

[14] Keir A. Lieber and Daryl G. Press, "Why States Won't Give Nuclear Weapons to Terrorists," *International Security* 38, no. 1 (2013): 80–104.

[15] Arthur L. Burns, "The Rationale of Catalytic War," Princeton University, Center of International Studies, Research Monograph, no. 3, 1959, 4.

None of these conclusions hold with certitude, however. The abolitionists are right to emphasize that even the best system of nuclear deterrence is afflicted by various risks that make perpetual success uncertain. But what is most troublesome about their solution—the complete and irrevocable elimination of all atomic weapons—is that for all the infirmities of nuclear deterrence, its deliberate excision could prove to be just as problematic for assuring international peace and security. After all, the pre-nuclear era also witnessed mass carnage on an unbelievable scale. And so long as the deep structure of global politics continues to be defined by an unrelenting struggle for power among states, there is every likelihood that the elimination of nuclear weapons would only end up making the world safe for conventional war—with the gargantuan casualties that would inevitably result, albeit over longer durations. Recognizing just this fact, one perceptive analysis concluded that "the apparent robustness of nuclear deterrence over the decades presents a high threshold for any alternative that seeks to replace it. Embracing an alternative, therefore, requires highly favorable assessments of its effectiveness,"[16] which is something that no advocate of nuclear elimination, or for that matter any other alternative to nuclear deterrence, has yet been able to demonstrate.

What complicates things further is that the abolition of nuclear weapons, even if it could be achieved, may not subsist as a permanent condition because the sheer potency of these instruments would constantly tempt states to recreate them. As Thomas Schelling once insightfully noted, because the knowledge of nuclear weaponry cannot be erased, a world of former nuclear powers would be little other than a world of latent nuclear powers.[17] Given the continuing rivalries of international politics, previous nuclear arms races would be replaced by new sprints to breakout because whichever state succeeded in reconstituting a nuclear arsenal first would have tremendous advantages with respect to either blackmailing its rivals or preemptively destroying their nuclear infrastructure. If these are some of the instabilities that would ensue, even a successful elimination of nuclear arsenals globally would not provide the "increasing measure of assured security for all nations" that the advocates of nuclear abolition otherwise sensibly seek.[18]

The last argument for eliminating nuclear weapons comes from a radically different direction and is driven by the recognition that these instruments remain the final handicap preventing the United States from being able to project its power effortlessly against various adversaries. This

[16] Dallas Boyd and James Scouras, "Escape from Nuclear Deterrence: Lessons for Global Zero from the Strategic Defense Initiative," *Nonproliferation Review* 20, no. 2 (2013): 348.

[17] Thomas C. Schelling, "A World Without Nuclear Weapons?" *Daedalus* 138, no. 4 (2009): 126.

[18] Shultz et al., "Deterrence in the Age of Nuclear Proliferation."

argument for abolition is not driven by concerns about international stability or the risks to world peace. Rather, it arises from a purposive calculation of what stands in the way of entrenching American hegemony globally and, as such, constitutes an imperialist justification for nuclear disarmament. At its core, it is grounded in three critical insights. First, although the United States possesses the most puissant nuclear arsenal in comparison with all other nations, the differences in the relative sophistication of various nuclear weapons do not yield greater-than-proportionate political benefits in comparison with their absolute performance. As a result, no matter how technologically innovative the U.S. nuclear weapons complex may be, it cannot produce weapons that allow Washington to freely neutralize the strategic reserves of its rivals. Second, the enormous damage that even small numbers of relatively primitive nuclear weapons can inflict in highly compressed timeframes makes them far more effective as defensive instruments of deterrence than as offensive instruments of warfighting. This implies, from a political rather than a technical perspective, that adversaries possessing even simple nuclear weapons can prevent the United States from applying coercive power against them far more effectively than the United States can employ its sophisticated nuclear weapons to neutralize their deterrents. Third, and finally, the growing effectiveness of many conventional weapons in the U.S. arsenal now permits the United States to substitute these capabilities in many (though not all) missions that previously could be executed only by nuclear weapons. As such, its need to procure nuclear weapons for many combat missions has become less pressing.

These three insights combine to argue for the comprehensive elimination of all nuclear weapons worldwide because these capabilities alone, in the possession of others, stand between the United States and its ability to apply military power against various adversaries successfully. As Secretary of Defense Les Aspin argued in 1993, "nuclear weapons can still be the equalizer against superior conventional forces. But today it is the United States that has unmatched conventional military power, and it is our potential adversaries who may attain nuclear weapons. We're the ones who could wind up being the equalizee."[19] Given this reality, a world without nuclear weapons would indeed be a world where U.S. power could be projected with impunity— and hence nuclear abolition ought to be a goal pursued by the United States resolutely and with alacrity.

There is much that is appealing in this rationale for nuclear disarmament from the viewpoint of U.S. interests. But what makes it so utterly attractive to the United States is exactly what prevents it from being actualized: the

---

[19] Les Aspin, "The Counterproliferation Initiative" (speech at the National Academy of Sciences, Washington, D.C., December 7, 1993).

stake that all other nations have in avoiding victimization by Washington. Because they recognize that they would be severely disadvantaged vis-à-vis conventional U.S. military power, which is likely to remain unchallenged for some time to come, both the peer competitors of the United States and its weaker adversaries are certain to reject its entreaties for comprehensive denuclearization. Whatever the benefits to international peace accruing from such an outcome, the dangers to these states' particular interests are exceptionally high. As a result, they are unlikely to contribute toward achieving a nuclear-free world, even if their rhetoric sometimes hews to the contrary. Thus, even the most attractive justification for nuclear disarmament from the perspective of the United States ends up with little chance of being fructified.

This pessimistic assessment of the prospects of nuclear abolition should not come as a surprise to U.S. policymakers; hence, it is indeed odd that statesmen like the Gang of Four and leaders like President Obama nonetheless peddle such escapist solutions at this juncture in international politics. Clearly, they have been moved greatly by their fears of the dangers ensuing from further proliferation. The desire to secure legitimacy for the U.S. campaigns against emerging nuclear states such as North Korea and Iran has provided further motivation, while the president's own yearning to buttress his legacy as a transformational figure has probably provided some impetus for his support of this utopian goal. But whatever the motivations may be, the fact remains that a genuine "global zero," understood as a world without nuclear weapons, not only is unattainable right now and may never be realized in the future but also, and more importantly, should not be pursued so long as the deep ordering principles of international politics remain unchanged. To chase such a chimera amid continuing interstate competition and the prospect of more nuclear powers worldwide is more than merely a fool's errand; it is actually a dangerous distraction from the more urgent tasks of ensuring that nuclear weapons remain reliable, survivable, safe, and secure—and thereby preclude actual use.

Attending to these tasks requires greater attention to the more mundane elements laid out both in Obama's visionary speech in Prague, such as securing fissile materials, revamping the architecture of international civilian nuclear cooperation, and strengthening the NPT, and in the Gang of Four's manifestos, such as reducing alert rates of existing nuclear forces, creating international nuclear fuel banks, and phasing out highly enriched uranium from civil commerce and research facilities. Even more importantly, however, it requires renewed focus on U.S. deterrent capabilities because, although these remain largely outside the public eye, they nevertheless still function as the fundamental "backstop" on which the nation's security, the protection of U.S. allies, and the durability of the global order ultimately depends. There is growing evidence that the lack of attention to the U.S. nuclear arsenal has spawned unsettling problems in many areas, ranging from the health of the production complex to the management of the weapons themselves. This is all the more critical because, as the evidence in this volume summarizes, nuclear weapons will remain a growth industry in large quadrants of Asia for quite some time to come.

Nuclear Weapons Are Alive and Well and Thriving in Asia

This volume of *Strategic Asia* examines the role of nuclear weapons in the grand strategies of key Asian states and their impact on regional and international stability. Although previous editions have touched on nuclear weapons, this is the first time since the inception of the series that an entire volume has been dedicated to reviewing the character and impact of various Asian nuclear programs.

The reasons for this interest are almost self-explanatory. The challenges posed by the nuclear programs in North Korea and Iran in recent years have highlighted the problems confronting the global nonproliferation regime and especially its centerpiece, the NPT. It is often easy to assume that because this near-universal treaty still enjoys strong international support, all its signatories will consider themselves bound by its obligations in perpetuity. Yet, as Bismarck might have said, "every treaty contain[s] an unwritten clause, *rebus sic stantibus*,"[20] meaning that its responsibilities compel only so long as the original circumstances that justified accession obtain. The North Korean and Iranian cases demonstrate all too clearly the limitations of legal fundamentalism, drawing attention instead to the centrality of power politics. Whatever pledge may once have been made to eschew nuclear weapons, a state will embark on a quest to acquire them if it believes that their possession promises to improve its security.

Because no nation can predict how its future strategic environment might change, promises to forgo nuclear weapons recorded in the NPT will always be contingent assurances. Breaking such solemn commitments is invariably a costly act; hence, it is unlikely that states will do so unless they judge the gains to be worth the consequent aggravations. The United States and the international community more generally should, therefore, strengthen the legal instruments of nonproliferation to the degree possible because they help deter casual exits from the NPT. But these actions must

---

[20] A.J.P. Taylor, *Bismarck: The Man and the Statesman* (New York: Vintage Books, 1967), 192.

be implemented without any illusions that even such successful treaties will suffice to keep countries from acquiring nuclear capabilities if their supreme national interests demand otherwise.

Given the contested geopolitics of Asia, which is defined by several enduring rivalries, many unresolved territorial disputes, significant local power transitions, and now the continent-wide anxieties provoked by the rise of China, it is not surprising that nuclear weapons have retained their critical importance thanks to their unique capacity to inflict "high-leverage strategic harm" unmatched by any other kind of military instrument.[21] Nuclear weapons can inflict enormous destruction in a very short period of time; they can threaten the vital concentrations of an adversary's national capabilities, even in the presence of effective frontier defenses; their efficacy, for the most part, does not hinge on their relative sophistication, even if a competitor possesses comparable capabilities; their susceptibility to successful defense is low; and the ease with which they can be tailored to achieve specific operational effects is higher than other weapons of mass destruction. All these attributes combine to make nuclear weapons splendid instruments of deterrence, tools that undermine the hierarchy of international power insofar as their comparatively low costs enable even weaker states to effectively defend themselves against otherwise more powerful rivals.

While the importance of nuclear weapons has receded in Europe—the cockpit of the Cold War—Asia's continuing economic dynamism, which now makes it the center of gravity in the global system, has produced a renewed interest in nuclear weaponry. Many of the states in the region have come to view these devices as indispensable for the preservation of their security. Uncertainties over the future of U.S. hegemony and, by implication, the reliability of U.S. extended deterrence only perpetuate the interest in nuclear weapons in various quarters of Asia, including in countries that have formally renounced the acquisition of these instruments but nonetheless possess sufficient latent capabilities to permit their rapid procurement should circumstances demand.

At least in Asia, therefore, the bold vision of a world without nuclear weapons—the ambition that Obama articulated in Prague in 2009 and reiterated in Berlin more recently—seems very far away, if not downright evanescent. The myriad nuclear challenges already present attest to that fact. Within the next year, for instance, the United States and its allies will likely have to make some hard decisions about their response to Iran's evolving nuclear program if a satisfactory diplomatic resolution cannot be reached.

---

[21] This concept comes from the testimony and prepared statement of Henry D. Sokolski, *Proliferation and Regional Security in the 1990s*, U.S. Senate, Committee on Governmental Affairs, 101st Congress, 2nd Session, October 9, 1990, 28–41, 65–88.

North Korea's nuclear activities, undertaken in clear violation of Pyongyang's NPT obligations, continue apace, challenging not simply an important component of the global order but equally the security of South Korea and Japan, the most important U.S. treaty allies in East Asia. Fearful of U.S. nuclear superiority, China has embarked on a systematic modernization of its own nuclear arsenal—a development that has spurred an Indian counter-response, which in turn has reinforced many troubling components of Pakistan's own nuclear program. Russia, struck by a continuing economic malaise amid its inextinguishable great-power ambitions, has deepened its dependence on nuclear weapons for security vis-à-vis both the United States and China and is actively exploring new roles for these devices in the context of an ever-evolving warfighting strategy. Even non-nuclear states are not immune to these developments: every major Asian state in this category—Japan, South Korea, Taiwan, and Australia—has enormous latent nuclear capabilities that would permit rapid nuclearization should a political decision be reached to that effect. And even countries that ordinarily would not be imagined as interested in nuclear weapons, such as Saudi Arabia, are now either demonstrating some interest in their acquisition or slowly acquiring the wherewithal that might make their acquisition possible in the distant future.

All in all, then, nuclear weapons in different forms—either in established armories or in latent capacity or in embryonic potential—are alive and well and thriving in Asia. A close look at their presence in the region and their impact on strategic stability, therefore, yields benefits from both a scholarly and a policy perspective. The chapters that appear in this volume are divided into three broad sections: the first part focuses on the programs of "acknowledged" nuclear powers, namely Russia, China, India, and Pakistan; the second part focuses on states with significant "latent" nuclear capacities of different kinds, such as North and South Korea, Iran, and Japan; and the third part contains, as all previous volumes of *Strategic Asia* have done, a special study, this time on the challenges facing U.S. extended deterrence in Asia amid the nuclear transformations occurring elsewhere in the region.

Where the acknowledged nuclear powers are concerned, each country chapter analyzes two broad issues in some detail: (1) the character of the nuclear weapons program at both a technical and a societal level, and (2) the impact of the program on strategic stability in a regional and international context along four specific dimensions whenever possible: deterrence stability, crisis stability, arms-race stability, and political stability, broadly understood to include diplomatic consequences and the prospects for arms control as well as the manipulative utility of nuclear weapons for signaling, escalation, and crisis management.

The structure of the chapters in the second section dealing with latent nuclear powers is slightly different. Here each chapter focuses on three central issues: (1) the nature of latency as manifested in each country's resident national capabilities in the areas of nuclear infrastructure, fissile materials, advanced computation, delivery systems, national research and development infrastructure, and human capital in the nuclear realm, (2) the external and domestic political, strategic, economic, and technological factors that could prompt a potential nuclear power to transform its latent capacity into actual nuclear weapons, and (3) the impact on the regional and global system, to include the nonproliferation regime, of a decision by the particular country to go nuclear.

Taken together, all the chapters collected in this volume confirm the expectation that the reliance on nuclear weapons witnessed in Asia will only increase in the years ahead. This reality not only will stress U.S. deterrent capabilities in challenging ways but also will make the recent calls for nuclear abolition even more anachronistic as an actionable agenda for public policy.

A closer look at the nuclear programs in Asia suggests that, in fact, there are seven different types of relationships where dependence on nuclear weapons is concerned. Of all the countries relevant here, only the United States comes closest to genuinely being a post-nuclear power in that it requires nuclear weapons principally because other states continue to possess them. In most, though not all, cases, Washington could defend its interests through its conventional military capabilities. Hence, more than any Asian state, the United States can—at least in theory—contemplate the divestiture of its nuclear weaponry.

Russia and China, in contrast, remain good examples of established nuclear powers that are highly dependent on nuclear weapons for protecting their security. Accordingly, both maintain arsenals of significant size, diversity, and technological sophistication, although in purely comparative terms Russian nuclear capabilities are larger and more complex than China's.

Of Asia's emerging nuclear powers, Pakistan and the Democratic People's Republic of Korea (DPRK) are likewise highly dependent on nuclear weapons for security. However much outsiders may feel that the sense of threat experienced by these countries is exaggerated, security managers in both states remain utterly convinced that only nuclear weapons stand between them and external domination. Hence, Pakistan and the DPRK are unlikely to ever forgo these capabilities, irrespective of what happens elsewhere in the world.

Odd as it may seem, India, in contrast, is an emerging nuclear power with a low dependence on nuclear weapons because it possesses sufficient conventional military power relative to both its principal adversaries,

Pakistan and China. Even though this balance could deteriorate vis-à-vis the latter, New Delhi feels compelled to maintain its nuclear arsenal more because other states possess these weapons—and hence could subject India to strategic blackmail—and less as instruments of active defense.

The latent nuclear states in Asia are of two kinds as well. The states that are highly dependent on nuclear weapons for security include Iran, Japan, the Republic of Korea, and, with qualifications, Taiwan. Policymakers in all these countries perceive significant nuclear threats to their security, all have the capacity to acquire nuclear weapons if they choose to, and, with the exception of Iran, all rely presently on the extended deterrence provided by the United States in lieu of developing their own arsenals.

Currently, the sole example of an Asian state possessing latent nuclear capabilities, but with an arguably low dependence on nuclear weaponry, is Australia. Thanks to favorable geography and the benefits of U.S. extended deterrence, Australia enjoys the best of both worlds: distance from the most significant threats, yet protection by the globe's most capable power. Should technology or politics ever alter these realities, however, Australia could develop significant nuclear capabilities. The country has a fascinating, though not well-known, history of entanglement with nuclear weapons.

Finally, a large—and growing—number of Asian (to include Middle Eastern) states possess embryonic nuclear potential either because they already have some elements of the nuclear fuel cycle, especially research or power reactors, or because they are embarked on advanced plans to invest in nuclear energy. The United Arab Emirates, Vietnam, Indonesia, and Saudi Arabia are good examples of countries in this category.

The seven detailed studies in this volume elaborate at length on the diversity of the motivations, capabilities, and implications of Asia's nuclear ferment. They leave no doubt that the principal challenge facing the international community will not be nuclear abolition of any kind but rather preserving strategic stability against the backdrop of a rising demand for nuclear weaponry.

Jacob Kipp's assessment of Russia's nuclear capabilities exemplifies this conclusion perfectly. Kipp describes how Moscow's current nuclear arsenal, both in its architecture and its numbers, reflects many of the capabilities it inherited from the Soviet Union. Unlike those heady days, however, when the Soviet nuclear forces and conventional military were at parity with, if not superior to, those of the West, the weakened Russian economy during the last two decades has resulted in a dramatic enervation of the country's conventional forces. This occurs at a time when Moscow still has serious geopolitical disagreements with NATO, and the United States in particular, while deeply fearing China's rising power despite being unable to acknowledge this apprehension.

In such circumstances, Russia's dependence on nuclear weapons has only intensified. These instruments remain the strongest assurance of its continued great-power status, while providing it with credible protection against the threats posed by new precision-strike weapons that may be employed in tandem with missile defense. Because nuclear weaponry still remains an arena of Russian comparative advantage, this industry continues to receive high budgetary priority, with military planners in Moscow contemplating ever more exotic doctrines for how such arms may be employed in support of Russian interests. Given the importance of nuclear weapons to Russia, its leaders—unsurprisingly—have dismissively rejected all ideas of nuclear abolition and become increasingly resistant to even considering further reductions if advanced conventional weapons, missile defenses, and the arsenals of other nuclear powers are not included in the negotiations.

Jeffery Lewis's study of China's nuclear modernization is in many ways an exercise in contrast. Unlike the Russian arsenal, Beijing's strategic capabilities historically have been small, more primitive technologically, and modest in what they sought to achieve. But these capabilities have nonetheless been just as important to China insofar as they validated its great-power status and simultaneously provided it with a sure last line of defense against multiple, and more powerful, adversaries that to this day include both Russia and the United States. Because security concerns pertaining to the latter have increased recently, while worries about the former have never quite disappeared, China is currently in the midst of a comprehensive program of nuclear modernization, including improvements to its delivery systems, warhead storage facilities, missile bases, and command-and-control network. The size of China's arsenal is increasing as well, and its traditional posture, which centers on fielding de-mated systems, is also likely to undergo a change when the sea-based leg of its deterrent becomes operational.

Accordingly, Lewis notes that China could be on the cusp of a significant transition in how it manages its nuclear arsenal. His analysis suggests, however, that the range of threats Chinese nuclear forces are intended to deter has not decreased. Although coping with U.S. power remains central to Beijing's calculus because of both extant geopolitical disputes and the uncertainties that always accompany potential power transitions, China's nuclear weapons target all its major regional rivals, including Russia, Japan, India, and Vietnam. They also play an important, though not always transparent, role in managing the dispute over Taiwan. Despite its past advocacy of nuclear abolition, therefore, Beijing has effectively deflected this goal by demanding that the larger nuclear powers irreversibly reduce their inventories before it entertains any ideas of cooperation. When this position is coupled to the possibility that China could in fact become a major rival of the United States—first in Asia and then globally—any dreams of involving Beijing in a campaign for nuclear abolition are certain to fail.

At first sight, the Indian nuclear program shares many similarities with its Chinese counterpart: both weapon stockpiles are relatively small, both are maintained as forces-in-being rather than as ready arsenals intended for prompt operations, both are oriented toward executing primarily punitive deterrence strategies rather than denial campaigns centered on damage limitation, and, today, both nuclear inventories are growing at a relatively measured pace. For all these resemblances, however, China's nuclear deterrent is orders of magnitude more capable than India's because of the greater numbers of weapons and delivery systems deployed, the huge difference in the yield of the largest warheads deployed, the significant disparity in the survivability of Chinese and Indian nuclear forces, and the superior quality of Chinese missilery in comparison with its Indian counterpart.

Gaurav Kampani's chapter in this volume systematically details how Indian policymakers are working feverishly to remedy these limitations in hardware, infrastructure, and procedures. This task has only become more onerous because of the rapid improvements in Beijing's nuclear capability, which are driven by fears of the United States. New Delhi's undertakings are also urgent because Sino-Indian relations are rivalrous at a time when Sino-Pakistani ties are still aimed at limiting India's freedom of action, when Indo-Pakistani security competition persists with high costs for both states, and when Pakistan is continuingly engaged in a dramatic expansion of its own nuclear weapons program. Although Kampani concludes that India has now put in place an assured destruction capability vis-à-vis Pakistan, the fact that it has a long way to go vis-à-vis China guarantees that Indian policymakers will not be entertaining ideas about nuclear arms control, let alone abolition, any time soon.

Christopher Clary's chapter on Pakistan's nuclear program represents a remarkable case study of how a country beset with grave internal security problems, a fragile economy, sharp social and political divides, and frayed civil-military relations still seeks refuge in nuclear weapons as the ultimate guarantee of national survival. Clary describes in detail the myriad dimensions of Pakistan's galloping nuclear expansion—a distention suggesting that the nation's military leaders believe that only more can be enough where nuclear adequacy is concerned. If the increase in arsenal size were the only issue at stake, the growth of Pakistan's nuclear capabilities would not generate excessive concern as long as these weapons were adequately safeguarded and the nuclear endeavor did not bankrupt the state. But Clary's analysis indicates that these threats still persist, although perhaps not as grievously as the public discourse might sometimes suggest. Moreover, they are amplified both by the particular direction in which Pakistan's nuclear expansion seems to be evolving and by the military's propensity to exploit nuclear weaponry for the cover they provide in regard to the sub-conventional challenges levied at India.

All these variables combine to produce a vicious circle of debilitating proportions. New Delhi seeks to checkmate Pakistani terrorism by threatening conventional military retaliation, which then provokes Pakistani investments in tactical nuclear weapons, an unfortunate solution gleaned from an overly studious reading of NATO's Cold War strategies. The threats of tactical nuclear use, then, must be backstopped by ever more ambitious theater and strategic weaponry, even though the risks to security increase and the economic burdens on the state are magnified. Whatever the limitations of Islamabad's strategic logic, however, one conclusion obtains clearly: Pakistan is in no danger of giving up its nuclear weapons, irrespective of what India—or, for that matter, any other country—does. The implications for the abolitionist vision should be obvious.

John Park's chapter about nuclear weapons on the Korean Peninsula serves as the perfect transition from acknowledged nuclear states to latent nuclear powers in this volume. Beginning first with North Korea, Park demonstrates that no matter what the DPRK's reasons for pursuing nuclear weapons originally were, these devices have now become a multipurpose instrument for enhancing national security. The weaknesses of the North Korean economy—even when assessed in its own right, let alone in comparison with South Korea—do not permit the regime to sustain an effective conventional military force. Consequently, nuclear weapons become both compensating supplements and straightforward deterrents vis-à-vis multiple adversaries. The DPRK's persisting national economic weakness also ensures that its broader nuclear capabilities remain critical instruments for extorting assistance from the international community and could, in extremis, even be traded abroad, as Pyongyang has already done, for example, with both nuclear reactors and long-range missilery.

The nuclear threats posed by the DPRK obviously affect South Korea directly, the first latent nuclear power examined in this volume. South Korea already possesses substantial nuclear capabilities and has emerged as a world-class exporter of nuclear reactors. It also pursued a nuclear weapons program in the 1970s. Although this effort was terminated under pressure from Washington, the benefits of U.S. extended deterrence seemed to provide adequate compensation for a while. However, the increasing angst in South Korea about the future of U.S. military capacities, Japan's strategic direction, and the dramatic progress of the DPRK's strategic program has now resulted in large majorities of the South Korean population endorsing the creation of a national nuclear deterrent. Although no shift in this direction is imminent, the case of South Korea only illustrates how the demand for nuclear weapons has not abated in Asia, even among U.S. allies who are otherwise trustworthy partners. If, as Park concludes, the DPRK's nuclear program is certain to expand in multiple directions so long as the current regime remains in power, the prospect of preserving nonproliferation gains in Northeast Asia, let alone securing nuclear abolition, will prove to be increasingly tenuous.

Robert Reardon's chapter on Iran provides ample evidence for why denuclearization in any meaningful sense will forever remain a chimera. Detailing the progress Iran has made in recent years with respect to uranium enrichment, nuclear weaponization, and the development of delivery systems, the chapter leaves little doubt that Iran is genuinely a latent nuclear power possessing all the capabilities that would permit it to cross the threshold quickly if and when it decides to do so. Because Iranian leaders have judged that possessing the capacity to build nuclear weapons serves their strategic interests just as efficaciously for now as actually building them, Reardon concludes that the regime will aim mainly to shorten the time to breakout: Iran will subsist just at the nuclear threshold for as long as is necessary, remaining in formal and arguably sufficient compliance with its NPT obligations principally to avoid any military attack by the United States. The ability to sustain such a posture indefinitely—where a state acquires the wherewithal to develop a nuclear arsenal but chooses not to fabricate one—highlights the weakness of the abolitionist agenda. It demonstrates how a country can exploit the virtual existence of nuclear weapons to secure political benefits even when the material artifacts themselves do not exist as such. It also serves as a potent example for the East Asian states that might one day seek the protection of nuclear capabilities without actually having to take the final step of actually fabricating nuclear weapons.

In Iran's case, simply acquiring the capacity to produce nuclear weapons appears to have bolstered the legitimacy of its theocratic rulers and enhanced their survival domestically, despite their failure to demonstrate any other success in economics or governance. It has raised the country's stature in the Persian Gulf and has already sent Iran's neighbors scrambling for new forms of protection. It has unnerved Israel, a technologically formidable rival, and posed difficult strategic quandaries for the United States. A military attack launched by Washington, Reardon argues, would set back the Iranian nuclear program, perhaps considerably, but would not eliminate it, unless the conflict led to the demise of the regime and the emergence of new liberal leaders who placed little value in nuclear weapons. Given's Iran's history, sense of destiny, and fears of its Sunni Arab neighbors, even such an outcome might not produce permanent nuclear abdication. A decision by the United States to let things stand as they are—assuming Israeli acquiescence—would reinforce the idea that even weak powers exuding a whiff of nuclear capability can deter the strong. It would thus lead to greater interest in nuclear weaponry on the part of Iran's neighbors, if for no other reason than to deter Tehran. Either way, Iranian nuclear capabilities look destined to become a durable feature of regional geopolitics in the foreseeable future. At its worst, this outcome would stimulate further nuclear proliferation in the vicinity—to include possibly Egypt, Saudi Arabia, and Turkey—thus making the hope of nuclear abolition even less plausible than it already is.

The question of whether Japan will eventually succumb to acquiring nuclear weapons probably remains the most defining test of the health of the international nonproliferation regime. Being the only victim of nuclear attack in human history, Japan has been a strong champion of nonproliferation— even as it has struggled with the question of whether nuclear weapons should be acquired as a means of protecting its security. At various points in the past, Japan re-examined its early postwar decision to remain a non-nuclear state, but ended up continuing to rely on U.S. security guarantees instead. Even as it did so, however, Japan developed a formidable mastery of the entire fuel cycle, accumulated large quantities of separated plutonium, and nurtured an imposing defense industry capable of producing advanced delivery systems.

This uneasy equilibrium has persisted for many decades, but as Richard Samuels and James Schoff's survey of the current Japanese debate emphasizes, it is simply no longer possible to assume that Tokyo's rejection of nuclear weaponry is indeed a permanent feature of its national security policy. China's ascent as the world's second-largest economy (overtaking Japan in 2010); China's increasing military capabilities and, more importantly, growing ability to deny the United States the freedom to operate along the Asian littorals; the unsettling questions about the credibility of the U.S. nuclear umbrella in the face of Chinese nuclear modernization; and finally, the DPRK's own expanding nuclear capabilities have all combined to increase Japanese doubts about the viability of Japan's nuclear abdication decision. While Samuels and Schoff note that dramatic reversals in Tokyo's policy are currently unlikely, they caution that the U.S. policy of seeking to reassure Japan will face steeper challenges than before. To the degree that U.S. power will continue to diminish even as the security threats to Japan do not promise to disappear, the temptation in Tokyo to seek refuge in nuclear weapons will only intensify, thus putting one more nail in the coffin of global abolition.

The last chapter in this volume, the special study authored by Linton Brooks and Mira Rapp-Hooper, examines the challenges posed to U.S.

extended deterrence in the Asia-Pacific region as a result of the continued problems associated with the second nuclear age. Even when the dangers in South Asia and the greater Middle East are excluded from the analysis, the authors conclude that U.S. extended deterrence in Pacific Asia will be much more challenging than it was during the Cold War because of the difficulties of simultaneously deterring and reassuring adversaries while also protecting allies, all in a stable equilibrium. Although this specific problem materialized and was managed more or less successfully during the competition with the Soviet Union, Brooks and Rapp-Hooper convincingly argue that the current challenge is much more burdensome because of the presence of multiple threats, serious security rivalries among the United States' own regional allies, and the absence of a single unified alliance system in Asia. Moreover, the U.S. competition with China is not yet a rivalry between two relatively satiated powers, as was the case with the Soviet Union after 1962. Rather, the contest with China implicates issues where Beijing is deeply dissatisfied, that impact the survival of the Chinese Communist Party itself, and that involve a rising power that will be progressively harder to deter as its own capabilities increase.

Managing this challenge in a way that does not stimulate further nuclear proliferation in Asia—in this case, among the United States' own allies—will tax the skills of policymakers in Washington. The recommendations offered by Brooks and Rapp-Hooper to aid this effort are utterly sensible and merit close attention because they emphasize the need to avoid unnecessarily changing extant U.S. declaratory policy. They also highlight the importance of preserving the traditional nuclear parity with Russia and maintaining the requisite levels of conventional warfighting capability to achieve success in regional contingencies while not imposing greater demands on U.S. strategic reserves. These efforts should be complemented by various confidence-building measures involving all states. The merit of this approach is that it seeks to buttress extended deterrence in uncertain times. Such a strategy allows the United States' allies to continue benefiting from its protection without the need for radical unilateral solutions, while creating a space for challengers such as China and North Korea to avoid levying more dangerous threats to enhance their security. Although Brooks and Rapp-Hooper are conscious that the approach they recommend will be tested most seriously in the cyber realm and in maritime confrontations short of absolute war, their solution is nonetheless grounded in the critical necessity of managing deterrence rather than in the romantic fantasy of jettisoning it.

What Does All This Mean for the United States? Dilemmas and Challenges Aplenty

The chapters in this volume demonstrate that the nuclear ferment in Asia is unlikely to subside any time soon. The continuing interstate competition in this part of the world—and the expectation on the part of many states that nuclear weapons will enhance their security against current and future threats—ensures that regional arsenals will grow in the years ahead. As the process continues apace, the likelihood increases that more states will be tempted to consider acquiring these weapons either to neutralize the threats that may be posed by the extant possessors or because their acquisition by others validates the notion that nuclear weapons are in fact excellent deterrents. The United States, therefore, must prepare for a reality that is quite different from the vision offered by nuclear abolitionism: an Asia that hosts many nuclear powers whose arsenals vary in capacity, architecture, and doctrine.[22]

At least in the foreseeable future, the Asian reliance on nuclear weapons will increase. While it is possible, maybe, to slow the growth of some arsenals and in some instances even to procure reversals, the fundamental fact that nuclear weapons will remain embedded in the high politics of Asia, as well as globally, cannot be wished away. That reality, in turn, should stimulate the United States not to further indulge in its daydream of eliminating nuclear weapons but rather to focus more resolutely on the challenges of managing deterrence. However burdensome this approach may be amid the proliferation of new nuclear powers, preserving stable deterrence even as the United States protects its primacy is the critical obligation facing Washington in the second nuclear age. The Obama administration has already promised that "as long as nuclear weapons exist, the United States will maintain a safe, secure and effective arsenal that guarantees the defense of the United States and our allies and partners."[23] If Washington makes good on this commitment, it may discover that the steps taken toward strengthening deterrence might actually render the hope of abolition even more futile. But that would merely be a recognition of the iron realities of international politics, not a reason to avoid investing in the only approach that can prolong the nuclear peace that has now held for close to 70 years.

The first step in this direction is to recognize clearly that the United States needs nuclear weapons today—and will continue to need them in the

---

[22] Bracken, *The Second Nuclear Age*, 189–90.

[23] White House, "Nuclear Weapons Employment Strategy of the United States," Fact Sheet, June 19, 2013, http://www.whitehouse.gov/the-press-office/2013/06/19/fact-sheet-nuclear-weapons-employment-strategy-united-states.

foreseeable future—for multiple reasons. The Obama administration's 2010 *Nuclear Posture Review* sensibly declared that "the United States will only consider the use of nuclear weapons in extreme circumstances to defend the vital interests of the United States or its allies and partners."[24] Yet this avowal must not be taken to such limits as to justify arguments declaring that "the strategic deterrent should do one thing, and one thing only: prevent the nuclear destruction of the United States by a peer like China or Russia."[25]

Clearly, deterring the use, and threats of use, of nuclear weapons against U.S. and allied interests will remain a central mission for U.S. nuclear weapons in perpetuity. But their utility in deterring conventional war against the United States and its allies is equally important because no adversary should ever draw the conclusion that attacks on U.S. interests that do not involve nuclear instruments are essentially risk-free—even if Washington has the resources to cope with such dangers through conventional means alone. This is particularly relevant because U.S. allies in many cases may be far from the U.S. conventional reinforcements capable of protecting their core national assets effectively, or because the conventional balance of power in particular geographies may not favor the United States and its allies today or over time. Consequently, deterring even conventional threats by preserving the risk of nuclear escalation remains an important benefit of U.S. nuclear forces and one that must not be discarded, given both the high cost of modern conventional wars and the critical importance of preventing U.S. allies from seeking nuclear weapons as a means of mitigating serious conventional threats.[26]

Finally, U.S. nuclear weapons also play a vital role as tactical warfighting instruments in certain specific, admittedly limited, contingencies. Although most of the traditional combat missions of nuclear weaponry have been taken over by conventional weapons, there are still some targets, such as hardened and deeply buried facilities, that are immune to conventional interdiction. The number of such targets in emerging and established nuclear states is in fact growing. If deterrence successfully prevails—as is to be hoped—attacks on these sites will never become an issue. Yet because only nuclear weapons

[24] White House, "Nuclear Weapons Employment Strategy of the United States."

[25] Tom Nichols, "Time to Change America's Atomic Arsenal," *Diplomat*, March 14, 2013, http://thediplomat.com/2013/03/14/time-to-change-americas-atomic-arsenal/?all=true. For a sophisticated discussion that defends this position broadly, see George Perkovich, "Do Unto Others: Toward a Defensible Nuclear Doctrine," Carnegie Endowment for International Peace, 2013.

[26] Frank Miller, "Disarmament and Deterrence: A Practitioner's View," in *Abolishing Nuclear Weapons: A Debate*, ed. George Perkovich and James M. Acton (Washington, D.C.: Carnegie Endowment for International Peace, 2009), 151.

today and prospectively can hold these targets at risk, their relevance for this mission—in the overall context of avoiding war—cannot be overlooked.[27]

Since nuclear weapons will, therefore, continue to be critical for tasks beyond simply deterring nuclear attacks on, or threats to, the U.S. and allied homelands and U.S. interests more generally, the Obama administration's desire to "reduc[e] the role of nuclear weapons in [U.S.] security strategy"[28] should not extend to promulgating declaratory policies that limit the utility of nuclear weapons for dealing with diverse dangers. In fact, the less said about how the United States might use nuclear weapons, the better. The character of these weapons, and the enormous destructive power they embody, is so well-known that nothing need be said about the circumstances that would trigger their use—except to occasionally reiterate that the United States remains willing to use them when dangers to its interests arise. There is little value in emphasizing that Washington will use nuclear weapons only in narrow circumstances—even if that is in fact the case—because there is no evidence whatsoever that nuclear proliferation among U.S. adversaries is stimulated by the specifics of its declaratory policy. Because the same may not be true of its friends, however, the fruits of silence are particularly golden in this instance. As a general rule, therefore, the desire to reduce the salience of nuclear weapons in world politics should not extend to devaluing the utility of nuclear weapons for deterrence because these instruments will continue to remain the *ultima ratio* in an environment that only promises more, not less, proliferation.[29]

The second task, where protecting deterrence is concerned, is reconsidering the quantitative requirements of nuclear sufficiency.[30] The U.S. nuclear arsenal has been steadily decreasing in size since its peak during the Cold War. This trend is undoubtedly sensible because U.S.-Russian relations are not acutely antagonistic, as they once were, and because both states have realized that their security requirements can be adequately satisfied with smaller numbers of strategic weapons. The fact that both the United States and Russia have reduced their inventories through negotiated agreements has imposed a desirable order on the process, but the process of nuclear

---

[27] National Research Council, *Effects of Nuclear Earth-Penetrator and Other Weapons* (Washington, D.C.: National Academies Press, 2005), 30.

[28] White House, "Nuclear Weapons Employment Strategy of the United States."

[29] For an excellent survey of the myriad issues implicated here, especially as they bear on the choices of U.S. allies, see Keith Payne et al., *Nuclear Guarantees, Extended Deterrence, and the Assurance of Allies* (Fairfax: National Institute for Public Policy, 2009).

[30] For useful overviews of this issue, see Amy F. Woolf, "U.S. Strategic Nuclear Forces: Background, Developments, and Issues," Congressional Research Service, CRS Report for Congress, RL33640, June 14, 2013; Glenn C. Buchan et al., *Future Roles of U.S. Nuclear Forces: Implications for U.S. Strategy* (Santa Monica: RAND, 2003); and Ivan Oelrich, "Missions for Nuclear Weapons after the Cold War," Federation of American Scientists, Occasional Paper, no. 3, January 2005.

reductions may be reaching—if it has not reached already—the limits of its success. There is a grave danger that future nuclear reductions may be driven more by the political necessity of advancing the abolitionist agenda than the requirements of ensuring stable deterrence.

To be sure, assessing the appropriate number of nuclear weapons for preserving stability is not an easy task because it implicates both nuclear strategy and the tenor of international relations. During the Cold War, the requirements of sufficiency were driven by the logic of U.S. nuclear strategy, which emphasized damage limitation and, accordingly, resulted in U.S. nuclear forces not only being pegged closely to Soviet force levels but also being tasked fundamentally for counterforce and countermilitary operations. A continued reduction in nuclear force levels—if undertaken as before with reference to Russia alone—could place the United States at a serious disadvantage at a time when Chinese nuclear capabilities are growing in size, sophistication, and survivability.

It is simply not clear whether the prospective force levels desired by the Obama administration, taking into account the president's recently announced willingness to shrink the U.S. inventory of operationally deployed strategic nuclear weapons by up to one-third, would permit the nation to sustain its traditional nuclear strategy centered on damage limitation when the potential Russian and Chinese target sets together are still large and, in the case of the latter, continuing to grow. This issue is academic if nuclear deterrence involving these states is completely stable and the threat of war is irrelevant. If this is so, deeper nuclear reductions of the sort contemplated by the administration have no downside, given that the possibilities of nuclear use are by definition ruled out. If this is not the case, however, and the United States must still prepare for the contingency of nuclear use—no matter how improbable—then the number of nuclear weapons and how they might be used become questions that cannot be avoided.

A low number of nuclear weapons might still produce deterrence stability, but it could require the United States to start targeting adversary populations per se, something Washington never did during the Cold War for sound strategic and moral reasons. If this strategy has to be adopted in the future, its implications ought to be thoroughly analyzed prior to pursuing any further reductions.[31] The separate question of whether deterrence and crisis stability can actually be sustained comfortably in a world of lower numbers—and how far weapon inventories can drop before instabilities

---

[31] For a superb analysis that is critical of low numbers and minimum deterrence in general, see Keith B. Payne et al., "Minimum Deterrence: Examining the Evidence," National Institute for Public Policy, 2013. For a contrary view, see James M. Acton, *Deterrence During Disarmament: Deep Nuclear Reductions and International Security*, Adelphi Paper 417 (Abingdon: Routledge, 2011).

arise—also deserves further examination through, among other things, detailed modeling that employs the best classified information about the characteristics of all other countries' weapons systems, their operating regimes, and their target sets. The dangers of the other nuclear states reaching for parity, at least numerically, with declining U.S. and Russian nuclear inventories also needs to be assessed. And, perhaps most importantly, the consequences of forfeiting U.S. nuclear superiority vis-à-vis China for the viability of extended deterrence in Asia require careful consideration. As the analyses in this volume suggest, both Japan and South Korea would be strongly tempted to acquire independent deterrents if the credibility of U.S. nuclear guarantees were to diminish as a result of any functional nuclear parity between Washington and Beijing.[32]

Finally, the larger question of whether further nuclear reductions by the United States—unilaterally, bilaterally, or as part of some larger collaborative process with other nuclear states—will ever extinguish the incentives for proliferation in a competitive international system merits some reflection. If the relationship between nuclear arms control and dampening proliferation is only tenuous, because at least some states might consider acquiring nuclear weapons for reasons that have nothing to do with whether the extant nuclear states maintain or forsake their weapons, then the entire endeavor of nuclear reductions for its own sake becomes questionable, nay even dangerous. If future efforts in this direction are pursued by Washington, they should be attempted only because they yield gains for strengthening deterrence and not as part of any quest for nuclear abolition.

The third task facing the United States in regard to managing deterrence is ensuring that its nuclear weaponry retains integrity over an indefinite future. It should be abundantly clear that, despite the aspirations of abolition, few, if any, nuclear states today appear ready to give up their strategic capabilities. Assuring the perpetual effectiveness of the U.S. arsenal is therefore critical because it remains the foundation for preventing both nuclear weapons threats and the dangers of consequential aggression from materializing.

Protecting the survivability and the flexibility of the U.S. nuclear deterrent force is the first step in this direction. Although the idea of eliminating one or more legs of the strategic triad has been aired in recent years, the temptation to do so must be eschewed because these three combat arms—the land-based missile force, ballistic missile submarines, and bombers—have complementary strengths and weaknesses that fortify deterrence *in toto*. Even

---

[32] For a different, but corroborating, analysis of this conclusion, see Kurt M. Campbell and Robert J. Einhorn, "Avoiding the Tipping Point: Concluding Observations," in *The Nuclear Tipping Point: Why States Reconsider Their Nuclear Choices*, ed. Kurt M. Campbell, Robert J. Einhorn, and Mitchell B. Reiss (Washington, D.C.: Brookings Institution, 2004), 321ff.

if further nuclear reductions are justified, the triad should be preserved not simply to ensure the survivability of the force as a whole (especially against a sophisticated peer like Russia) but because it provides Washington with enormous flexibility in coping with a nuclear environment that will be characterized by diverse sources and types of threats.

The biggest challenge to the viability of the triad today is probably less ideational than budgetary. It is hard to prove that the United States could preserve its deterrence options just as effectively if it were to lose one leg of the nuclear force, but finding the resources to sustain comprehensive modernization of what is an aging deterrent is another matter. And the deterrent is indeed old: the mainstay of the land-based force, the Minuteman III intercontinental ballistic missile, for example, entered service in the 1970s; the first of the Ohio-class nuclear-powered ballistic missile submarines entered service in 1985; and the B-52 bomber, which is the workhorse of the triad's air leg, dates back to the 1960s. Although all these systems and their other stable mates have been repeatedly modernized, it is clear that they will all need to be replaced during the next two decades at a price tag of hundreds of billions of dollars—when resources are scarce and the competition from new threats, such as cyber and space, remains unabated.[33]

The challenges of modernizing the triad are complemented by another equally vexatious problem, namely assuring the reliability of U.S. nuclear warheads in perpetuity without further "hot" testing. The tension between attempting to limit proliferation while simultaneously preserving the effectiveness of the nuclear deterrent comes most clearly to a head on this issue and is embodied by the debate about ratifying the Comprehensive Nuclear-Test-Ban Treaty (CTBT). Washington pursued the CTBT on the expectation that the United States would be able to assure the reliability of its nuclear warheads without having to explosively test them again. The accumulated knowledge of nuclear weapons acquired over decades of testing, the availability of high-speed computers to run detailed simulations, the possibility of sub-critical tests, and the presumption that the aging components of stockpiled weapons could be replicated and replaced by high-fidelity substitutes without reducing their effectiveness, all combined (along with other assumptions) to justify the belief that the U.S. stockpile would be reliable even if it were not validated through periodic underground detonations.[34]

---

[33] Megan Scully, "The New Nuclear Age," *CQ Weekly*, March 3, 2012.

[34] Rose Gottemoeller, "The Last U.S. Nuclear Test—20 Years Later: Status and Prospects for the Comprehensive Test Ban Treaty" (speech at the Center for International and Strategic Studies, Washington, D.C., September 27, 2012).

The confidence of these science-based assessments, however, seems questionable for many reasons, including because the interaction effects of the modifications made to individual subsystems of a nuclear weapon during its life extension program are not well understood and hence cannot be modeled with confidence. As the JASON panel of independent scientists reviewing this and other issues concluded,

> Unfortunately, we do not know to what extent the performance of nuclear weapons is non-deterministic. There are no homogeneous series of tests, and the occasional significant deviation from expectation is as plausibly the result of a deterministic process as of indeterminacy. On the other hand, indeterminacy is important, because it may pose the ultimate limit to reliability.[35]

Doubts about stockpile reliability will likely increase over time, despite its importance given that continued proliferation is certain. Hence, U.S. policymakers should re-examine their past rejection of the Reliable Replacement Warhead if the country still stands by, as it should, a theory of deterrence centered on the certainty of effective retaliation. Equally important is the need to rethink how the United States proceeds with respect to ratification of the CTBT. Considering all the uncertainties, the optimal course of action for the United States today would be to avoid ratification of this treaty, while hewing to its obligations for as long as is necessary. There is already a de facto global moratorium on explosive testing, in part because of the national decisions made by all nuclear states save North Korea. Washington, accordingly, should commit to upholding its CTBT obligations, but without encumbering itself by cementing this commitment—even though abjuring these restraints is possible under *force majeure*—until it is certain beyond reasonable doubt that the reliability of the U.S. nuclear stockpile is assured despite whatever changes may likely occur in regard to proliferation or nuclear inventories elsewhere.[36]

The importance of preserving the integrity of the U.S. nuclear deterrent in an uncertain future, where the only certain trend promises to be further proliferation, also highlights the importance of preserving the U.S. nuclear weapons production complex and, particularly, the human capital—the scientists and the engineers with a specialty in nuclear weapons design and fabrication—which turns out to be the most precarious resource of all.[37]

---

[35] D. Eardley et al., "Quantification of Margins and Uncertainties (QMU)," MITRE Corporation, JASON Program Office, March 2005, 13.

[36] Kathleen Bailey and Thomas Scheber, "The Comprehensive Test Ban Treaty: An Assessment of the Benefits, Costs, and Risks," National Institute for Public Policy, 2011, http://www.nipp.org/CTBT%20 3.11.11%20electronic%20version.pdf.

[37] U.S. Department of Defense, *Nuclear Posture Review Report* (Washington, D.C., April 2010), 40–43, http://www.defense.gov/npr/docs/2010%20Nuclear%20Posture%20Review%20Report.pdf.

Unfortunately, the history of the last decade does not inspire confidence on this front. Critical facilities essential to the manufacture of nuclear weapons are languishing for either budgetary reasons or a lack of strategic direction—and the environmental hazards at many of these sites still persist. The personnel associated with the development of current U.S. nuclear warheads are slowly retiring and will probably exit the nuclear weapons development complex entirely by the end of this decade. Further, the National Nuclear Security Administration, the nodal body that oversees U.S. nuclear weapons for the Department of Energy, is still hobbled by troubling management and oversight deficiencies.[38] The bottom line, therefore, is stark but should not be controversial: the ability of the United States to maintain a reliable and effective nuclear deterrent indefinitely into the future is compromised by the shortcoming of its nuclear complex. Unless determined efforts are made to redress these weaknesses, the country could end up functionally disarming itself in circumstances where other states would still possess nuclear weapons.

Conclusion

The perils of nuclear proliferation, which will probably continue unabated, understandably drive the current enthusiasm for abolishing all nuclear weaponry. The studies in this volume suggest, however, that active security competition still persists in Asia, the new locus of power in the emerging world system. There is no evidence whatsoever that interstate rivalries are vanishing either here or elsewhere in international politics. Consequently, the quest to eliminate nuclear weapons—a dream that goes back to the beginning of the nuclear age but which has now been adopted as U.S. policy by President Obama—will likely fail. As even the most ardent advocates of abolition realize, the eradication of nuclear weaponry cannot obtain without a fundamental transformation in the character of politics in the earthly city. The pervasiveness of conflict, which characterizes all aspects of human interaction and social structure, will have to disappear first before abolition becomes viable precisely because nuclear weapons are such extraordinary instruments of violence. To imagine that conflict can be eradicated within history, however, is utopian, and eliminating nuclear weapons in its pursuit could end up making the cure worse than the disease.

Even if this elimination were to successfully proceed in a phased and verifiable fashion—as the abolitionists usually advocate—it would still be destabilizing, unless the human condition were so altered as to eliminate

---

[38] For a useful survey of the challenges facing the U.S. nuclear weapons production complex, see Taylor A. Bolz, ed., *In the Eyes of Experts: Analysis and Comments on America's Strategic Posture* (Washington, D.C.: United States Institute of Peace Press, 2009), 99–189.

the prospect of recidivism entirely. Not even the boldest of the nuclear abolitionists can contend that this might be achieved. Given this reality, U.S. policymakers should recognize that there is no escape from the enduring reality of nuclear weapons in competitive politics, and their commitment to abolish these weapons enshrined in the NPT is, therefore, little other than a "noble lie." The ethic of purity and the ethic of responsibility, then, combine to demand that statesmen persist with those prosaic choices that have maintained international security thus far: upholding the system of deterrence that prevents nuclear use, conventional aggression, and strategic coercion. Continuing to painstakingly implement such a policy is far less flashy than the phantasmagorical pursuit of nuclear abolition, but it is much more prudent, dependable, and effective.

STRATEGIC ASIA 2013–14

ESTABLISHED NUCLEAR POWERS

EXECUTIVE SUMMARY

This chapter assesses Russia's posture as a major nuclear weapons state and examines the role of Russian nuclear forces within the complex security environment of Eurasia.

MAIN ARGUMENT:
Russia does not believe that nuclear war is imminent and sees areas for cooperation with the U.S. and other powers to reduce proliferation. Russia has maintained nuclear parity with the U.S. through the modernization of its nuclear forces and the negotiation of strategic arms control agreements. In the absence of large conventional forces, the government has adopted a doctrine of nuclear "first use" and conducted exercises simulating first use in the case of conventional attacks on Russia and its allies. Russian experts are concerned about instability in a number of regions judged vital to Russian interests, especially if open conflict were to provoke U.S. and NATO out-of-area interventions that lack the approval of the UN Security Council. The U.S. development of a global ballistic missile defense system and "prompt global strike" conventional systems raises fears in Moscow that such capabilities could undermine the deterrence potential of Russia's strategic nuclear forces.

POLICY IMPLICATIONS:
- The Russian elite will not embrace "global zero" as a means to sustain strategic stability in an emerging multipolar world order.

- Instability in Eurasia and NATO out-of-area operations has demonstrated the potential for local wars to become regional conflicts with risks of further escalation, leaving Russia with limited nuclear options to address threats to its vital interests.

- While Russia had hoped to develop new systems of non-nuclear or pre-nuclear deterrence for the emerging era of "no contact" warfare, the recent announcement of the failure of military reforms raises the prospect that it will continue to rely on nuclear deterrence.

Russia as a Nuclear Power in the Eurasian Context

Jacob W. Kipp

Speaking on Sino-Russian relations in 2003, Evgeny Sergeev remarked that "sometimes it is safer to hold on to the tiger's tail than to let go." This comment also seems to fit Russia's approach to nuclear weapons in the post–Cold War world. Once a country has grabbed hold of the "nuclear tiger," it may prove hard to let go. In spite of all the reductions in the size of its nuclear arsenal since the end of the Cold War, via bilateral arms control agreements and unilateral declarations of intent, Russia still views nuclear deterrence as the key factor in strategic stability and the core of its national security. This is more than a matter of inertia, and has its roots in the highly unstable Eurasian security environment in which Russia has operated over the last two decades. The Balkans, the Caucasus, the Middle East, Central Asia, and the Far East have seen ethnic and religious strife turn into civil wars and then lead to foreign intervention. While for a long time many in the West saw these events as part of a natural advance of democratic institutions and only later as a clash of civilizations, Russia's elite has seen in these conflicts challenges to the existing order and threats to the stability of Russia itself.

From the vantage point of 1991 and the collapse of the Soviet Union, Russia has had a difficult time adjusting to its domestic transformation from a command to a market economy and defining its international position. With the end of the Soviet Union, the concept of a bipolar world vanished.

Jacob W. Kipp is an Adjunct Professor of Russian military history at the University of Kansas. He can be reached at <jacobkipp@cs.com>.

Russia found itself a weaker international player seeking to define its place in Eurasia and now more vulnerable to internal and external instability on its periphery. A hard decade of economic crisis and decline gave way to a period of recovery under the mantle of a strong, centralized state, which began to claim a special place in Eurasia. One legacy of the Soviet Union that Russia inherited was its arsenal of nuclear weapons. This alone could not make Russia a superpower, but it did provide a measure of strategic stability while Russia sought to ensure internal stability and define its new place in Eurasia.

Russia inherited the Soviet arsenal at a time when the prospects of general nuclear war had sharply declined from the previous decade. Soviet leadership had invested heavily in the country's nuclear arsenal in order to achieve parity with the United States and deter potential attacks.[1] The United States' anticipated deployment of highly mobile nuclear missiles to Europe, its covert aid to the Afghan resistance, and President Ronald Reagan's intense rhetoric led the KGB to search for key indicators of the impending nuclear first strike.[2]

What made this period of the late Cold War so dangerous was that technological innovations in nuclear command and control had increased the risk of a nuclear crisis. On the U.S. side, targeting the Soviet leadership was a top priority in the operation plan for conducting nuclear war. At the same time, the Soviet military-political leadership had developed its own solution to ensure an effective counterstrike in case of decapitation. This initiative, known as *Perimetr* or "Dead Hand," provided for launch authorization if the military and political leadership could not act following a nuclear attack. The algorithms did not exclude human action but placed it directly in the hands of those in missile silos and aboard nuclear-powered ballistic missile submarines (SSBN) on the assumption that no national chain of command would still be functioning.[3]

Ultimately, the interactions between the second Reagan administration and the Soviet leadership under Gorbachev never resolved the issue of missile defense. Yet they did set in motion the demilitarization of Central Europe,

---

[1] Parity in this case was achieved by expanding the number of nuclear weapons and delivery systems. There were asymmetric aspects of each power's nuclear arsenal, but the size of both arsenals assured that neither side could achieve a disarming first strike and thus would face the prospect of a retaliatory attack capable of ensuring mutual destruction. The estimated size of the Soviet nuclear arsenal in 1986 was about 45,000 weapons.

[2] Christopher Andrew and Oleg Gordievsky, *KGB: The Inside Story of Its Foreign Operations from Lenin to Gorbachev* (New York: HarperCollins, 1990), 383–85.

[3] Nicholas Thompson, "Inside the Apocalyptic Soviet Doomsday Machine," *Wired*, September 21, 2009; Valerii Iarynich, "Bez prava verit" [Without the Right to Believe], *Otechestvennye zapiski*, no. 2 (2003), http://magazines.russ.ru/oz/2003/2/iaryn.html; and "Sistema garantirovannogo iadernogo udara 'Perimetr'" [System of Guaranteed Retaliatory Nuclear Strike "Perimeter"], Masterok, web log, December 5, 2012, http://masterok.livejournal.com/501495.html.

the elimination of entire classes of delivery systems, and the reduction in both sides' nuclear arsenals through bilateral arms control agreements and unilateral statements of intent. In 1989 the destruction of the Berlin Wall symbolically marked the end of Soviet hegemony in Eastern Europe, and by the end of 1991, after an unsuccessful coup, the Soviet Union ceased to exist. However, its nuclear arsenal lives on.

This chapter begins by providing an overview of the nuclear legacy that Russia inherited from the Soviet Union. The next two sections then examine Russia's efforts to modernize its nuclear forces and the role of nuclear weapons in its national security strategy. Following a discussion of recent developments, the chapter concludes by considering the geopolitical impact of Russia's nuclear policies and drawing implications for the United States.

The Soviet Nuclear Legacy

Following the dissolution of the Soviet Union in December 1991, the Russian Federation inherited the Soviet nuclear arsenal and much of its nuclear industry. This happened with the consent of the successor states and the support of the United States, which viewed keeping the arsenal intact and under positive, active control to be in both its own interest and the interest of the international community. Bilateral arms control negotiations with the Soviet Union during the final years of the Cold War had led to the Intermediate-Range Nuclear Forces Treaty of 1987, which eliminated intermediate range (300–3,400 miles) ballistic and cruise missiles capable of carrying nuclear and conventional warheads. This agreement was followed by the first Strategic Arms Reduction Treaty (START), which was signed in July 1991 and reduced strategic nuclear offensive forces to just over 10,000 bombers, intercontinental ballistic missiles (ICBM), and submarine-launched ballistic missiles (SLBM) for each side. Although Russia enjoyed a slight advantage over the United States in total number of ICBMs and SLBMs (9,416 vs. 8,210) and a significant advantage in total throw-weight (6,326 vs. 2,361 megatons), the U.S. strategic nuclear forces possessed an advantage in terms of accuracy.[4] A large quantity of ballistic missiles that had been based in Ukraine, Kazakhstan, and Belarus were gradually relocated to Russia. Likewise, a smaller number of manned strategic bombers that had been deployed outside Russia were redeployed.

In addition to strategic nuclear weapons, the Russian Federation also inherited a large nonstrategic nuclear arsenal made up of tactical and

---

[4] Pavel Podvig, "The Russian Nuclear Arsenal," Center for International Security and Cooperation, Stanford University, November 2005, http://russianforces.org/podvig/2005/11/the_russian_nuclear_arsenal.shtml.

operational weapons with specific intended functions in the conduct of theater warfare. The estimated size of the arsenal in the late 1980s was 15,000–20,000 weapons, and many of these were deployed outside Russian territory. The same requirement to bring strategic nuclear weapons under Russian control applied to nonstrategic nuclear weapons. With the dissolution of the Soviet Union, Russia confirmed its intention to continue the process of reducing or eliminating various categories of nonstrategic nuclear weapons. This included nuclear-capable short-range missiles (having a range of three hundred miles or less), mines, and artillery shells from its ground forces, and nuclear missiles and torpedoes from ships. A Russian estimate at the time placed the country's nonstrategic nuclear arsenal at 13,759 platforms and 11,305 warheads.[5] In this case, Russia was announcing for the first time cuts not only in platforms but also in warheads. Since then, the government has offered repeated statements about the progress of these reductions as a percentage of its total force but has not provided concrete and transparent figures.[6]

Russia also inherited the Soviet Union's nuclear and defense infrastructure to support, sustain, and develop its nuclear arsenal. Specifically, it inherited the Soviet Ministry of Atomic Power and Industry, which was renamed the Federal Atomic Energy Agency in 2004, and then the State Atomic Energy Corporation in 2008. Some parts of the nuclear military-industrial complex were located in other successor states, but the core of the nuclear industry was located inside Russia. The Russian military assumed oversight of nuclear weapons subsystems through the Ministry of Defense and the General Staff, which ensured Russia's nuclear strike capabilities beyond warheads and delivery systems. These included early-warning radar, reconnaissance and communication satellites, nuclear weapons storage depots, and C4ISR (command, control, communication, computer, intelligence, surveillance and reconnaissance) systems that would support the launch of a nuclear attack. However, the electronics industry in the defense sector was and remains a chronic underperformer, unable to match world-class standards in computers, radars, sensors, guidance systems, and optics. Makhmut Gareev wrote recently about Russia's "long-standing gap in the electronic components, space communications, media intelligence, electronic warfare, network-centric means of automated control systems, and high-precision weapons."[7] This situation has put Russia at a technological disadvantage to not only the United

---

[5] Vladimir Belous, "Nuclear Warheads: What Do We Do? Good Intentions and Harsh Reality," *Nezavisimaya Gazeta*, June 17, 1992, 2.

[6] Gunnar Arbman and Charles Thornton, "Russia's Tactical Nuclear Weapons—Part I: Background and Policy Issues," Swedish Defence Research Agency, FOI-R1057-SE, November 2003, http://drum. lib.umd.edu/bitstream/1903/7912/1/thorntonrussia.pdf.

[7] Makhmut Gareev, "Iskusstvo reshitel'nykh deistvii" [The Art of Decisive Actions], *Voenno-promyshlennyi kur'er*, June 12, 2012, 3.

States but also China and has pushed Moscow to purchase high-tech systems, such as unmanned aerial vehicles, abroad, including from Israel.[8]

The Modernization of Russia's Nuclear Forces

In spite of serious economic dislocations as a result of the transition from a centrally planned economy to a market economy, the Russian government under Boris Yeltsin, Dmitri Medvedev, and Vladimir Putin has sustained the modernization of the country's nuclear arsenal, even as it has negotiated reductions in strategic offensive nuclear weapons and continued its less transparent reductions in nonstrategic nuclear weapons. The nuclear weapons infrastructure has been maintained and modernized. Although the stockpiles are significantly reduced from the size of the Soviet Union's arsenal, Russia still retains its position as a major nuclear power.

Strategic Nuclear Forces

As of April 2013, the Arms Control Association estimated that Russia's strategic nuclear arsenal comprises 1,480 deployed warheads with another 1,022 non-deployed warheads.[9] Russia's strategic nuclear forces are organized into five divisions of land-based rocket forces making up two rocket armies. As of September 2012, these forces contained 395 missiles and 1,303 warheads. The modernization of the ICBM force continues with a mix of liquid- and solid-fueled, silo-based, and road-mobile single-warhead and MIRV-enabled ICBMs.[10] The force includes 58 heavy R-36MUTTX and R-36m2 (SS-18) missiles, 70 UR-100N UTTX (SS-19) missiles, 171 road-mobile PT-2PM Topol (SS-25) missiles, 60 silo-based RT-2PM2 Topol-M (SS-27) missiles, 18 road-mobile RT-2PM Topol-M missiles, and 18 road-mobile RS-24 Yars missiles. Of the eight SSBNs in the Russian Navy, four each are deployed with the Northern and the Pacific Fleets. Nuclear-capable strategic aviation, for its part, is based on three airfields and includes 45 aircraft equipped to deliver 508 long-range cruise missiles.[11]

Moscow has announced an investment of $70 billion over the next decade in nuclear weapons modernization, which Putin has described as an existential priority for national security:

---

[8] I.M. Popov, "Setetsentricheskaia voina: Gotova li k nei Rossiia?" [Network-centric War: Is Russia Ready for It?], *Sovetskaia Rossiia*, January 19, 2009.

[9] See "Nuclear Weapons: Who Has What at a Glance," Arms Control Association, April 2013.

[10] A MIRV is a multiple independently targetable reentry vehicle.

[11] "Strategicheskie iadernye sily Rossiiskoi Federatsii" [Strategic Nuclear Forces of the Russian Federation], Wikipedia (Russian).

> We should not tempt anyone by allowing ourselves to be weak. It is for this reason that we will under no circumstances surrender our strategic deterrent capability, and, indeed, will in fact strengthen it. It was this strength that enabled us to maintain our national sovereignty during the extremely difficult 1990s, when, let us be frank, we did not have anything else to argue with.[12]

Moreover, in addressing the priorities for defense procurement, Putin gave the modernization of strategic nuclear forces top priority.

Russian experts have noted that this investment will fund new mobile, solid-fueled missiles of the Yars class. It will also support improvements in the navy's strategic nuclear systems, especially the development of the Bulava (RMS-56) solid-fueled missile and the Lainer (R29RMU2) liquid-fueled heavy missile, as well as the construction of eight Borei-class SSBNs. In addition, Russia has made major investments in the PAK-DA nuclear-capable bomber and in dual-capable, short-range Iskander missiles, which will number ten brigades by 2020.[13]

However, the military has demonstrated certain institutional problems that make the realization of these plans problematic. The Soviet military-industrial complex dominated a centrally planned economy and simply consumed resources at the expense of the national economy as a whole. Over the last two decades, the infrastructure of that economy has seen a decline in production capacity, quality control, and systems integration. At the same time, the pool of skilled labor within the military-industrial complex has aged and found other employment.

Evidence of these problems in Russia's strategic weapons programs includes the long delays both in the production of the first Borei-class SSBN, the *Yury Dolgoruky*, and in the successful conclusion of the state tests for the Bulava SLBM, a solid-fuel missile deployed on the new Borei-class SSBNs. Sea trials for the *Yury Dolgoruky*, initially scheduled to be completed in 2002, were not conducted until 2010 due to budget constraints and because of problems associated with the submerged launch of the Bulava missile. Meanwhile, the Bulava was designed by the Moscow Institute of Thermal Technology (MITT) on the basis of its design of the Topol-M ICBM and produced at the same plant at Votkinsk. A series of failures of test firings in 2009 led to the resignation of Yuri Solomonov, the general director and chief designer at MITT. Since 2009, however, there have been a series of successful launches of Bulava SLBMs, the most recent of which was in November 2011, when

---

[12] Vladimir Putin, "Byt' sil'nymi: Garantii natsional'noi bezopasnosti dlia Rossii" [Being Strong: The Guarantee of National Security for Russia], *Rossiiskaia gazeta*, February 20, 2012, http://www.rg.ru/2012/02/20/putin-armiya.html.

[13] "Britanskie voennye eksperty uvereny: Mir uzhe vstupil v novuiu iadernuiu gonku" [British Military Experts: The World Has Already Entered Arms Race], *Trud*, October 31, 2011.

two were launched from the *Yury Dolgoruky* in the Barents Sea.[14] To date, one new Borei-class submarine is in service; a second, the *Alexander Nevsky*, is undergoing state sea trials; and a third, the *Vladimir Monomakh*, will begin its factory sea trials later in 2013. No operational launch has been carried out to date on the *Alexander Nevsky*, the second SSBN of the class. This boat will not enter service until it has also carried out a submerged launch of a Bulava SLBM, which is expected to take place this summer.[15]

Tactical Nuclear Forces

Since 1999, the Russian government has remained quiet on the exact size of the country's tactical nuclear arsenal, its deployment, and its modernization. In 2004, when the U.S. government raised the issue of whether Russia was fulfilling its obligations to reduce its tactical nuclear arsenal in Europe, the Russian Foreign Ministry raised objections to the word "obligations":

> First of all, the word "obligations" in this particular context is not correct. We are speaking about one-sided initiatives of 1991–1992, which were "strictly a matter of good will" on Russia's side. These measures looked not only to the reduction of tactical nuclear weapons but to a whole series of measures in the area of disarmament.[16]

The statement by the Foreign Ministry went on to affirm that Russia was fulfilling its self-imposed commitments through the liquidation of 50% of the nuclear weapons in the navy's arsenal of tactical missiles, as well as reducing stocks of air-defense missiles and aerial bombs. The statement further noted that Russia's tactical nuclear weapons were only deployed in Russia, unlike the U.S. tactical nuclear weapons stationed in Europe.

There have been very few official comments on the status of tactical nuclear weapons over the past few years, though the Russian press has published analytical works relating to these issues. The current role of these weapons emerged in the late 1990s during increased tensions between Russia and NATO and reflects the assumption that Russian conventional

---

[14] "MO gotovitsia priniat' APL *Iurii Dolgorukii* i bulava do kontsa goda" [MO Is Preparing to Accept for Service SSN *Iurii Dolgorukii* and Bulava before the End of the Year], RIA Novosti, December 26, 2012, http://ria.ru/arms/20121226/916283326.html.

[15] "VMF RF poluchit APL 'Aleksandr Nevskiy' posle puska s neye 'Bulavy'" [The Navy of the RF Will Acquire NPS *Aleksandr Nevsky* after It Is Used for Launching Bulava], RIA Novosti, February 4, 2013, http://ria.ru/defense_safety/20130204/921143027.html.

[16] "Press-Tsentr: Otvet ofitsial'nogo predstavitelia MID Rossii na vopros rossiiskikh SMI na press-konferentsii v RIA 'Novosti otnositel'no initsiativ Rossii po sokrashcheniiu takticheskogo iadernogo oruzhiia, 7 Oktiabria" [Russian Foreign Ministry Official Responds to Russian Journalists' Questions during the Press Conference at RIA "New Information on Russia's Initiatives in Nuclear Arms Reductions"], *Diplomaticheskii vestnik*, November 30, 2004.

forces—both then and now—have limited combat stability in case of aggression against Russia or one of its allies.

Command and Control

One of the major shifts since the end of the Cold War has been in the area of strategic command and control of the Russian armed forces. With the end of the Communist Party's monopoly on power and the emergence of the president of Russia as commander-in-chief of the armed forces, there has been an ongoing struggle to define the roles of the president, the minister of defense, the chief of the general staff, and the heads of Russia's other "power ministries" (*siloviki*). The latter exercise control of military and paramilitary forces belonging to other ministries and agencies of the Russian state, including the Ministry of Internal Affairs, the Federal Security Service, the Ministry of Extraordinary Situations, and the Federal Agency of Government Communications and Information. The number of services has been reduced from five (army, navy, air force, national air defense forces, and strategic rocket forces) to three (ground forces, air forces, and navy), along with forces of special designation (strategic rocket forces, aerospace defense forces, and airborne forces). The total manpower deployed is roughly one million, which is a significant reduction from the Cold War figure of over four million, with the vast majority of personnel cuts being made in ground troops. The Russian armed forces are composed of professional officers, conscripts who serve for one year, and contract soldiers. The current minister of defense, Sergei Shoigu, has set the target for contract personnel in the armed forces at 240,000 by the end of 2013 and 425,000 by the end of 2017.[17]

Strategic command and control of Russia's nuclear forces has evolved over the last two decades. The troika of the president, minister of defense, and chief of the general staff share the responsibility for authorizing the employment of nuclear forces. In this manner, the Russian state seeks to ensure the capacity to launch a retaliatory strike. Negative control of Russian nuclear forces arises from the system's highly automated nature. General Vladimir Dvorkin described the system in the following manner: "The system…has so many different stages and levels and links. All the way from the highest link, which [includes] the control center of the General Staff, and [reaches] all the way down to the launch pads. Nobody can tamper with it at any time."[18] This

---

[17] "K 2017 v sluzhashchie po kontraktu riadovogo i serzhantskogo sostava dolzhny naschityvat' 425 tysiach" [By 2017 the Number of Enlisted Men and Noncommissioned Officers under Contract Should Reach 425 Thousand], *Ekho Moskvy*, June 1, 2013, http://www.echo.msk.ru/news/1086292-echo.html.

[18] "Russian Roulette: An Interview with General Vladimir Dvorkin," *Frontline*, February 1999, http://www.pbs.org/wgbh/pages/frontline/shows/russia.

system protects against the unauthorized use of nuclear weapons but also provides for automatic release in case of system decapitation by enemy forces. However, in the aftermath of the dissolution of the Soviet Union, Russia lost key parts of its early-warning system in the Baltic region and the Caucasus. The system has recovered some of its capabilities but would be hard pressed to deal with differentiating between nuclear-armed missiles and those carrying conventional warheads as part of prompt global strike.[19] This situation could force Russia toward a launch-on-warning posture, especially in the context of a robust U.S. system for missile defense.[20]

The Role of Nuclear Weapons in Russia's National Security Strategy

The Putin Era and "First Use" of Nuclear Weapons: Whence the Threat?

The events of April–June 1999 had a profound effect on Russian domestic politics and foreign policy. NATO met in Washington in late April to celebrate its 50th anniversary and welcome three new members (Poland, the Czech Republic, and Hungary) to their first NATO summit. At the meeting, the alliance committed itself to further expansion "open to all European democracies, regardless of geography, willing and able to meet the responsibilities of membership, and whose inclusion would enhance overall security and stability in Europe."[21] NATO also approved a strategic concept that embraced out-of-area operations and crisis management as necessary for Atlantic-European security.[22] Following the summit, press reports suggested that some member governments were urging the employment of ground forces to bring about the end of the conflict in Yugoslavia on terms dictated by NATO. On May 7, 1999, U.S. Air Force B-2 bombers attacked a special target selected by the CIA and designated as a Yugoslav facility engaged in arms proliferation. The target in question turned out to be the Embassy of the People's Republic of China. China responded by condemning the attack with its loss of life as a barbaric act. During this same period, as tensions

---

[19] Pavel Podvig, "History and the Current Status of the Russian Early Warning System," *Science and Global Security* 10, no. 1 (2002): 21–60, http://iis-db.stanford.edu/pubs/20734/Podvig-S%26GS.pdf; and Pavel Podvig, "Russia and the Prompt Global Strike Plan," PONARS Policy Memo, no. 417, December 2006, http://csis.org/files/media/csis/pubs/pm_0417.pdf.

[20] Stephen J. Cimbala, "Russian Nuclear Command and Control: Mission Malaise?" *Journal of Slavic Military Studies* 14, no. 2 (2001): 1–28.

[21] "The Washington Declaration," NATO, Press Release, April 23, 1999, http://www.nato.int/docu/pr/1999/p99-063e.htm.

[22] "The Alliance's Strategic Concept," NATO, April 24, 1999, http://www.nato.int/cps/en/natolive/official_texts_27433.htm.

in the Russian Caucasus increased, rumors began to spread in Moscow about renewed terrorist actions in and around Chechnya during the coming summer, leading to speculation about a NATO intervention in Russia's own smoldering crisis.

On April 29, 1999, in the midst of the NATO bombing campaign against Yugoslavia, the Security Council of the Russian Federation met to discuss the current status and future of Russia's nuclear weapons complex. The council issued two sealed decrees on the development and employment of nonstrategic nuclear weapons.[23] Yeltsin, then president and council chairman, asserted that renewal of all the links in the Russian nuclear weapons complex was a top priority for the scientific elite, military, political leadership, and defense industry. Putin, then counsel secretary, spoke of a program that "authorized the conception of the development and utilization of nonstrategic nuclear weapons" as part of nuclear deterrence.[24] The Russian media, citing well-placed sources, described plans for a new generation of tactical nuclear weapons, developed not just for battlefield use but with the goal of making limited nuclear war possible.[25]

Although the significance of a shift toward nonstrategic nuclear weapons for force development was not immediately apparent, it was clear that an overt shift in the policy governing nuclear first use was occurring. In June 1999, as the conflict over Kosovo was ending, Russia conducted its first large-scale military exercise since the Cold War. Zapad-99 simulated a conventional attack on Belarus by Western forces and included the use of Russian nuclear weapons to de-escalate the conflict. During the exercise, Russian bombers simulated cruise missile strikes against operational targets in Europe and North America. The tactical goal was to end a local war before it could escalate into a broader conflict with risks of a strategic nuclear exchange. However, in the aftermath of the NATO air campaign over Yugoslavia, the likely political intent of the exercise was to warn the West about the risks that local wars pose to strategic stability.[26]

---

[23] "Iadernyi vek otkryl dveri novomu perodu istorii" [Nuclear Century: The Gate into a New Historical Period], *Voenno-istoricheskii zhurnal*, no. 1 (2000).

[24] Vitalii Denisov, "V sovete bezopasnosti osnova voennoi moshchi Rossii" [The Security Council Is the Foundation of Russia's Military Might], *Krasnaia zvezda*, April 30, 1999.

[25] Pavel Fel'gengauer, "Ogranichennaia iadernaia voina? Pochemu net!" [Limited Nuclear War? Why Not!] *Segodnia*, May 6, 1999.

[26] Vladimir Grigor'ev, "Koridory vlasti: uprezhdaiushchii iadernyi udar" [Corridors of Power: Preventive Nuclear Strike], *Profil*, July 12, 1999; and "Rossiia planiruet brat' Zapad na ispug kazhdye dva goda" [Russia Plans to Frighten the West Every Two Years], *Kommersant*, July 10, 1999.

Nuclear Strategy in a Changing Geopolitical Environment

Since 2000, Russian military doctrine has stipulated the circumstances under which nuclear weapons will be employed.[27] Nuclear weapons will not be used against signatories of the Nuclear Non-Proliferation Treaty. Russia does, however, explicitly claim the right to use such weapons in retaliation for the use of nuclear or other WMDs against it or its allies, as well as in cases of large-scale aggression by conventional forces that would threaten the national security of Russia.[28]

While Western experts tend to focus on strategic nuclear forces when assessing nuclear arsenals, Russian force planners do not underestimate the role of nonstrategic nuclear weapons in strategic stability. The Russian view of the country's nonstrategic and tactical nuclear arsenal reflects a unique geostrategic context, which can best be described as Eurasian. It takes into account Russia's geopolitical position and the complex continental environment with multiple and diverse security challenges and threats.

Russia's avowed primary objective is strategic stability, and it continues to see strategic nuclear weapons as both the technical and political manifestation of such stability.[29] Moscow is willing to engage in arms reductions so long as they do not alter the strategic status quo or preclude Russia's own modernization program. Despite President Barack Obama's promotion of a path to complete nuclear disarmament, the influential Russian strategist Sergei Karaganov summarized Russia's position when he offered a polite rejection of any dramatic moves that might undermine stability. To Karaganov, the immorality of nuclear weapons is unquestioned, but their power imposes restraint on countries through the threat of Armageddon. He writes:

> They are an effective means of preventing large-scale wars and mass destruction of people—something that humanity has engaged in throughout its history with surprising perseverance, destroying peoples, countries and cultures…. The world has survived only thanks to the nuclear sword of Damocles hanging over it.[30]

Karaganov makes a point regarding the useful secondary effects of strategic nuclear weapons on other powers that sheds light on their role in Russia's nuclear strategy. He asserts, for example, that China's economic and political success in the post–Cold War world was made possible by

---

[27] This section draws on the author's analysis in "Russian Doctrine on Tactical Nuclear Weapons: Contexts, Prisms, and Connections," in *Tactical Nuclear Weapons and NATO*, ed. Tom Nichols, Douglas Stuart, and Jeffrey D. McCausland (Carlisle: Strategic Studies Institute, 2012), 116–54.

[28] Security Council of the Russian Federation, *Voennaia doktrina Rossiiskoi Federatsii* [The Military Doctrine of the Russian Federation], February 5, 2010, http://www.scrf.gov.ru/documents/33.html.

[29] V.L., "Bomba spravliaet iubilei" [The Bomb Celebrates Its Anniversary], *Nezavisimoe voennoe obozrenie*, November 26, 2010.

[30] Sergei Karaganov, "Global Zero and Common Sense," *Russia in Global Affairs*, no. 2 (2010): 28.

the Russian strategic nuclear arsenal, which supposedly inhibited actions by other powers against China, especially by making China's posture of minimal strategic deterrence seem relatively benign.[31] Similarly, while Karaganov sees a dangerous transition in NATO from a defensive alliance into an instrument for intervention, Russia's recovery makes operations like Kosovo seem "unthinkable."[32] Instead, NATO is now involved in more distant out-of-area operations.

Karaganov rejects what he labels as "antinuclear mythology": that nuclear arms reductions by the major powers will convince lesser powers to give up their nuclear arms or convince states threatened by external and internal threats to forfeit the security these weapons may provide. Such arrangements might be in the interests of the two original nuclear powers but cannot be justified purely on moral grounds. He argues that states must act in their own interests in the absence of an international regime preventing the intervention of other powers. For example, Libya's renouncement of nuclear weapons after the 2003 Iraq War did not protect that state from external intervention into its civil war.

Karaganov maintains that in Russia's case the presence of both strategic and tactical nuclear weapons imposes restraint and compensates for the country's weakness in conventional forces in the west and east. Strategic nuclear weapons deter the United States and NATO from out-of-area adventures at Russia's expense and permit China to be the economic engine of Asian development, without the risk of U.S. military intervention against it. At the same time, according to Karaganov, Russia's tactical nuclear weapons deter China from intervention in the Russian Far East and Siberia. This point was also made in 2004 by Yuri Baluevsky, then chief of the general staff:

> The prevention of such a possibility [Chinese aggression] by only political methods via the maintenance of friendly relations or via reliance on the power of conventional weapons could prove ineffective. The Chinese factor dictates a continuation of political reliance on nuclear weapons and on strategic cooperation with the West.[33]

---

[31] Karaganov, "Global Zero," 28.

[32] Ibid., 29.

[33] Iu. N. Baluevskii, "Voenno-politicheskaia obstanovka, problemy natsional'noi i mezhdunarodnoi (regional'noi) besopasnosti" [Military-Political Environment, Issues of National and International (Regional) Security], in *Voennaia bezopasnost' Rossiiskoi Federatsii v XXI veke: Sbornik Statei* [Military Security of the Russian Federation in the 21st Century], ed. Iu. N. Baluevskii (Moscow: TsVSI, 2004), 22.

Responding to a Revolution in Military Affairs

Realists such as Karaganov seek to use nuclear weapons to provide Russia with some immediate security and even some leverage on its periphery. In the future, however, the deterrence capability of nuclear weapons might be reduced by the development of more advanced conventional weapons.[34] In addition, the modernization of missile defense systems raises questions about the long-term value of Russia's strategic forces, as does the modernization of Chinese conventional forces. These trends have cast doubt on Russia's deterrence capabilities in Siberia and the Far East, which were the subject of the 2010 Vostok exercise. Although the enemy in this exercise was hypothetical, some observers concluded that the exercise encompassed scenarios involving Chinese, U.S., and Japanese forces. In this case, the exercise embraced the first use of nuclear weapons to de-escalate a conflict.[35]

As previously mentioned, the shift to a nuclear policy of first use occurred in 1999 in the face of the deep precision-strike capabilities demonstrated by the United States and NATO in Yugoslavia. The first use of nuclear weapons for de-escalation (*deeskalatsiia*) would not be an act of political signaling but would specifically target the military systems supporting such capabilities. Russian leaders assumed that the greatest danger to national security stemmed from local wars that could invite foreign intervention and escalation. This perspective was first presented by military officers from the Frunze Academy as a response to the "informatization" of warfare. It applies military systemology to the conduct of combat operations in order to knock out key support subsystems, including reconnaissance and command and control, but without specific reference to the employment of nuclear weapons. In this manner, a country can defend itself merely by crippling an opponent's battle-management systems and depriving its attacking forces of their precision rather than by attempting to annihilate an opponent.[36] As this author observed at the time, Russian specialists pointing to such a change in the nature of warfare did not find a favorable audience in high places. Yeltsin's team was more focused on peace-enforcement operations on Russia's

---

[34] Oleg Falichev, "Amerikanskaia ruletka" [American Roulette], *VPK: Voenno-promyshlennyi kur'er*, April 10, 2009, http://vpk-news.ru/articles/1861.

[35] Oleg Falichev, "Krupneishee operativno-strategicheskoe uchenie VS Rossii nosilo issledovtel'skii kharakter" [The Most Significant Operational-Strategic Exercise Had an Exploratory Nature], *VPK: Voenno-promyshlennyi kur'er*, July 29, 2010.

[36] V.D. Riabchuk et al., *Elementy voennoi sistemologii primenitel'no k resheniiu problem operativnogo iskusstva i taktiki obshchevoiskovykh ob'edinenii, soedinenii i chastei: voenno-teoreticheskii trud* [Applying Elements of Military Systemology to Finding Solutions of Problems in Operational Art and Tactics for Combined Arms Large Formations, Formations, and Units: Military-Theoretical Work] (Moscow: Izdatel'stvo Voennoi Akademii imeni M.V. Frunze, 1995).

periphery and on cutting the heavy costs of defense on a weak economy trying to transition to a market system.[37]

The core problem of the debate was best described by Aleksandr Golts, a military journalist and the author of a major study on the failure of military reform in Russia. In 2003, the minister of defense, Sergei Ivanov, informed President Putin that military reform in Russia had been completed. In fact, reform had amounted to reducing the size of the army and making minor structural changes. Russia's army had become a smaller, more poorly armed version of the Soviet army with the same social and disciplinary problems. Golts's conclusion was simple: Russia had lost eleven years with nothing to show for it.[38] A champion of a smaller, professional army, Golts described the period from the collapse of the Soviet Union to 2004 as the long and painful death of a military system with roots in Petrine Russia and based on the conscript army created by Dmitri Miliutin in the 1870s.

Defeat in war had often resulted in military reform in Russia, but the Soviet Union's collapse led to no such transformation. The military system that Russia inherited was slowly collapsing after the dissolution of the Soviet state and economy. The first sign of this was the ineffectiveness of the Russian Army in the First Chechen War. In 2003, it was still fighting a second Chechen insurgency, if a bit more efficiently. Russian strategists realized that the key to winning modern wars was not mass industrial production but rather the capacity to engage in "information warfare," in which the U.S. military was leading the world. Golts emphasized the sad decline of Russia's conventional combat capabilities in the face of this challenge. Christopher Donnelly reached a similar conclusion when summarizing the findings of a group of Western military analysts looking back at a decade of Russian military reform. For Russia, the 1990s were a decade without substantial progress, except in reducing the number of men at arms.

The new technological possibilities associated with modern warfare were radically recasting the meaning of some key Russian concepts associated with nuclear weapons. This was due both to the reduced size and technological obsolescence of the Russian nuclear force and to the informatization of warfare and the possibilities created by deep precision-strike conventional systems, which have been demonstrated in local wars from the first Gulf War

---

[37] Jacob W. Kipp, "The Nature of Future War: Russian Military Forecasting and the Revolution in Military Affairs, a Case of the Oracle of Delphi or Cassandra?" *Journal of Soviet Military Studies* 9, no. 1 (1996): 1–45. On the struggle to create a Russian armed forces for conventional high-tech, precision-strike warfare, see Jacob W. Kipp, "Russian Doctrine on Tactical Nuclear Weapons," 116–54; and Jacob W. Kipp, "Russia's Future Arms Control Agenda and Posture," in *Russia and the Current State of Arms Control*, ed. Stephen J. Blank (Carlisle: Strategic Studies Institute, 2012), 1–62.

[38] Aleksandr Golts, *Armiia Rossii: Odinnadtsat' poteriannykh let* [Russia's Army: Eleven Lost Years] (Moscow: Izdatel'stvo Zakharov, 2004).

to NATO's air operations against Libya. Alexei Fenenko has argued that the Russian understanding of nuclear deterrence not only was different from the West's understanding but also failed to grasp the real implications of this new type of warfare:

> An alternative to nuclear deterrence today appears before us as forcing opponents to accept a certain set of conditions or the destruction of certain subjects of world politics. Therefore, contemporary discussions about the exhausting of "nuclear deterrence" reflect the appearance of an entirely new reality, that is, a world where policy of preventing wars means forceful acts including the use of nuclear weapons or their analogues.[39]

More recently, Andrei Kokoshin discussed precisely this new version of deterrence but linked it to the "analogous" means mentioned by Fenenko. Kokoshin pointed to Russia's development of a number of hypersonic systems capable of using non-nuclear, sub-nuclear, or electromagnetic-pulse weapons to attack high-value targets, including ground-based centers for radio-electronic reconnaissance, major warships of analogous type, communication centers, and command and control facilities.[40] Attacks on such military targets would carry with them less collateral damage. With respect to pre-nuclear deterrence, the target would shift to "analogous objects of civilian infrastructure" located outside urban centers but affecting economic production, including "power stations (excluding nuclear), which supply energy to the metropolises."[41]

The Race for Time and Network-centric Warfare

Russian military theorists, particularly the late general Vladimir Slipchenko, categorized informatization as a "sixth generation" of warfare that is in the process of superseding "fifth generation" warfare—nuclear war—which has become both politically and militarily untenable. Slipchenko doubted the ability of nuclear weapons to deter sixth-generation wars and anticipated major wars being conducted as "no contact" conflicts without

---

[39] A.V. Fenenko, "*Orbis terrarum*: Budushchee iadernogo sderzhivaniia—diskussii i realii" [Orbis Terrarum: The Future of Nuclear Deterrence—Discussions and Realities], *Polis-Politicheskie issledovaniia*, October 31, 2004.

[40] Andrei A. Kokoshin, "O sisteme neiadernogo (pred'iadernogo) sderzhivaniia v oboronnoi politike Rossii" [On the System of Non-Nuclear (Pre-nuclear) Deterrence in Russia's Defense Policy] (Moscow: Izdatel'stvo moskovskogo universiteta, 2012), 12–13.

[41] Ibid., 21. See also Andrei A. Kokoshin, "Ensuring Strategic Stability in the Past and Present: Theoretical and Applied Questions," Belfer Center for Science and International Affairs, Harvard Kennedy School, June 2011, http://belfercenter.ksg.harvard.edu/publication/21157/ensuring_strategic_stability_in_the_past_and_present.html.

the use of nuclear weapons when the forces and concepts driving this transformation have reached maturity.[42]

Recent efforts at reforming the Russian Army carried the catchy title of "new look."[43] This term conveyed a sweeping modernization of Russia's conventional forces, including a shift from a division- to a brigade-based combat structure and enhanced C4ISR associated with network-centric warfare.[44] The push for reform began after the Russo-Georgian War of August 2008 and was based on weaknesses exposed during that conflict.[45] By spring 2012, it was quite clear that the reform movement faced serious problems and mounting opposition from serving officers and defense contractors, who were upset by the ministry's purchases of foreign military technology and outsourcing of traditional military functions to private contractors.[46]

The reform efforts ended with Putin firing the minister of defense, Anatoli Serdiukov, under suspicion of corrupt practices and the retirement of the chief of the general staff. To replace the disgraced minister, he appointed new leadership in the ministry of defense: Sergei Shoigu, the former minister of extraordinary situations, became minister of defense, and Colonel General Valerii Gerasimov became chief of the general staff. Putin charged them with restoring confidence in the Ministry of Defense and overseeing the modernization of Russian military equipment. In assessing the first acts of the new team, however, one foreign observer wrote that military reform "drown[ed] in a sea of nostalgia."[47]

Serdiukov's "new look" reforms were supposed to raise the combat stability of Russian conventional forces and thereby reduce the need for nuclear first use in a crisis situation. One of the supporters of these reforms categorized the development of C4ISR capabilities to support network-centric warfare as a "race for time."[48] Aleksandr Kondratev, a leading proponent of this reform, had followed its origins in the U.S. military and later noted

---

[42] Vladimir Slipchenko, *Beskontaktnye voiny* [No Contact Warfare] (Moscow: Izdatel'stvo, 2001), 218.

[43] Roger McDermott, "'New Look' Russian Army Officially Formed," *Eurasia Daily Monitor*, November 24, 2009, http://www.jamestown.org/programs/edm/single/?tx_ttnews%5Btt_news%5D=35767&tx_ttnews%5BbackPid%5D=407.

[44] Roger N. McDermott, *The Reform of Russia's Conventional Armed Forces: Problems, Challenges, and Policy Implications* (Washington, D.C.: Jamestown Foundation, 2011).

[45] Mikhail Barabanov, Anton Lavrov, and Viacheslav Tseluiko, *Tanki avgusta: Sbornik statei* [Tanks of August: Essays] (Moscow: Tsentr Analiza Strategii i Tekhnologii, 2009).

[46] Roger N. McDermott, Bertil Nygren, and Carolina Vendil Pallin, eds., *The Russian Armed Forces in Transition: Economic, Geopolitical, and Institutional Uncertainties* (New York: Routledge, 2012).

[47] Roger McDermott, "Russian Military Reform Drowns in a Sea of Nostalgia," *Eurasia Daily Monitor*, February 12, 2013.

[48] A. Kondratev, *Setetsentrizm ili gonka za vremenem* [Network-centrism or the Race for Time], *Pentagonus*, September 27, 2011, http://pentagonus.ru/load/1/obshhie_voprosy/a_kondratev_setecentrizm/18-1-0-751.

the rapid progress being made by the People's Liberation Army (PLA) in acquiring network-centric capabilities. Kondratev stressed the threat posed by China's modernization of its armed forces and suggested that Russia was losing the race not only to the United States but also to China. The PLA took a different tack on network-centric warfare from the U.S. military and emphasized warfare in five dimensions: ground, sea, air, space, and cyberspace. Kondratev credited China with studying both U.S. military theory and its application during the wars of the last decade. On that basis, China had grasped the combat advantages of superior C4ISR capabilities, which it associated with information and radio-electronic warfare. The United States clearly had the advantage in both hardware and mature theory, but the PLA was pushing to become a network-centric force in the near term.[49] In a recent essay, Kondratev identified the common and distinct features of China's approach to network-centric warfare and emphasized its exploration of different methods for attacking identifiable centers of gravity in enemy forces, including the enemy's networks.[50]

By spring 2010, a number of those involved in bringing about Russia's "new look" were concerned that the PLA was moving rapidly toward a high-tech conventional force that was increasingly prepared for network-centric warfare.[51] The PLA conducted a major exercise, Stride 2009, which appeared to some Russian observers like a simulation of a military intervention in Central Asia or Russia.[52] A year later, addressing the deployment of two newly organized brigades along the Russian-Chinese border, the commander of the Siberian Military District stated that Russia was "obligated to keep troops there because on the other side of the border are five Chinese armies, and we cannot ignore that operational direction." In a related report, this commander characterized the new brigades as a deterrent force serving as a reminder to the PRC that "despite the friendly relations with China, our army command understands that friendship is possible only with strong countries, that is, those who can quiet a friend down with a conventional or nuclear club."[53]

---

[49] A. Kondratev, "Nekotorye osobennosti realizatsii kontseptsii 'setetsentricheskaia voina' v vooruzhennykh silakh KNR" [Some Unique Aspects of the Implementation of the "Network-centric Warfare" Conception in the PRC's Armed Forces], *Zarubezhnoe voennoe obozrenie* (2010): 11–17.

[50] A. Kondratev, "'Setetsentricheskie kontseptsii vedushchikh zarubezhnykh stran" [Network-centric Warfare Conceptions in Major Foreign Powers], *Armeiskii sbornik*, no. 3 (2013): 36–42.

[51] Kondratev, "Nekotorye osobennosti realizatsii kontseptsii," 11–17. The following discussion draws on Jacob W. Kipp, "Asian Drivers of Russia's Nuclear Force Posture," Nonproliferation Policy Education Center, August 26, 2010.

[52] "Ucheniia" [Military Exercises], *Zarubezhnoe voennoe obozrenie*, no. 8 (2009); and Aleksandr Khramchikhin, "Starye osnovy novoi doktriny" [Old Roots of the New Doctrine], *Voenno-promyshlennyi Kur'er*, no. 6 (2010): 5.

[53] "Russia Strengthens the Border with China," *Argumenty nedeli*, March 4–10, 2010.

Russia's modernization efforts, as described by Kondratev, are aimed at improving the country's capacity to arm, create, train, deploy, and keep combat-ready forces capable of conducting network-centric warfare. In the absence of such forces, deterrence depends on the credibility of the nuclear option to deter or repulse conventional attacks. Given the economic and demographic realities of Siberia and the Russian Far East, which are increasingly dominated by China, Russia has sought by nonmilitary means to preclude the emergence of a Chinese military threat. However, Russian observers also realize that an imminent military threat for Beijing can emerge out of regional instability, especially in the case of military intervention in North Korea, which is beyond Russia's unilateral means to control.

Recent Developments

The most recent Russian military doctrine, released in 2010, continues to characterize nuclear weapons as the primary deterrent against both nuclear and conventional attacks on Russia's interests, territorial integrity, and sovereignty.[54] The doctrine does not explicitly state that Russia will use nuclear weapons in preemptive attacks against such threats, as had been discussed in the fall of 2009, but leaves the decision to use such weapons in the hands of the Russian president. The context for such a decision, however, will be defined by the nature of the challenges and threats that Russia faces across Eurasia. One partially leaked document describes two threats that could lead to the use of nuclear weapons: (1) attacks on vital economic and political structures, early-warning systems, national command-and-control systems, and nuclear weapons systems, and (2) an invasion by enemy ground units into Russian territory that cannot be halted by conventional means. It is likely that these two threats respectively refer to a NATO action in Eastern Europe and an assault by the PLA in the Russian Far East.[55]

Which threat commands greater attention from the Russian national security elite seems to depend on the immediate geostrategic situation confronting Russia. As relations with the United States and NATO become rockier, as they did in fall 2011 over ballistic missile defense in Europe, some military leaders view the West as posing the most serious threat to Russia and openly champion even closer collaboration with China to counter that threat.[56] Leonid Ivashov, for example, regarding the combined threat of hypersonic,

---

[54] Security Council of the Russian Federation, *Voennaia doktrina Rossiiskoi Federatsii.*

[55] Vladimir Mokhov, "Osnovy natsional'noi bezopastosti" [The Foundation of National Security], *Krasnaia zvezda*, February 6, 2010. See also Kipp, "Asian Drivers of Russia's Nuclear Force Posture."

[56] Elena Krementsova, "Leonid Ivashov: Pentagon khokhochet nad nashimi ugrozami" [Pentagon Laughs at Our Threats], *Ekspress*, December 2, 2011, http://www.eg.ru/daily/politics/29081.

precision-strike cruise missiles and a mature global missile defense system, observed in November 2011 that "only China can save" Russia.[57] Likewise, in April 2013, Yuri Baluevsky, the former chief of the general staff and member of the Russian Security Council, stated that the United States is preparing for a "first nuclear strike on Russia and China" by building a global missile defense system to reduce their retaliatory strike to one hundred missiles.[58] Conversely, defense analyst Aleksandr Khramchikhin recently commented on China's preparation for a "major war." While Western analysts focus on the PLA's naval and air modernization, he is concerned by the modernization of China's ground forces and the conduct of large-scale maneuvers oriented toward continental theaters of military operations.[59] Thus, Washington's push for arms control based on a trilateral approach involving Washington, Moscow, and Beijing has not bloomed.[60]

During his election campaign in 2012, Putin spoke of the need for a smart defense to counter "new threats." These threats arise out of military-technical developments enhancing conventional capabilities in such a way that they could call into question the deterrent power of strategic offensive nuclear weapons. Putin announced that his next term as president would be devoted to the transformation of the Russian armed forces to meet this new challenge. Such a transformation would involve the recasting of the Russian defense industry to meet the challenge of "weapons based on new physical principles" and would encompass warfare in space, information warfare, and cyberwarfare. Putin emphasized the warfighting capabilities of these new technologies: "Such high-tech weapons systems will be comparable in effect to nuclear weapons but will be more 'acceptable' in terms of political and military ideology. In this sense, the strategic balance of nuclear forces will play a gradually diminishing role in deterring aggression and chaos."[61]

A recent response to this push for advanced weapons has been discussion of a return to a class of weapons mentioned in 1999 during the Kosovo crisis. Igor Artamonov and Roman Riabtsev, members of the Russian Academy of Rocket and Artillery Sciences, published a two-part article devoted to preparing Russia to fight "no-contact warfare" by employing "an asymmetric response" to the demands of network-centric warfare. The article focuses

---

[57] Krementsova, "Leonid Ivashov: Pentagon khokhochet nad nashimi ugrozami."

[58] "U.S. Ready for Preventive Nuclear Strike on Russia—Former General Staff Chief," Interfax, April 2, 2013.

[59] Aleksandr Khramchikhin, "Kitai gotov k bol'shoi voine" [China Is Prepared for a Large-Scale War], Voenno-promyshlennyi kur'er, June 22, 2013, 2.

[60] James Lewis, "Is the New New START Multilateral?" Examiner, April 10, 2013, http://www.examiner.com/article/is-the-new-new-start-multilateral.

[61] Putin, "Byt' sil'nymi: Garantii natsional'noi bezopasnosti dlia Rossii."

on "the development of nuclear weapons of small and super-small yields."[62] Although this argument might bring international condemnation for lowering the nuclear threshold, the authors regard such measures as necessary. They estimate that Russia's armament program by 2020 will not deliver an adequate force to fight sixth-generation warfare but will only be appropriate to conduct counterterrorism operations and peace enforcement. Putin, for his part, did not specify against what threats these new weapons might be directed. Artamonov and Riabtsev were more explicit:

> [The Russian Armed Forces] would not be enough to deal with a technologically equal and numerically superior enemy significantly (army of China—more than 2.3 million people, with a mobilization reserve [of] more than 30 million), or with the opposite side, about equal in number, but much superior technology (army of the United States—a little less than 1.5 million people; the European NATO countries—a little more than 1.5 million military personnel).[63]

In October 2012, Russia conducted a major exercise of its nuclear forces under the supervision of Putin. The exercise involved all elements of Russia's nuclear triad—long-range aviation, naval, and ground-based systems. Putin observed the testing of "the automated control system, as well as new control algorithms," as part of an initiative to place combat training missions for the strategic nuclear forces under a single operating plan. This exercise was reportedly "the first conducted on such a scale in the modern history of Russia."[64] Around the time that the Russian military press announced this exercise, the U.S. press reported that Russia was conducting drills involving the movement of strategic and tactical nuclear weapons in European Russia under the 12th Main Directorate of the Ministry of Defense. Although some Pentagon officials expressed no comment or considered the exercise a routine event, many were alarmed.[65] The nuclear drill may have been connected to the upcoming Zapad-2013 exercise, a joint operational and strategic drill to be conducted by Russian and Belarusian forces in September 2013. Speculation that a simulation of nuclear first use will be part of the exercise can be found in foreign press reports. The Polish press, for example, describes

---

[62] Igor Artamonov and Roman Riabtsev, "'Bog voiny' XXI veka" [The God of War of the XXI Century], *VPK: Voenno-promyshlennyi kur'er*, April 24, 2013.

[63] Igor Artamonov and Roman Riabtsev, "Asimmetrichnyi otvet Rossii" [Russia's Asymmetric Response], *VPK: Voenno-promyshlennyi kur'er*, April 17, 2013.

[64] Vladimir Zaeudnitskii, "Na peredovoi upravleniia voiskami" [In the Forefront of the Command and Control of Troops], *Krasnaia zvezda*, February 20, 2013.

[65] Bill Gertz, "Russia Launched Massive Nuclear Drill, Pentagon Alarmed," *Washington Times*, March 5, 2013, http://www.washingtontimes.com/news/2013/mar/5/russians-launched-massive-nuclear-drill-sounded-al.

a scenario involving a Russian nuclear strike on Warsaw.[66] The press in Belarus also mentions the possibility of nuclear first use if Russian and Belarusian conventional forces were defeated by a NATO attack.[67]

In the current climate of renewed talk about the use of nuclear weapons, the official Russian response to Obama's proposal in Berlin for the United States and Russia to cut their strategic nuclear arsenals by as much as a third has been overwhelmingly negative. Putin stated that Moscow could not expose itself to the risks of a disarming and decapitating first strike and thus would not act to undermine the effectiveness of its strategic offensive nuclear arsenal.[68] Other reports had Putin rejecting Obama's proposals as utopian and little more than "rosy dreams."[69] The Russian foreign minister Sergey Lavrov responded by stipulating that any future talks on further reductions in strategic nuclear weapons must include all other nuclear powers, declared and undeclared.[70] The foreign minister also stressed the need for Russia to fulfill all treaty obligations under START III. Sergei Ivanov, Putin's chief of staff, even suggested that Russia should take this opportunity to reconsider compliance with the Intermediate-Range Nuclear Forces Treaty, given that many states within range of Russian targets still possess, have developed, or are developing such weapons, including North Korea, China, Pakistan, India, Iran, and Israel. Ivanov asked why the United States and Russia should be banned from having such a class of weapons.[71]

Thus, there does not seem to be any desire in Moscow to consider cuts in nuclear weapons, which remain for the time being Russia's primary means of deterrence and the foundation of its strategic stability. Even the recent bilateral agreement to renew the Cooperative Threat Reduction Program for nuclear and chemical weapons, which dates back to 1992, is considered to be much weaker in its present form and unlikely to serve its original mission of transparency, threat reduction, and counterproliferation.[72]

---

[66] Agaton Koziński, "Manewry Zapad-2013: Rosja i Białoruś przećwiczy prewencyjny atak jądrowy na Warszawę. A NATO?" [Zapad-2013 Maneuvers: Russia and Russian Practice Preventive Nuclear Strike on Warsaw and What About NATO?], *Polskatimes*, April 2, 2013.

[67] Aleksandr Alesin, "Ucheniia 'Zapad-2013' perepolshili Pol'shu i Litvu" [The Exercises 'Zapad-2013' Have Alarmed Poland and Lithuania], *Politika*, February 18, 2013, http://naviny.by/rubrics/politic/2013/02/18/ic_articles_112_180876/.

[68] "Putin: Rossii nel'zia iskliuchat' opasnost' nanrseniia obezruzhivaiushchego udara" [Putin: Russia Cannot Ignore the Danger of the Launching of a Disarming Strike], *Vzgliad*, June 19, 2013.

[69] "Putin ne vosprinimaet vser'ez rozovye mechty Obamy" [Putin Does Not Take Seriously Obama's Rosy Dreams], *Mir i politikia*, June 20, 2013.

[70] "Lavrov: Sokrashchenie SNB nado obsuzhdat' so vsemi iadernami derzhavami" [Lavrov: Reduction in Strategic Nuclear Weapons Must Be Considered by All Nuclear Powers], Vesti.Ru, June 22, 2013.

[71] "Russia Honoring INF Treaty, but This Can't Last Endlessly—Kremlin Chief of Staff," Interfax, June 21, 2013.

[72] "New Russian-U.S. Agreement on Nunn Lugar Vastly Dilutes Program's Reach," *Bellona*, June 19, 2013.

Geopolitical Implications

Russian nuclear policy under Vladimir Putin has exhibited a distinctly Eurasian focus and character. The Eurasian context has forced Russia, which found its geopolitical status diminished after the Cold War, to confront an international environment where it has been more object than subject, reacting to developments rather than shaping them. Weaker economically and politically than the Soviet Union, Russia has made nuclear weapons an explicit part of its response to potential crises from a number of diverse and complex sources of instability, both within the country and on its periphery. Over the last two decades, Russia has confronted security crises in the Balkans, the Baltic, the Caucasus, the Middle East, Central Asia, and the Far East. In the face of such instability, Moscow has sought to create international instruments to promote collective security in the form of the Collective Security Treaty Organization and the Shanghai Cooperation Organisation (SCO). The first includes some of the successor states from the Soviet Union (Armenia, Belarus, Kazakhstan, Kyrgyzstan, and Tajikistan), led by Russia, but has proved largely ineffective in dealing with regional crises, such as the 2010 civil war in Kyrgyzstan. The SCO, which includes the five Central Asian states, Russia, and China, has focused on threats to stability in Central Asia and provides the foundation of an emerging strategic partnership between Russia and China. Beijing and Moscow share a concern for radical Islam in the region and seek to counter U.S. influence by promoting multipolarity. The shared perspectives on radical Islam in Central Asia and hostility to the U.S. hegemon do not, however, preclude Russian anxiety over China's growing power in Asia in the face of Russia's own weakness in Eastern Siberia and the Russian Far East.

The range of threats across Eurasia has required that Russia maintain conventional military forces of a size and diversity appropriate for dealing with everything from terrorism and civil unrest to local, regional, and general wars. Economics and demographics, however, make it impossible for Moscow to settle for the conventional answer of mass mobilization and industrial war. Efforts at reform have not yet brought about a conventional force with the flexibility and mobility to meet the above threats or counter the advanced military capabilities of the United States if it were to intervene in a conflict. Russia has thus adopted a posture featuring limited conventional means; a declaratory policy of nuclear first use to de-escalate any crisis threatening vital state interests, territorial integrity, or national sovereignty; and reliance on strategic nuclear forces to sustain deterrence. Yet Russian analysts have observed that the increasing emphasis on network-centric warfare could call into question the survivability of Russia's nuclear forces. Recently, the country's defense experts have specifically discussed how an emerging global missile defense system and prompt global strike pose just such a threat.

This Russian vision of a threat from the United States and the West would seem from a Western perspective to be absurd. But the Russian elite live with the chaos of the collapse of the Soviet Union and the ensuing decade of economic, social, and political crises. Vladimir Putin's claim to political legitimacy comes from his recreation of a powerful centralized Russian state, which, if not a superpower, has become an influential regional power with recognized areas of interest. From a Russian perspective, the chief challenge from the West has come from three sources. One has been what the Russian elite refers to as the "color revolutions." These brought regimes to power in Ukraine and Georgia that were seen as inherently anti-Russian in their policies. Even the subsequent outcomes of these revolutions have not reduced Russian fears about informational assaults and psychological warfare, as can be seen in Putin's response to mass demonstrations in Moscow in 2012–13 and the Duma's recent law requiring NGOs engaged in political activities and receiving foreign financial assistance to register as "foreign agents." The second source has been NATO's expansion into post-Soviet states in Eastern Europe. In this case, membership plans for Georgia and Ukraine brought these two "dangers" together for a time. As George F. Kennan had warned, NATO expansion to Russia's borders has contributed to deteriorating bilateral relations between Moscow and Washington.[73]

The third source of danger from the West cited by Russia's national security elite is U.S.-NATO missile defense plans and the United States' creation of conventional global strike capabilities, which could undermine the deterrence capabilities of Russia's own strategic nuclear weapons and call into question the country's strategic stability. Just recently, Dmitry Rogozin, deputy prime minister and chair of the Military-Industrial Commission, spoke at a conference devoted to national security and informed the world that Russia would lose a general war with the United States in six hours because of the combination of its robust missile defense and an advanced conventional prompt-global-strike system.[74] Russian experts addressing changes in the targeting of U.S. nuclear forces see those emerging capabilities as a threat to the future survivability of Russia's offensive nuclear forces.[75] In his conference statement, Rogozin was attempting to justify increased defense spending on advanced military technology over the rest of this decade.

---

[73] George F. Kennan, "A Fateful Error," *New York Times*, February 5, 1997.

[74] Dmitrii Popov, "Rossiia proigraet Amerike voinu za 6 chasov" [Russia Will Lose a War with America in 6 Hours], *Moskovskii komsomolets*, June 29, 2013, 2.

[75] Markell Boitsov, "Natselivanie iadernykh sil SShA" [The Targeting of U.S. Nuclear Forces], *Nezavisimoe voennoe obozrenie*, July 19, 2013, 1.

The combination of threat perceptions from the West encompassing psychological-informational subversion in the form of the penetration of Western values, geopolitical expansion, and military-technical developments makes it very difficult to see any hope for further bilateral arms control or for another reset of relations between the United States and Russia. The relative decline of Europe's political weight to influence U.S.-Russian relations seems to be a direct result of Moscow's calculation that the economic crisis within the European Union has reduced the ability of the major European powers to coordinate their security policies, especially at a time of declining defense spending. Moscow had counted on Europe to constrain foreign intervention by Washington, but that now seems less likely.[76]

The sharpest manifestation of this problem was Russia's war with Georgia over South Ossetia and Abkhazia in August 2008. Russian conventional forces intervened in a civil war not as peacekeepers or under an international mandate, but as an external force determined to impose its version of order on the South Caucasus. Behind this conflict stands a critical doctrinal issue at the heart of Russian national security policy. Should external powers seek to intervene in response to the Russian military intervention, Russia reserves the right to respond with nuclear weapons. There was no foreign military intervention to aid Georgia, but continued fighting, a Russian advance on Tbilisi, or a Russian air attack on U.S. military transport aircraft bringing Georgia's first brigade back to Tbilisi from Iraq could have forced such a response.

In the aftermath of the conflict, the Russian military's "new look" reforms were supposed to provide its conventional forces with the means to engage in such operations without relying on nuclear deterrence. The collapse of those efforts under the weight of charges of corruption and incompetent leadership in late 2012 has left Russia with a strategic dilemma as it faces instability across Eurasia. The reformers of 2008 had identified the poor performance of the Russian military in force structure, air-space management, and C4ISR. They attributed these weaknesses to the fact that the armed forces were a distinctly "legacy force," based on aging Soviet equipment, force structure, and doctrine. Post-Soviet Russia continued to rely on tanks and infantry following the model of mass industrial war.[77] For well over a decade now, Russia has declared that the inadequacy of its conventional forces in numbers and capabilities gives it the right to first use of nuclear weapons to de-escalate a conflict in the face of foreign intervention in a local war where Russian

---

[76] Sergei Karaganov, "West's Decline Will Play a Mean Trick on Russia," *Moscow Times*, January 22, 2013.

[77] Barabanov, Lavrov, and Tseluiko, *Tanki avgusta: Sbornik statei*. For a view of the same war as a triumph of mechanized warfare as fought by the Russians, see Igor Dzhadan, *Piartidnevnaia voina: Rossiia prinuzhdaet k miru* [The Five-Day War: Russia Imposes Peace] (Moscow: Izdael'stvo "Evropa," 2008).

strategic interests or territorial integrity is threatened. In Georgia, the conflict ended too quickly for any threat of foreign military intervention to materialize. By setting limited political and military goals and resolving the conflict quickly, Russia successfully avoided the nuclear dilemma.

Five years later, and after the reset in U.S.-Russia relations, the situation has not measurably improved. The single bright spot has been Russia's continued engagement in the groups of powers seeking to deal with the most pressing problems of nuclear proliferation: North Korea and Iran. But Russia has depended on its strategic partnership with China to keep from being isolated and subject to pressure from the West. On issues associated with North Korea, Moscow has consistently followed Beijing's lead—for example, during the crisis after North Korea sank the South Korean patrol vessel *Cheonan* in 2010.[78]

More recently, the Russian response to the Arab Spring evolved from concerned observation into limited cooperation via the United Nations on Libya and into open dispute with the West over Syria. On the latter issue, Russian support for the Assad regime has benefitted from China's willingness to reject Western efforts to impose Bashar Assad's removal as the first condition for the settlement of the civil war. Indeed, in response to the series of crises that have developed as a result of the Arab Spring, Moscow and Beijing have found more reasons to cooperate under the assumption that external intervention by foreign powers could turn the Syrian civil war into a local war with the risks of regional escalation. Behind this assumption stand both powers' concerns over Islamic radicalism and ties between foreign fighters in Syria and domestic sources of Islamic resistance and terrorism. Moscow's position, in particular, stresses the fact that because Assad is the *de jure* head of state, Russian assistance to the regime must be considered legitimate.

At the same time, Moscow is also aware of the complex dynamics shaping the entire Middle East. As regional instability increases from the effects of the Syrian civil war, support for the regime may become meaningless as the state collapses into warlords and ethno-religious enclaves. Such an outcome, especially in the case of a widening conflict among Sunni and Shia across the region, could have an impact on Russia's own periphery in the Caucasus and bring about the very sort of conflict that Moscow has sought to avoid. In this particular environment, nuclear weapons introduce their own set of complications, which recall some of the worst moments of the great-power

---

[78] Stephen Blank, "The Paradox of Russo-Chinese Relations," e-International Relations, June 22, 2012, http://www.e-ir.info/2012/06/22/the-paradox-of-russo-chinese-relations. See also Jacob W. Kipp, "Moscow Seeks Room to Maneuver as Crisis on the Korean Peninsula Intensifies," *Eurasia Daily Monitor*, June 18, 2010.

confrontations in the Middle East during the Cold War. In this case, the nuclear equation involves multiple players and includes the possibility of disarming preemptive strikes (e.g., in the case of Iran) with second- and third-order effects beyond the capacities of the actors to forecast.

Beyond the Middle East, Russia faces the threat of new instability in Central Asia as a result of U.S. and NATO disengagement after 2014. For more than a decade, U.S. and NATO forces limited the spread of radical Islam and terrorism from Afghanistan. With the withdrawal of those forces, Russia will soon discover whether its own collective security structures—the Collective Security Treaty Organization and the SCO—will be equal to the increased threats posed by instability in Afghanistan. Given the linkage to radical Islam, which is a cause of the evolving crisis in the Middle East and Afghanistan, Russia can expect continued cooperation from China, but it is unclear which power will inherit the role of securing Central Asia.

Reading the recent pronouncements of the current heads of the Chinese and Russian states, one is left with the impression that there are no security problems between them. Putin categorized Sino-Russian relations during his visit to China as a strategic partnership:

> Today the Russian-Chinese relations are on the rise, they are the best in their centuries-long history. They are characterized by a high degree of mutual trust, respect for each other's interests, support in vital issues; they are a true partnership and are genuinely comprehensive.[79]

He then enumerated specific areas of their pragmatic cooperation: "the situation in the Middle East and North Africa, the nuclear problem on the Korean Peninsula, and the situation around the Iranian nuclear program."[80]

The comments of the new Chinese president Xi Jinping have been of much the same character. During his visit to Moscow in March 2013, he asserted that "Sino-Russian relations are one of the most significant bilateral relationships in the world. They not only correspond to our interests but also serve as a guarantee of balance in the world."[81] Xi left the impression of being both an ally and a lover of Russian culture. The Russian military press in its turn honored the Chinese leader with the title "Comrade Xi."[82] Although

---

[79] Vladimir Putin, "Interview to the ITAR-TASS News Agency," ITAR-TASS, March 22, 2013, http://eng.kremlin.ru/news/5152. On Putin's signals of a shift toward improving Sino-Russian relations following his election in 2012, see Jacob W. Kipp, "Whither Russia: Looking East and Ready to Embrace it," *Eurasia Daily Monitor*, May 14, 2012.

[80] Putin, "Interview to ITAR-TASS News Agency."

[81] "Predsedatel' KNR Si Tszin'pin ostalsia dovolen itogami vizita v Rossiiu" [President of the PRC Xi Jinping Is Pleased with the Results of His Visit to Russia], *Rossiiskaia gazeta*, March 23, 2013.

[82] "Si Tszin'pin v Moskve: Koshmar dlia Ameriki" [Xi Jinping in Moscow: A Nightmare for America], *Voennoe obozrenie*, March 27, 2013, http://topwar.ru/25937-si-czinpin-v-moskve-koshmar-dlya-ameriki.html.

other press reports described tensions regarding arms deals, the overall tenor was one of Sino-Russian solidarity.[83] Xi took the opportunity in Moscow to highlight the continuing shared position of China and Russia regarding Syria and warned against Western intervention in the civil war.[84]

This image of positive bilateral relations does not tell the entire story of the two countries' interactions, however, as Russia seeks to come to terms with its own reduced status in world affairs and China's emergence as an industrial and military power. Marcel de Haas has argued that the present level of cooperation between Moscow and Beijing is more a tactical response to U.S.-NATO intervention in the Arab Spring than a long-term strategic partnership. He postulates that the Russian elite does see a potential strategic threat in China. These concerns center on the growing power of the PLA, China's increasingly tense relations over border disputes in the Pacific since 2010, China's economic incursion into Central Asia, Russia's own economic and demographic weakness in Eastern Siberia and the Russian Far East, and China's unwillingness to renounce claims to Russian territory in these regions.[85] Whereas China stands tall as an emerging economic power and geopolitical actor, Russia is openly mocked as "Nigeria in snow" because of its corruption and government inefficiency.[86] On the other hand, Stephen Blank has argued that renewed arms sales between Beijing and Moscow, including China's purchase of Su-35 advanced fighters, are evidence of a deepening strategic partnership primarily oriented against the United States. Blank identifies several areas of shared concerns, ranging from Syria and North Korea to ballistic missile defense.[87]

In July 2013 the PLA Navy and Russian Navy conducted joint maneuvers in the Gulf of Peter the Great. The latest and largest of these joint exercises involved surface warships, submarines, and naval aviation and included a

---

[83] "Itogi vizita Si Tszin'pina v RF: Druzhba na pochve krolikovodstva i spor iz-za oruzhiia" [The Results of Xi Jinping's Visit to the RF: Friendship Based on Rabbit Husbandry and Disagreements with Regard to Armaments], Newsru.com, March 25, 2013, http://www.newsru.com/russia/25mar2013/vizit.html.

[84] Vladimir Soldatkin, "In Moscow, New Chinese Leader Xi Warns against Meddling," Reuters, March 23, 2013, http://www.reuters.com/article/2013/03/23/us-china-russia-moscow-idUSBRE92M02F20130323.

[85] Marcel de Haas, "Russian-Chinese Security Relations: Moscow's Threat from the East?" Netherlands Institute of International Relations (Clingendael), March 2013, http://www.clingendael.nl/publications/2013/20130327_rc_securityrelations.pdf; and Thomas Lynch, "A Shift in the Sino-Russian Relationship," EastWest Institute, March 28, 2013, http://www.ewi.info/shift-sino-russian-relationship. On China's vision of its evolving role in Central Asia, see Charles Hawkins and Robert R. Love, eds., *The New Great Game: Chinese Views on Central Asia* (Fort Leavenworth: Foreign Military Studies Office, 2006).

[86] Andrei Polunin, "Nigeriia v snegu" [Nigeria in the Snow], *Svobodnaia pressa*, February 27, 2013, http://svpressa.ru/society/article/64866.

[87] Stephen Blank, "Shared Threat Perceptions Begin Renewal of Sino-Russian Arms Trade," *Eurasia Daily Monitor*, February 15, 2013.

range of scenarios against a hypothetical opponent, one that could mount air attacks against warships at sea, conduct antisubmarine warfare, engage in surface combat, and undertake acts of piracy against merchant ships. The Russian and Chinese press noted that Japan and the United States were conducting their own naval exercises at the same time in the adjacent Sea of Japan and speculated that the Japanese and U.S. forces were collecting intelligence about Chinese electronic warfare.[88] Shortly thereafter the Russian Ministry of Defense and General Staff mounted a surprise exercise covering Siberia and the Russian Far East. The Russian press emphasized the size of the exercise (160,000 troops, 1,000 tanks and infantry fighting vehicles, 130 aircraft and helicopters, and 70 warships), the movement of the units from their bases to the exercise areas, and the preparedness of the commands to move without a warning alert.[89] The combat scenarios here also featured a hypothetical opponent, but one that would demand the movement of Russian forces over great distances requiring air, automotive, and rail transport. In addition, the exercise called for long-range aviation to engage in the "so-called strategic deterrence of the hypothetical enemy."

The situation that Moscow faces in the Far East makes the identification of a single probable opponent a matter of political significance, as well as military posture. Russia must address its own regional weakness there as it continues to face potential conflicts with Japan and the United States over the Kuril Islands and potential demands for concessions from China in the event of a Sino-American confrontation. North Korea, however, remains the most dangerous place for a political confrontation to turn into open warfare on Russia's doorstep. While one can speculate about what states could be probable opponents in a conflict requiring strategic nuclear deterrence and large-scale ground, air, and sea combat operations, Sergei Karakaev, commander of the Strategic Rocket Forces, had no trouble naming the state in December 2011. He declared that Putin "was right; we can destroy the United States in less than half an hour."[90]

---

[88] Sergei Medvedev, "'Piratam' dan otpor" [The Pirates Were Repulsed], *Krasnaia zvezda*, July 9, 2013; and Konstantin Lobkov and Andrei Gavrilenko, "Po volnam vzaimodeistviia" [On the Waves of Cooperation], *Krasnaia zvezda*, July 9, 2013.

[89] Petr Asanov, "Vnezapho ne zhachit vrasplokh" [Surprise Does Not Mean Caught Off Guard], *Krasnaia zvezda*, July 19, 2013.

[90] Viktor Baranets, "Komanduiushchi' RVSN general-leitenant Sergei Karakaev: 'Vladimir Vladimirovich byl prav—My mozhem unichtozhit SShA bystree chem za polchasa'" [CinC SRF General-Lieutenant Sergei Karakaev: 'Vladimir Vladimirovich Was Right—We Can Destroy the USA in Less than a Half Hour"], *Komsomol'skaia pravda*, December 17, 2011.

Conclusion

In 2010 the Obama administration addressed U.S.-Russian relations in its first and only *National Security Strategy* thus far. At that time, the "reset" was in full bloom, and the document reflected the optimism then felt in Washington about bilateral relations. Russia's nuclear arsenal did not seem to pose a thorny problem. It was merely one aspect of a developing relationship based on mutual interests, which included reducing nuclear weapons; preventing nuclear proliferation; fighting terrorism, especially in Afghanistan; and developing trade and investment. Russia was expected to promote "the rule of law, accountable government, and universal values" so that it could be a "responsible partner in Europe and Asia."[91]

Not much of that optimism remains. Although Russia did enjoy U.S. support in achieving WTO membership, Obama's re-election to a second term did not fundamentally change the pessimistic cast of U.S.-Russian relations. While Obama has stated that he intends to seek negotiated cuts with Russia and thereby bring to an end the Cold War nuclear postures, Moscow's response has been frosty at best. The Russian elite now assumes that U.S. progress in creating the foundations for global missile defense and conventional strategic-strike systems has raised questions regarding the adequacy of Russia's strategic nuclear forces as a means to ensure strategic stability in Eurasia. It seems that the two sides have been talking past each other.

For the United States, it is possible to view nuclear arms reductions as a means to removing a remote but devastating threat to national existence. In the Russian case, the threats are not confined to some remote prospect of strategic nuclear exchange but the very real possibilities of regional conflicts over access to raw materials and disputes among ethnic groups and religious sects. Recently, Dmitri Rogozin postulated five hypothetical scenarios for future conflicts facing Russia: no-contact warfare, mass industrial war, local wars, terrorism (including state-sponsored terrorism), and a conflict in the Arctic.[92]

In all of these situations, Russia relies on nonstrategic nuclear forces to provide a linkage between weak conventional forces and its strategic deterrence. This is most apparent in the Russian Far East, where Russia's weakness makes it an object to be acted on rather than an independent actor. Its strategic partnership with China reflects shared concerns for stability in Central Asia in the face of Islamic radicalism. Moscow, however, must

---

[91] White House, *National Security Strategy* (Washington, D.C., May 2010), 44.

[92] See Sergei Ptichkin, "Chto znachit byt' sil'nym" [What It Means to Be Strong], *Rossiiskaia gazeta*, July 1, 2013.

confront the reality of the growing power of China and the possibility of it seeking strategic depth in Siberia and the Russian Far East at Russia's expense. In this case, nonstrategic nuclear weapons are the implicit safeguard, making U.S.-Russian bilateral arms control negotiations over such weapons a nonstarter.

EXECUTIVE SUMMARY

This chapter considers the evolution of China's nuclear posture and the current status of its nuclear modernization programs and draws implications for the Asia-Pacific region and the U.S.

MAIN ARGUMENT:
China is continuing to modernize its strategic forces, including by adding new capabilities such as conventionally armed missiles. The modernization of its nuclear force is driven by a complex set of motivations, including the perceived need for continual technological advancement, responses to perceived strategic challenges, and ideological considerations. China's nuclear capability is oriented toward maintaining a credible strategic retaliatory capability, primarily through the development of increasingly advanced medium-range and intercontinental ballistic missiles. This process, combined with broader changes in all aspects of life in China, raises questions about whether such modernization will occur within the historical framework of the country's policy on nuclear weapons or mark a fundamental transition.

POLICY IMPLICATIONS:
- The dynamics of strategic stability between the U.S. and China will be fundamentally different from what existed between the U.S. and the Soviet Union, primarily because of significant disparities in power and capability as well as profound differences in how Washington and Beijing see one another and the role of nuclear weapons in their bilateral relationship.

- The major policy choice for the U.S. involves whether to accept a Chinese "assured destruction capability" as a strategic fact and, if so, whether to publicly acknowledge this fact.

- A negotiated joint statement on strategic stability, in which the two countries agree to work toward stabilizing the current strategic balance, may provide a basis for ongoing discussions.

China's Nuclear Modernization: Surprise, Restraint, and Uncertainty

Jeffrey Lewis

If the history of the United States' understanding of China's nuclear capabilities and force development could be summarized in one word, it would be "surprise." When the People's Republic of China (PRC) tested its first nuclear device in 1964, U.S. policymakers and analysts were not only surprised that China possessed enough fissile material to conduct a test but were further surprised to learn that it had used highly enriched uranium rather than plutonium for its first device. China's turbulent internal politics, as well as its different historical and ideological circumstances, have conspired to produce an approach to nuclear weapons and deterrence that is a puzzle to most U.S. observers. The Chinese arsenal appears relatively small and vulnerable, almost provocatively so to a Western observer. China possesses a few hundred warheads available for deployment on ballistic missiles, but the warheads are stored separately from the missiles and are constrained by a policy of "no first use" (NFU) that requires the country's nuclear forces to ride out a first strike.

Given this history, assessments of China's current and future nuclear posture and strategy should be grounded in a humble acknowledgement of the limitations of external analysis. Although information about Chinese strategic forces is far better today than it was in 1964, significant limitations remain.

Jeffrey Lewis is Adjunct Professor and Director of the East Asia Nonproliferation Program at the James Martin Center for Nonproliferation Studies at the Monterey Institute of International Studies. He can be reached at <jeffrey.lewis@miis.edu>.

The PRC's current capabilities and the intentions of its leadership, as well as its future plans for the strategic force, remain obscured by a combination of intentional opacity, historical and ideological dogma of uncertain practical significance, and a seemingly genuine uncertainty in Beijing about several key issues.

With such caveats in mind, China is continuing to modernize its strategic forces, including through the introduction of new capabilities such as conventionally armed strategic missiles, indications of interest in missiles capable of carrying multiple warheads, and the construction of the foundation of a viable submarine-based deterrent. This process raises fundamental questions about the future of China's nuclear modernization—whether it will occur within the country's traditionally restrained approach to nuclear weapons, or whether new capabilities will enable Chinese leaders to choose a fundamentally different path.

The first section of this chapter surveys the evolution of China's nuclear program and is followed by an examination of the key features of China's current nuclear strategy, capabilities, and posture. The next section discusses the reasons for Chinese strategic restraint and considers questions about the country's NFU policy. The chapter then concludes by assessing the regional and global impact of China's nuclear modernization and by drawing implications for the United States.

The History of China's Nuclear Weapons and Missile Development

China's acquisition of nuclear weapons and ballistic missiles was initially driven by a desire to possess the same "sophisticated weapons" as other major powers. From the very beginning in the late 1950s, the Chinese leadership was committed to developing large, multi-megaton thermonuclear warheads that could be delivered at intercontinental ranges by ballistic missiles. This was an audacious goal for the poor, technologically inept PRC of the Great Leap Forward era. Yet China moved quickly in its nuclear testing program to develop thermonuclear warheads—burning thermonuclear fuel in its third nuclear test (prior to demonstrating a deliverable fission device) and successfully conducting a staged thermonuclear explosion in its sixth test. At the same time, China pursued an ambitious missile development program called "eight years, four missiles" (*banian sidan*).[1] Although the four missiles are usually described as aspirations in terms of range, with

---

[1] John Wilson Lewis and Xue Litai, *China Builds the Bomb* (Stanford: Stanford University Press, 1988), 211–12.

illustrative targets—Okinawa, Guam, Hawaii, and Washington, D.C.—it is more accurate to say that the selection of four missiles was actually driven by technical targets: a large single-stage missile with one engine, a missile with clustered engines, a staged missile, and finally an intercontinental ballistic missile (ICBM).

For decades, the PRC's strategic programs appear to have been driven by a peculiar type of technological determinism, as Chinese leaders followed the technical, but not strategic, lead of the United States and other advanced military powers.[2] This approach to nuclear weapons and ballistic missiles reflected a broader Maoist approach of setting high (often unrealistic) goals for the country's industrial development without defining a way to achieve those objectives. In some cases, such as Mao Zedong's Great Leap Forward to surpass Britain in steel production within ten years, this approach led to devastating results. Yet it was fairly successful in rapidly developing a Chinese strategic capability. The heads of the PRC's defense research community articulated a rationale for science and technology programs that emphasized catching up with foreign defense developments, with the expectation that this process would result in the nationwide development of key industries and technology. Consistent with this ideological outlook, Chinese officials continued to assert that nuclear weapons were "paper tigers," despite China's possession of them, and articulated a policy of not being the first to use such weapons under any circumstances.

This emphasis on technological goals, rather than near-term acquisition of usable weapons systems, defined the unique circumstances that led to China's acquisition of nuclear weapons. Chinese leaders initially expected substantial Soviet assistance in this process, but after the Soviet Union suspended support in 1960 and the chaos of the Great Leap Forward engulfed China, a split developed over the issue of strategic programs. The R&D community sought to continue the programs, whereas the defense production community wanted to free up money for the ships, tanks, and aircraft that would be needed to defend China from the United States or the

---

[2] An account by Nie Rongzhen on China's nuclear development provides a useful illustration of the type of technological determinism at play. Nie recalls the motivations for military modernization programs and notes that by the PRC's founding the great powers had already achieved modernization, especially in the atomic sphere. At the time of the Korean War, he notes that China's technology was backward, which he believes contributed to its many difficulties during the war. Nie further theorizes that wars of the modern era are wars of technological advances. He believes that the United States even "dared to bully China" during the Korean War because the PRC was technologically backward. In order to be free of this, it needed rapid technological advancement and the modern scientific research required for a strong economy and national defense. For China, nuclear development was not for the sake of prestige per se but rather to attain a level of technological development necessary to resist coercion from and to compete with technologically advanced countries. See Political Department of the PLA General Armament Department, *Liangdan yixing: Gongheguo fengbei* [Nuclear, Missile, and Satellite Program: Achievements of the Republic] (Beijing: Jiuzhou tushu chubanshe, 2000), 2–4.

Soviet Union. In the summer of 1961, the Central Committee resolved the controversy, selecting strategic programs for modernization at the expense of conventional forces. Marshal Nie Rongzhen, the head of China's defense science and technology complex after 1958, carried the day, arguing that strategic programs would serve as an organizing endeavor for national science and technology.[3] This rationale linked the development of sophisticated weapons to the broader theme of China's national economic development and emphasized the possession of advanced capabilities rather than their battlefield uses.

This approach underpinned China's unusual force structure. The dominance of the R&D community meant that resources were devoted to technological improvements, with relatively little emphasis placed on acquiring large numbers of missiles or nuclear weapons. Moreover, the dominance of technology-acquisition goals meant that new systems were developed with comparatively little emphasis on operational concepts. The People's Liberation Army (PLA) itself was hardly in a position to do more than accept the systems developed by the defense community. In 1966, China established the Second Artillery Force out of a disbanded public security unit and the artillery elements responsible for missile testing. Perhaps due to the turmoil of the Cultural Revolution, the Second Artillery "only slowly developed rigorous operational and targeting plans."[4]

This approach continued into the 1980s, as Deng Xiaoping consolidated power. Deng's economic reforms resulted in a substantial reduction in the resources available for strategic weapons programs. During this period, China suspended efforts to develop an operational sea-based deterrent and reorganized existing solid-fuel missile programs, resulting in substantial delays in the modernization of its missile force. To the extent that resources were made available, this was typically in the context of state-driven investments in high technology, such as the 863 Program—an effort to stimulate innovation across several technological areas, including computer processing and space travel.[5] Starting in the late 1970s, China also invested heavily in the development of an enhanced radiation warhead, or "neutron bomb," but did not deploy this capability despite successful tests in 1984

---

[3] Jeffrey Lewis, *The Minimum Means of Reprisal: China's Search for Security in the Nuclear Age* (Cambridge: American Academy of Arts and Sciences, 2007).

[4] John Wilson Lewis and Xue Litai, "Making China's Nuclear War Plan," *Bulletin of the Atomic Scientists* 68, no. 5 (2012): 47–48.

[5] On the development of the 863 program, see Evan Feigenbaum, *China's Techno-Warriors: National Security and Strategic Competition from the Nuclear to the Information Age* (Stanford: Stanford University Press, 2003); and Gregory Kulacki and Jeffrey Lewis, "A Place for One's Mat: China's Space Program, 1956–2003," American Academy of Arts and Sciences, 2009.

and 1988.[6] As a result, China's development of strategic capabilities continued to remain disconnected in important ways from questions of strategy, doctrine, and requirements.[7]

Second Artillery Modernization

Since the 1990s, the PLA has replaced the R&D community as the dominant factor in defense policy. As the budget and professionalism of the PLA grew in the 1990s, so too did its political influence on policy matters relating to defense. In 1998, China folded the institutional remnants of what has been called its techno-nationalist elite into the General Armaments Department of the PLA. Moreover, interviews with Chinese officials and experts suggest that the mistaken U.S. bombing of the Chinese embassy in Belgrade in 1999 served as an additional catalyst for increased investment in strategic capabilities.[8]

As a result, the Second Artillery Force has become better funded and vastly more professional than it was in the past. China is rapidly achieving major technological developments and integrating them into its strategic forces, including solid-fuel ballistic missiles and advanced information technologies. With a new leadership in power, it is worthwhile to ask how China's changing technological, political, and security situation will shape its strategic forces in the years to come.

The PLA's growing role necessarily complicates and enriches the narrative regarding China's investment in strategic forces and capabilities. Starting in the 1990s, concepts such as survivability appear to have joined technological improvement as drivers of nuclear modernization. Specifically, perceived advances in U.S. military capabilities appear to have informed greater Chinese investments in certain advanced strategic forces, while other investments are more likely derived from technologically driven motivations.

In some cases, however, the motivations driving Chinese nuclear modernization are unclear. Starting in the mid-1980s, China undertook to replace its existing liquid-fuel missiles with solid-fuel replacements.

---

[6] On China's decision-making regarding the development of an enhanced radiation warhead, see Jonathan Ray, "Red China's Capitalist Bomb: Chinese Efforts to Develop an Enhanced Radiation Warhead" (master's thesis, Monterey Institute of International Studies, 2013).

[7] Politics also played a role. The September 1985 resignation of several important figures from the Central Military Commission, including Nie Rongzhen and Zhang Aiping, was accompanied by the elevation of Nie's son-in-law Ding Henggao to the chairmanship of the Commission for Science, Technology, and Industry for National Defense. See Benjamin C. Ostrov, *Conquering Resources: The Growth and Decline of the PLA's Science and Technology Commission for National Defense* (Armonk: M.E. Sharpe, 1991), 73.

[8] On the impact of the 1999 bombing on Chinese investment in strategic capabilities, see Gregory Kulacki and Jeffrey Lewis, "Understanding China's Antisatellite Test," *Nonproliferation Review* 15, no. 2 (2008): 335–47.

This process took much longer than might have been expected. The DF-21 did not begin to replace the DF-3 until the late 1990s, and the DF-31 and DF-31A did not enter service until the mid-2000s, serving as functional replacements for the DF-5 and DF-5A. Recent press reports suggest that China may be in the process of developing a new road-mobile ICBM that may be able to carry multiple warheads.[9] It tested the new JL-2 submarine-launched ballistic missile (SLBM) in 2012.[10] Eventually, China will deploy these systems—JL-2 deployment is expected imminently—but it is important to understand the long lead times associated with the programs. The decision to develop the DF-31 was made in 1985, a world away from when the missile actually entered into the field in 2005. Chinese leaders were likely driven by a perceived need to achieve advanced technologies comparable to other major powers. They were also aware of the benefits of such systems for enhancing the effectiveness and survivability of China's strategic forces in the face of challenges posed by U.S. (and to a lesser extent Russian) investments in intelligence, surveillance, and reconnaissance (ISR); conventional precision-strike capabilities; and missile defense.[11]

The development of conventionally armed ballistic missiles signals a significant evolution in terms of service profile and autonomy for the Second Artillery, while also suggesting the continuing technological impetus for Chinese military modernization. When Chinese officials initially began discussing conventionally armed ballistic missiles in the 1980s, foreign observers were generally surprised. Although the country's ballistic missiles were widely inaccurate in their early variants, making conventional uses seem implausible at the time, the Chinese were early enthusiasts for arming them with conventional warheads (probably because China's missile force benefited from a favorable comparison with the archaic PLA Air Force). John Lewis and Hua Di, in explaining a conventional variant of the DF-15, noted that the development "may seem odd to Western strategists."[12] Today, conventional missions receive equal billing in Chinese texts, including in the *Science of Campaigns* and *Science of Second Artillery Campaigns*, which may represent a significant shift in how the Second Artillery views its core purpose. More

[9] Office of the Secretary of Defense, *Annual Report to Congress: Military and Security Developments Involving the People's Republic of China 2013* (Washington, D.C., 2013), 6.

[10] Ibid., 31; and "Ballistic and Cruise Missile Threat," National Air and Space Intelligence Center, May 2013, 23.

[11] Yao Yunzhu, "Chinese Nuclear Policy and the Future of Minimum Deterrence," in *Perspectives on Sino-American Strategic Nuclear Issues*, ed. Christopher P. Twomey (New York: Palgrave MacMillan, 2008), 222–24; and Chu Shulong and Rong Yu, "China: Dynamic Minimum Deterrence," in *The Long Shadow: Nuclear Weapons and Security in the 21st Century*, ed. Muthiah Alagappa (Stanford: Stanford University Press, 2008), 161–87.

[12] John Wilson Lewis and Hua Di, "China's Ballistic Missile Programs: Technologies, Strategies, Goals," *International Security* 17, no. 2 (1992): 5–40.

than half of all Second Artillery launchers are now deployed for conventional missions. Although there are some apparently independent missions, such as a "warning strike," the Second Artillery's conventional missions largely support joint PLA operations. They include providing fire support for PLA ground forces and amphibious-landing and counter-landing campaigns, as well as supporting the PLA Air Force and PLA Navy in wartime missions.[13]

The modernization of the Second Artillery also needs to be understood within the broader context of China's overall defense modernization. In addition to developing new ballistic missiles and launchers, China has invested in other strategic capabilities, especially those relating to space. It began work on "hit to kill" anti-satellite and missile defense technologies in the mid-1980s, although the central leadership did not provide significant funding for the program until the broad increase in defense-technology spending following the 1999 Belgrade embassy bombing.

China has tested its hit-to-kill interceptor a number of times since 2005, in both anti-satellite and ballistic missile defense modes. Following a series of non-intercept tests in 2005 and 2006, China used an SC-19 missile to intercept and destroy the Chinese FY-1C weather satellite on January 11, 2007.[14] On January 11, 2010, China launched another SC-19 missile from the Korla Missile Test Complex and successfully intercepted a CSS-X-11 medium-range ballistic missile (MRBM) launched from the Shuangchengzi Space and Missile Center. It conducted a third hit-to-kill test, again in a missile defense mode, on January 28, 2013. China also is reportedly investing in lasers, presumably for ranging, imaging, and interfering with reconnaissance satellites.[15]

China appears to be pursuing advanced technologies broadly rather than solely pursuing specific modernization initiatives to support a particular strategy. The model appears to be to seek certain general capabilities, with decisions about procurement and operational concepts deferred until later. Chinese leaders are aware of strategic challenges, of course, but the late process may trouble the development of operational concepts for new capabilities. For example, the command-and-control issues presented by newly mobile missile forces such as ballistic missile submarines appear to present a persistent challenge for Chinese operational planners. As noted

---

[13] Ron Christman, "Conventional Missions for China's Second Artillery Corps," *Comparative Strategy* 30, no. 3 (2011): 198–228. See also Michael S. Chase and Andrew S. Erickson, "The Conventional Missile Capabilities of China's Second Artillery Force: Cornerstone of Deterrence and Warfighting," *Asian Security* 8, no. 2 (2012): 115–37.

[14] Kulacki and Lewis, "Understanding China's Antisatellite Test." The abbreviation "SC" is the U.S. intelligence designator for the Shuangchengzi Space and Missile Center, signaling that this was the nineteenth type of missile identified at that test site.

[15] See, for example, Office of the Secretary of Defense, *Annual Report to Congress: Military Power of the People's Republic of China 2006* (Washington, D.C., 2006), 24.

above, China stores its nuclear warheads separately from delivery vehicles, with an extensive and separate system for handling warheads. While the PLA appears to have examined the challenge this raises for its missile submarines, it is not clear that defense planners have developed concepts for deploying and communicating with the submarines on operational patrols, either in peacetime or a crisis. Similarly, the evolving rationale for China's hit-to-kill efforts would suggest that the PLA has yet to decide whether it will deploy the system as an anti-satellite weapon, a missile defense, both, or not at all. Although the PLA is perfectly capable of articulating requirements and shaping the defense R&D process, Chinese policymakers still appear to value broad technological parity as an ideological matter.

Key Features of China's Nuclear Forces, Posture, and Policies

The principal feature of China's nuclear arsenal today is that it is based primarily on ballistic missiles operated by the Second Artillery Force, which also controls China's land-based conventional missile forces. China's 2008 defense white paper indicated that the Second Artillery "is mainly responsible for deterring other countries from using nuclear weapons against China, and for conducting nuclear counterattacks and precision strikes with conventional missiles."[16] Furthermore, the white paper states:

> The Second Artillery Force sticks to China's policy of no first use of nuclear weapons, implements a self-defensive nuclear strategy, strictly follows the orders of the CMC [Central Military Commission], and takes...as its fundamental mission the protection of China from any nuclear attack. In peacetime the nuclear missile weapons of the Second Artillery Force are not aimed at any country. But if China comes under a nuclear threat, the nuclear missile force of the Second Artillery Force will go into a state of alert, and get ready for a nuclear counterattack to deter the enemy from using nuclear weapons against China. If China comes under a nuclear attack, the nuclear missile force of the Second Artillery Force will use nuclear missiles to launch a resolute counterattack against the enemy either independently or together with the nuclear forces of other services.[17]

---

[16] Information Office of the State Council of the PRC, *China's National Defense in 2008* (Beijing, January 2009), 29, http://www.fas.org/programs/ssp/nukes/2008DefenseWhitePaper_Jan2009.pdf.

[17] Ibid. The white paper also states that "the conventional missile force of the Second Artillery Force is charged mainly of the task of conducting medium- and long-range precision strikes against key strategic and operational targets of the enemy."

Delivery Systems for China's Nuclear Weapons

According to the U.S. Department of Defense, China's nuclear arsenal currently consists of 50–75 ICBMs, including approximately 30 road-mobile, solid-fuel DF-31 and DF-31A ICBMs (see **Table 1**). This force is complemented by liquid-fuel, intermediate-range ballistic missiles (IRBM) and road-mobile, solid-fuel MRBMs, such as the DF-21, for regional deterrence missions.[18] In addition, the U.S. Department of Defense describes China's growing arsenal of nuclear-capable ground- and air-launched cruise missiles, as well as short-range ballistic missiles, as having conventional warheads. China has also developed a land-attack cruise missile, the DH-10. This system is nuclear-capable, although it appears that the PLA has not deployed nuclear-armed variants. There are indications that China may be developing air- and submarine-launched variants of the DH-10 for China's strategic bombers and new nuclear-powered submarines.

This accounting suggests that China possesses an operationally deployed force of approximately 100–200 warheads, with some uncertainly arising over how many of the DF-21 ballistic missiles are armed with nuclear warheads. (The first 50 DF-21 missiles are most likely nuclear-armed.)

T A B L E 1   Delivery vehicles for China's nuclear arsenal, 2013

Type	System	Range (km)	Number
ICBM	DF-4	5,400+	50–75
	DF-5	13,000+	
	DF-31	7,200+	
	DF-31A	11,200+	
IRBM	DF-3	3,000+	5–20
MRBM	DF-21	1,750+	75–100*
SLBM	JL-2	7,200+	Not yet deployed

S O U R C E : Author's estimates based on multiple editions of the Office of the Secretary of Defense's *Annual Report to Congress: Military and Security Developments Involving the People's Republic of China*; and "Ballistic and Cruise Missile Threat," National Air and Space Intelligence Center.

N O T E : Asterisk indicates that only the first 50 DF-21s may be nuclear-armed.

---

[18] Office of the Secretary of Defense, *Annual Report to Congress* (2013). This small force of nuclear-armed medium- and intermediate-range missiles is deployed in areas that suggest China values the ability to hold targets at risk in eastern Russia, India, and throughout East Asia.

The U.S. intelligence community expects this number to grow, either through China acquiring more of the existing types of missiles or through deploying new systems. China is currently modernizing its missile force and introducing new solid-fuel missiles to replace the first generation deployed between 1966 and 1996. It has replaced the DF-3, DF-4, and DF-5 with the DF-21, DF-31, and DF-31A. China also appears to be developing additional missiles, including another MRBM (identified as the CSS-X-11) and possibly a new ICBM (sometimes called the DF-41).[19] Recent images from Chinese social media show three previously unidentified transporter-erector launchers.

China is currently developing a new nuclear-powered ballistic missile submarine (SSBN) (the Type-094 Jin-class), as well as a new SLBM (the JL-2). Although technical problems have slowed the deployment of this system, as stated above, the new JL-2 SLBM was successfully tested in 2012.[20] China currently has one Xia-class (Type-092) SSBN, which it constructed in the 1980s, with sixteen launch tubes. Despite these developments, China's sea-based deterrent remains in its infancy. PRC officials continue to refer to the Second Artillery as the main or primary deterrent force, despite the impending entry of the PLA Navy into the business of deterrent operations. China does not appear to have invested in command-and-control or other communications capabilities that would support an operational sea-based deterrent. Moreover, the PLA Navy has no experience in conducting operational patrols with nuclear warheads mated to missiles. It will surely acquire such capabilities over time, but significant questions remain as to how China will operate its fleet of SSBNs. It is possible that, rather than maintaining a continuous at-sea deterrent in the form of strategic patrols or the use of a bastion, China may patrol episodically and wait for a crisis to flush submarines to sea.

As mentioned above, one unique aspect of China's strategic deployment practices is that it keeps its nuclear warheads stored separately, often "tens of kilometers" from their ballistic missiles, according to one former U.S. defense official.[21] China appears to maintain storage locations or depots for warheads that are distinct from the units deployed with ballistic missiles. Additionally, it appears to keep conventional and nuclear units at separate locations,

---

[19] The 2010 edition of the Office of the Secretary of Defense's *Annual Report to Congress* stated that China "may also be developing a new road-mobile ICBM." See Office of the Secretary of Defense, *Annual Report to Congress: Military and Security Developments Involving the People's Republic of China 2010* (Washington, D.C., 2010), 2.

[20] See Office of the Secretary of Defense, *Annual Report to Congress* (2013), 31.

[21] "Re-framing De-alert" (seminar organized by the EastWest Institute, Yverdon Les Bains, Switzerland, June 21–23, 2009), available at http://www.ewi.info/reframing_dealert. See also Mark A. Stokes, "China's Nuclear Warhead Storage and Handling System," Project 4029 Institute, March 12, 2010, http://project2049.net/documents/chinas_nuclear_warhead_storage_and_handling_system.pdf.

although this judgment is difficult to make with any degree of certainty and questions exist about the deployment of conventional and nuclear-armed DF-21 ballistic missiles.

The Size of China's Nuclear Arsenal

The relatively small size of China's deployed nuclear forces—a few hundred warheads—is consistent with its limited production of fissile material.[22] The PRC has military facilities for separating plutonium and enriching uranium. Based on atmospheric test data through 1980, China's nuclear weapons have large amounts of plutonium in their primaries. Production of highly enriched uranium appears to be for thermonuclear secondaries, as well as for naval propulsion.[23] (Modern thermonuclear weapons are said to be "staged" with a "primary" fission explosive igniting a "secondary" fusion explosion.)

China's initial highly enriched uranium and plutonium were produced at a pair of facilities near Lanzhou and Jiuquan in Gansu Province. These facilities were replicated in interior "third line" facilities near Jinkouhe (also sometimes called Heping) and Guangyuan in Sichuan. China's first-line facilities were converted to civilian use in the 1980s and subsequently shut down. Today, the PRC is building civilian enrichment and reprocessing facilities at these sites. It also appears to have decommissioned its facilities at Guangyuan, but the status of highly enriched uranium production at Jinkouhe is less clear.

Overall, the size of China's arsenal is probably constrained by past plutonium production, which open-source estimates place between 1 and 5 tons.[24] A classified 1999 U.S. Department of Energy estimate, leaked to the *Washington Times*, listed China's weapons plutonium stockpile as 1.7–2.8 tons.[25] The lower estimate probably reflects reduced production from the second reactor, which may have been operated at a much lower level than previously thought. If China has approximately 2 tons of plutonium and

---

[22] For a declassified U.S. assessment of China's stockpile, see "China's Nuclear Weapons Testing: Facing Prospects for a Comprehensive Test Ban," CIA, Office of Scientific and Weapons Research, September 30, 1993; and "China Seeking Foreign Assistance to Address Concerns about Nuclear Stockpile under CTBT," *Proliferation Digest*, March 29, 1996.

[23] See Lars-Erik De Geer, "Chinese Atmospheric Nuclear Explosions from a Swedish Horizon: A Summary of Swedish Observations of Chinese Nuclear Test Explosions in the Atmosphere, 1964–1980" (paper presented at the Fourth SCOPE-RADTEST International Workshop, Beijing, October 1996).

[24] David Wright and Lisbeth Gronlund, "Estimating China's Production of Plutonium for Weapons," *Science and Global Security* 11, no. 1 (2003): 61–80; and Hui Zhang, "China's HEU and Plutonium Production and Stocks," *Science and Global Security* 19, no. 1 (2011): 68–89.

[25] Robert S. Norris and William M. Arkin, "World Plutonium Inventories," *Bulletin of the Atomic Scientists* 55, no. 5 (1999): 71.

uses 4 kilograms of plutonium per warhead, the total stockpile size would be approximately five hundred warheads.[26] If less material has been produced, or if China makes less efficient use of fissile material than the United States does, the total stockpile size might be smaller.

Some outside experts have questioned U.S. intelligence estimates of the size of China's strategic forces. Although General Robert Kehler, commander of U.S. Strategic Command, recently reiterated that "the Chinese arsenal is in the range of several hundred" warheads and that he does "not believe that China has hundreds or thousands more nuclear weapons than what the intelligence community has been saying," there is a persistent interest in the possibility of a large number of uncounted nuclear weapons.[27] The view that China's arsenal is much larger than previously believed is particularly prevalent in Russia, where figures such as Viktor Yesin and Alexei Arbatov have made similar claims.[28]

Proponents of larger estimates are correct that China's military has made substantial investments in tunneling and placing key facilities underground. The Second Artillery is no exception and maintains a large engineering regiment devoted to enhancing the survivability of China's deterrent. These efforts are covered extensively in state media. China deployed its earliest ICBM, the DF-4, in caves from which Chinese units could "roll out" the missile on rails to launch.[29] China's system of tunnels, often referred to as the "underground Great Wall," originated in the mid-1980s and appears

---

[26] This estimate assumes that China would replicate a compact U.S. or Russian thermonuclear warhead, which on average contains 4 kilograms of plutonium in the primary. For further details, see Hui Zhang, "Nuclear Modernization in China," in *Assuring Destruction Forever: Nuclear Weapon Modernization around the World*, ed. Ray Acheson (New York: Reaching Critical Will, 2012).

[27] Phillip A. Karber, "Strategic Implications of China's Underground Great Wall," Georgetown University, September 26, 2011, available at http://www.fas.org/nuke/guide/china/Karber_UndergroundFacilities-Full_2011_reduced.pdf; and William Wan, "Georgetown Students Shed Light on China's Tunnel System for Nuclear Weapons," *Washington Post*, November 29, 2011, http://articles.washingtonpost.com/2011-11-29/world/35280981_1_nuclear-weapons-georgetown-students-military-journals.

[28] On Yesin's estimates, see Viktor Yesin, "Tretiy posle SShA i Rossii: O yadernom potentsiale Kitaya bez zanizheniy i preuvelicheniy" [Third after the U.S. and Russia: China's Nuclear Capabilities without Understatement or Exaggeration], *Voyenno-promyshlennyy kuryer*, May 2, 2012, http://vpk-news.ru/articles/8838; and Jeffrey Lewis, "Yesin on China's Nukes," Arms Control Wonk, web log, June 29, 2012, http://lewis.armscontrolwonk.com/archive/5460/yesin-on-chinas-nukes. On Arbatov, see Alexei Arbatov, Vladimir Dvorkin, and Sergey Oznobishchev, eds., "Prospects of China's Participation in Nuclear Arms Limitations," Institute of World Economy and International Relations, Russian Academy of Sciences, 2012, http://www.imemo.ru/en/publ/2012/12031_EN.pdf.

[29] In May 1977 the Central Military Commission formally adopted this concept. Zhang Aiping reportedly referred to the concept as "shooting a firecracker outside the front door." For a more thorough discussion, see Lewis and Hua, "China's Ballistic Missile Programs."

designed to bolster the survivability of its land-based ballistic missiles.[30] China's warhead storage also relies extensively on tunnels.[31]

Although tunnels complicate efforts to assess the size of China's nuclear forces, there are practical issues related to force structure, beyond the number of deployed missiles, that help bound the size of China's missile force, such as the number of bases and launch brigades. The forces that operate China's missiles live and exercise above ground. Leaked documents and accounts relating to Chinese and Saudi Arabian deployment of the DF-21 illustrate how changes in barracks and other external facilities can be used to track the status of missile deployments. China's production of fissile material, particularly plutonium, also constrains estimates of the size of its nuclear forces. Although it would seem reasonable to ask whether the country's total stockpile is a few hundred or several hundred warheads, there is little evidence justifying a rejection of the baseline estimate provided by the U.S. intelligence community in favor of a postulated force that approaches numerical parity with the United States and Russia. Although there is some deterrence benefit for China to uncertainty about the size of its nuclear forces, that benefit exists only for smaller arsenal sizes. There would be little advantage in concealing an investment in a deterrent that is underestimated by such a large margin.

China's No-First-Use Policy

Authoritative Chinese military publications suggest a number of signals that China might send in a crisis, such as placing its nuclear forces on alert or announcing that it would not be bound by its NFU pledge. Western experts are often quick to interpret these materials as embracing nuclear coercion. However, much of what has been viewed as a debate about NFU is actually a debate about generating realistic options within that framework. This is not to say that there is not real irritation with the NFU policy or that certain operational proposals—such as renouncing NFU to attempt to stop ongoing conventional attacks on strategic forces—do not undermine the pledge. The effort to retrofit operational approaches with China's NFU policy has not been smooth or without controversy. Many Chinese-language military sources note the constraints and limitations of operating under an NFU pledge. Alastair Iain Johnston, in particular, has carefully documented these

---

[30] For a discussion of Chinese tunneling efforts, see Hui Zhang, "The Defensive Nature of China's 'Underground Great Wall,'" *Bulletin of the Atomic Scientists*, January 16, 2012, http://www.thebulletin. org/defensive-nature-chinas-underground-great-wall.

[31] Stokes, "China's Nuclear Warhead Storage and Handling System," 13, 65.

debates in a number of articles.[32] One lingering question is whether the desire of strategic thinkers to provide Chinese leaders with realistic operational concepts for China's strategic forces will hollow out the NFU pledge or lead to a fundamental change in policy, especially as the PLA becomes more professional and the PRC leadership becomes less ostentatious about its commitment to ideology.

In terms of targeting nuclear weapons, China appears to adhere to a policy of holding high-value targets at risk. In Western circles, academics sometimes distinguish between counterforce and countervalue targeting.[33] This distinction makes little sense in a Chinese context, however, where leaders see the ability to target military forces, such as military bases within the region, as having a psychological effect. Chinese textbooks and other materials emphasize the shock value of retaliatory nuclear strikes against a range of targets in bringing a nuclear conflict to a close. In this vein, a more relevant distinction would be between deterrence by punishment and deterrence by denial. These sources clearly emphasize the role of punishment in creating the psychological conditions necessary to stop a nuclear campaign against China rather than the role of nuclear weapons in degrading an adversary's ability to continue to wage war. By contrast, Chinese writings about conventional missile operations are much clearer about the contribution of missile strikes to other conventional operations.[34]

Explaining Chinese Nuclear Restraint

Why has China built such a small nuclear force? Why does it exacerbate the inherent vulnerability of such a force by storing its warheads separately and maintaining a retaliatory posture? As previously described, advocates for nuclear weapons in China's defense hierarchy were initially located within the R&D community, while the bureaucracy responsible for defense production advocated spending scarce funds on the production of tanks, ships, and aircraft. However, the traditional rivalry between the research and production

---

[32] For an excellent review of these materials, see Alastair Iain Johnston, "China's New 'Old Thinking': The Concept of Limited Deterrence," *International Security* 20, no. 3 (1996): 5–42. For a more contemporary account, see M. Taylor Fravel and Evan Medeiros, "China's Search for Assured Retaliation: The Evolution of Chinese Nuclear Strategy and Force Structure," *International Security* 35, no. 2 (2010): 48–87.

[33] In the United States, "countervalue" targeting is synonymous with targeting cities and other civilian targets, whereas "counterforce" targeting refers to targeting military assets. As a result, U.S. officials talk about tailoring deterrence to hold at risk those targets that the adversary values most, while quite sincerely denying that U.S. policy is countervalue targeting, since the United States would only use nuclear weapons against legitimate military targets.

[34] See, for example, *Di'er paobing zhanyi xue* [The Science of Second Artillery Campaigns] (Beijing: Zhongguo renmin jiefangjun chubanshe, 2004).

communities declined during the Cultural Revolution when few members of either group were able to avoid persecution. Since the 1990s, the PLA has successfully moved to place both defense R&D and production under the General Armaments Department.

The first generation of Chinese leaders also had Maoist ideas about the role of nuclear weapons. China's NFU policy should be understood in this context. It is a statement about the ideologically correct way to understand the nature of nuclear weapons rather than a promise made to other states. Consider, for example, Mao's famous remark that "the atomic bomb is a paper tiger." This comment is often treated either as disingenuous, since China was determined to acquire nuclear weapons, or as evidence of a dangerous irrationality in Chinese attitudes toward such weapons. It is neither. As Mark Ryan found in his study of the formation of Chinese attitudes about nuclear weapons during the Korean War, the first generation of Chinese Communist leaders made highly accurate assessments about the physical limitations of nuclear weapons and the political constraints on the United States' use of them.[35] Having successfully endured nuclear threats from the United States, these leaders saw nuclear weapons as tools of political coercion that could be met with resolve and eventually possession of similar capabilities.

Mao's remark is also not disingenuous, a point that deserves further explanation. Chinese Communist leaders first used the term "paper tiger" to refer to reactionaries, not nuclear weapons, in 1946. The reference is a metaphorical allusion to "an older Maoist revolutionary maxim which holds that men and politics, rather than weapons and economic power, are the determining factors in war."[36] In this context, referring to nuclear weapons as paper tigers merely indicates that the balance of nuclear weapons is not likely to be decisive in a conflict and that the technical details matter very little. Given that China continues to deploy nuclear forces that are numerically inferior to those of the United States and Russia, it appears that Chinese leaders have yet to revisit these strategic premises in a fundamental way.

NFU, then, is best understood as a statement about the role of nuclear weapons and an ideological construct that China imposed for political reasons on their development. There is considerable concern in the United States about whether the PRC's real plans are consistent with NFU or whether there is a debate in Chinese circles about the pledge. To some extent, these questions miss the point that in China nuclear policy precedes strategy. NFU is a political edict, with operational questions about how and when China

---

[35] Mark A. Ryan, *Chinese Attitudes toward Nuclear Weapons: China and the United States during the Korean War* (Armonk: M.E. Sharpe, 1989), 179.

[36] Ralph L. Powell, "Great Powers and Atomic Bombs Are 'Paper Tigers,'" *China Quarterly* 23 (1965): 55–63.

would actually use nuclear weapons delegated to pay grades far too low to pass judgment on the pronouncements of Mao.

How long such ideological factors will continue to shape China's nuclear force is an open question. There are, to be sure, ongoing debates on the prudence of the NFU policy. Indeed, the most recent Chinese defense white paper does not include the standard language about NFU, prompting concern among Western experts.[37] What remains unclear, however, is what constitutes evidence of a debate that might result in a significant change in policy or behavior. There appear to be at least two parallel processes: a high-level political debate at the apex of the Chinese political hierarchy, and arguments at the working level in the military and academia to develop operational concepts for existing weapons systems.[38] It is difficult to know whether or how the debates surrounding operational concepts relate to and influence broader political debates about the implications of NFU, if they do at all. When evaluating evidence of internal debates, it also is important to understand what kinds of evidence refer to which process.

Often the debates at what might be called a "working level" reflect the inability of lower-ranking officials to interpret ambiguous direction by the senior leadership. In 1978, for example, Deng Xiaoping stated that he had "the greatest interest in mobility on land; that is, in the use of modern weapons for fighting guerilla war."[39] The formal process of developing plausible operational concepts for the Second Artillery began in the early 1980s, apparently in an effort to respond to Deng's guidance. The Second Artillery assigned Major General Li Lijing, then deputy director of the Military Academic Committee, to organize the drafting of what would become *The Science of Second Artillery Campaigns* (*Di'er Paobing Zhanyi Xue*).[40] Over the years, the Second Artillery has struggled to create plausible operational concepts within the strictures of NFU.

This process appears to continue today. In recent years, Chinese military experts appear to have become especially concerned about precision strikes against strategic forces or other targets, such as nuclear power plants and dams, that could cause mass casualties. Although China's forces, posture, and training appear consistent with a fundamentally retaliatory mission, the doctrinaire nature of NFU appears to invite coercion.

---

[37] See Yao Yunzhu, "China Will Not Change Its Nuclear Policy," Pacific Forum CSIS, PacNet, no. 28, April 23, 2013, http://csis.org/files/publication/pac1328.pdf.

[38] These debates are described in Michael S. Chase, "China's Transition to a More Credible Nuclear Deterrent: Implications and Challenges for the United States," *Asia Policy* 16 (2013): 85–88; and Fravel and Medeiros, "China's Search for Assured Retaliation," 78–80.

[39] Lewis and Hua, "China's Ballistic Missile Programs," 26; and Lewis, *Minimum Means of Reprisal*, 70.

[40] Lewis and Xue, "Making China's War Plan."

Recent events have renewed questions regarding China's nuclear policy and strategy, including the NFU pledge. Last year, new Chinese president Xi Jinping gave a speech to the Second Artillery in which he emphasized that the force should be on "high alert" (*gao jibei zhuangtai*)—a rarely used phrase previously applied to U.S. and Russian nuclear weapons programs.[41] This spring, China published a new defense white paper that describes the retaliatory mission of its nuclear forces but, as stated above, omits familiar and ubiquitous language relating to the NFU pledge.[42] Ultimately, it does not appear that China is preparing to either alter the alert status of its nuclear weapons or reject outright its NFU policy.[43] But in the ensuing discussions Chinese experts made it clear that the country's leaders will continue to assess the proper role for nuclear weapons to play in national security.[44]

Impacts on Strategic Stability and Regional Security

Chinese strategic planners must manage a highly complex strategic environment that involves both cooperation and competition with a wide variety of nuclear and non-nuclear powers. Many of China's regional relationships involve significant economic integration mixed with a profound sense of strategic rivalry, which is often exacerbated by lingering territorial disputes. While nuclear issues do not always play an explicit role in these dynamics, they are a major component of the broader geopolitical environment within which all players evaluate risk. Moreover, in relationships where nuclear weapons play a more explicit role, the broader strategic interactions and issues of the relationship cannot be separated from the nuclear dynamics. China's strategic modernization needs to be understood in its proper regional security context, including the potential for crises over the status of Taiwan, on the Korean Peninsula, and related to territorial disputes, especially maritime disputes with Japan.

---

[41] The speech is described in Wei Feng and Zhang Haiyang, "Nuli jianshe qiangda de xinxihua zhanlüe daodan budui" [Efforts to Build a Strong Information Technology Strategic Missile Force], *Renmin ribao*, December 13, 2012.

[42] Information Office of the State Council of the PRC, *The Diversified Employment of China's Armed Forces* (Beijing, April 2013), http://news.xinhuanet.com/english/china/2013-04/16/c_132312681. htm; and James Acton, "Is China Changing Its Position on Nuclear Weapons?" *New York Times*, April 18, 2013, http://www.nytimes.com/2013/04/19/opinion/is-china-changing-its-position-on-nuclear-weapons.html.

[43] See, for example, the remarks of Lieutenant General Qi Jianguo, PLA deputy chief of general staff, in "New Trends in Asia-Pacific Security: Q&A" (panel discussion at the Shangri-La Dialogue, Singapore, June 2, 2013), http://www.iiss.org/en/events/shangri%20la%20dialogue/archive/shangri-la-dialogue-2013-c890/fourth-plenary-session-0f17/qa-57d8.

[44] Yao Yunzhu, "China Will Not Change Its Nuclear Policy," China-U.S. Focus, April 22, 2013, http://www.chinausfocus.com/peace-security/china-will-not-change-its-no-first-use-policy.

U.S.-China Nuclear Dynamics

For both Chinese and U.S. officials, a crisis over the status of Taiwan remains the primary planning scenario for a major engagement involving U.S. and Chinese military forces, including their strategic capabilities. The issue of Taiwan is one that has vexed relations between the United States and China from the beginning. The Chinese side views reunification as a core national interest. Efforts to secure the return of Hong Kong, Macao, and eventually Taiwan are also part of a legitimizing narrative that links the rule of the Communist Party to China's emergence from foreign domination. In 1996 the Central Military Commission adopted a policy of "stabilize the south, garrison the north" (*wen nan, bao bei*) that shifted the country's planning focus toward Taiwan and its "foreign supporters."[45] The result is that, in the intervening years, China's formal planning apparatus has organized around Taiwan scenarios.

For the United States, too, the issue of Taiwan is a central one. The United States maintains a global set of security commitments based on a collective judgment that the catastrophe of World War II, as well as the ensuing division of Europe in the Cold War, arose primarily from the failure of the Western democracies to oppose aggression by Germany and Japan. In this context, it is impossible for Western policymakers to imagine abandoning a democratic Taiwan, absent a reckless provocation from an independence-minded Taiwanese leader. Thus, whereas Chinese leaders see a domestic issue related to China's eventual unification, policymakers in Washington see a test case for broader global commitments that extend through Northeast Asia and across the globe.

An important turning point for U.S. thinking about Taiwan was China's 1995 and 1996 military exercises, which included missile launches, amphibious exercises, and live-fire demonstrations intended to influence Taiwan's first democratic presidential election. Since then, Taiwan has moved toward the center of U.S. planning scenarios, and China has once again become a key consideration in U.S. nuclear planning. Leaked portions of the 2002 *Nuclear Posture Review* listed "a military confrontation over the status of Taiwan" as one of three scenarios that exemplified an "immediate contingency"—a planning construct that sized the number of nuclear forces on day-to-day alert.[46]

Chinese policymakers appear to believe that the United States, all things being equal, would use nuclear threats to attempt to compel China to accept

---

[45] John Wilson Lewis and Xue Litai, *Imagined Enemies: China Prepares for Uncertain War* (Stanford: Stanford University Press, 2006).

[46] Philipp C. Bleek, "Nuclear Posture Review Leaks; Outlines Targets, Contingencies," *Arms Control Today* 32, no. 3 (2002).

an independent Taiwan. They regard their own nuclear weapons as defensive safeguards against U.S. nuclear coercion, which they allege the United States used in the Taiwan Strait crisis of 1955. Similarly, U.S. policymakers often suggest that China might use the threat of nuclear weapons against the United States or U.S. allies such as Japan to prevent the United States from coming to the aid of Taiwan.

This sort of mirror-imaging is evident in the famous incident in which a Chinese official was alleged to have said that the United States would not "trade Los Angeles for Taipei."[47] Many U.S. officials understood the remark to be a threat to use nuclear weapons against the United States if U.S. forces came to the aid of Taiwan. Charles Freeman, the U.S. official to whom the remark was addressed, appears to have interpreted it in the opposite direction—that the United States would not use nuclear weapons to coerce China to accept an independent Taiwan because of the threat of retaliation against the United States. A memorandum of a conversation with Freeman in October 1996 further clarifies that the statement was intended to convey retaliatory plans for a Taiwan Strait scenario; that is, it was a deterrence-based formulation rather than an indication of a willingness to strike first during a crisis.[48] Although there is a debate about the fundamental nature of the statement, the remark is consistent with an NFU policy.

The fundamental challenge appears to be that each side believes the other intends to use its nuclear weapons coercively, which leads both parties to interpret statements on deterrence as coercive threats. This tendency may lead to certain pathologies in the relationship, as each side systematically misinterprets the signals sent by the other.

The China-U.S. strategic dyad is further complicated by issues relating to U.S. security commitments in Northeast Asia, including to Japan. The United States must take special care that China-U.S. dynamics do not undermine its security commitments to regional allies. This is an important U.S. interest, given the role that alliance commitments have played in discouraging nuclear weapons proliferation in Japan, South Korea, and Taiwan.

The operational role of extended deterrence is another challenging issue for the United States. Although it is commonplace to make reference to the U.S. nuclear umbrella, in fact the United States has no formal commitment to

---

[47] See Chas Freeman, "China: Avoiding a Self-fulfilling Prophecy," Carnegie Endowment for International Peace, March 13, 2001. The original quote was reported in 1996 in the *New York Times*. See Patrick E. Tyler, "As China Threatens Taiwan, It Makes Sure U.S. Listens," *New York Times*, January 24, 1996.

[48] "Memorandum of Conversation with Charles Freeman, Jr.," White House, October 9, 1996. According to Freeman, the key phrase was, "if you hit our homeland, we will hit you." The discussion was leaked, without this crucial sentence, to the *New York Times* by two individuals present at the White House meeting.

employ nuclear weapons on behalf of any of its allies. The United States has security commitments to several Asian allies, but these commitments deal with aggression generally. For example, the 1960 Treaty of Mutual Cooperation and Security between the United States and Japan commits Washington and Tokyo to "act to meet the common danger" represented by "an armed attack against either party in the territories under the administration of Japan."[49] The United States clearly maintains nuclear weapons that might be used in the defense of Japan or other allies, but the conceptual challenge posed by extended nuclear deterrence is how to credibly impute a nuclear character to the alliance. This has been especially challenging in the case of Japan, which has a well-known nuclear "allergy" that precludes the NATO practice of forward-deploying U.S. nuclear weapons and limits the ability to discuss such matters in a frank and open manner.

The result, one might argue, is that Japanese policymakers tend to look for proxies that demonstrate the U.S. commitment, both in general terms and in terms of dealing with nuclear threats. From a Japanese perspective, the U.S.-China strategic dyad has important effects on regional security issues. Japanese policymakers are especially sensitive to what they describe as the "creeping peacetime expansion" of Chinese activities in disputed territorial areas. They appear to believe that the broader U.S.-China strategic balance affects China's overall willingness to use military deployments over territorial issues. Although U.S. policymakers have not historically viewed China's maritime activities as a function of the strategic balance, they do take seriously issues of regional security. During the process that led to the 2010 *Nuclear Posture Review*, for example, Japanese officials and academics strongly argued that efforts to enhance strategic stability between the United States and China should not come at the expense of regional security.[50] The review report consequently contains significant emphasis on strengthening regional security architectures in order to balance stability in a U.S.-China dyad with the regional security concerns of U.S. allies and partners.[51]

Chinese views of U.S. extended-deterrence commitments appear mixed. On the one hand, Chinese scholars and officials repeatedly voice their support for a robust U.S. role in the Asia-Pacific and often privately credit extended deterrence with preventing Japan, South Korea, and Taiwan from acquiring indigenous nuclear capabilities. On the other hand, many simply reject extended nuclear deterrence out of hand as blatant nuclear coercion.

---

[49] "Treaty of Mutual Cooperation and Security between Japan and the United States of America," January 19, 1960.

[50] See Jeffrey Lewis, "Trip Report on U.S.-Japan Dialogue on the Nuclear Posture Review Hosted by the New America Foundation," May 2010, available by request from the author.

[51] U.S. Department of Defense, *Nuclear Posture Review Report* (Washington, D.C., April 2010).

Particularly troubling for these Chinese interlocutors is the notion that the United States might come to the aid of an ally facing a dire conventional attack.

These dynamics are complicated by the reluctance of each side to engage with certain historical legacies of the Cold War. U.S. policymakers continue to be divided by the notion of whether to accept what has come to be called "mutual vulnerability" with China. During the first year of the Obama administration, U.S. policymakers debated how best to describe the relationship between the two countries. Ultimately, the administration chose to state that "maintaining strategic stability in the U.S.-China relationship is as important to this administration as maintaining strategic stability with other major powers."[52] The new nuclear weapons employment guidance signed by the president states that "the United States seeks to maintain strategic stability with Russia and China," placing China in a category with Russia that is distinct from that of countries such as North Korea and Iran.[53] Together, these statements appear to represent a tacit recognition of China's deterrent and the practical inability of the United States to reliably negate it. The administration has understandably avoided more explicit formulations, despite support from a number of high-level groups, including the secretary of state's International Security Advisory Board and a Council on Foreign Relations task force, which argued that "mutual vulnerability" is a fact to be managed through maintaining strategic stability.

Beijing, for its part, has continued to insist that Washington adopt an explicit NFU policy and views a public pledge as a test for whether the United States would seek to coerce China. However, in a number of conversations with Chinese officials and experts, few were aware that an NFU pledge was a major feature of Soviet diplomacy during the Cold War. Moreover, they were largely unaware that most U.S. experts believe that this pledge was a propaganda device to divide the NATO alliance and that the Soviet Union planned to violate it on the first day of a major conflict in Europe. Chinese experts are often surprised to hear that their U.S. counterparts interpret Chinese calls for NFU in a similar light.[54]

---

[52] U.S. Department of Defense, *Ballistic Missile Defense Review Report* (Washington, D.C., February 2010); and U.S. Department of Defense, *Nuclear Posture Review Report* (2010).

[53] U.S. Department of Defense, "Report on Nuclear Employment Strategy of the United States," June 2013.

[54] See Gregory Kulacki and Jeffrey Lewis, "Bu shouxian shiyong hewuqi: Zhong-Mei he duihua de kunjing yu chulu" [No First Use of Nuclear Weapons: The Dilemma and Way Out for the China-U.S. Nuclear Dialogue], *Waijiao pinglun* 29, no. 5 (2012).

Russia

China's relationship with Russia is important, if often overlooked. As the Sino-Soviet split deepened in the 1960s, the two countries fought a series of deadly border skirmishes in 1969 that may have brought them much closer to war than is generally believed. In the depth of the 1969 crisis, Mao's then heir apparent, Lin Biao, drafted an order placing the country in a state of alert. Lin appears to have also taken some steps to ready the country's nascent nuclear missile force, although important questions remain about Lin's exact orders.[55]

The Soviet Union remained China's major concern through the 1980s. John Lewis and Hua Di recount an internal discussion in which a Chinese missileer sought to explain the relative unimportance of accuracy when dealing with multi-megaton warheads by stating that "if a missile landed on the Bolshoi instead of the Kremlin, it would be equally effective."[56] Although relations today are improved, and the two sides have settled the major border disputes that led to clashes in 1969, they cannot be said to be without lingering tension.

Despite the fact that Moscow and Beijing share similar political orientations and concerns about U.S. primacy, relations continue to be marked by distrust. Russian officials still assert, for example, that further offensive nuclear reductions with the United States require the participation of other nuclear weapons states, particularly China. Although such statements may be partly tactical, Russian officials do appear to hold exaggerated views of the size and alert rate of China's nuclear arsenal. Russia's possession of a large stockpile of tactical nuclear weapons appears driven in part by these concerns about China. Five of its nine surface-to-surface missile brigades, for example, are deployed east of the Urals.[57] Moreover, Russia is investing in new nuclear weapons capabilities that appear to be oriented toward China, including a new missile that may be in violation of the 1987 Intermediate-Range Nuclear Forces Treaty, largely in response to China's intermediate-range nuclear forces.[58]

---

[55] Lewis and Xue, *Imagined Enemies*.

[56] Lewis and Hua, "China's Ballistic Missile Programs," 5–40.

[57] International Institute for Strategic Studies, *The Military Balance 2013* (London: Routledge, 2013), 199–244.

[58] Russian president Vladimir Putin referred to the nuclear forces of certain "neighbors" in responding to President Obama's proposal for another round of nuclear weapons reductions. See, for example, Sergei Loiko, "Russia Reacts Coolly to Obama's Nuclear Proposals," *Los Angeles Times*, June 19, 2013.

The Korean Peninsula

Officially, China's policy remains one of support for North Korea. China came to North Korea's aid during the Korean War—Peng Dehuai was one of the four signatories to the armistice—and has a formal security commitment to Pyongyang. Actual relations between the PRC and North Korea are, however, considerably more complex. Kim Il-sung had a closer relationship to the Soviet Union than China, though he worked to balance each power against the other. Kim worked to eliminate both pro-Soviet and pro-Chinese cadres from his government, much as Mao sought to eliminate pro-Soviet factions from the Chinese Communist Party. Kim Jong-il continued this policy, keeping the Chinese—and what he perceived as their tendency to lecture on the need for reform—at a safe distance.

Today, the relationship between Beijing and Pyongyang appears to be highly complex. Chinese leaders seem increasingly frustrated with their North Korean counterparts, while continuing to support North Korea politically and economically in hopes of preserving the regime's stability. As a result, although Chinese foreign policy continues to see the viability of North Korea as a fundamental interest, there are growing calls within China to reassess the relationship. These debates appear to break down on generational lines: younger voices argue that a more pragmatic assessment of China's interests should trump historical or ideological affinities, whereas more senior officials emphasize traditional concerns about having a U.S. ally on their border in the event of a unified Korea, the potential for significant inflows of refugees if Pyongyang collapses, and the historical and ideological linkages between China and North Korea. That tension remains unresolved within the Chinese bureaucracy.

There is a risk that North Korea may draw China into open conflict with the United States. Should the regime collapse or initiate a general war on the Korean Peninsula, Beijing may find itself compelled to come to Pyongyang's aid, seal its border to prevent an influx of refugees, or enter North Korea to secure nuclear materials. Regardless of the specific scenario, North Korea's possession of an increasingly operational nuclear capability raises complicated questions about how North Korean thinking about the use of nuclear weapons would interact with Chinese support for Pyongyang during a military conflict on the peninsula. It is difficult to imagine a million Chinese "people's volunteers" once again flooding into North Korea to fight the U.S. and South Korean militaries, but China could provide logistical or other support to the Korean People's Army in the opening phases of a conflict.

Territorial Disputes

A third set of issues centers on China's numerous territorial disputes, including with Japan over the Senkaku/Diaoyu Islands, with India over its shared border, and with numerous Southeast Asian countries over control of the South China Sea. While all three disputes have flared up recently, the most prominent is the one involving the Senkaku/Diaoyu Islands, which have been administered by Japan since the United States reverted control of Okinawa and the Ryukyu Islands in 1972. China has, since the 1990s, undertaken regular naval deployments to establish its claim on the islands and the surrounding exclusive economic zone (EEZ). In recent years, it has more aggressively contested Japan's administration. Civilian and military vessels have also been used to support China's claims on a much more frequent basis. Although nuclear weapons do not play an overt role in managing Chinese maritime incursions, some Japanese analysts believe that nuclear weapons represent a latent capability that matters a great deal in overall assessments of the strategic balance. They argue that reductions below those in the New START Treaty could result in a power vacuum that China would seek to fill.[59]

India and Pakistan

The China-India strategic dyad is unusual and perhaps more properly thought of as a triad encompassing Pakistan. China and India have significant and unresolved border disputes. Although the material value of the disputed territories is low, the disputes represent unresolved legacies of the colonial period, a time that each side regards as an aberration in its historical development. The two countries fought a border war in 1962, one that resulted in China seizing significant areas claimed by India in the Himalaya Mountains. In addition to this territory, China claims a significant portion of India's Arunachal Pradesh area.

China has largely preferred to threaten India by proxy through providing significant nuclear and missile assistance to Pakistan. The scope of this assistance remains surprising, even for a state that was a vocal opponent of the nonproliferation regime. Through the early 1980s, China provided significant nuclear weapons assistance to Pakistan, including the provision of a design for nuclear weapons small enough to fit on a missile (a miniaturized implosion device using highly enriched uranium that China first tested in 1966).[60] Pakistan further miniaturized that design for its own stockpile of uranium weapons. This design information spread to contacts in Libya and

---

[59] See Lewis, "Trip Report on U.S.-Japan Dialogue."

[60] For a review of China's assistance to Pakistan, see David Albright, *Peddling Peril: How the Secret Nuclear Trade Arms America's Enemies* (New York: Free Press, 2010).

Switzerland through the network of Pakistani nuclear scientist A.Q. Khan. China also provided significant technical assistance to Khan's uranium-enrichment efforts, although it is unclear how much of this trade was related to China's own nascent centrifuge programs. The United States and China had a significant dispute in the 1990s over China's provision of ring magnets suitable for use in Pakistan's centrifuge program. Although Beijing denies providing nuclear weapons assistance, it continues to aid Pakistan's civilian nuclear program, assisting with the construction of new reactors. China has also provided Pakistan with ballistic missiles, including the M-11.

Chinese officials tend to avoid direct statements about India's nuclear forces. Still, when negotiating the Comprehensive Nuclear-Test-Ban Treaty, Chinese negotiators insisted on India's ratification as a condition for the treaty to enter into force. Indian officials are much less reticent about making references to China's nuclear weapons. For example, when India conducted nuclear tests in 1998, remarks by then defense minister George Fernandes relating to China were largely seen as an effort to frame the test in terms of the Sino-Indian balance.[61]

Over the past decade, China has replaced the older liquid-fuel DF-3 with the solid-fuel DF-21, providing a modern regional deterrent capability, including against targets in India. New DF-21 IRBMs deployed near Da Qaidam in Qinghai Province, as well as new DF-31s in central China, may provide coverage of major strategic targets in India, including with conventionally armed missiles. Similarly, India's test of an Agni-V ICBM in April 2012 would appear to give New Delhi the capability to target Beijing—indeed, the Indian press dubbed the missile a "China killer."[62]

Implications for China's Nuclear Policy

The variety of challenges that China faces that involve nuclear weapons suggests a highly complex strategic environment in which shifts in policy and strategy could have multiple, cross-cutting implications on several issues. For example, Chinese strategists will necessarily be forced to consider the implications that an arms-limitation agreement with the United States and Russia would have for its strategic dynamic with India, as well as its ability to pursue conventional military objectives. More significantly, the distrust and

---

[61] For example, see "Aiming Missiles: India Claims Biggest Threat Is China, Not Pakistan," *Economist*, May 9, 1998.

[62] "India Launches New Generation Strategic Missile Agni 5," Defense Research and Development Organisation, Press Release, April 19, 2012, http://drdo.gov.in/drdo/English/dpi/press_release/Agni_5.pdf. On the phrase "China killer," see "Agni-V, India's 'China Killer,'" Indo-Asian News Service, April 19, 2012, http://www.deccanherald.com/content/243201/agni-v-indias-china-killer.html.

uncertainty that permeate all of China's nuclear relationships will necessarily complicate its ability to consider strategic limitation as anything other than an attempt to coerce China or to undermine its strategic retaliatory capability.

Implications for U.S. Policy

Time and again, outside observers of China's nuclear policy and strategy have been surprised by the scope of its nuclear capabilities and the speed of its modernization. Modesty should therefore be the catchword of all analyses of China's nuclear force posture and strategy: the outside world cannot fully know the country's strategic capabilities, understand how its leaders think about nuclear weapons, or predict how those leaders may leverage nuclear weapons in a crisis or conflict. Analysts are left to make judgments and recommendations based on their best knowledge at the time—a constant challenge for any national security or military strategy.

Although the possibility of a nuclear exchange with China is very remote, the United States must plan for a number of security contingencies within Northeast Asia, contingencies that could involve nuclear weapons. The major one, of course, concerns the status of Taiwan. Other scenarios include a conflict on the Korean Peninsula and an escalation of territorial disputes, such as the one between China and Japan over the Senkaku/Diaoyu Islands. In these contingencies, the fundamental policy challenge for the United States concerns how it views China's nuclear weapons. Does China have what might be termed an "assured destruction" capability against the United States? If so, should Washington take steps to negate such a capability? Or should it formally acknowledge a Chinese assured-destruction capability as a strategic reality?

Debates during the previous decade over whether China is a "small Russia" or "large North Korea" appear to have given way to a consensus within the United States that China's nuclear forces are small but sufficient. The 2010 *Ballistic Missile Defense Review* and 2010 *Nuclear Posture Review* underscored Washington's desire for strategic stability in its nuclear relationship with China, with the 2010 *Nuclear Posture Review* even establishing the high-level goal of initiating a dialogue with China on this issue. Although stopping short of a formal acknowledgement of mutual vulnerability, the Obama administration appears to be proceeding on the basis of this as a tacit, if unspoken, matter of fact.

As a practical matter, then, the United States appears to currently accept a level of mutual deterrence with Beijing in the absence of a major, unforeseen geopolitical crisis. Notably, the new guidance on the employment of U.S. nuclear weapons, signed by President Obama in 2013, emphasizes the importance of maintaining "strategic stability with Russia and China" rather than maintaining strategic forces capable of response options for either country.[63]

Whether the United States should publicly articulate this acceptance of mutual vulnerability and deterrence is a separate, but important, policy question. Within the United States, there is a significant body of opinion that would reject an explicit embrace of mutual vulnerability. For example, the preceding incarnation of the secretary of state's International Advisory Board warned that Washington should state clearly that it "will not accept a mutual vulnerability relationship" and take steps to "avoid the emerging creep to a Chinese assured destruction capability."[64] A recent report by the Center for Strategic and International Studies framed the challenge, particularly for extended deterrence, in clear and nonpolemical terms, underscoring concerns that U.S.-China strategic stability will come at the expense of regional security and alliances:

> [A] situation of vulnerability does exist and will likely become more entrenched as Chinese capabilities continue to develop, yet [some observers] are deeply concerned that public and formal acknowledgement of "mutual vulnerability" will achieve little more than raising questions from nervous allies. In this view, the issue is more a matter of diplomatic messaging than one of strategic assessment. Vulnerability is reality—but it is almost certain that Beijing already knows this. More probable is that Beijing is actually seeking to extract a public and formal acknowledgement of the condition in order to achieve several objectives including causing fissures in U.S.-Asia alliance relationships. Any diplomatic acknowledgement is therefore unlikely to significantly influence China's choices on its nuclear policies. Such an acknowledgement would, however, have a deleterious influence on U.S. assurance efforts with respect to Japan and other important allies and partners.[65]

Given that Chinese leaders have pressed for a formal, explicit statement— usually in the guise of an NFU pledge—U.S. policymakers must decide whether to pursue a dialogue on strategic stability in the absence of some resolution on the question of aligning declaratory policy and strategic realities. Their Chinese counterparts have shown little interest in such a dialogue, although it remains unclear if this reflects Chinese assessments of U.S. policy, internal leadership dynamics, or other factors.

---

[63] This guidance effectively replaced the nuclear weapons employment guidance signed by the George W. Bush administration in National Security Presidential Directive 14 on June 28, 2002.

[64] See International Security Advisory Board, "China's Strategic Modernization, Report from the ISAB Task Force" (unpublished draft, 2008), http://www.fas.org/nuke/guide/china/ISAB2008.pdf.

[65] Elbridge A. Colby and Abraham M. Denmark, eds., "Nuclear Weapons and U.S. China Relations: A Way Forward," Center for Strategic and International Studies, report of the PONI Working Group on U.S.-China Nuclear Dynamics, 2013, 20, http://csis.org/files/publication/130307_Colby_USChinaNuclear_Web.pdf.

Going forward, Washington and Beijing would do well to build on a notion of strategic stability that reflects the unique features of their relationship. Given the significant asymmetry between U.S. and Chinese nuclear forces—in number, type, and alert status—it is hard to imagine simply transplanting U.S.-Soviet notions of stability. If strategists are to imagine measures to strengthen strategic stability, including the prospects for formal arms control agreements, they must understand the associated challenges.

The U.S.-China dyad, as noted in the preceding section, has unique challenges and pathologies that might usefully be addressed. Differences in how U.S. and Chinese policymakers think about nuclear weapons may complicate efforts to sustain strategic stability in peacetime and could result in real misperceptions during a crisis. Chinese leaders, on the one hand, appear to believe that their nuclear weapons are essential to avoid being coerced by the U.S. threat of nuclear use or conventional strikes into accepting a humiliating settlement in a regional contingency. U.S. policymakers, on the other hand, view their nuclear weapons as defensive, enabling the United States to come to the aid of beleaguered allies and friends such as Taiwan, Japan, and South Korea. Where Chinese leaders see implicit nuclear coercion, the United States sees the extension of deterrence and the fulfillment of security commitments. These incompatible narratives raise troubling questions about crisis stability and the role of signaling with nuclear forces.

Another potentially dangerous pathology relates to Chinese efforts to signal resolve. Chinese leaders, as has been noted, appear to believe that placing forces on alert or renouncing NFU would stop the United States from continuing its efforts at coercion. If Washington, however, believes that it is not coercing Beijing but reassuring allies, then it would be easy to imagine the United States interpreting a decision by Beijing to put mobile missiles into the field as a highly escalatory step, if not a preparation for an attack. Given past experiences with U.S.-China crisis management, the potential for miscalculation would appear to be significant.

It seems unlikely that formal arms control agreements on numerical limits would address this specific pathology. The challenges arise not only from asymmetry in capabilities but also from the asymmetry in viewpoints that has led each side to create such different forces. The evolution of China's strategic forces reflects a local and contingent view of nuclear weapons, as a result of distinct historical, ideological, and bureaucratic experiences. The degree to which this view is different from that which prevails in the United States is evident in China's smaller, less diverse, and less alert nuclear forces. (Under the terms of the New START Treaty, for example, China has no deployed nuclear weapons.)

One possible solution might be to draw not from U.S.-Soviet history but from the U.S.-Chinese relationship and negotiate a "joint statement on strategic stability." Indeed, U.S. and Chinese officials have been able to bridge significant gaps in the past. In 1972 the Nixon administration was able to dramatically open relations with China through a process that resulted in the Shanghai Communiqué, which rested on the slenderest reed of agreement between Washington and Beijing—that there was only one China (even though they could not agree on the status of Taiwan). The communiqué succeeded because both sides could agree that the status quo, though not entirely desirable, should not be altered by force. As a result, this unorthodox document has proved a surprisingly durable basis for reconciliation despite the persistence of Taiwan as a severe flashpoint between the two countries.

Drawing on the lessons of the Shanghai Communiqué, China and the United States could build on their shared view that the fundamental role of nuclear weapons is to deter nuclear attacks. Since neither country wants to use nuclear weapons to change the status quo, it would be wise to firmly ground the strategic relationship in a joint statement on strategic stability. This statement might also provide a basis for ongoing discussions of the more technical problems concerning both sides.

An agreement on strategic stability would comprise pledges from each country. The United States could offer a security assurance that makes clear that it does not seek to achieve nuclear superiority or to negate China's deterrent. The policy statements outlined in the *Ballistic Missile Defense Review Report* and *Nuclear Posture Review Report* are already close to such a pledge. For its part, China could make clear that it does not seek numerical parity with the United States or to otherwise undermine U.S. security commitments in Asia. A political statement by China that recognizes the reality of these commitments would be difficult for Beijing, but it could assuage concerns in Washington, Tokyo, and Seoul that strategic stability may come at the expense of regional security.

The basis of this joint statement would not be an NFU pledge but rather a bargain in which both sides stated clearly their shared interests in moving forward on the basis of the current nuclear balance. Admittedly, such a statement would leave unresolved some important disagreements. The United States would remain concerned about China's improving nuclear forces, while China would remain wary of U.S. missile defense efforts. But if both sides agree to work toward stabilizing, rather than changing, the current strategic balance, then they will be in a better position to resolve or manage these issues.

Specifically, a joint statement on strategic stability would have three advantages. First, working toward a common goal would change the subject. The goal of a joint statement could force each party to set aside the formulaic calls for no first use and transparency that crowd out meaningful discussion during the already limited opportunities for dialogue. A formal communiqué creates an opportunity for both parties to explain how modernization programs reinforce rather than undermine the status quo. Second, a joint statement might enable a set of limited transparency measures. Chinese objections to U.S. calls for transparency tend to emphasize that such approaches are open-ended. If the United States and China were to agree to the pledges suggested above, however, they might also be able to agree to tailored transparency measures intended to build confidence in specific commitments. Finally, and most importantly, the dialogue leading to a joint statement on strategic stability could provide important benefits in the event of a crisis. Although they have the hardware to communicate in a crisis, such as the U.S.-China defense telephone link, both sides need to complement that hardware with softer cultural infrastructure that would make such a link more effective. This process would not, of course, solve all communication problems. But in a moment of heightened emotions and stakes, with limited decision-making time, the experience in negotiating a joint statement on strategic stability might reinforce the countries' shared interest in avoiding a nuclear exchange.

EXECUTIVE SUMMARY

This chapter provides an overview of the operational advances in India's nuclear capabilities over the past decade and analyzes their regional and global implications.

MAIN ARGUMENT:
At the technical level, India has the means for an assured strike capability against Pakistan. But it will take at least another decade before India acquires similar assurance against China. The pernicious nature of the Indo-Pakistani ideological rivalry, Pakistan's continued resort to low-intensity warfare, and China's huge nuclear lead do not bode well for deterrence and crisis stability in the Asia-Pacific. Although India's emergence as a nuclear weapons power is a positive development for the U.S. in managing China's rise, the price for that development is active diplomatic intervention in South Asia to ensure crisis stability and close vigilance to ensure that Pakistan's expanding nuclear arsenal remains safe and secure.

POLICY IMPLICATIONS:
- In the short term, the nuclear competition in the Asia-Pacific is prone to deterrence instability. Deterrence instability stems from material gaps in India's nuclear hardware, especially pertaining to China. The U.S. has the choice of continuing its present course of approaching India's nuclear drive with relative passivity or assisting India more aggressively through the supply of hardware.

- As long as Pakistan retains its strategy of low-intensity warfare against India, the threat of recurring crises in South Asia will remain, as will the demand for U.S. intervention and crisis management.

- The size of Chinese nuclear forces in the future may be partially determined by India's rival nuclear force. Chinese force expansion would complicate further reductions in the U.S. nuclear arsenal below one thousand.

India: The Challenges of Nuclear Operationalization and Strategic Stability

Gaurav Kampani

Fifteen years have passed since India stepped out of the nuclear closet and staked its claim to nuclear power status. Within the cohort of countries with nuclear weapons, India is generally regarded as a "reluctant" proliferator, having sat on the nuclear fence for sixteen years.[1] Scholars often attribute New Delhi's indecision to a strategic culture that is averse to nuclear weapons as well as to a leadership that is generally shy about taking political risks. Further, scholars and policy practitioners attribute India's quest for nuclear weapons to prestige as much as security. Until 2005–6, seven years after conducting nuclear tests, the pace of India's nuclear operationalization was slow. This led many to believe that Indian political leaders cared more about the symbolism associated with nuclear weapons than their military utility. Thereafter, the process picked up steam, especially with the military's participation in nuclear force planning. During the last seven years, India has made impressive strides toward deploying a nuclear triad of aircraft, mobile land-based missiles, and sea-based assets. Senior national security managers have also insisted that they take the task of building operational capabilities—the institutional and infrastructure invisibles such as command, control, communications, intelligence, logistics, procedures, planning, safety, and training—very

Gaurav Kampani is a Transatlantic Postdoctoral Fellow for International Relations and Security (2013–15) at the Norwegian Institute of Defence Studies in Oslo, the Center for Security Studies in Zurich, and the RAND Corporation in Washington, D.C. He can be reached at <gkampani@gmail.com>.

---

[1] After conducting a nuclear test in 1974, the Indian government began weaponizing in spring 1989. Although India conducted a second round of nuclear tests in 1998 and subsequently claimed the status of a nuclear power, it had acquired nuclear weapons sometime during 1990–92.

seriously. However, critics maintain that India's arsenal is technically unreliable and suffers from huge institutional and organizational lacunae.

During the last decade, India's and Pakistan's pursuit of nuclear weapons, China's nuclear force modernization, and North Korea's nuclear tests have put Asia at the center of the "second nuclear age." Although the rivalry between the nuclear powers in Asia does not approach the intensity of the Cold War competition between the Soviet Union and the United States, relations in the India-China and especially the India-Pakistan nuclear dyads are particularly tense. Since beginning their nuclear quest in the 1970s, India and Pakistan have fought one war and confronted each other in four serious crises that almost led to war. China and India have also clashed along their land border, and China has undermined India's security by materially aiding Pakistan in the development of its nuclear arsenal. Not surprisingly, therefore, serious concerns arise about maintaining strategic stability in the Asia-Pacific over the next several decades.

This chapter assesses how India perceives nuclear weapons as advancing its national interests in order to present a picture of the operational distance the country has traveled in the last decade. The first section offers a historical overview of India's nuclear weapons program and situates India's nuclear drive within the context of national security objectives. Next, the chapter surveys the hardware capabilities of both its weapons and delivery systems and analyzes the technical challenges that India must overcome to acquire a truly secure second-strike capability. The chapter then discusses the regional impact of India's emergence as a nuclear power with respect to deterrence stability, crisis stability, and arms race stability. Finally, the conclusion assesses these developments for U.S. policy in the Asia-Pacific and the world at large.

This chapter makes four arguments. First, India already possesses the technical means for an assured strike capability against Pakistan but will need at least another decade to acquire a similar capability vis-à-vis China. Second, institutional, organizational, and procedural capacities are as vital as hardware for force employment purposes. The latter constitute the Achilles heel of India's nuclear force and are acquiring increasing attention from national security managers. Third, the pernicious nature of the ideological rivalry between India and Pakistan, the latter's ongoing reliance on terrorism and low-intensity warfare, and China's huge nuclear lead over India do not bode well for deterrence and stability in the region. Nonetheless, the nuclear arms competition is more stable than external actors often perceive it to be. Finally, although India's emergence as a nuclear weapons power is a positive development for the United States in managing China's rise, the price for that development is active U.S. intervention in the region to ensure stability during crises and continued vigilance to ensure that Pakistan's expanding nuclear arsenal remains safe and secure.

Situating Nuclear Weapons within India's Strategic Objectives

India's nuclear policy operates at two different levels in the international system. At the global level, nuclear weapons symbolize the country's quest for power in a hierarchical international system. The weapons also underwrite New Delhi's strategic autonomy and provide rhetorical "reassurance to the people of India that their national security interests are paramount and will be promoted and protected."[2] The operational focus of India's arsenal, however, is directed exclusively at Pakistan and China, nuclear powers with which India anticipates continued geopolitical rivalry and the possibility of war in the 21st century. Speculation abounds on the operational reach of the Indian arsenal in this decade and the next. Doctrinal revisions made by the Indian government in 2004, investments in a triad capability, and the possibility of a program to develop intercontinental ballistic missiles have raised concerns that India might follow the trajectory of France's *force de frappe* (strike force) with the goal of achieving a *tous azimuts* (omnidirectional) capability.[3] Although a combination of interagency rivalry, political symbolism, and economic growth might underwrite that effort, technical, economic, and organizational obstacles make it unlikely that India will achieve such a capability in this decade.

India's operational nuclear capabilities are believed to lag behind Pakistan's and are regarded as significantly behind those of China.[4] Following its 1998 nuclear tests and formal claims to nuclear power status, the Indian government did not create the robust institutional capacities to wield nuclear weapons until 2003–4.[5] This slow tempo of operational planning gave rise to theories that the 1998 tests did not constitute a radical break with India's past and that Indian leaders remain invested in nuclear weapons as political and not military instruments. In 2001, for example, Ashley Tellis famously summed up the Indian posture as "strategically active though

[2] Atomic Archive, "Indian Government Statement on Nuclear Tests," May 11, 1998, http://www.atomicarchive.com/Docs/Deterrence/IndiaStatement.shtml.

[3] "Cabinet Committee Reviews Operationalization of India's Nuclear Doctrine," Government of India, Press Release, January 4, 2003; Verghese Koithara, *Managing India's Nuclear Forces* (Washington, D.C.: Brookings Institution Press, 2012), 106–21; and Bharat Karnad, *India's Nuclear Policy* (New Delhi: Pentagon Press, 2008), 101–2.

[4] Karnad, *India's Nuclear Policy*, 92–94.

[5] Pravin Sawhney, "Bombed," *Force*, February 2004, 8–10.

operationally dormant."[6] Nearly a decade after Tellis made that observation, India's former chief of nuclear forces, Rear Admiral (ret.) Vijay Shankar, described Tellis's characterization as "wordsmithing at its best."[7] Outside of the public eye, India is quietly changing how it has traditionally done business to address shortcomings in its nuclear operations. With the military's gradual institutionalization of nuclear planning during the last decade, hardware reliability, responsive infrastructure, and effective management have become India's primary operational goals.[8]

Indian nuclear planning is fixated primarily on Pakistan. National security managers regard China, the original trigger for New Delhi's interest in nuclear weapons in the 1960s, as a potential source of political blackmail and psychological intimidation.[9] Despite India being routed by China in the 1962 border war, Indian leaders have historically considered the Chinese threat with far greater equanimity than is often communicated publicly.[10] The Himalayas constitute a natural geographic barrier between the two countries that would limit the scale and scope of conventional operations. During the Cold War, particularly in the late 1960s and early 1970s, Indian policy planners also believed that both the Soviet Union and the United States, in order to maintain the balance of power in Asia, would intervene to prevent Chinese nuclear intimidation.[11] Notwithstanding such muted concerns, successive Indian governments remained committed, some more steadfastly than others, to investing in programs that could contribute to an actualized nuclear capability in the future. The 1974 nuclear test was the most visible expression of that sentiment. Lesser known is the inception of a program in the early 1970s to develop a medium-range ballistic missile capable of delivering a one-ton warhead up to 1,500 kilometers (km).[12]

In the early 1980s, the immediate nuclear threat from Pakistan revitalized India's nuclear weapons program.[13] The idea that Pakistan poses a threat to India is somewhat counterintuitive given the latter's gross advantages in

---

[6] Ashley Tellis, *India's Emerging Nuclear Posture: Between Recessed Deterrent and Ready Arsenal* (Santa Monica: RAND Corporation, 2001), 279.

[7] Author's interviews with Vijay Shankar, who served as commander-in-chief of India's Strategic Forces Command from 2006 to 2008, in New Delhi, July 31, 2010, and August 11, 2010.

[8] Ibid.

[9] Tellis, *India's Emerging Nuclear Posture*, 58–75, 273–80.

[10] Andrew B. Kennedy, "India's Nuclear Odyssey: Implicit Umbrellas, Diplomatic Disappointments, and the Bomb," *International Security* 36, no. 2 (2011): 133–34.

[11] Ibid., 134.

[12] Ashok Parthasarathi, *Technology at the Core: Science and Technology with Indira Gandhi* (New Delhi: Pearson, 2007), 168–80.

[13] Kargil Review Committee, *From Surprise to Reckoning: The Kargil Review Committee Report* (New Delhi: Sage Publications, 2000), 183–213.

size, geographic depth, conventional force numbers, and overall resource availability. However, Pakistan's superior internal lines of communication, reserve forces, and shorter mobilization times, as well as the division of the Indian army along the northern and western borders, attenuates most conventional advantages that India enjoys in theory.[14] Even with its crude numerical advantage, India realized in the early 1980s that in conditions of nuclear asymmetry it would be unable to concentrate its forces, enabling a weaker conventional enemy to destroy Indian forces in a piecemeal manner. This argument, presented by General Krishnaswamy Sundarji in the famous "Mhow papers," became the core of India's revived rationale for a nuclear weapons program in the early 1980s.[15]

A related rationale for Indian weaponization was that in conditions of nuclear asymmetry Pakistan might attempt to snatch disputed territory such as Kashmir from India, especially if the Indian political leadership were paralyzed for want of a nuclear option.[16] Hence, India's approach since the mid-1980s has been to counter the possibility of nuclear blackmail from Pakistan. Since its inception, Pakistan also has a history of subcontracting foreign and defense policies to nonstate proxies.[17] From the late 1980s onward, Pakistan has revived that strategy in Kashmir and elsewhere by capitalizing on local disaffection and supporting insurgent and terrorist groups in India. Islamabad has been emboldened by the assumption that its nuclear arsenal would both immunize it from an Indian conventional riposte and catalyze international intervention.[18] The Indian response to this approach has gradually evolved into a strategy of punishing Pakistan conventionally through limited operations, while either preventing escalation to the nuclear level or terminating war at the lowest possible rung of escalation should nuclear operations commence.[19]

The China-India rivalry, as Susan Shirk describes it, is one-sided. Threats are perceived more by India than by China, in light of the disparity of resources and the prevailing nuclear asymmetry.[20] From India's perspective,

---

[14] V.K. Sood and Praveen Sawhney, *Operation Parakram: The War Unfinished* (New Delhi: Sage Publications, 2003), 145–70.

[15] See "Combat Paper no. 1" in "Effects of Nuclear Asymmetry on Conventional Deterrence," ed. Krishnaswamy Sundarji, College of Combat, May 1981.

[16] Kargil Review Committee, *From Surprise to Reckoning*, 187.

[17] S. Paul Kapur and Sumit Ganguly, "The Jihad Paradox: Pakistan and Islamist Militancy in South Asia," *International Security* 37, no. 1 (2012): 111–41.

[18] Kargil Review Committee, *From Surprise to Reckoning*, 53–80.

[19] Ali Ahmed, "In Tribute: Recalling the 'Sundarji Doctrine,'" *U.S.I. Journal* 88, no. 571 (2008): 108.

[20] Susan L. Shirk, "One-Sided Rivalry: China's Perceptions and Policies toward India," in *The India-China Relationship: What the United States Needs to Know*, ed., Francine R. Frankel and Harry Harding (New York: Columbia University Press, 2004), 75–76.

four issues are potential causes for conflict: the unresolved border dispute, Chinese nuclear and missile assistance to Pakistan, China's potential support for insurgencies in India, and the water security of rivers originating in the Himalayas. India's support for a potential Tibetan insurgency in the Tibet Autonomous Region, its attempts to disrupt Chinese energy supplies traversing the sea lines of communication in the Indian Ocean, or rivalry in Southeast Asia could serve as other causes for conflict. None of these issues immediately threaten to induce a nuclear conflict because both countries possess powerful conventional forces that could address such contingencies. However, there is great unease in New Delhi over China's projected growth trajectories, emergence as the world's second-largest economic power, opaque decision-making, fluctuation between confrontational and cooperative behavior in border disputes with neighbors, and options to leverage the nuclear asymmetries that favor China. Above all, the issue that most concerns Indian policy planners is China's potential to confine India to South Asia and deny it a great-power role and status commensurate with India's perceptions of itself as one of the world's great civilizations.[21]

India's Nuclear Capabilities

Historical Background

India's nuclear program, like France's, was dual-use from its inception. Between the program's founding in 1947 and the early 1960s, the Indian government did not consciously pursue a weapons program even though India's Atomic Energy Commission acquired all the stages of the nuclear fuel cycle.[22] The quest for a weapons program began in the wake of the 1962 border war with China and the Chinese nuclear test in 1964.[23] Following these developments, Prime Minister Lal Bahadur Shastri authorized the development of a nuclear device in November 1964.[24] This program, known as the "subterranean nuclear explosive program," culminated in a nuclear test in 1974, but the device tested was not the prototype of a weapon.

Between 1974 and 1980, India's nuclear weapons program lay dormant. Much speculation abounds on the reasons for India's lone nuclear test in 1974 and the lack of follow-on tests. The likely answer to this puzzle is a

---

[21] Ashley J. Tellis, "China and India in Asia," in Frankel and Harding, *India-China Relationship*, 134–77.

[22] Karnad, *India's Nuclear Policy*, 35–55.

[23] Sumit Ganguly, "India's Pathway to Pokhran II: The Prospects and Sources of New Delhi's Nuclear Weapons Program," *International Security* 23, no. 4 (1999): 151–53.

[24] George Perkovich, *India's Nuclear Bomb: The Impact on Global Proliferation* (Berkeley: University of California Press, 1999), 83–85.

combination of India's confidence in its ability to manage the Chinese nuclear threat in the short term, resource constraints, and the lack of a diversified industrial infrastructure.[25] By the late 1970s, the "balance of threat"[26] in South Asia began to change for the worse, as clear indicators emerged of Pakistan's nuclear quest. In a classic internal balancing act, Indira Gandhi's government revived a weapon R&D program in 1980–81.[27] Subsequently, in 1983, her government instituted a ballistic missile program.[28] Through the 1970s and 1980s, the Indian air force also imported dual-use combat aircraft capable of performing nuclear missions. Together, these programs became part of an "options" strategy—that is, a strategy for India to acquire all the components of a working nuclear force without breaking the bank or attracting extreme international opprobrium.

India verged on nuclear tests in 1982–83 but relented under U.S. pressure.[29] Work on the program continued in secret, however. Ultimately, in 1989 then prime minister Rajiv Gandhi, confronted by Pakistan's nuclear advances and the failure of his global nuclear disarmament plan, authorized a program of weaponization and appointed then defense secretary Naresh Chandra to oversee the effort.[30] The Indian government assembled a secret committee in summer 1990, in the wake of the 1989–90 Kashmir crisis, to plan nuclear weapons use. The committee's recommendations institutionalized the practice of (1) maintaining unassembled nuclear weapons, (2) separating warheads from delivery systems, and (3) distributing the custody of fissile material cores, non-nuclear firing assemblies, and delivery systems among three different agencies.[31] Scholars dubbed this institution as one of "recessed" or "non-weaponized" deterrence.

Fission weapons likely became available in 1990–91, and India achieved the capability to deliver nuclear weapons reliably and safely via the Mirage

---

[25] "Nuclear Policy," memo from L.K. Jha to Prime Minister Indira Gandhi, May 3, 1967, P.N. Haksar Files, Sub. F. – 111, Nehru Memorial Library, New Delhi; and Perkovich, *India's Nuclear Bomb*, 121, 173–76.

[26] I borrow this phrase from Stephen Walt, who argues that states' balancing behavior is triggered not just by a shift in the balance of power but by their perceptions of threats inherent in that shift based on the opposing state's strength, geographical proximity, offensive capabilities, and offensive intentions. Although Walt's argument concerns states' external balancing versus bandwagoning behavior, I extend his concept to internal balancing. See Stephen M. Walt, "Alliance Formation and the Balance of World Power," *International Security* 9, no. 4: (1985): 3–43.

[27] Raj Chengappa, *Weapons of Peace: The Secret Story of India's Quest to Be a Nuclear Power* (New Delhi: Harper Collins Publishers, 2000), 246–47.

[28] Indranil Banerjie, "The Integrated Guided Missile Development Programme," *Indian Defence Review*, July 1990, 99–109.

[29] Chengappa, *Weapons of Peace*, 257–61.

[30] Ibid., 332–36.

[31] Author's interviews with K. Subrahmanyam, Noida, India, October 2009.

2000 fighter sometime between 1994 and 1996.[32] In 1995–96, India verged on nuclear tests again under the impending threat of the Comprehensive Nuclear-Test-Ban Treaty (CTBT), which national security managers feared would close the political window for testing. However, the country's economic reforms, dependence on the International Monetary Fund for structural support, and the potential for the United States to disrupt the economic transition led then prime minister P.V. Narasimha Rao to once again postpone tests.[33] The Atal Bihari Vajpayee government finally ordered tests in May 1998, ending India's policy of ambiguity by formally claiming nuclear power status. Following this event, the quasi-governmental National Security Council Advisory Board released the Draft Nuclear Doctrine (DND) in 1999. The DND made explicit India's employment of a "no first use" doctrine, formalized the institutional separation in command and control between civilian and military agencies, and spelled out an ambitious program for building a nuclear triad.[34] Although the Indian government at the time downplayed the proposed force architecture, the trajectory of India's nuclear force development has closely followed recommendations contained in the DND.

The Organization of India's Nuclear Forces

The end of external ambiguity about India's nuclear weapons program paved the way for the collapse of internal ambiguity as well. The development helped relocate the program from its narrow technical confines and embed it into a broader template of institutions, organizations, and procedures, a process that has given meaning to the idea of force employment.

Institutional reforms related to national security exploded in the aftermath of the 1999 Kargil War and the Kargil Committee Report.[35] The movement for these reforms, which had begun gaining strength in the late 1980s and early 1990s, received full expression in the 2000 group of ministers' report on national security reforms.[36] The report touched on every aspect of higher-level defense management: long-term national security planning, intelligence collection, and aggregation; "jointness" among the three armed

---

[32] Author's interviews with a senior officer in the Indian Air Force, New Delhi, December 2009 and February 2010.

[33] Author's interviews with a senior Indian defense official, New Delhi, October and November 2009.

[34] "India's Draft Nuclear Doctrine," *Arms Control Today* 29, no. 5 (1999).

[35] The Indian government appointed the Kargil Review Committee in the aftermath of Pakistan's aggression against India in Kargil in summer 1999. The committee's report reviewed the events leading up to the clash in Kargil and recommended national security reforms to prevent such events from recurring. For additional information, see Kargil Review Committee, "Appointment, Approach and Methodology," in *From Surprise to Reckoning*.

[36] Anit Mukherjee, "Failing to Deliver: Post-Crises Defence Reforms in India, 1998–2010," Institute for Defence Studies and Analyses (IDSA), IDSA Occasional Paper, no. 18, 2011, 9–22.

services; and the recasting of civil-military relations.[37] The operational management of the nuclear force was also part of the reform process.[38]

The principal vector of institutional reform in the military was Arun Singh's Task Force on Management of Defence (see **Figure 1**).[39] It proposed reforms in the context of the revolution in military affairs and India's status as a nuclear weapons state. The heart of its recommendations concerned replacing the existing Chiefs of Staff Committee (COSC) with the Integrated Defence Staff (IDS) led by a chief of defence staff (CDS). Prior to the reforms, joint planning between the services was the province of the COSC, which consisted of the three service chiefs. The chairmanship of the COSC devolved by rotation to the most senior chief, but chairmanship of the COSC was nominal and did not signify the principle of "first among equals." Nor did the three service chiefs and their services coordinate hardware acquisitions, doctrine development, and operational plans with each other. The net result of such institutional practices was the near absence of hardware and operational synergy between the services.

Nuclearization created an even more acute operational dilemma because of India's institutional legacy of maintaining a de-mated force. The control of nuclear warheads is divided between two civilian scientific agencies: the Bhabha Atomic Research Center and the Defence Research and Development Organization (DRDO), which control the fissile cores and non-nuclear firing assemblies, respectively. However, the air force, army, and navy each retain separate control of nuclear-capable combat aircraft, ships, and ballistic missiles. Military reformers therefore sought to recast their institutions to instill greater coordination and joint planning between the services.

Compared with the past, when the chairman of the COSC was only a nominal head, Singh's task force conceived the CDS as the first among equals. With assistance from a vice chief of defence staff and with the IDS acting as his secretariat for staffing functions, the CDS would "administer the strategic forces" and "provide single-point military advice to the government."[40] Pursuant to the task force's recommendations, the government instituted the IDS in 2001. A tri-service Strategic Forces Command (SFC) was subsequently instituted within the IDS in May 2002 to coordinate and manage nuclear forces. However, it was not until 2003–4 that the military actually gained

---

[37] Satish Chandra, "Slow, but Steady: Evolution of the National Security System," *Force*, October 2005, 49–51.

[38] Arun Prakash, "India's Higher Defence Organization: Implications for National Security and Jointness," *Journal of Defence Studies* 1, no. 1 (2007): 13–31.

[39] Prakash, "India's Higher Defence Organization."

[40] Ibid.

institutional authority in nuclear force planning and management alongside the scientific agencies.[41]

Since the middle of the last decade, the SFC's organizational presence within India's nuclear planning has grown substantially. In 2010, Vice Admiral (ret.) Vijay Shankar, former commander in chief of the SFC, estimated the command's staff strength at a "little below 100." This count, according to Shankar, is a "large staff for a command, especially when compared to other conventional operational commands, where staff strength does not exceed 50–60."[42] With organizational expansion, the SFC now has departments that

FIGURE 1   India's higher defense organization

NOTE: Asterisk indicates that the CDS was proposed by the Arun Singh Task Force at the head of the COSC. The position of CDS, however, does not yet exist.

---

[41] Sawhney, "Bombed," 10; and Karnad, *India's Nuclear Policy*, 94–95.

[42] Sawhney, "Bombed," 10.

cover logistics; a works department for building infrastructure; a technical section that has representation from all three services; a department of land, air, and sea vectors responsible for generating standard procedures for various stages of operational readiness in peacetime and war; an electronics department that focuses on general release codes for nuclear weapons, general computing, and communications requirements; an independent intelligence analysis group that processes raw data from various government agencies; and its own specialized medical staff.[43]

In January 2003, India made public the establishment of a National Command Authority (NCA). The NCA consists of two halves: the Political Council and the Executive Council. The prime minister chairs the Political Council, whose composition has not been made public.[44] However, given India's past institutional practices, it most likely consists of the Cabinet Committee on Security (comprising the ministers of home affairs, defence, finance, and external affairs), the national security advisor, the cabinet secretary, and the prime minister's principal secretary. Other special invitees would possibly include the principal scientific advisor to the prime minister, the scientific advisor to the defence minister, the chairman of the Atomic Energy Commission, and the three service chiefs in a non-voting capacity. The Political Council is the "sole body [that] can authorize the use of nuclear weapons."[45]

The Executive Council is chaired by the national security advisor and "provides inputs for decision-making by the NCA and executes the directives given to it by the Political Council."[46] The composition of the Executive Council has also not been made public. However, it almost certainly includes the three service chiefs, the commander in chief of the SFC, the principal scientific advisor, and the heads of the Atomic Energy Commission, the DRDO, and intelligence agencies. Within the NCA, a program strategy staff with representatives from the armed services, the DRDO, the Atomic Energy Commission, and the foreign ministry provides strategic inputs to the national security advisor on the quality and reliability of India's nuclear weapons and delivery systems, foreign intelligence, and long-term planning for the arsenal. In addition, a separate Strategic Armaments Safety Authority advises the national security advisor and the NCA on the safety and security of India's nuclear assets.[47]

---

[43] Author's interviews with Shankar.

[44] "Cabinet Committee on Security Reviews Progress in Operationalizing India's Nuclear Doctrine," Prime Minister's Office, Government of India, Press Release, January 4, 2003.

[45] Ibid.

[46] Ibid.

[47] Shyam Saran, "Weapon That Has More Than Symbolic Value," *Hindu*, May 4, 2013, http://www.thehindu.com/opinion/lead/weapon-that-has-more-than-symbolic-value/article4681085.ece.

Weapons and Fissile Material

Fission weapons are the mainstay of India's nuclear arsenal. These very likely have a yield in the range of 12–15 kilotons, although some analysts believe that the yield could be boosted to 30 kilotons.[48] Because designing reliable boosted weapons usually entails repeated testing, doubts persist that Indian scientists can build and deploy such weapons with confidence on the basis of a single test. The proven fission design in India's inventory has a significantly reduced yield-to-weight ratio in comparison with the device tested in 1974. It is also believed to be sufficiently light and rugged for delivery by combat aircraft and ballistic missiles. During the 1998 test series, the fission device was the only device tested in weaponized form.[49]

It is unclear whether India has weaponized low-yield fission devices in the sub-kiloton range. Such devices are prohibited by India's nuclear doctrine, and the Indian government does not acknowledge their existence or planned use. Statements by political leaders and national security managers make clear that India does not view nuclear weapons as usable on the battlefield. However, the question persists, within both the armed forces and the strategic community at large, of how India might achieve a proportionate retaliatory response to limited battlefield strikes by Pakistan and China with tactical nuclear weapons.

India's claim that it possesses or is capable of deploying thermonuclear and boosted-fission weapons has met with enormous skepticism both within the country and abroad. Although in the immediate wake of the 1998 tests the Indian nuclear establishment claimed that it had successfully tested a thermonuclear device, those claims were contradicted by visual data of the device's crater morphology and the seismic signal from the test series. There were also conflicting claims and even revisions of the data by the Indian scientists involved in the tests.[50] Moreover, the nuclear scientists' claims were disputed by members of India's own nuclear and defense establishment who were involved with the weapon-design, testing, and data-verification programs.[51] In 2008, this controversy exploded in public when the DRDO's former director of technology made public that the DRDO—the agency charged by the atomic establishment with the instrumentation for the test

---

[48] Tellis, *India's Emerging Nuclear Posture*, 519–22; and Koithara, *Managing India's Nuclear Forces*, 125.

[49] Pranay Sharma, Ajaz Ashraf, and K. Santhanam, "The Myth Bomber," *Outlook* (India), October 5, 2009, http://www.outlookindia.com/article.aspx?262027.

[50] Tellis, *India's Emerging Nuclear Posture*, 508–19.

[51] P.K. Iyengar, "Non-Fissile Doubts," *Outlook* (India), October 26, 2009, http://www.outlookindia.com/article.aspx?262331. For additional context, see the public protest note to the Indian government by several senior Indian scientists, many of whom worked for India's Department of Atomic Energy. P.K. Iyengar et al., "On Thermonuclear Weapon Capability and Its Implications for Credible Minimum Deterrence," *Mainstream* XLVIII, no. 1 (2009).

data as well as with gathering and verifying that data—had disputed the nuclear scientists' claims of success in a classified report to the government and recommended a program of further tests.[52]

In the wake of this controversy, the Indian government appointed a secret committee to review the claims and counterclaims.[53] Little is known about the committee's composition and terms of reference. Its findings and recommendations to the government are also classified. In public, however, the Indian nuclear establishment insists that India is capable of deploying thermonuclear warheads whose yields can be boosted up to 200 kilotons. Nonetheless, the weight of evidence suggests that the thermonuclear device has not been weaponized.

Triad

As stated in the DND fourteen years ago, India remains committed to developing nuclear forces based on "a triad of aircraft, mobile land-based missiles, and sea-based assets."[54] The Indian Air Force has several nuclear-capable aircraft, which include the Mirage 2000, Jaguar, MIG-27, and Sukhoi-30 MKI. During the 1990s, a small number of Mirage 2000s were converted to perform nuclear missions.[55] Several analysts also believe that the Sukhoi-30 MKI may have been tailored for nuclear missions, although the evidence is conflicting.[56] The air leg of India's triad is by far the most flexible and reliable but suffers from penetration limitations, especially in targeting China. Some of the range and communications hurdles that impeded the air leg in the 1990s have been partially addressed in the last decade through the acquisition of mid-air refueling systems and airborne early warning aircraft.[57]

Since the early 2000s, India's operational effort has shifted to developing and deploying land-based ballistic missiles, which afford the advantages of longer range, easier storage and maintenance, and greater mobility. The Agni I is a 700-km, road-mobile missile. The 2,000-km Agni II is

---

[52] Sharma, Ashraf, and Santhanam, "The Myth Bomber."

[53] Author's interview with M.R. Srinivasan, Bangalore, July 8, 2010. Srinivasan was chairman of the Atomic Energy Commission and secretary of the Department of Atomic Energy from 1987 to 1990.

[54] See "India's Draft Nuclear Doctrine," *Arms Control Today* 29, no. 5 (1999): 33.

[55] Chengappa, *Weapons of Peace*, 382–84.

[56] M.V. Ramana, "India," in *Assuring Destruction Forever: Nuclear Weapon Modernization Around the World*, ed. Ray Acheson (New York: Women's International League for Peace and Freedom, 2012), 34–43.

[57] Indo-Asian News Service, "Indian Air Force to Have Mid-air Refueling Capabilities on All Combat Aircraft," NDTV, December 9, 2012, http://www.ndtv.com/article/india/indian-air-force-to-have-mid-air-refuelling-capability-on-all-combat-aircraft-303115; and "Surya's Chariots: India's AWACS Program," *Defense Industry Daily*, March 5, 2013, http://www.defenseindustrydaily.com/indian-awacs-moving-forward-on-2-fronts-04855.

rail-mobile, although it is also available in a road-mobile configuration. Both the Agni I and Agni II have entered production and been tested in an operational configuration by the SFC.[58] The 3,500-km, rail-mobile Agni III has completed development tests and is in the process of entering operational service.[59] Two other variants, the Agni IV and V, are being tested.[60] The 4,000-km Agni IV was likely designed to test new technologies such as composite rocket motors, an inertial navigation system with laser ring gyroscope, a micro-navigation system, and a digital controller system.[61] It is unclear whether the missile will enter operational service or only be used to validate technologies that will become incorporated into the Agni V and VI. In 2012, the DRDO tested the 5,000-km Agni V, and more tests are planned before 2015.[62] The Agni VI, currently under development, will be road-mobile like the other missiles in the Agni family and have the same range as the Agni V, but it will deliver a heavier payload. Whereas the first five Agni variants are all capable of deploying a one-ton warhead,[63] the Agni VI reportedly will have a three-ton payload and deploy three warheads with multiple independently targetable reentry vehicle (MIRV) technology.[64] See **Figure 2** for a map of Indian missile ranges.

Finally, as first stated in the DND in 1999, India remains seriously invested in developing a secure, sea-based second-strike capability. Its current sea-based capability consists of a small number of 350-km liquid-fuel Prithvi missiles deployed on two offshore patrol vessels. Because of the limited range of both the ships and the missiles, this force represents a token capability

[58] "Agni-I Missile Test-fired as Part of Army's User Trial," *Indian Express*, December 1, 2011, http://www.indianexpress.com/news/agnii-missile-testfired-as-part-of-armys-user-trial/882757/1; and T.S. Subramanian, "Agni-II Missile Successfully Test Fired," *Hindu*, April 7, 2013, http://www.thehindu.com/news/national/agniii-missile-successfully-test-fired/article4590964.ece.

[59] Y. Mallikarjun, "Agni-III Test-fired Successfully," *Hindu*, September 21, 2012, http://www.thehindu.com/news/national/agniiii-testfired-successfully/article3922230.ece.

[60] T.S. Subramanian, "Agni-IV Test-flight a 'Stupendous Success,'" *Hindu*, November 15, 2011, http://www.thehindu.com/news/national/article2629274.ece; and T.S. Subramanian and Y. Mallikarjun, "In Wheeler Island, a Perfect Mission Sparks Celebrations," *Hindu*, April 20, 2012, http://www.thehindu.com/news/national/article3332940.ece.

[61] "Long Range Strategic Missile Agni-IV Test-fired," *Hindu*, September 19, 2012, http://www.thehindu.com/sci-tech/science/article3914340.ece.

[62] Y. Mallikarjun and T.S. Subramanian, "Agni-V Propels India into Elite ICBM Club," *Hindu*, April 19, 2012, http://www.thehindu.com/news/national/article3330921.ece.

[63] "India Successfully Test-fires Agni I Ballistic Missile," *Indian Express*, November 25, 2010, http://www.indianexpress.com/news/india-successfully-testfires-agni-i-ballist/715859; Y. Mallikarjun, "Fresh User Trial of Agni-II on Monday from Wheeler's Island Off Orissa Coast," *Hindu*, May 14, 2010, http://www.thehindu.com/news/national/article429490.ece; and "Agni-III Test Fired by India," *Indian Express*, July 9, 2006, http://expressindia.indianexpress.com/news/fullstory.php?newsid=70753.

[64] Ajai Shukla, "Advanced Agni-6 Missile with Multiple Warheads Likely by 2017," *Business Standard*, May 8, 2013, http://www.business-standard.com/article/economy-policy/advanced-agni-6-missile-with-multiple-warheads-likely-by-2017-113050800034_1.html.

FIGURE 2   Indian missile ranges

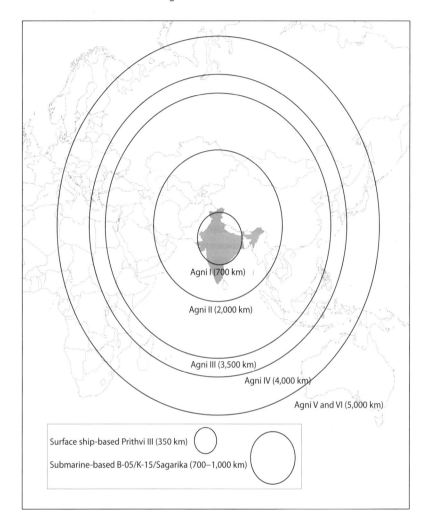

SOURCE: The missile range map uses data drawn from a compendium of open-source literature. Missile ranges reported by Indian defense agencies are conflicting and there are no independent means available in the open-domain to make accurate technical assessments. Because Indian defense agencies are known to exaggerate capabilities, the missile ranges should be regarded as rough estimates and treated with caution.

against Pakistan.[65] However, India will acquire a true sea-based deterrent when its planned fleet of three nuclear-powered ballistic missile submarines (SSBN) begins entering service later this decade.

The first of these boats, the S-2, is currently undergoing sea trials.[66] The vessel's power plant consists of a 90-megawatt reactor that uses low-enriched uranium, and its overall displacement weight is 6,000 tons.[67] The S-2 has four launch tubes for a ballistic missile with an estimated range of 700–1,000 km.[68] This missile, variously known as the K-15, Sagarika, and more recently the B-05, has been under development since the early 2000s.[69] Thus far, India's missile development agency has only used underwater pontoons for test launches of the B-05.

The S-3 and S-4 will follow the development of the S-2 but incorporate modifications and improvements capable of being retrofitted to the S-2 hull and supported by its power reactor. The S-5, however, will be a fundamental redesign of the S-2 class,[70] which is essentially a "technology demonstrator" for follow-on systems. Building the S-2 and its successor vessels will help India consolidate its industrial infrastructure for submarine design and construction. Like a carrier task force, however, nuclear submarines have huge operational time lags. Hardware acquisition brings with it requirements for a large ancillary infrastructure for safety, maintenance, refueling, navigation, and crew training in operations, communications, and nuclear launch procedures.[71]

The Regional Impact of India's Nuclear Capabilities

Over the last decade, India has fundamentally expanded the scale and scope of its material nuclear capabilities. It has also attempted to embed those capabilities within new institutional and organizational contexts. Both transformations have not reached maturity yet, and existing gaps in India's material and organizational capabilities render deterrence and crisis

---

[65] Koithara, *Managing India's Nuclear Forces*, 137.

[66] The S-2 will be known as the *Arihant* after it enters operational service.

[67] Arun Prakash, "A Step Before the Leap," *Force*, September 2009, http://forceindia.net/FORCEINDIAOLDISSUE/arunprakash12.aspx.

[68] Pravin Sawhney and Vijay Shankar, "Is the Navy's Newest Sub Worth the Price?" *Hindu*, January 25, 2012, http://www.thehindu.com/opinion/op-ed/is-the-navys-newest-sub-worth-the-price/article2829121.ece.

[69] Pallava Bagla, "A White Rocket Rose from the Water," *Outlook* (India), February 11, 2013, http://www.outlookindia.com/article.aspx?283764.

[70] Sawhney and Shankar, "Is the Navy's Newest Sub Worth the Price?"

[71] Vijay Shankar, "Chakra, the Filler of Strategic Space," *Hindu*, January 25, 2012, http://www.thehindu.com/todays-paper/tp-opinion/chakra-the-filler-of-strategic-space/article2829869.ece.

management vis-à-vis Pakistan and China problematic. Nonetheless, the nuclear arms competition in the Asia-Pacific, although worrisome, is not as pernicious as the one that consumed the superpowers during the Cold War.

Deterrence Stability

Deterrence stability is contingent upon a secure second-strike capability, robust institutions and organizations that help actualize that capability, well-developed procedures, and training of personnel to ensure institutional and organizational coordination. In India's case, deterrence stability vis-à-vis Pakistan is a lesser concern because both states are emerging nuclear powers and confront similar technical, organizational, and procedural problems. China, which enjoys a three-decade lead in the development, deployment, and management of nuclear forces, poses a greater challenge to India.

Although India's arsenal of fission weapons and air-, land-, and sea-based missile delivery systems provide it with an assured strike capability against Pakistan, this condition does not extend to China. The failure of India's thermonuclear weapon design, the moratorium against further testing, and doubts about the reliability of any deployed boosted-fission weapons have created nuclear asymmetry that favors China. However, several influential analysts believe that stability is possible, despite the existing asymmetry, because the nuclear devices that India likely possesses would be sufficient to kill hundreds of thousands of people.[72] That said, until it develops and deploys intermediate-range ballistic missiles successfully, India will lack the capability to target mainland China in its entirety.

Apart from the lethality and reliability of Indian nuclear weapons, there are several operational issues limiting the conduciveness of India's land-based Agni class of missiles to deterrence stability in the region. These include weight, ease of mobility, and strain on rail and road infrastructure. India's unique institutions of deployment—involving the separation of fissile cores from the warhead and the warhead from the missile—increase the logistical and coordination challenges that exist between the military and civilian scientific institutions.[73] Finally, the SFC has only recently begun independently testing ballistic missiles in an operational mode.[74]

Several operational limitations also beset India's current class of SSBNs, the S-2. The vessel's reactor, for example, is believed to have a short refueling

---

[72] K. Subrahmanyam and V.S. Arunachalam, "Deterrence and Explosive Yield," *Hindu*, September 20 2009, http://www.thehindu.com/opinion/op-ed/article22870.ece.

[73] Koithara, *Managing India's Nuclear Forces*, 108–15, 123–32.

[74] For examples, see Y. Mallikarjun, "Agni-I Soars Successfully," *Hindu*, December 12, 2012, http://www.thehindu.com/news/national/agni1-soars-successfully/article4190985.ece; and Subramanian, "Agni-II Missile Successfully Test-Fired."

cycle. Because reactor refueling can take between 18 and 24 months, India will remain without a submarine on patrol for significant gaps of time until the S-3 and S-4 enter service.[75] In addition, the short range of the B-05 ballistic missile slated for deployment aboard S-2 SSBNs means that India will lack a significant sea-based strike capability against China for another decade.[76] Other limitations follow from the low number of missile tubes, which restricts the number of warheads that could be deployed on board each vessel. The Indian Navy ultimately hopes to deploy a submarine with a displacement of 10,000–12,000 tons and with 16–24 missile tubes. Such a vessel would be capable of launching MIRV missiles with a range of 4,000–8,000 km, supported by a 200-megawatt reactor. This dream vehicle could operate safely out of the Bay of Bengal or the Arabian Sea and finally provide India with a secure second-strike capability against China.[77] Its development, however, will likely take another decade or more.

Beyond these technical issues, force reconstitution and operational employment raise institutional and organizational problems for India's military. There are two causes for concern, the first of which is institutional. Two civilian scientific entities—the Bhabha Atomic Research Centre and DRDO—retain custody of the fissile cores and non-fissile trigger assemblies, while the army and navy possess a small ballistic missile force, and the air force controls all dual-use combat aircraft in peacetime. Neither the military nor the scientific agencies, however, have jurisdiction over the other. Further, the Indian government has not acted on the recommendations of the Arun Singh task force to create a "single point" authority—the proposed CDS—to command the nuclear force. Thus, institutional and organizational gridlock, should it occur, cannot be resolved by either the military or scientific agencies. These conflicts can only be resolved at the level of the national security advisor in the Prime Minister's Office. Such cumbersome institutional arrangements do not bode well for intra- and inter-agency cooperation during war.

The second problem concerns India's weak physical infrastructure, which encompasses secure communication networks, redundant command and control nodes, safe storage and launch hideouts for the nuclear force, and robust transport links for the secure passage of warheads, fissile cores, and delivery vehicles.[78] During the mid-2000s for example, the SFC judged the infrastructure of the Indian nuclear force, especially its communications

---

[75] Prakash, "Step Before the Leap."

[76] Koithara, *Managing India's Nuclear Forces*, 136–38; Prakash, "Step Before the Leap;" and Sawhney and Shankar, "Is the Navy's Newest Sub Worth the Price?"

[77] Koithara, *Managing India's Nuclear Forces*, 128–31; and Prakash, "Step Before the Leap."

[78] Koithara, *Managing India's Nuclear Forces*, 145–49.

and transport networks, to be subpar.[79] "If Pakistan decides to launch [an attack] in such a way that it takes out your command and control…it [will also] take out some of your nuclear nodes," asserts former chairman of the COSC, Admiral (ret.) Arun Prakash, "and [if] they inflict enough damage… then even our response may not be assured."[80]

The military would prefer to have complete custody of India's nuclear forces to improve employment efficiency, which is the institutional practice in all other existing nuclear weapons states. But given the Indian political class's historical aversion to nuclear weapons and the dependency those ideas have engendered through reification, India's operating conditions in the past decade have involved the worst of two worlds: a disaggregated arsenal embedded within weak institutional and physical structures. However, there is evidence that the Indian Navy may acquire greater operational control over the country's nuclear forces when its SSBNs enter operational service.[81]

Crisis Stability

Unlike deterrence stability, which is a function of a state's technical, institutional, and organizational capacities, crisis stability stems from the ability of nuclear powers to communicate their intent accurately during a crisis and control the organizational response of their forces such that it matches the intended communications. Nuclear crisis stability operates at both the external and domestic levels. Externally, it depends on the state of political relations between nuclear powers; clearly articulated doctrines and nuclear red lines raise the bar for deterrence and help maintain stability. Domestically, crisis stability flows from the capacity of nuclear powers to coordinate their own nuclear and conventional forces in a manner that signals resolve and reduces the likelihood for miscalculation and error.

Three problems in the current management of India's nuclear forces create the potential for crisis instability. The first concerns the compatibility of India's conventional military strategy of "limited war under nuclear conditions" and its declared nuclear doctrine of "massive retaliation." The second problem is the gap between New Delhi's declaratory nuclear policy and actual employment strategy. Finally, the Indian military's conventional and nuclear forces remain weakly coordinated.

The document that best captures Indian thinking on the declaratory aspects of nuclear policy is the DND, which was made public in 1999. The

---

[79] Karnad, *India's Nuclear Policy*, 97–98.

[80] Author's interview with Arun Prakash, Dehradun, April 2009.

[81] Author's interview with Brajesh Mishra, New Delhi, October 2009. Mishra was India's national security advisor from 1998 to 2004.

DND formalizes the core elements of India's nuclear posture, first developed in the early 1990s: no first use, retaliation only against the use of nuclear weapons, recessed deployment, and assertive command and control.[82] The doctrine proposes "punitive" retaliatory attacks and leaves the door open for proportionate deterrence or retaliatory attacks that are calibrated to match a nuclear attack against India. India's Cabinet Committee on Security issued a subsequent document on the "operationalization" of the nuclear doctrine in January 2003. The committee replaced the "punitive retaliation" clause of the DND with "massive retaliation" regardless of the scale of attacks against India.[83]

The problem with India's declaratory doctrine of "massive retaliation" is that it does not speak to the conventional military doctrine, which proposes to fight a limited conventional war under nuclear conditions. The Indian army devised the latter doctrine to deal with the problem of Pakistan's sub-conventional war strategy. Since the late 1980s, Pakistan has used the security of its nuclear arsenal to provide material and ideological support to insurgents and terrorists fighting the Indian government. Prior to 1999, the Indian military responded to Pakistani provocations through a strategy of denial and dissuasion. Thereafter, it switched to a strategy of denial and punishment. Instead of simply denying Pakistani-sponsored insurgents and terrorists victory, the Indian army sought to punish their sponsor, the Pakistani military itself, through swift retaliatory blows and limited incursions and occupation of Pakistani territory along the border. This doctrine, known as "Cold Start," is now at the center of India's proposed conventional response to any serious provocations by Pakistan.[84]

Pakistan's nuclear strategy in turn has evolved to defeat India's new punishment strategy by adopting what Vipin Narang terms "asymmetric escalation." What this essentially means is that Pakistan proposes to use nuclear weapons first and early.[85] At the declaratory level, India's response alternates between two extremes: either do nothing or undertake massive attacks that will impose unacceptable losses on the enemy. India's nuclear doctrine thus contradicts its conventional war strategy. Whereas Cold Start envisages a war of limited aims with limited means, massive retaliation proposes a war with unlimited means for unlimited ends.

---

[82] "India's Draft Nuclear Doctrine."

[83] "Cabinet Committee Reviews Operationalization of India's Nuclear Doctrine."

[84] Walter C. Ladwig III, "A Cold Start for Hot Wars? The Indian Army's New Limited War Doctrine," *International Security* 32, no. 3 (2007/08): 158–90.

[85] Vipin Narang, "Posturing for Peace? Pakistan's Nuclear Postures and South Asian Stability," *International Security* 34, no. 3 (2009/10): 38–78.

The more likely reality is that India's operational employment policy does not actually seek to punish a nuclear aggressor through massive retaliation. Senior military leaders have suggested that the SFC's operational plans encompass a range of options that include nuclear demonstration shots, the tactical use of nuclear weapons against conventional military targets on the battlefield, and large-scale attacks against an enemy's cities.[86] However, the dissonance between India's stated and actual employment policy creates room for doubt and miscalculations.

Senior military leaders in the SFC and COSC view sub-conventional, conventional, and nuclear operations as belonging to a single spectrum of operations. They believe that low-yield tactical nuclear weapons, which China and Pakistan both possess, could be used for strategic political effect on the battlefield with relatively low casualties. Conventional operations could therefore seamlessly escalate into a nuclear exchange.[87] A nuclear attack by an adversary, at least in its early stages, would very likely assume the form of a symbolic strike, a demonstration, or warning shot against some tactical Indian formation in the field.[88] The risk of Chinese nuclear strikes in the Himalayan theater of operations is generally considered to be low at present.[89] But one former chairman of the COSC has argued privately that this risk is perceived as low because India is "grossly ill-informed about the Chinese military psyche, thought process, and mind sets…[having] failed to devote adequate resources to a serious study of these factors."[90] Senior Indian military leaders aver that such attacks, if they were to materialize, would demand a highly calibrated Indian counter-response to terminate war at the lowest possible level of nuclear exchange.[91] However, such a nuanced politico-military strategy would be difficult to execute given the existing state of compartmentalization between India's conventional and nuclear war commands.

Conventional and nuclear operations under the current dispensation are the independent responsibilities of the three services (army, navy, and air force) and the SFC. The SFC, the agency responsible for nuclear operations, is housed within the IDS, the body which serves as the secretariat and coordinating arm for the COSC. But "there is no link between the SFC

---

[86] Tellis, *India's Emerging Nuclear Posture*, 363–65.

[87] Author's interview with Prakash; and author's interviews with Ajit Bhavnani, New Delhi, April 2009 and February 2010. Bhavnani was commander-in-chief of the SFC from 2004 to 2006.

[88] Author's interviews with Shankar.

[89] Author's interview with a former chairman of the Chiefs of Staff Committee, New Delhi, July 2010.

[90] Author's e-mail correspondence with Arun Prakash, April 2009.

[91] Author's interview with a former chairman of the Chiefs of Staff Committee, New Delhi, July 2010; and author's personal communication with Prakash.

and IDS," according to a former SFC commander in chief; rather, "the SFC reports only to the chairman [of the] COSC."[92] As a result, the IDS is unable to synergize tasks with the SFC. In any war, the primary focus of the three service chiefs would be on fighting their own separate conventional wars. This includes the chairman of the COSC—the nominal head of the SFC—who is first a service chief and then head of IDS.[93] Senior Indian military leaders maintain that in a future crisis the SFC would essentially function directly under the Prime Minister's Office through the national security advisor, bypassing the defense ministry and the military's normal chain of command.[94] Thus, according to two former commanders in chief of the SFC and chairmen of the COSC, India's nuclear command system "is broken."[95]

A decade after the 1998 nuclear tests, General (ret.) Ved Malik, a former army chief, publicly raised the question of whether the services "had been able to interface…nuclear capability with conventional capabilities."[96] To this question, a former commander in chief of the SFC, Air Marshal (ret.) Ajit Bhavnani, replied in private that "this compartmentalization still exists… and…we've tried our best…. We've said that it is important for everyone in the military to understand the nuclear issues…. All I can say [is that] from 2001 until today there has been an evolutionary change in the understanding of nuclear warfare."[97] Senior SFC commanders claim that procedures now exist for coordinating conventional and nuclear operations. Yet they all concede that paper plans and coordinating procedures are weak substitutes for horizontal organizational integration between the SFC and IDS. Such institutional compartmentalization does not bode well for crisis stability.

Arms-Race Stability

Alongside questions of deterrence and crisis stability, the prospect of a nuclear arms race has been an issue of great concern in South Asia since the early 1980s, when India and Pakistan launched their secret nuclear weapon programs. Those earlier concerns harked back to Robert Jervis's concepts of "security dilemmas" and "spiral" effects. Nonetheless, U.S. pressure proved successful in slowing the pace of both programs. Similarly, in the 1990s the clandestine nature of these programs imposed some stability on the nuclear

---

[92] Author's interview with a former commander in chief of the SFC, New Delhi, April 2009.

[93] Author's interview with Prakash, April 2009.

[94] Koithara, *Managing India's Nuclear Forces*, 175–76.

[95] Author's interview with Vijay Shankar, August 2010.

[96] V.P. Malik, "Operation Shakti: A Decade Later," *U.S.I. Journal* 88, no. 572 (2008), http://www.usiofindia.org/Article/?pub=Journal&pubno=572&ano=337.

[97] Author's interview with Bhavnani, April 2009.

arms competition in the region. Fearful of nonproliferation pressures and the threat of U.S. sanctions, both India and Pakistan found it hard to coordinate their weaponization efforts across multiple internal agencies.

However, fears of an open-ended arms race resurfaced after 1998, the year India and Pakistan conducted nuclear tests and formally laid claim to nuclear power status. Since then, a popular refrain is that a new nuclear arms race has descended on South Asia and the Asia-Pacific region more broadly, which is now home to three new nuclear powers and four modernizing nuclear weapons programs. This belief partly draws on India's ambitious plans to deploy a nuclear triad. Although then foreign minister Jaswant Singh sought to reassure international audiences that India would not engage in an open-ended nuclear arms race and only seek a "credible" minimum nuclear capability, he qualified that claim by arguing that "minimum cannot be a fixed physical quantification; it is a dynamic concept but firmly rooted in the strategic environment, technological imperatives and national security needs and the actual size, components, deployment and employment of nuclear forces will be decided taking into account all these factors."[98]

In the last decade, India has made good on its plans to develop a triad, although the force is still far from completion. In 1999, it also launched a program to develop a two-tiered missile defense system designed to offer protection against short- and medium-range missiles.[99] Viewed in conjunction, these programs theoretically threaten offense dominance against Pakistan, if not China.

Despite these developments, several factors make the arms competition in Asia more stable than its Cold War predecessor. The first is New Delhi's self-imposed moratorium on further nuclear testing. Although India is not a party to the CTBT and the moratorium on testing is *de facto* and not *de jure*, the Indo-U.S. civil nuclear agreement and the resumption of international sales of power reactors have raised the threshold for resuming nuclear testing.[100] Further, the limited data collected from the two rounds of nuclear tests in 1998 makes the development of new nuclear weapon designs unlikely. This places limits on the acquisition of new delivery systems such as cruise missiles that would require major modifications in warhead design.

---

[98] See Jaswant Singh, "Interview with Jaswant Singh, India's Minister for External Affairs," *Hindu*, by C. Raja Mohan, November 29, 1999, available at http://www.acronym.org.uk/spsingh.htm.

[99] "DRDO Ballistic Missile Defense System, India," Army-technology.com, http://www.army-technology.com/projects/drdo-bmd.

[100] Justine Isola, "If India Tests? The Implications for the Indo-U.S. Civil-Nuclear Deal," IDSA, IDSA Issue Brief, August 26, 2010, http://www.idsa.in/system/files/IB_IndiaUSNuclearDeal.pdf. See also P.K. Iyengar, A.N. Prasad, A. Gopalakrishnan, and Bharat Karnad, *Strategic Sell-Out: Indian-U.S. Nuclear Deal* (New Delhi: Pentagon Press, 2009).

Admittedly, the phrase "credible minimum" has become an oxymoron in the last decade because of the scale of India's nuclear ambition, exemplified by investments in a triad, expansion of warhead and delivery system numbers, and investments in the infrastructure invisibles that make a nuclear force operable.[101] However, this development is endogenous, driven substantially by changes in the methodology of nuclear force planning. Until the mid-2000s, the Indian government's approach to damage estimates, the statistical basis for nuclear force planning, was very likely based on projections of fissile material availability and crude estimates of the reliability of weapon systems. Air Marshal Bhavnani, who oversaw the process during 2004–6, alluded to this reality when he complained that

> one of these grey areas in India has always been that civilian control has been so strong over security matters on matters related to strategic security, etc. The senior military people do not fit into their scheme of things…when calculating, when strategizing, when coming out with solutions for making nuclear strategy. So in that aspect, when a person has less knowledge about nuclear issues, he then feels that perhaps ten or fifteen nuclear weapons are good enough. We do not think so.[102]

The greater availability of fissile material in the aftermath of the 2005 Indo-U.S. nuclear rapprochement and the deeper institutionalization of the SFC appear to have changed that reality. Senior SFC commanders such as Bhavnani's successor, Rear Admiral Shankar, insist that "Everything is numbers based…on operations research-based probabilistic analysis. The former is necessary to arrive at facts…in contrast to the intuitive gut-instinct analysis of the nuclear scientists, politicians, and their civilian advisors in the past."[103] In other words, a larger and more diverse arsenal is not some pernicious effect of an arms race; rather, it more likely stems from the application of formal methods to the determination of nuclear force size.

India's principal effort—in both the past decade and the current one—has been to develop land-based intermediate-range ballistic missiles in order to close the strategic gap with China. Pakistan is no longer a serious driver of India's nuclear hardware development. Given the huge lead that China enjoys over India, the land-based long-range missiles that India proposes to deploy by the end of this decade will only create nominal parity between the two sides. India will not possess a secure sea-based retaliatory capability against China until well into the next decade.

---

[101] Karnad, *India's Nuclear Policy*, 63–106.

[102] Author's interview with Bhavnani, April 2009.

[103] Author's interview with Shankar, August 2010.

At the same time, the sea leg of India's triad will no doubt exacerbate Pakistani anxieties and spur further modernization efforts. However, even prior to this development, Pakistan's arsenal was already growing more rapidly than India's, being shaped by perceived threats from the United States in the last decade as much as from India.[104] By contrast, Indian leaders have resisted pressures from their military to respond in kind to Pakistan's development of tactical nuclear weapons.[105] On the other hand, if past policy behavior is any guide, Beijing may prefer to respond to India's attempts at closing the strategic gap with China by arming Pakistan rather than by addressing the Indian buildup directly.

The DRDO's recent announcement that the Agni-VI ballistic missile will deploy three independently targetable warheads has also aroused anxieties that MIRV technology will undermine strategic stability.[106] The evidence suggests, however, that a MIRV capability is India's solution to the failed 1998 tests of thermonuclear and boosted-fission weapon designs. With only simple fission designs that have sharp limits on explosive yield, increased throw-weight of missiles is India's attempt at achieving better damage-estimate ratios.[107] MIRV technology, however, is destabilizing because it offers the theoretical possibility of a successful first-strike against an adversary. This technology also encourages preemptive strikes on the part of adversaries during a crisis because of its inherent capacity for successful preemption.[108] Although a small Indian ballistic missile force with MIRV technology is unlikely to destabilize the India-China dyad, given the diverse and distributed nature of the latter's nuclear forces, offense dominance in the India-Pakistan dyad remains a theoretical possibility. Much would depend, however, on how India parlays MIRV technology into a future ballistic missile force. The political context could also significantly allay or exacerbate Pakistan's apprehensions.

Alongside MIRV, a successful ballistic missile defense has the potential to undermine strategic stability in the region. India has evinced interest in missile defense since 1999. In the last decade, DRDO has developed a two-layered anti–ballistic missile defense: the exo-atmospheric Prithvi air defense and the

---

[104] Hans M. Kristensen and Robert S. Norris, "Pakistan's Nuclear Forces, 2011," *Bulletin of the Atomic Scientists* 67, no. 4 (2011): 91–99.

[105] Interview with D.B. Shekatkar, "'Yes, Pakistan Has Tactical Nukes,'" *Outlook* (India), June 10, 2002, http://www.outlookindia.com/article.aspx?215977; Nitin A. Gokhale and Murali Krishnan, "Small is Scary," *Outlook* (India), June 10, 2002, http://www.outlookindia.com/article.aspx?215975; and "In Conversation with Defense Minister Pranab Mukherjee," *Force*, September 2004, 33.

[106] Shukla, "Advanced Agni-6 Missile."

[107] Koithara, *Managing India's Nuclear Forces*, 129–31.

[108] Vipin Narang and Christopher Clary, "Capability Without Strategy," *Indian Express*, May 22, 2012, http://www.indianexpress.com/news/capability-without-strategy/952086.

endo-atmospheric advanced air-defense missile.[109] Phase one of the program is aimed at intercepting short- and medium-range ballistic missiles. Phase two, which has not yet entered the development stage, aims at intercepting missiles in the intermediate range.[110] After a decade of development, the DRDO has claimed a 99% successful interception rate in phase one of the program and pronounced the BMD system mature and ready for partial deployment.[111] Such claims, if accepted at face value, are grounds for enormous concern. When viewed in conjunction with India's emerging triad and MIRV capability, a missile defense system with an interception capability that is 99% successful could offer the theoretical possibility of destroying an enemy's nuclear forces in a first strike. The reality, however, is more prosaic. India's missile defense system, whatever its long-term promise, is far from operational. Thus far, the DRDO has conducted only seven tests, six of which were successful. All seven tests were conducted under highly controlled conditions, with the launch sites for the hostile and interceptor missiles separated by merely 70 km. Further, the DRDO tested the interceptor missiles against India's Prithvi short-range liquid-fuel ballistic missiles. The latter have a slower rate of ascent during the boost phase compared with the liquid- and solid-fuel rocket systems in Pakistan's and China's inventories. Above all, India's armed services have not verified the DRDO's claims independently.[112] For all these reasons, the perceived threat to strategic stability in the Asia-Pacific region from India's BMD system is more hypothetical than real.

Implications for the United States

After China's and Israel's nuclear activities in the 1960s, India's program is the most ambitious attempt to build an air-, land-, and sea-based nuclear force. The nuclear rapprochement with the United States has substantially aided India's efforts. It has opened the door for greater access to fissile material

---

[109] "DRDO Ballistic Missile Defense System, India."

[110] Rajat Pandit, "India Tests Missile Shield, DRDO Says It Will Be Operational by 2014," *Times of India*, November 24, 2012, http://articles.timesofindia.indiatimes.com/2012-11-24/india/35317919_1_terminal-high-altitude-area-defence-bmd-system-aegis-bmd-3.

[111] Hemant Kumar Rout, "More Teeth to Defence System," IBN Live, February 14, 2012, http://ibnlive.in.com/news/more-teeth-to-defence-system/230239-60-117.html; and "India's Ballistic Missile Shield Ready for Deployment, Says Top Scientist," *Global Times*, May 6, 2012, http://www.globaltimes.cn/NEWS/tabid/99/ID/707977/Indias-ballistic-missile-shield-ready-for-deployment-says-top-scientist.aspx.

[112] Pravin Sawhney, "India's Ballistic Missile Defence Capability Is Grossly Exaggerated," DNA, April 4, 2011, http://www.dnaindia.com/analysis/1527966/analysis-indias-ballistic-missile-defence-capability-is-grossly-exaggerated; and Manoj Joshi, "Government Baffled over DRDO Chief's Claim on Missile Shield," *India Today*, July 18, 2012, http://indiatoday.intoday.in/story/government-baffled-over-drdo-chief-claim-on-missile-shield/1/208850.html.

and dual-use technologies, while making possible India's purchase of sensitive nuclear arsenal–related technologies from other advanced industrial states, which Washington had opposed in the past. The United States has thus become a party to India's emergence as a nuclear weapons power.

The nuclear exception the United States made for India by changing its domestic laws has created a precedent for accommodating other nuclear powers in the future. To be sure, India is a democracy with which the United States shares common values. Further, as a non-signatory to both the Nuclear Non-Proliferation Treaty and the CTBT, India violated no international law by conducting nuclear tests and claiming nuclear power status. Yet the Bush administration's exception for India has opened the door, however slightly, to the institutional means the United States might use to deal with a potential nuclear breakout in Asia, especially one that concerned an ally such as Japan or South Korea. Or in happier political times, it sets a precedent for how the United States might strike a nuclear *modus vivendi* with Pakistan or a nuclear Iran.

The implications of India's emergence as a serious nuclear weapons power are twofold. In the medium term, the maturing Indian triad will end the asymmetry in the existing balance of power in Asia. The combination of economic modernization, conventional force modernization, and nuclear hardware will enable India to narrow the material gap with China, paving the way for a duopoly of power. Undoubtedly, structural power needs ideas and institutions in order to create agency. Nonetheless, nuclear forces will provide India with the added confidence to stand up to potentially threatening or bullying Chinese behavior in the future, as well as the self-reassurance to participate in regional partnerships and quasi-alliances. As the United States turns its attention to managing the next great-power competition of the 21st century, the narrowing of the material gap between the two Asian giants will be a positive entry in the U.S. power ledger.

In the short term, however, the nuclear competition in the Asia-Pacific is prone to deterrence and crisis instability. Deterrence instability stems from current material gaps in India's nuclear hardware, especially with respect to China. The United States has the choice of continuing its present course of approaching India's nuclear drive with relative passivity, or Washington can address the gaps more aggressively through the kind of "negative guidance" it extended to France in the last century. That said, U.S. rivalry with China does not approach the level of Soviet-U.S. competition during the Cold War. Indian distrust of the United States is also high because of a quarter century of technology denials and nonproliferation pressures. However, sooner rather than later the United States might need to consider providing India with nuclear assistance of the variety that China extends to Pakistan.

The gaps in India's institutional and organizational capacities also have the potential to create crisis instability in the region. But this is an issue of greater concern in India-Pakistan relations than in the India-China dyad. In the latter, there is merely the potential threat of a first-class crisis with nuclear overtones. In the former, that concern is present and overwhelmingly located in a low-intensity war that has been the source of persistent tension in South Asia for over six decades. It has ignited several wars between India and Pakistan and generated serious crises that almost led to wars. In the past, the United States has managed crises in South Asia by urging restraint and intervening actively to defuse them. As long as Pakistan retains its strategy of low-intensity warfare and of delegating foreign policy objectives to nonstate proxies, the threat of recurring crises in South Asia remains, as does the demand for U.S. intervention and crisis management.

With India, Pakistan, China, and North Korea in the midst of developing and modernizing their nuclear forces, there is no doubt that Asia is now the epicenter of a second nuclear age. The arms buildup, however, is not analogous to the one that characterized the Cold War for several reasons. For one, the prevailing moratorium on nuclear testing (North Korea notwithstanding) puts limits on the development of new nuclear warhead designs. Further, the hardware capabilities that India is currently developing constitute an effort to fill gaps between its staked claims to nuclear power status and the actual means of achieving that status. Determinations of arsenal size now flow from operations research and damage estimate parameters, as do decisions on India's MIRV program. However, professional planning in India, especially in the nuclear realm, remains closely subject to political controls. There is no evidence yet of runaway weapon numbers determined by scientific and military agencies, which should be of some reassurance to the United States.

The impact of India's nuclear buildup on Chinese force planning is still unclear. China retains the advantage of significant nuclear asymmetries vis-à-vis India. In the past, Beijing has responded to pressure from India by boxing it in South Asia through a buildup of countervailing Pakistani capabilities. The strategy proved successful as long as the United States prevented India from purchasing sensitive nuclear and dual-use technologies from international markets, but this condition no longer prevails. In the future, it is possible that China may respond to India's nuclear buildup directly. A decision by China to expand its nuclear force would have implications for the robustness of Washington's extended-deterrence guarantees to allies in the Asia-Pacific and would complicate further reductions in the U.S. nuclear arsenal below one thousand warheads.

Unlike China, Pakistan remains extremely sensitive to Indian nuclear force planning and will likely expand and diversify its arsenal, which is already the fastest growing in the world, as India's triad matures. The implications of a Pakistani buildup for the United States go beyond deterrence and crisis stability in South Asia. They concern the safety and security of Pakistan's nuclear arsenal; the likelihood of theft, sabotage, or terrorism; and the possibility that some future Pakistani government might seek to sell nuclear weapons to clients in the Middle East, following Iran's decision to proliferate. The loss of sensitive personnel, scientific talent, and nuclear material in the event of a fundamentalist revolution in Pakistan or the state's partial collapse also increases the threat of a terrorist event in the United States or Europe involving a nuclear weapon or a "dirty bomb." Thus, the price of the nuclear buildup in South Asia will be continued U.S. vigilance over the region's safety and security.

Conclusion

In the last decade, India's focus has shifted decisively from the symbolic aspects of nuclear weaponry to developing operational capabilities. No doubt, the nuclear arsenal undergirds India's status as a great power. However, two Indian national security advisors, former and current, have explicitly identified security concerns as the principal drivers behind nuclear force improvements.[113] After the 1998 tests and the Indian government's justifications for them, these are the strongest statements concerning the country's nuclear motivations. In this decade and the next, it is highly likely that India's efforts will remain focused on force improvements, both hardware and software. Hardware improvements will come at the level of delivery systems and the support infrastructure. Software improvements will continue at the level of institutional and organizational coordination between nuclear command authorities and executive agencies.

Although the country's operational capabilities are improving substantially, the focus of those capabilities is still regional. In theory, India could acquire an omnidirectional strike capability sometime in the next decade, especially given its historical pattern of developing "technology demonstrators." But it remains uncertain whether a future government would actualize that capability into an operational force. Much would depend

---

[113] "India's Nuclear Weapons a Deterrent against Global Power Threats: Shiv Shankar Menon," *International Business Times*, August 22, 2012, http://www.ibtimes.co.in/articles/376120/20120822/ nuclear-weapons-national-security-shiv-shnkar-menon.htm; and "Nuclear Weaponisation Vital for Country's Security: Narayanan," *Indian Express*, July 31, 2012, http://m.indianexpress.com/ news/nuclear-weaponisation-vital-for-country-s-security-narayanan/981845.

on the state of the international system and the makeup of India's internal regime. A relatively secure and open international system with reformist institutions capable of accommodating rising powers would provide fewer incentives for India to behave aggressively. Likewise, an internal political regime committed to pluralism, economic growth, and open markets would have fewer incentives to invest in capabilities that provide no tangible benefits for India's security.

From New Delhi's perspective, the current expansion and diversification of India's nuclear force emanates from endogenous demands of operational planning and not any specific advances in Pakistani and Chinese force developments. The Indian military's institutionalization of nuclear decision-making has changed the methodology for nuclear force planning from one based on heuristics to one based on statistical damage estimate probabilities. India's stable of fission warheads is also the likely reason behind its pursuit of MIRV technology. In the absence of further testing to reliably validate boosting or develop a true thermonuclear capability, the onus for hardware improvements is centered on developing the ballistic missile force's throw-weight capacity.

The growth of operational nuclear forces in both India and Pakistan has increased the risk of a conventional war turning nuclear. This risk is tempered, however, by the Indian political leadership's pattern of restraint during crises. Further, terrain and robust Pakistani conventional capabilities limit the Indian military's capacity to execute its Cold Start strategy. Finally, Indian military leaders believe that external predictions about Pakistan's propensity for nuclear use are based on the brute reality of the country's tactical nuclear weapon arsenal rather than on a realistic assessment of the Pakistani military's ability to employ nuclear forces on the conventional battlefield. In the case of China, Indian military leaders believe the threat of a conventional war turning nuclear is low at present.

By making a nuclear exception for India, the United States has created an institutional precedent for accommodating other nuclear weapons powers in the future. Likewise, by ending its policy of denying India nuclear and dual-use technologies, the United States has become an indirect party to the country's emergence as a nuclear weapons power. This is a positive development for the balance of power in Asia and the management of China's rise. However, its downside is the increased risk of deterrence and crisis instability as well as nuclear terrorism.

EXECUTIVE SUMMARY

This chapter reviews developments in Pakistan's nuclear arsenal since 1998 and projects likely developments through 2020.

MAIN ARGUMENT:
Pakistan remains one of the most likely sources of nuclear risk globally—through theft of Pakistani nuclear material, unauthorized use of weapons during conflict, or intentional use in war. This stems from the large number of dangerous groups based in Pakistan, regional instability in its neighborhood, and the country's increasing reliance on nuclear weapons rather than conventional military force for deterrence. The future of Pakistan's nuclear weapons program is the development of a larger arsenal with more types of delivery vehicles and an expanding role for nuclear arms in warfighting. While not yet committed to a battlefield role for nuclear weapons, Pakistan is developing the constituent components necessary for such missions, giving it a battlefield capability that the country's adversaries must account for in the event of crisis or conflict. In other words, even without fully developing a battlefield nuclear force, Pakistan has taken the steps necessary to create a battlefield "force in being" that can affect the decisions of other states, even at this nascent stage.

POLICY IMPLICATIONS:
- The U.S. has little leverage to directly alter Pakistan's increasing reliance on nuclear weapons or to shape the country's nuclear choices.

- The two factors that are most likely to arrest the growth of the Pakistani nuclear arsenal are resource constraints and improved relations between India and Pakistan.

- Pakistani civilian leaders are more likely to force a reassessment of nuclear decisions than their military counterparts. As a consequence, U.S. policy initiatives to bolster civilian leaders may ultimately facilitate greater moderation in the expansion of the Pakistani arsenal.

The Future of Pakistan's Nuclear Weapons Program

Christopher Clary

Fifteen years ago, in May 1998, Pakistani officials announced that they had tested six nuclear devices, completing a round of reciprocal nuclear tests that had begun two weeks earlier when Indian representatives announced five nuclear tests. After having bombs in the basement for so long, the period of overt weaponization in South Asia began. Before the eventful month of May 1998, both states had unproven designs; Pakistan had conducted no overt nuclear tests, and India's 1974 "peaceful nuclear explosion" device was viewed as unreliable and so massive as to be undeliverable.[1] Both states had uneven delivery dyads in 1998, relying primarily on manned aircraft and secondarily on ballistic missiles. These missiles were mostly in development and had undergone only a handful of flight tests. Both India and Pakistan likely had very small arsenals at the time of the tests, with warheads perhaps numbering in the single digits.[2]

In the immediate aftermath of the May tests, both governments assured the world that they would avoid the mistakes of the established nuclear powers. Pakistan's foreign secretary Shamshad Ahmad explained to the international

Christopher Clary is a PhD candidate in the Department of Political Science at the Massachusetts Institute of Technology and a Stanton Nuclear Security Predoctoral Fellow at the RAND Corporation. He can be reached at <clary@mit.edu>.

[1] On India's 1974 device, see Ashley J. Tellis, *India's Emerging Nuclear Posture: Between Recessed Deterrent and Ready Arsenal* (Santa Monica: RAND Corporation, 2001), 196–98.

[2] Robert S. Norris and William M. Arkin record two and three warheads in their historical estimate of the respective Indian and Pakistani arsenals in 1998. Although this estimate seems too small, it likely is of the correct order of magnitude. See Robert S. Norris and William M. Arkin, "Global Nuclear Weapons Inventories, 1945–2010," *Bulletin of the Atomic Scientists* 66, no. 4 (2010): 82.

community: "It is not our purpose to enter into an arms race. The history of the Cold War showed that such disastrous races are counterproductive and definitely not sustainable."[3] The following year, Ahmad reaffirmed this stance to an Islamabad think tank: "Let me state clearly and unequivocally that Pakistan can and will find ways and means to maintain credible nuclear deterrence against India without the need to match it—bomb for bomb, missile for missile."[4]

Despite those statements of restraint, the fifteen years since 1998 have witnessed abundant developments by both South Asian nuclear powers. Although still constrained by limited resources, Indian and Pakistani policymakers appear to have determined that the requirements for credible minimum deterrence are considerably more expansive than they anticipated in the initial months after the 1998 nuclear tests. Pakistan has emphasized nuclear weapons development in the last fifteen years to compensate for its conventional-force disparity with India. As a result, its program has developed at a pace equal to if not more impressive than India's, despite greater fiscal limitations.

Barring a severe economic crisis, this strategy is likely to continue. Pakistan's security managers are pursuing a larger nuclear weapons arsenal, featuring diverse delivery vehicles, that the Pakistan military can rely on to deter rivals in crisis and war. The most significant development in recent years has been the creation of a battlefield nuclear "force in being" that provides Pakistan the option of battlefield use of nuclear weapons, even if Pakistani decision-makers have not fully incorporated such thinking into their doctrine. The net result of this and other developments has been more weapons at heightened levels of readiness, posing a greater nuclear threat in peacetime, crisis, and war. Pakistani officials assess that these risks are tractable—despite Pakistan's difficult internal threat environment—given concerted and professional efforts at nuclear stewardship by the country's military. Observers outside Pakistan, however, may be less comfortable with the negative externalities concomitant with relying on a nuclear threat to deter foes.

This chapter will examine Pakistan's ongoing and foreseeable nuclear developments, first reviewing the status of Pakistan's fissile-material production. Next, it turns to assess whether these trends in fissile-material production are consistent with the continuing primacy of the mission to deter India for Pakistan's strategic forces, or whether such numbers imply

---

[3] Kenneth J. Cooper and John Ward Anderson, "A Misplaced Faith in Nuclear Deterrence," *Washington Post*, May 31, 1998.

[4] Shamshad Ahmed, "India's Nuclear Doctrine: Implications for Regional and Global Peace and Security" (statement presented at the Institute of Strategic Studies, Islamabad, September 7, 1999).

expanding missions. While admitting that other threats, most notably concerns about the United States, may increasingly factor into Islamabad's nuclear force strategy, the chapter concludes that deterring India remains the paramount goal. It then surveys the growing number and types of Pakistan's delivery vehicles, again finding evidence of an India-centric force. The chapter finally assesses the collective impact of these trends on regional stability and draws policy implications for the United States.

The Production of Fissile Material and Pakistan's Growing Nuclear Arsenal

Historically, resource constraints, especially on fissile-material production, severely limited Pakistan's options for force structure and employment. Now, however, Pakistan is widely assessed to have the world's "fastest growing" stockpile of fissile material.[5] Public estimates of the size of that stockpile should be taken as notional and require considerable guesswork based on scant data. Even so, these estimates suggest that Pakistani decision-makers are striving for a nuclear arsenal in the range of two hundred to three hundred warheads, giving Pakistan nuclear capabilities roughly of the same magnitude as the United Kingdom, France, and China.[6] Such a force would provide the country with options that it could not previously consider.

Pakistan's fissile-material stockpile includes both highly enriched uranium (HEU) and plutonium.[7] The program is shifting from a traditional emphasis on HEU toward a greater reliance on plutonium, which will allow Pakistan to produce a greater number of lighter warheads. The Khushab complex contains three plutonium-production reactors, with a fourth reactor under construction. The Khushab-I reactor has been operational since 1998, while the Khushab-II and Khushab-III sites may have come online in 2009

---

[5] Hans M. Kristensen and Robert S. Norris, "Pakistan's Nuclear Forces, 2011," *Bulletin of the Atomic Scientists* 67, no. 4 (2011): 91; Andrew Bast, "Pakistan's Nuclear Surge," *Newsweek*, May 15, 2011, http://www.thedailybeast.com/newsweek/2011/05/15/fourth-nuclear-reactor-at-pakistan-s-khushab-site.html; and David E. Sanger and Eric Schmitt, "Pakistani Nuclear Arms Pose Challenge to U.S. Policy," *New York Times*, January 31, 2011, http://www.nytimes.com/2011/02/01/world/asia/01policy.html.

[6] Norris and Arkin report that the United Kingdom has 225 warheads today, down from a peak of 492 in the 1970s; China has 240 warheads, which is its peak; and France has 300 warheads, down from a peak of 540 in the early 1990s. See Norris and Arkin, "Global Nuclear Weapons Inventories."

[7] The following section draws extensively on Zia Mian, A.H. Nayyar, and R. Rajaraman, "Exploring Uranium Resource Constraints on Fissile Material Production in Pakistan," *Science and Global Security* 17, no. 2–3 (2009): 77–108.

and 2010, respectively.[8] Satellite imagery from April 2012 suggests that the latter two facilities are at least externally complete and that Pakistan is making substantial progress on the construction of a fourth reactor at Khushab, though its initial operational date is likely still several years away. While in the past there has been some disagreement over the size of the reactors, the nongovernmental consensus appears to be that the three extant reactors are 50–megawatt thermal (MWt) heavy-water reactors.[9] Each reactor would likely consume 13 tons of natural uranium per year, producing approximately 11.5 kilograms (kg) of weapons-grade plutonium.[10]

Today, Pakistan has a stockpile of perhaps 150 kg of plutonium, to which the three existing Khushab reactors could collectively add approximately 35 kg per year. If Khushab-IV were to become operational in 2016, this would increase the annual rate of the complex's plutonium production to approximately 46 kg. By 2020, the upper limit for Pakistan's stockpile of weapons-grade plutonium might be as high as 480 kg.

Along with the plutonium route, Pakistan employs centrifuge cascades to enrich uranium, primarily at the Khan Research Laboratories facility at Kahuta, although enrichment facilities at Chaklala, Gadwal, Golra, and Sihala are also referenced in U.S. government documents and nongovernmental analyses.[11] These sources assess that Pakistan had produced approximately

---

[8] These are assumptions made in Mian, Nayyar, and Rajaraman, "Exploring Uranium Resource Constraints," 84. See also Paul Brannan, "Steam Emitted from Second Khushab Reactor Cooling Towers; Pakistan May Be Operating Second Reactor," Institute for Science and International Security (ISIS), ISIS Imagery Brief, March 24, 2010, http://isis-online.org/uploads/isis-reports/documents/Second_Kushab_Rector_24Mar2010.pdf; and David Albright and Robert Avagyan, "Construction Proceeding Rapidly on the Fourth Heavy Water Reactor at the Khushab Nuclear Site," ISIS, ISIS Imagery Brief, May 21, 2012.

[9] Mian, Nayyar, and Rajaraman, "Exploring Uranium Resource Constraints"; Albright and Avagyan, "Construction Proceeding Rapidly"; and Thomas B. Cochran, "What Is the Size of Khushab II?" Natural Resources Defense Council, September 8, 2006, http://docs.nrdc.org/nuclear/nuc_06090801A.pdf.

[10] Mian, Nayyar, and Rajaraman, "Exploring Uranium Resource Constraints." Tamara Patton uses open-source imagery analysis to conclude that the Khushab-II and Khushab-III sites have the capacity to produce 15 and 19 kg of weapons-grade plutonium annually. See Tamara Patton, "Combining Satellite Imagery and 3D Drawing Tools for Nonproliferation Analysis: A Case Study of Pakistan's Khushab Plutonium Production Reactors," Science and Global Security 20, no. 2–3 (2012): 137. While Patton's evidence is impressive, this chapter uses the more conservative and more commonly used estimates from Mian et al.

[11] U.S. Department of Commerce, "India and Pakistan Sanctions and Other Measures," Federal Register, November 19, 1998, 64322–42, http://www.bis.doc.gov/pdf/india-pakistanentities-nov98.pdf; Zia Mian, "The Future of Military Fissile Material Production Facilities in South Asia Under an FMCT" (presentation at the FMCT Scientific Experts Meeting on "Technical Issues Related to a Fissile Material Cut-off Treaty," Geneva, May 30, 2012), http://fissilematerials.org/library/IPFM-Geneva-30-May-2012.pdf; and Mark Fitzpatrick, Nuclear Black Markets: Pakistan, A.Q. Khan, and the Rise of Proliferation Networks: A Net Assessment (London: International Institute for Strategic Studies, 2007), 18–19.

3,000 kg of HEU by 2012.[12] Going forward, estimating Pakistan's uranium-enrichment capacity requires many assumptions about the efficiency of the country's centrifuges and the uranium feedstock available for enrichment. Zia Mian, A.H. Nayyar, and R. Rajaraman conclude that by 2020 Pakistan could enrich as much as 6,000 kg of HEU.[13]

By varying assumptions about reactor size, reprocessing capacity, uranium-enrichment capacity, or raw uranium ore available, even the best nongovernmental analyses produce a wide range of estimates for Pakistan's total fissile-material production today and in the future. Estimates of how many weapons Pakistan will have likewise vary because of uncertainty regarding the quantity of plutonium or HEU used in weapon designs. Analysts typically assume that 4–6 kg of plutonium or 12–16 kg of HEU are required for a nuclear weapon, which means that Pakistan could have possessed between 130 and 290 weapons equivalent of fissile material in 2012. This range widens substantially over time given uncertainty in annual production estimates. By 2020, Pakistan could have between 210 and 620 weapons equivalent of fissile material, depending on the assumptions used in the analysis (see **Figure 1**).

It is possible that the typical estimates of fissile material required for each device are too conservative. As Thomas Cochran and Christopher Paine argued several years ago, if states are seeking weapons with smaller yields of approximately 1–5 kilotons (kt), they could use less fissile material even with simple weapons designs. Smaller-yield warheads might be of greater interest to Pakistan if it seeks to devote a portion of its arsenal to devices for battlefield nuclear missions. For 1-kt devices, Cochran and Paine argue that even a state with low technical capability could use as little as 3 kg of plutonium or 8 kg of HEU—in other words, 66%–75% of the material typically assumed for devices that are 10–20 kt. By 1951, the United States was testing designs employing even less fissile material that achieved yields of 1 kt.[14] Besides using less material in smaller-yield warheads, states can use material more efficiently through composite warheads, where a 2–3 kg plutonium core is surrounded by an HEU shell. While composite warheads require much less plutonium, the fact that both a plutonium core and an HEU shell are needed means that the overall gains of a composite-core design are modest. If Pakistan's weapons engineers had a composite warhead design with which they were comfortable,

---

[12] "Countries: Pakistan," International Panel on Fissile Materials, February 3, 2013, http://fissilematerials.org/countries/pakistan.html; Mian, "The Future of Military Fissile Material;" and author's personal communication with Zia Mian, April 25, 2013.

[13] Mian, Nayyar, and Rajaraman, "Exploring Uranium Resource Constraints."

[14] Thomas B. Cochran and Christopher E. Paine, "The Amount of Plutonium and Highly-Enriched Uranium Needed for Pure Fission Nuclear Weapons," Natural Resources Defense Council, April 13, 1995, http://www.nrdc.org/nuclear/fissionw/fissionweapons.pdf.

FIGURE 1   Pakistan's estimated fissile material

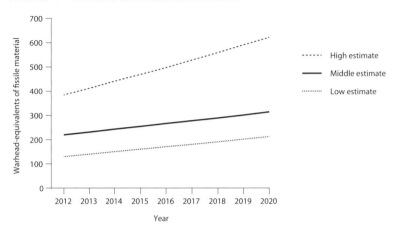

SOURCE: Zia Mian, A.H. Nayyar, and R. Rajaraman, "Exploring Uranium Resource Constraints on Fissile Material Production in Pakistan," *Science and Global Security* 17, no. 2–3 (2009): 77–108; and "Countries: Pakistan," International Panel on Fissile Materials, February 3, 2013, http://fissilematerials.org/countries/pakistan.html; and author's calculations.

NOTE: Figure 1 provides high, middle, and low estimates. High estimates assume more fissile-material production and smaller warhead sizes. Low estimates assume less fissile-material production and larger warheads. Because not all fissile material is necessarily fabricated into a finished warhead, the arsenal is likely smaller than the warhead "equivalents" possible.

they could produce perhaps 11% more warheads from the same quantity of plutonium and HEU, if the efficiency gains achieved by early U.S. warhead designs are indicative.[15]

Such calculations should not be taken as an argument that Pakistan is likely to have 600 or more warheads by 2020. This figure almost certainly constitutes an upper bound. When government estimates leak into the public sphere, they occasionally suggest that nongovernmental calculations of the potential size of the Pakistani arsenal are too high. An anonymous government official estimated in a 2011 article that the arsenal comprised 90–110 weapons and questioned some nongovernmental assessments higher than that figure.[16] Even so, others with extensive work in government seem to suggest quantities of fissile material consistent with the calculations presented here. Bruce Riedel, who was previously involved with U.S. intelligence and policy on South Asia, estimates the size of the Pakistani arsenal at over

---

[15] Cochran, "What Is the Size of Khushab II?"; and Richard Rhodes, *Dark Sun: The Making of the Hydrogen Bomb* (New York: Simon & Schuster, 1995), 227.

[16] Sanger and Schmitt, "Pakistani Nuclear Arms."

200 weapons.[17] What the entirety of the evidence suggests is that it is quite plausible for Pakistan to possess a force of approximately 200–300 weapons by 2020, which would enable the country to pursue different nuclear postures from what it could adopt with a force of only tens of warheads.

The discussion of possible nuclear missions that follows assesses the process whereby Pakistani force planners determine how many warheads are sufficient for deterrence. The rapid expansion of Pakistan's nuclear infrastructure, combined with its continued diplomatic objections to a Fissile Material Cutoff Treaty (FMCT), suggests that an adequate number will not be reached in the near or medium term.

The Changing Missions for the Arsenal

Given the growing size of Pakistan's nuclear force, what can be inferred about the current and future mission for the Pakistani arsenal? The key analytic question is whether Pakistan's considerable efforts at nuclear force modernization make sense in the context of an Indian adversary that may well have fewer nuclear weapons.[18] If the nuclear arsenal remains India-specific, why outrace rather than match your foes' efforts?

The analysis indicates that while other concerns may modestly contribute to force-sizing decisions, Islamabad is still overwhelmingly focused on deterring India. The fast pace of development is motivated by concerns about Indian counterforce and ballistic missile capabilities, potential battlefield roles for Pakistani nuclear weapons, and long-term calculations about parity with India. There are also hints that Pakistan's worsening relations with the United States may also be a factor in its calculations of deterrence sufficiency.

India nonetheless remains the *raison d'être* for the Pakistani nuclear program. Its primacy is evident in Pakistan's delivery-vehicle developments, which have pointedly eschewed efforts to create missiles that could reach targets beyond eastern India. Officials, politicians, and pundits regularly reaffirm this focus in public and private statements. Feroz Khan, in his quasi-official history of India's nuclear program, concludes that "the Pakistanis see no role for nuclear weapons other than to deter India from waging a

---

[17] Bruce Riedel, "The United States, India, and Pakistan: To the Brink and Back" (presentation at the Brookings Institution, Washington, D.C., February 26, 2013), http://www.brookings.edu/~/media/events/2013/2/26%20india%20pakistan/20130226_india_pakistan_armageddon_transcript.pdf.

[18] Hans M. Kristensen and Robert S. Norris estimated in 2012 that India had 80–100 weapons and fissile material for 100–130 warheads. This compares to their 2011 estimate of Pakistan's 90–110 weapons and fissile material for 160–240 warheads. See, for example, Hans M. Kristensen and Robert S. Norris, "Indian Nuclear Forces, 2012," *Bulletin of the Atomic Scientists* 68, no. 4 (2012): 96–101; and Kristensen and Norris, "Pakistan's Nuclear Forces, 2011," 91–99.

conventional war. This was the original purpose of the program and it stands to this day."[19] Pakistan's nuclear program is viewed domestically as having largely fulfilled that mission. Depending on the specific interlocutor, the successful outcomes of the 1986–87 Brasstacks crisis, the 1990 compound crisis, the 2001–2 military standoff, and the 2008 Mumbai crisis are attributable to the nuclear program. While the 1999 Kargil War ended unfavorably for Pakistan, India's reluctance to escalate that conflict is attributable to deterrence, Pakistani analysts argue.

But why does Pakistan need so many warheads? Its nuclear force should be more than capable of carrying out countervalue attacks to deter threats to the country's survival. The problem, of course, is that it is not only trying to deter Indian nuclear attacks against Pakistan or even existential conventional threats. When faced with existential dangers, the Pakistani force poses a credible threat to Indian cities. But India has devised strategies for limited war in an effort to avoid threats to Pakistan's major population centers or the viability of its armed forces. By permitting such Indian "salami tactics"—that is, limited conventional military attacks that do not cross Pakistan's stated red lines for nuclear use—Islamabad could find its deterrent to be much less valuable than it had hoped.[20]

One goal of a larger nuclear force, with more moving parts, is to make it easier to generate risk. More concretely, when a serious crisis unfolds, warheads can be mated, moved out of peacetime locations, and perhaps moved toward the battlefield. The latter action increases danger in two ways: it places those missiles in a use-them-or-lose-them situation and elevates the risk of accidents. Use-or-lose situations are doubly dangerous if missile commanders have the ability to launch without explicit authorization. Yet even if Pakistani command-and-control arrangements are centralized, those central authorities would be placed in a situation where some portion of their forward-deployed force might be destroyed by combat. Precisely because such moves generate risk, they also signal to other states the seriousness of the crisis and the resolve of Pakistani decision-makers. It is worth stressing that while most of this risk falls on India, outside powers—notably the United States—are sensitive to nuclear dangers; hence, such risk generation is in part designed to draw in third-party intervention.[21]

---

[19] Feroz Hassan Khan, *Eating Grass: The Making of the Pakistani Bomb* (Stanford: Stanford University Press, 2012), 380.

[20] For an early exposition on "salami tactics," see Thomas C. Schelling, *Arms and Influence* (New Haven: Yale University Press, 1966), 66, 77.

[21] See the related discussion in Vipin Narang, *Nuclear Strategy in the Modern Era: Regional Powers and International Conflict* (Princeton: Princeton University Press, forthcoming), especially chap. 3 and 10.

Larger forces also allow for the prospect of iterated nuclear use, where Pakistan deploys some of its force in a battlefield role but reserves a substantial portion of the arsenal for countervalue strikes against India. While still horribly dangerous, this strategy is more credible with a large force than a small one. Indian decision-makers, seeing nuclear use on the battlefield, would be forced to decide if countervalue strikes against Pakistan were rational, knowing full well that such a response would open up their cities to retaliation. As suggested above, even if Pakistani planners do not anticipate ever using battlefield weapons, the arsenal as configured creates a battlefield force-in-being that might still stymie Indian freedom of action.

Pakistan's current pace is also more explicable over longer time horizons. Pakistani commentators point out that while India may not have manufactured many nuclear devices to date, in the long run it has the potential to dramatically outpace Pakistani production.[22] Many of these commentators argue that Indian fissile-material production has been frustrated by uranium shortages that previously forced a trade-off between energy- and plutonium-production nuclear power reactors, since reactors optimized for energy or weapons-grade plutonium output both require uranium. Admittedly, Indian decision-makers have historically favored energy production over plutonium production, but with the U.S.-India civil nuclear agreement making possible foreign imports for the civilian program, such difficult choices will no longer be necessary. More significantly, whatever technology India acquires for enrichment and reprocessing, as well as for its ambitious breeder-reactor program, will not forever remain compartmented to the civilian side of the program. Individuals and knowledge are porous. The net result, Pakistani observers argue, is a much greater capacity for India to produce fissile material.[23] Additionally, Pakistani force planners cannot entirely dismiss the possibility that India might one day use its sizable stockpile of perhaps 3,300–3,900 kg of reactor-grade plutonium, set aside ostensibly to fuel its future breeder-reactor program, to fabricate weapons.[24]

---

[22] For a similar argument by a U.S. scholar, see Michael Krepon, "Nuclear Race on the Subcontinent," *New York Times*, April 4, 2013, http://www.nytimes.com/2013/04/05/opinion/global/nuclear-race-on-the-subcontinent.html.

[23] See, for example, Maleeha Lodhi, "Pakistan's Nuclear Compulsions," *News International*, November 6, 2012, http://www.thenews.com.pk/Todays-News-9-141314-Pakistan%E2%80%99s-nuclear-compulsions; and Mansoor Ahmed, as quoted in Michael Krepon, "The Tortoise and the Hare: A Rebuttal," Arms Control Wonk, web log, April 23, 2013, http://krepon.armscontrolwonk.com/archive/3754/the-tortoise-and-the-hare-a-rebuttal.

[24] "Global Fissile Material Report 2010—Balancing the Books: Production and Stocks," International Panel on Fissile Materials, December 2010, 117, http://fissilematerials.org/library/gfmr10.pdf. For an explicit statement about Pakistani concern of civil-to-military diversion, see "The South Asian Nuclear Balance: An Interview with Pakistani Ambassador to the CD Zamir Akram," *Arms Control Today*, December 2011, http://www.armscontrol.org/act/2011_12/Interview_With_Pakistani_Ambassador_to_the_CD_Zamir_Akram.

The reason India's nuclear numbers matter to Pakistan is that the Pakistani military does not entirely discount the possibility of an adversary's first strike, despite India's "no first use" declaratory policy. In 2006, Lieutenant General Khalid Kidwai told a U.S. audience that Pakistan's force must be sufficient "to deter a counterstrike against strategic assets."[25] Peter Lavoy, an American academic turned government official who has spent considerable time with personnel from Pakistan's Strategic Plans Division (SPD), which oversees the respective strategic forces maintained by the army, navy, and air force, wrote in 2008 that Pakistan sought "a survivable strategic force capable of withstanding sabotage, conventional military attacks, and at least one enemy nuclear strike."[26]

In the U.S.-Soviet nuclear competition, parity concerns were driven by both fears of an adversary counterforce first strike and a desire to be able to launch a disarming first strike of one's own. In the South Asian context, there is no evidence that Pakistan seeks a disarming first strike against India's arsenal, but there is some evidence that Pakistan fears India could target its weapons. The extent of the fear, and the degree to which Pakistan believes its nuclear forces can survive a nuclear attack, would determine how many additional warheads it would need to account for the risk of a first strike. Pakistan's fears that India might target its nuclear assets with conventional forces are partially justified. Repeatedly in Track 1.5 and Track 2 forums, retired Indian military personnel attest that missile launchers in the battlefield would and should be targeted in the context of a full-scale conflict because such launchers could be performing a conventional mission. Moreover, because such launchers might also be carrying nuclear warheads, Indian military personnel are willing to take the risks that are concomitant with targeting them: namely, the slow degradation of Pakistan's nuclear force, the small chance of an accidental detonation, or the larger chance of the dispersal of radiological material.[27]

When these counterforce fears are combined with India's nascent capacity for ballistic missile defense, force requirements can grow quickly. Imagine if a Pakistani force planner were to believe it is necessary for deterrence purposes that 100 warheads reach Indian targets. Further imagine that this individual

---

[25] Robin Walker, "Pakistan's Evolution as a Nuclear Weapons State: Lt. Gen. Khalid Kidwai's CCC Address," Naval Postgraduate School, November 1, 2006, http://www.nps.edu/academics/centers/ccc/news/kidwaiNov06.html.

[26] Peter R. Lavoy, "Islamabad's Nuclear Posture: Its Premises and Implementation," in *Pakistan's Nuclear Future: Worries Beyond War*, ed. Henry D. Sokolski (Carlisle: U.S. Army War College, 2008), 131, 159.

[27] Launchers, if destroyed, might have a warhead mated on the missile, meaning the launcher, delivery vehicle, and missile would no longer be available for deterrent missions. Since Pakistan might rely on one launcher to deliver multiple missiles, the destruction of a launcher might neutralize weapons even if delivery vehicles or warheads survived a conventional attack.

were confident that 70% of the force would survive even determined Indian counterforce activity. He might further assess that Indian ballistic missile defenses could intercept 20% of the missiles launched at India. Such fears quickly inflate the notional force of 100 warheads to 180 warheads in order to reach the same number of targets despite Indian actions. If a Pakistani force planner had mild doubts about the reliability of his country's warheads and missiles (for the sake of calculation, assume 95% reliability for warheads and missiles), the "necessary" force could easily reach 200 warheads.[28]

In other words, it should be evident that Pakistan might feel compelled to build a sizable force, even if it were implementing concepts of finite deterrence that do not seek parity or counterforce strikes on India. That is, current estimates of Pakistani fissile-material production are consistent with an Indian-centric nuclear force and are not so large that it is necessary to introduce other missions to explain the arsenal's size. Even so, there are reasons to believe that the United States is a growing factor for Pakistani force-sizing decisions.

Pervez Hoodbhoy, a liberal Pakistani nuclear physicist, reports that his contacts within the Pakistan military are increasingly fearful that the United States might attempt to disarm Pakistan if it felt such a mission might succeed.[29] The U.S. raid on Abbottabad in 2011 was understandably worrisome to military leaders since they were apparently unable to detect or stop the intrusion.[30] The fears triggered by the raid are even more explicable given regular media reports of U.S. planning for operations to secure the Pakistani arsenal.[31] Graham Allison, a U.S. academic and former defense official, states that "the U.S. tried to prevent Pakistan from becoming a nuclear weapons state.... It is not delusional for Pakistan to fear that America is interested in de-nuking them. It is prudent paranoia."[32] Such fears might translate into Islamabad undertaking more active dispersal and deception operations to

---

[28] For a similar set of calculations, see Jamal Hussain, "Deterrence in a Nuclear Environment," *Defence Journal*, 2003, http://defencejournal.com/2003/mar/deterrence.htm.

[29] Pervez Hoodbhoy, "Introduction," in *Confronting the Bomb: Pakistani and Indian Scientists Speak Out*, ed. Pervez Hoodbhoy (New York: Oxford University Press, 2013), xxxvii–xxxviii.

[30] For a timeline of Pakistani information about the raid, see Peter L. Bergen, *Manhunt: The Ten-Year Search for Bin Laden from 9/11 to Abbottabad* (New York: Crown Publishers, 2012), 231–37.

[31] See, for example, Seymour M. Hersh, "Watching the Warheads," *New Yorker*, November 5, 2001, http://www.newyorker.com/archive/2001/11/05/011105fa_FACT; Rowan Scarborough, "U.S. Has Plan to Secure Pakistan Nukes if Country Falls to Taliban," Fox News, May 14, 2009, http://www.foxnews.com/politics/2009/05/14/plan-secure-pakistan-nukes-country-falls-taliban; and Seymour M. Hersh, "Defending the Arsenal," *New Yorker*, November 16, 2009, http://www.newyorker.com/reporting/2009/11/16/091116fa_fact_hersh.

[32] Jeffrey Goldberg and Marc Ambinder, "The Ally from Hell," *Atlantic*, October 28, 2011, http://www.theatlantic.com/magazine/archive/2011/12/the-ally-from-hell/308730.

complicate the ability of outsiders to locate Pakistani weapons.[33] Those same fears, however, could also lead to larger arsenals if Pakistani planners conclude that dispersal and deception are insufficient. Such countermeasures would not change the fundamental mission of the arsenal—to deter India—but would instead indicate that security managers have concluded that carrying out this mission requires an arsenal of sufficient size and survivability to deter third-party seizure.

With that said, the current size and disposition of Pakistan's nuclear force appears to be so large as to deter even the most risk-acceptant U.S. planner. The Abbottabad raid, which involved only one site that essentially had no ground defenses, was difficult and nearly failed following the crash of one helicopter. The Abbottabad raid also involved months, and possibly years, of efforts to validate intelligence regarding the targeted location. If Pakistan's nuclear forces are dispersed across ten or twenty sites; if a portion of the arsenal is occasionally moved from location to location, including to dummy locations; and if those locations are guarded by trained military personnel—all assumptions that are plausible based on available reporting—then the odds of a successful raid to seize the Pakistani arsenal dwindle to nearly nothing. The addition of a naval leg to the Pakistani arsenal would complicate matters even more. As Hoodbhoy cautions, "even if a single Pakistani nuke (out of roughly 100) escapes destruction, that last one could be unimaginably dangerous."[34] Even so, if relations between the United States and Pakistan worsen considerably, it seems possible that such fears could further inflate Pakistan's nuclear force requirements and shape the country's choices about peacetime basing, despite the primacy of India in Pakistani deterrence goals.

The following section will survey the major developments in the Pakistani arsenal, with particular focus on new delivery vehicles. These developments further suggest the India-specific nature of the arsenal, as well as growing Pakistani interest in threatening battlefield targets as a way to deter limited conventional military attacks from India.

Major Developments in the Arsenal

In addition to the quantitative expansion of the Pakistani arsenal, there have been corresponding qualitative changes, mostly involving a growing diversity of delivery systems (see **Table 1**). Of these, the most significant development involves heightened Pakistani pursuit of a battlefield nuclear

---

[33] Goldberg and Ambinder, "The Ally from Hell."

[34] Robert Windrem, "U.S. Prepares for Worst-Case Scenario with Pakistan Nukes," NBC News, August 3, 2011, http://openchannel.nbcnews.com/_news/2011/08/03/7189919-us-prepares-for-worst-case-scenario-with-pakistan-nukes?lite.

TABLE 1   Pakistan's delivery systems

Type	Title	Range (km)	First tested	Numbers (if available)
Aircraft	F-16 A/B	925	—	45 planes in inventory
	F-16 C/D	1,360	—	18 planes in inventory
	Mirage 5 PA	1,300	—	53 planes in inventory
Ballistic missiles	Hatf-1	70–100 (50*)	1989	Fewer than 50 Hatf-1, -3, -4, and -9 launchers (combined)
	Hatf-2 (Abdali)	180	1989	Unknown
	Hatf-3 (Ghaznavi)	200	2002	Fewer than 50 Hatf-1, -3, -4, and -9 launchers (combined)
	Hatf-4 (Shaheen-1)	750	1999	Fewer than 50 Hatf-1, -3, -4, and -9 launchers (combined)
	Hatf-5 (Ghauri-1 and -2)	1,250	1998	Fewer than 50 Ghauri launchers
	Hatf-6 (Shaheen-2)	2,500 (2,000*)	2004	Unknown
	Hatf-9 (Nasr)	60	2011	Fewer than 50 Hatf-1, -3, -4, and -9 launchers (combined)
Cruise missiles	Hatf-7 (Babur)	750 (350*)	2005	Unknown
	Hatf-8 (Ra'ad)	350	2007	Unknown
	Naval variant	Unknown	In development	—

SOURCE: *Jane's Air-Launched Weapons*; *Jane's Strategic Weapon Systems*; *Jane's All the World's Aircraft*; *Jane's Aircraft Upgrades*; *Jane's World Air Forces*; International Institute for Strategic Studies, *The Military Balance 2013* (London: Routledge, 2013); and "Ballistic and Cruise Missile Threat," National Air and Space Intelligence Center, May 2013, http://www.fas.org/programs/ssp/nukes/nuclearweapons/NASIC2013_050813.pdf.

NOTE: Asterisks indicate smaller range estimates given in "Ballistic and Cruise Missile Threat."

capability, signaled through the testing of very short-range missiles. Pakistan also continues to develop both ground- and air-launched cruise missiles and has expressed interest in fielding a seaborne cruise-missile capability. These capabilities would complement the long-range ballistic missiles and dual-use–capable manned fighter aircraft that Pakistan has possessed for nearly fifteen years.[35]

Battlefield Nuclear Weapons

Pakistan announced on April 19, 2011, that it had tested a 60-km range missile, the Hatf-9 Nasr, which it claimed "carries warheads of appropriate yields with high accuracy [and has] shoot and scoot attributes."[36] The director-general of the SPD stated that the test was important to "consolidat[e] Pakistan's strategic deterrence capability at all levels of the threat spectrum" and that the Hatf-9 Nasr would provide Pakistan with a "short range missile capability" in the "hierarchy of military operations" to complement Pakistan's medium- and long-range capabilities. The Nasr test followed a subtle shift in tone in Track 1.5 and Track 2 forums around 2010, when individuals familiar with SPD's thinking began to argue that Pakistan might respond with nuclear weapons "between the trip wire [of conventional war] and last resort."[37] By September 2011, after the Nasr test, it was relatively easy to find informed Pakistani analysts talking in such international forums about the benefits of graduated nuclear options for deterrence.[38] These twin technological and rhetorical changes suggest not only that the targets for a Pakistani first use have possibly shifted to the battlefield but also that the number of scenarios in which Pakistan envisions the use of nuclear weapons might have expanded modestly.

Short-range delivery platforms for battlefield missions have greater viability given the numerical increase in Pakistani warheads. In 2001–2, the limited use of 10 weapons for battlefield missions might have required nearly

---

[35] Feroz Hassan Khan reports that the Pakistan Air Force and the Pakistan Atomic Energy Commission were satisfied with tests of air-dropped mock nuclear warheads in 1995. See Khan, *Eating Grass*, 187.

[36] Inter-Services Public Relations (Pakistan), Press Release, April 19, 2011, http://www.ispr.gov.pk/front/main.asp?o=t-press_release&id=1721&search=1.

[37] Feroz H. Khan and Nick M. Masellis, "U.S.-Pakistan Strategic Partnership: A Track-Two Dialogue for Long-Term Security Cooperation, Fifth Iteration," Defense Threat Reduction Agency, Advanced Systems and Concepts Office, Workshop Report, October 2010, 24, http://www.hsdl.org/?view&did=722129.

[38] Feroz H. Khan and Nick M. Masellis, "U.S.-Pakistan Strategic Partnership: A Track II Dialogue, Sixth Iteration," U.S. Naval Postgraduate School, Center on Contemporary Conflict (CCC), Project on Advanced Systems and Concepts for Countering WMD, January 2012, http://www.hsdl.org/?view&did=709607.

half of Pakistan's extant arsenal, if public estimates are accurate.[39] That same limited-use mission today might only require 10% of the arsenal, a figure that could drop to 5% in the near future. Redoing the arithmetic in absolute terms frames the issue even more starkly: in 2001–2, Pakistan might have had 10 devices remaining for a second strike after a limited first use, whereas today it could have 90 devices in reserve and by 2020 it could have as many as 200. The credibility of India's massive retaliation doctrine is obviously very different in a scenario where Indian decision-makers, confronting the limited use of weapons to attack Indian troops on Pakistani soil, face the prospect that Pakistan retains hundreds of devices compared with a scenario in which Pakistan has already utilized a substantial portion of its arsenal. In 2001, Ashley Tellis calculated that it might take 37 weapons of 15 kt (or 57 weapons of 8 kt) to operationally disable an Indian armored division. Such high numbers led Tellis to dismiss serious Pakistani interest in battlefield roles for nuclear weapons.[40] In the foreseeable future, it is likely that Pakistan could devote as many as 100 weapons to battlefield missions and still possess a substantial reserve for attacking strategic targets. While this does not make nuclear warfighting likely, it does make the prospect possible in ways that were not true a decade ago.

The steps Pakistan has taken so far suggest that it is interested in a battlefield nuclear weapons capability that compels its adversaries to consider the possible employment of nuclear arms even if battlefield weapons do not play a prominent role in Pakistani doctrine. In Tellis's 2001 analysis, he suggested that Indian commanders could spread armored forces across wider frontages with greater depths. Although this tactic would complicate Pakistani targeting, it would also diffuse Indian armored combat power and thus still be beneficial to Pakistan.

Retired Pakistani officers and nongovernmental Pakistani analysts participating in Track 1.5 and Track 2 forums now regularly suggest that Pakistan might also be interested in developing nuclear artillery to further diversify the delivery means available to it in battlefield missions. These are still rumors. The highest-caliber artillery piece in the Pakistan Army is 203 mm (the M110 and M115 howitzers), considerably smaller than the Nasr's diameter. The United States first tested nuclear artillery of this diameter in 1957, employing a design that would become the W-33 warhead. U.S. nongovernmental analysts speculate that the W-33, while an HEU gun-style

---

[39] Although ten weapons is an arbitrary number for a limited-use battlefield mission designed primarily to send a political signal, it also has battlefield effects. As will be discussed in greater detail below, more weapons might be required to ensure military results against Indian armored forces.

[40] Tellis, *India's Emerging Nuclear Posture*, 133–34. For similar calculations, see Zia Mian and A.H. Nayyar, "Pakistan's Battlefield Use of Nuclear Weapons," in Hoodbhoy, *Confronting the Bomb*.

device, employed a more complicated "double gun" design to achieve critical mass.[41] In other words, even if one accepts that Pakistan might have miniaturized warheads to fit atop the Nasr, there would be additional technical hurdles to the design and manufacture of nuclear artillery shells. Keep in mind that while the United States was able to design 203-mm nuclear artillery by 1957, it did so only after conducting over one hundred nuclear tests. The degree that Pakistan could compensate for its lack of testing through computer modeling and assistance from China is an open question.

Cruise Missiles

Pakistan has also pursued ground- and air-launched cruise missiles over the past decade.[42] The ground-launched Babur (sometimes referred to as the Hatf-7) was first tested in August 2005. The air-launched Ra'ad (or Hatf-8) was first test-fired in August 2007. Both missiles likely have circular error probabilities (CEP) under 20 meters (m), though Pakistani official sources have claimed even smaller CEPs in the range of 3–10 m. Both weapons are allegedly capable of carrying 500-kg warheads, with Pakistani official press releases being quite explicit that the cruise missiles are designed to potentially carry nuclear weapons. The announced range of the Ra'ad is 350 km, while the Babur is advertised as being able to reach targets up to 750 km away (though a 2013 U.S. government publication lists both missiles as having only a 350-km range). The Babur has undergone at least nine tests and likely achieved initial operating capability in 2010, while the Ra'ad has undergone at least four tests, with its current operational status unknown.[43]

Ballistic Missiles

These newer short-range and cruise missiles complement Pakistan's force of longer-range missiles. This force includes the Ghaznavi (Hatf-3, likely an M-11 variant), with a range of 250 km; the Shaheen-1 (Hatf-4, possibly an M-9 variant), with a range of 750 km; the Ghauri (Hatf-5, a Nodong variant), with a range of 1,250 km; and the Shaheen-2 (Hatf-6), with a range of 2,000 km. The U.S. National Air and Space Intelligence Center (NASIC) estimates that Pakistan possesses fewer than 50 combined Ghaznavi,

---

[41] Carey Sublette, "Nuclear Weapons Frequently Asked Questions," Nuclear Weapon Archive, July 3, 2007, section 4.1.6.1, http://nuclearweaponarchive.org/Nwfaq/Nfaq4-1.html#Nfaq4.1.6.1.

[42] This paragraph draws from Vipin Narang and Christopher Clary, "Doctrine, Capabilities, and (In)stability in South Asia" (presentation at the Stimson Center, Washington, D.C., March 12, 2013).

[43] "Hatf-7 (Babur)," *Jane's Strategic Weapon Systems*, September 27, 2012; "Ra'ad (Hatf-8)," *Jane's Air-Launched Weapons*, October 26, 2012; and "Ballistic and Cruise Missile Threat," National Air and Space Intelligence Center, May 2013, http://www.fas.org/programs/ssp/nukes/nuclearweapons/NASIC2013_050813.pdf.

Shaheen-1, and Hatf-9 launchers; fewer than 50 Ghauri launchers; and an unknown number of Shaheen-2 launchers. The number of missiles may be much larger than the number of launchers.[44]

The ranges presented here are somewhat conservative, relying mostly on NASIC's released estimates rather than public claims by the Pakistani government that assert longer ranges. NASIC estimates do not include the so-called Shaheen-1A, a variant tested in 2012 that Pakistan claims has both a longer range and greater accuracy than its predecessor.[45] Except for the Ghauri missile, which had its first flight tests in April 1998, initial testing for all these designs occurred in a burst of activity from 1999 (the Shaheen-1) to 2004 (the Shaheen-2). Although which missiles are fully operational and which are still in development is unknown, it does seem reasonably clear that Pakistan can reach all of mainland India with the Shaheen-2 missile and can reach India's commercial and political capitals of Mumbai and New Delhi with the Ghauri, the Shaheen-1 and -2, and perhaps the Babur.

In addition, Pakistan might have interest in employing conventionally armed ballistic and cruise missiles in counterforce roles. Depending on their accuracy and the types of sub-munitions they can carry, these missiles might be attractive for disrupting troops in the rear, suppressing sortie generation at Indian air bases, and attacking military or political command and control targets. They might also be useful as a signaling mechanism if targeted against cities. When Iran and Iraq used Scud missiles against one another in the "war of the cities" period late in the Iran-Iraq war, the direct military effect was negligible, with only a few hundred dead and wounded. The broader psychological effects were more substantial, with perhaps several million Iranians fleeing Tehran after weeks of Iraqi missile barrages. Pakistan's missiles are likely to be considerably more accurate than vintage 1980s Scud missiles and would carry larger warheads than the comparatively small 135–250 kg warheads in Iraq's force.[46]

Perhaps wary of such trends, India has proved increasingly interested in pursuing ballistic missile defenses. Yet almost all the information on the program is from statements by the Indian Defense Research and Development Organization, which claims that the program seeks to achieve incredibly high

---

[44] All range figures are from "Ballistic and Cruise Missile Threat." See also "Hatf 4 (Shaheen 1)," *Jane's Strategic Weapon Systems*, May 3, 2013; "Hatf 5 (Ghauri)," *Jane's Strategic Weapon Systems*, September 7, 2012; "Hatf 6 (Shaheen 2)," *Jane's Strategic Weapon Systems*, September 7, 2012; and "Missile Race in South Asia," *Jane's Foreign Report*, March 2, 2000.

[45] Inter-Services Public Relations (Pakistan), Press Release, April 25, 2012, http://ispr.gov.pk/front/main.asp?o=t-press_release&id=2044.

[46] Anthony H. Cordesman and Abraham R, Wagner, *The Lessons of Modern War, Volume II: The Iran-Iraq War* (Boulder: Westview Press, 1990), chap. 10, http://csis.org/files/media/csis/pubs/9005lessonsiraniraqii-chap10.pdf.

intercept rates of 99.8%.[47] Even though hard-nosed Pakistani defense planners are unlikely to take these statements at face value, Indian developments are still probably stimulating greater Pakistani interest in the wide array of countermeasures that could lower the success rate of Indian interceptors. Pakistani press releases on the short-range Nasr system are explicit about its ability to defeat ballistic missile defenses, which is likely a function of its short flight times and ability to be fired in salvos rather than other technical factors like inflight maneuvering.[48] Additionally, Pakistan's interest in cruise missiles may in part derive from their ability to evade most missile defense systems.

Naval Variants

The final area of major development in the Pakistani arsenal involves submarine- or ship-launched nuclear-capable cruise missiles. Feroz Khan reports that Pakistan's Maritime Technology Organization is nearing completion of a naval variant. He further states that such a project, upon completion, would fall under the Naval Strategic Forces Command and complete the "third leg of the triad" complementing the existing aircraft and ground-based missile delivery options.[49] Although the addition of a sea-based element would certainly complicate any attempt to destroy the entirety of the Pakistani arsenal, its practical utility is considerably decreased by the relatively short ranges of Pakistan's cruise missiles and the range limitations of diesel-electric submarines. At least in the near to medium term, such a sea-based deterrent could likely only strike targets in western and southern India and would not threaten New Delhi, which is over 1,000 km from the ocean. While Pakistan could theoretically use a sea-based force against targets in eastern India, the long journey to the Bay of Bengal (presumably facing considerable Indian antisubmarine warfare) would be dangerous and unwise.

The Implications of Pakistan's Force Modernization for Regional Stability

Given the India focus of Pakistan's nuclear program, what are the implications of its force modernization for the stability of the subcontinent? The answer varies depending on one's outcome of interest. South Asia remains prone to sub-conventional violence, with India being unable to deter Pakistani

---

[47] Omer Farooq, "India Expects to Use Missile Interception System as a Weapon, Top Scientist Says," Associated Press, December 4, 2006.

[48] Inter-Services Public Relations (Pakistan), Press Release, February 11, 2013, http://www.ispr.gov.pk/front/main.asp?o=t-press_release&id=2240.

[49] Khan, Eating Grass, 396–97.

support of violent nonstate actors. This legacy of proxy support is in turn partially responsible for the endemic levels of terrorism within Pakistan, which generate instability and dangers to the Pakistani arsenal. At one level higher, conventional warfare remains unlikely because India's conventional military edge is less substantial than is commonly believed. Moreover, even if India were dominant conventionally, the country's civilian leaders have shown little willingness to undertake the nuclear risks associated with war. In the event of a conventional war, however, there should be minimal incentive for either country to use nuclear weapons first, although Pakistan's strategy is to manipulate risk to achieve both immediate deterrence (to prevent a crisis from becoming a war) and intrawar deterrence (to prevent a war from escalating from limited to full scale). Nonetheless, despite the low prospects for war, the risk of an arms race is increasing, propelled by the dyadic security dilemma, the multilateral nature of security competition in Asia, and the technological impulses of military-scientific communities.

This section will review each component of stability: nonstate threats, the prospects for both conventional and nuclear war in South Asia, and the danger of a peacetime arms race between Pakistan and India.

Nonstate Threats

The existence of violent nonstate actors in Pakistan presents not just a threat to India and the United States but also a threat to Pakistan—and by implication such nonstate actors might endanger Pakistan's nuclear assets. The country has suffered widespread terrorist violence over the last decade. In recent years, much of that violence has been directed at state organs and security institutions. These include locations associated with the nuclear weapons program, leading to understandable concerns about insider and outsider threats to the Pakistani nuclear arsenal.[50] Such an attack, in the worst case, might result in a nonstate actor stealing or detonating a Pakistani weapon or detonating an improvised nuclear explosive device from Pakistani fissile material.

Pakistan has shown considerable seriousness in its efforts to secure its nuclear materials and warheads. It established a dedicated command-and-control organization; organized a force of more than 20,000 personnel to guard nuclear weapons; developed some functional equivalent to U.S. permissive-action links that require a code to permit weapons use; created a personnel-reliability program to screen out potentially dangerous individuals from sensitive jobs; enacted a program for material protection,

---

[50] Shaun Gregory, "The Terrorist Threat to Pakistan's Nuclear Weapons," Combating Terrorism Center, CTC Sentinel, July 2009, http://www.ctc.usma.edu/wp-content/uploads/2010/06/Vol2Iss7-Art1.pdf.

control, and accounting; and employed a variety of other technical and procedural controls to ensure that dangerous actors are unable to seize nuclear material or weapons.[51]

The problem is not that Pakistan takes the task of safety and security any less seriously than other nuclear states, but rather that it faces a much more difficult task because of the threat environment in which it operates. George Perkovich has correctly argued the following:

> [T]he general level of violence, insurrection, and political instability in Pakistan poses the greatest long-run threats to the security of Pakistan's nuclear arsenal, either from insiders or outsiders, than do specific nuclear security practices of the Pakistani security establishment. Focusing, as many U.S. officials and commentators do, on the presumed insecurity of Pakistan's nuclear assets distracts attention and effort from the more fundamental objective of redressing militancy and disorder within Pakistan.[52]

Some Pakistani commentators are too quick to dismiss these concerns. It is common to hear even informed Pakistani interlocutors say that if a weapon were to fall into the hands of terrorist groups, they would be unable to detonate the weapon or launch it at a target.[53] While this may be true, there is the additional and perhaps more serious risk that the fissile material contained within the weapon could be fashioned into an improvised nuclear device that could still achieve kiloton yields. In some ways, HEU that has been converted into a metal but has not yet been fashioned into a nuclear weapon is one of the most dangerous components of the Pakistani arsenal.

Although the sum of these nonstate risks is difficult to quantify, it is at least possible that the odds that nonstate actors might acquire and use nuclear weapons are greater than the possibility that the Pakistani state would order

---

[51] For more on these measures, see Christopher Clary, "The Ongoing Evolution of Pakistan's Nuclear Command and Control" (presentation at the annual conference of the International Studies Association, San Francisco, April 3–6, 2013); Naeem Salik and Kenneth N. Luongo, "Challenges for Pakistan's Nuclear Security," *Arms Control Today*, March 2013; Christopher Clary, "Thinking about Pakistan's Nuclear Security in Peacetime, Crisis and War," Institute for Defense Studies and Analyses, IDSA Occasional Paper, no. 12, September 2010, http://www.idsa.in/system/files/OP_PakistansNuclearSecurity.pdf; Lavoy, "Islamabad's Nuclear Posture;" and Kenneth N. Luongo and Naeem Salik, "Building Confidence in Pakistan's Nuclear Security," *Arms Control Today*, December 2007.

[52] George Perkovich, "The Non-Unitary Model and Deterrence Stability in South Asia," Stimson Center, November 13, 2012, http://www.stimson.org/images/uploads/research-pdfs/George_Perkovich_-_The_Non_Unitary_Model_and_Deterrence_Stability_in_South_Asia.pdf.

[53] See comments by former Pakistan Atomic Energy Commission scientist N.M. Butt, "Good Morning Pakistan," trans. BBC Monitoring South Asia, *PTV News*, April 13, 2010, available at http://www.accessmylibrary.com/article-1G1-223813243/pakistan-tv-show-discusses.html.

the use of such weapons in a conflict.[54] Both risks are quite low in absolute terms but high enough in relative terms to merit their prominent place on the international security agenda.

The Prospect of War

To date, Indian political elites have shown themselves to be uninterested in pursuing a high-cost punitive campaign against Pakistan for the latter's support of violent groups operating in India. This reluctance is the primary firebreak between the sub-conventional instability generated by violent nonstate actors and the outbreak of conventional hostilities.[55] This strategic disinterest could end, however, if the salience of national security to Indian voters increases, perhaps concomitant with the expansion of the Indian middle class. So long as many militant groups continue to operate from Pakistan with varying degrees of state support, terrorist attacks in India will continue to be like passing streetcars for Indian politicians: they will provide potential *casus belli* that can be used when convenient.

Alternatively, India's conventional military edge could increase to such an extent that limited military actions might be possible with little chance of conventional or nuclear escalation. Today and in the near term, India's military edge is simply not so great to allow the Indian military to operate against Pakistan with impunity.[56] As the discussion below on the potential for a peacetime arms race will argue, that state of affairs is unlikely to persist indefinitely.

Finally, and perhaps most likely in the near term, a terrorist attack against India could be so massive or symbolically resonant that it overcomes political disinterest. Put differently, sub-conventional instability could overwhelm the forces that have generated "ugly stability" at the conventional level.[57] Pakistan is doing all it can to ensure that its combined conventional and strategic forces deter Indian attack, but continued sub-conventional provocations—perhaps with or without Pakistani state sponsorship or acquiescence—might cause

---

[54] This is an assessment about which reasonable analysts can disagree. Bruno Tertrais concludes, for example, that "the main risks today are not those of 'weapons falling into the wrong hands' and even less an 'Islamist takeover of the country.' They are risks of deliberate use and perhaps partial loss of control of the nuclear complex in wartime; and low-level leaks of expertise or materials, or a radiological incident in peacetime." Bruno Tertrais, *Pakistan's Nuclear Programme: A Net Assessment* (Paris: Fondation pour la Recherche Stratégique, 2012), 4.

[55] Narang argues that Indian leaders have been deterred from cross-border attacks in recent years because of Pakistan's nuclear decisions since 1998. Narang, *Nuclear Strategy in the Modern Era*, chap. 10.

[56] Christopher Clary, "Deterrence Stability and the Conventional Balance of Forces in South Asia," Stimson Center (forthcoming).

[57] See Ashley J. Tellis, *Stability in South Asia* (Santa Monica: RAND Corporation, 1997), http://www.rand.org/content/dam/rand/pubs/documented_briefings/2005/DB185.pdf.

a future Indian leader to accept the risks of military conflict in the hopes of decreasing the likelihood of terrorist violence.

The Prospect of Nuclear Escalation

Assuming war begins, how strong is the incentive for either party to use nuclear weapons first out of the belief that this tactic is likely to generate a better outcome? The incentive for first use derives from a state believing that (1) escalation to nuclear war is inevitable and (2) by striking first it can substantially limit the damage it will suffer.

From the perspective of contemporary Pakistan, the incentive to strike first remains low in both respects. First, while Pakistani force planners may not entirely believe India's pledge to refrain from first use, there is also no evidence that they believe Indian first use is likely during a conflict. Second, Pakistan's reliance on mobile missiles should provide it considerable assurance in being able to maintain a survivable deterrent even if India attempted a counterforce strike. While mobile missiles traveling toward the battlefield might face slow-motion attrition as the result of Indian conventional attacks, longer-range missiles in the rear are relatively safe from either conventional or nuclear attack. Additionally, given the relatively low yields associated with India's nuclear tests in 1974 and 1998, Pakistan might be reasonably confident that nuclear weapons housed in silos or tunnels would survive attempted counterforce strikes even if their locations were known to Indian nuclear planners. In other words, a mix of mobile and hardened launch locations means that India would not limit its potential for damage significantly from striking first. Third, India's size, reliance on mobility, and development of a credible sea-based deterrent all suggest that the benefits to Pakistan of striking first are also minimal.

Given these constraints, the most likely path to nuclear escalation involves either the unauthorized use of nuclear weapons during a full-scale war or the limited employment of Pakistani nuclear weapons on the battlefield to prevent imminent defeat by Indian conventional forces.

The risk of unauthorized use is not entirely clear. SPD officials Khalid Banuri and Adil Sultan state:

> To preclude any possibility of inadvertent or unauthorized use of nuclear weapons, Pakistan has developed physical safety mechanisms and firewalls both in the weapon systems themselves and in the chain of command. No single individual can operate a weapons system, nor can one individual issue the command for nuclear weapons use. The evolution of the NCA ensures that

no unauthorized use of nuclear weapons could ever take place, yet the weapon can be operationally ready on short notice.[58]

The question is whether Pakistan, like many nuclear states, increases the readiness of its nuclear forces during an evolving crisis or conflict. If so, at the highest state of readiness short of a nuclear launch order, what mechanisms are in place to prevent a launch other than a "two-man rule" requiring two individuals to concur that a launch is necessary? Does either the delivery vehicle or the weapon require command codes before it will function, and are those command codes only given with the launch order? Based on public statements by SPD officials, the risk of unauthorized launch appears low during peacetime. Whether that risk remains small during war is another matter.[59]

The question of whether Pakistan would intentionally employ battlefield weapons is ultimately a question of leadership psychology on both sides of the dyad. Would Indian civilian and military leaders authorize war plans that place Pakistan in a position where employing battlefield nuclear weapons becomes militarily or politically necessary? If placed in such a situation, would senior Pakistani leaders be willing to risk massive Indian retaliation? Even if Pakistani leaders are dubious about India's threats of massive retaliation in response to limited battlefield nuclear use by Pakistan, they cannot entirely discount the possibility that India would carry out its stated doctrine.[60] Based on the analysis presented above, Pakistan's battlefield capability seems presently configured as a force-in-being rather than a warfighting arsenal. Unlike the U.S.-NATO posture during the Cold War, there is little evidence that Pakistani doctrine or strategy assumes battlefield use of a nuclear device. Instead, Pakistan's strategy appears designed to manipulate the risk of use so that it increases with the severity of the conflict. Battlefield nuclear weapons carry much greater potential for what Thomas Schelling called "a threat that leaves something to chance."[61] One all-or-nothing decision to use nuclear weapons might be difficult for a national leader to make, but a series of incremental steps that increase nuclear danger and might inadvertently lead to nuclear escalation is more imaginable. Precisely because of these dangers,

---

[58] Khalid Banuri and Adil Sultan, "Managing and Securing the Bomb," *Daily Times*, May 30, 2008, http://www.dailytimes.com.pk/default.asp?page=2008\05\30\story_30-5-2008_pg3_6.

[59] Bruno Tertrais asks a related question of whether codes are transmitted at the last minute or whether codes are available to military commanders and only supposed to be opened and used when given political authorization. See Tertrais, *Pakistan's Nuclear Programme*, 24.

[60] This doctrine was stated most recently by Shyam Saran, chairman of India's National Security Advisory Board, in Indrani Bagchi, "Strike by Even a Midget Nuke Will Invite Massive Response, India Warns Pak," *Times of India*, April 30, 2013, http://articles.timesofindia.indiatimes.com/2013-04-30/india/38928972_1_pakistan-shyam-saran-india.

[61] Thomas C. Schelling, *The Strategy of Conflict* (Cambridge: Harvard University Press, 1960), chap. 8.

Pakistan might be attracted to battlefield weapons as a means to preserve deterrence at all levels of conflict.

The Danger of a Peacetime Arms Race

Despite only modest risks of intentional or unintentional use of nuclear weapons in conflict, the prospect for a peacetime arms race in South Asia is substantial. An arms race could be spurred by a growing conventional asymmetry between India and Pakistan, a structural context that makes it difficult for India to arrest this asymmetry through arms control, and technological communities that are likely to exacerbate the situation.

First, Pakistan is likely to rely increasingly on nuclear weapons as its conventional asymmetry with India grows. While today India's conventional-force advantage over Pakistan is only modest—a fact that is likely to deter conflict—in the medium to long term India will outpace Pakistan in any conventional arms race. This fact is immediately clear in a comparison of defense expenditures for India and Pakistan since 1988 (see **Figure 2**). India has gone from spending nearly four to five times as much as Pakistan in 1988 to nearly seven to eight times as much in 2012.[62] This trend is occurring despite the fact that Indian defense spending is declining as a percentage of GDP over the same period. So far, this disparity has not translated into India's conventional dominance because Indian defense procurement is still characterized by long timelines owing to cumbersome rules and a proliferation of veto players that slow purchases and induction. Over the long run, however, the disparity in defense expenditure between India and Pakistan will begin to translate into a wider capability asymmetry. In this situation, Pakistan will have little recourse but to rely increasingly on nuclear weapons, likely manifesting itself in both greater numbers of weapons overall and more devices for battlefield roles in particular.

Obviously, military expenditure is not decided exogenously. India could decide to restrain expenditures if it were to feel that arms control is beneficial to its interests. The problem is that India is in its own conventional competition with China, and here it is the laggard in defense expenditures. India has gone from spending virtually the same amount as China on defense in 1989 to only one-third as much today (see **Figure 3**). This disparity has emerged despite the fact that China's defense expenditure as a percentage of GDP has remained fairly constrained during this time period.

To some extent, India could keep up with China without beating Pakistan in an arms race through making certain choices with regard to the composition

---

[62] Stockholm International Peace Research Institute (SIPRI), "SIPRI Military Expenditure Database," http://www.sipri.org/research/armaments/milex/milex_database.

FIGURE 2   Military expenditures of India and Pakistan

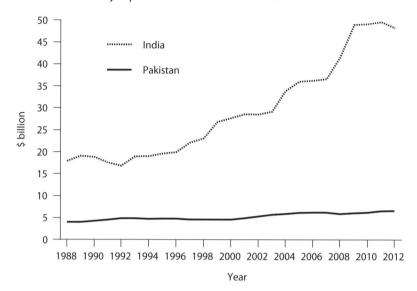

SOURCE: Stockholm International Peace Research Institute (SIPRI), SIPRI Military Expenditure Database, http://www.sipri.org/research/armaments/milex/milex_database.

FIGURE 3   Military expenditures of China, India, and Pakistan

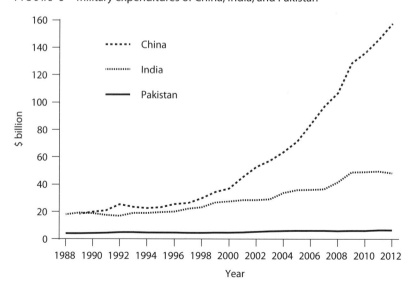

SOURCE: SIPRI, SIPRI Military Expenditure Database.

of defense procurements. Tanks, for instance, serve little function on the mountainous Sino-Indian border. The majority of defense items, however, are useful for both Indo-Pakistani and Sino-Indian contingencies. As India buys fighters, helicopters, transport planes, missiles, artillery, military satellites, and many other things, Pakistan will have to assume that the bulk of that capability will be used against it, even if India is purchasing the equipment primarily out of fear of China. This basic structural asymmetry makes arms control nearly impossible.

This situation is exacerbated by tendencies in both countries, but particularly India, to allow considerable autonomy in the choices made by defense scientists. In both capitals, there seems to be a pattern of permitting scientists to develop and build items because they are able to rather than because they meet a strategic need. This is most evident in India's pursuit of very short-range ballistic missiles (Prahaar), ballistic missile defenses, multiple independently maneuverable reentry vehicles, and increasingly accurate medium- and intermediate-range ballistic missiles.[63] For Pakistan, its scientists and engineers have assembled an impressive nuclear complex capable of producing fissile material. At some future date, the country's fissile material stockpile may be sufficient to meet strategic requirements, but will this complex be told to stop production? The inertial pressures to continue to produce ever-larger stockpiles will be powerful, and it remains to be seen whether this will exacerbate the arms competition in South Asia.

Who Decides? Civil-Military Relations and Pakistan's Nuclear Future

Opposite the forces of inertial growth are budgetary realities. Resource constraints in both India and Pakistan already impinge on what defense planners would procure if money were not a factor. There are repeated signs that Pakistan's economy might be approaching severe crisis—for example, the country's fiscal deficit already exceeds 8% of GDP. A December 2012 *Economist* article concluded that "without reform Pakistan courts economic disaster, a financial crisis that might blow the precarious economy away like straw."[64] With the U.S. drawdown in Afghanistan and a concomitant decrease in U.S. reliance on Pakistan, international donors may be less willing to provide the assistance necessary to avert such crises. In the context of severe economic pressure, military expenditure—even if prioritized—may be much less than Pakistan's defense planners would otherwise prefer.

---

[63] Vipin Narang and Christopher Clary, "Capability without Strategy," *Indian Express*, May 22, 2012, http://www.indianexpress.com/news/capability-without-strategy/952086/.

[64] "Pakistan's Economy: Plugging Leaks, Poking Holes," *Economist*, December 8, 2012, http://www.economist.com/news/asia/21567999-who-will-pay-pakistans-state-plugging-leaks-poking-holes.

So far, these resource constraints have slowed rather than eliminated the arms competition in South Asia. If they become more acute, they might force a more fundamental reassessment in Pakistan about the benefits of continued adversarial relations and the need for substantial expenditures on conventional and nuclear deterrence.

Who would lead this reassessment? How would the Pakistani state determine its nuclear needs had been met? How would it know enough is enough? On paper, there is a collective process: the National Command Authority (NCA) chaired by the prime minister,[65] which includes the ministers of foreign affairs, defense, and interior along with their uniformed colleagues, the chairman of the Joint Staff Headquarters and the army, navy, and air force chiefs. The Strategic Plans Division serves as the secretariat for the NCA. Despite the civilians at the top, this is a military-dominated process. Four of nine NCA members are military officers, the secretariat is a military organization, and civil-military relations in Pakistan are still such that civilians are reluctant to confront the military on core issues.

The question is thus whether Prime Minister Nawaz Sharif is prepared to confront the military on this issue. Given the other challenges faced by the Sharif government in the coming year, it seems unlikely that a battle over nuclear matters will be a high priority. What is opaque to outside analysts, however, is the cost associated with the increase in fissile-material production. Building new nuclear reactors, maintaining centrifuge operations, reprocessing nuclear fuel, and developing new missiles are all costly activities, but so is acquiring and maintaining other forms of military equipment. Zia Mian concludes:

> There is almost no information about the funding of Pakistan's nuclear weapons programme and little useful information about Pakistan's overall military spending. It is clear, however, that a significant fraction of Pakistan's financial resources go to its nuclear weapons programme, but that this cost is not a large share of its overall military spending.[66]

If Pakistan's budgetary pressures are severe, the military (which makes up at least 15% of all federal outlays) may be forced to slow its growth.

---

[65] When the Pakistani government announced the National Command Authority in 2000, it said the "head of government" would serve as chairperson, a role served by Pervez Musharraf as chief executive and then president of Pakistan. Initially, President Asif Ali Zardari also performed that function after assuming office, but when Zardari re-authorized the NCA in 2009, he designated the prime minister as chairperson and abolished the vice chairman position previously allotted to the prime minister. Now that Nawaz Sharif is prime minister, this change is likely to remain in effect. Paul K. Kerr and Mary Beth Nikitin, "Pakistan's Nuclear Weapons: Proliferation and Security Issues," Congressional Research Service, CRS Report for Congress, RL34248, February 13, 2013, 13–14, see note 97.

[66] Zia Mian, "Pakistan," in "Assuring Destruction Forever," ed. Ray Acheson, Women's International League for Peace and Freedom, 2012, 51.

Whether nuclear developments would have priority over conventional-force modernization in a resource-constrained environment is uncertain. At the moment, however, this is all hypothetical. The first budget of the Sharif era proposed a 10% increase in defense expenditures, despite serious budgetary pressures.[67] Even so, going forward it is the budgetary benefit—rather than any foreign policy or strategic goal—that seems most likely to motivate future changes in nuclear decision-making in Pakistan.

Policy Implications

U.S. interests are endangered directly and indirectly by current Pakistani policies. More weapons increase the risk of loss, theft, or accident. If deterrence fails, war risks nuclear escalation, which would likely cause the greatest loss of life from one event since the Great Leap Forward—including thousands of dead Americans, given the large number of U.S. citizens regularly present on the subcontinent. The most likely pathway for the failure of deterrence involves a terrorist attack on Indian soil, and such an event is both more likely to occur and more likely to trigger war so long as Pakistan acquiesces and supports at least some terrorist groups.

Although Washington thus has strong incentives to attempt to alter Pakistani policies on nuclear proliferation and support for terrorism, the United States will continue to have great difficulty in making progress in these areas. While the Pakistani arsenal was developed and remains focused on deterring India, it has had the unintended consequence of amplifying international fears of the dangers of Pakistani state failure. The probability of that outcome is overblown but is still higher than for any other nuclear state except North Korea.[68]

Most generally, Washington could either pursue greater coercive pressures on Pakistan in an effort to alter Pakistani policies or attempt continued accommodation in a belief that, given sufficient time and support, stabilizing and moderating forces will prevail. U.S. attempts to alter Pakistani calculations have struggled, however, because for U.S. coercion to succeed, threats of punishment (through sanctions and restrictions on defense sales) must be (1) sufficiently severe to alter Pakistan calculations, (2) insufficiently severe to cause major instability in Pakistan, and (3) credible. The three requirements are interrelated. U.S. policymakers are unlikely to

---

[67] Agence France-Presse, "Pakistan Raises Annual Defense Budget by 10 Percent," *Defense News*, June 13, 2013; and "Federal Budget 2013–2014," Ministry of Finance, Government of Pakistan, http://www.finance.gov.pk/fb_2013_14.html.

[68] See, for example, Anatol Lieven, "Pakistan's Passing Grade," *National Interest*, May 11, 2009, http://nationalinterest.org/article/pakistans-passing-grade-3118; and Clary, "Pakistan's Nuclear Security."

apply sanctions if they believe this policy will destabilize the Pakistani state, and this makes the threat of sanctions incredible to leaders in Islamabad and Rawalpindi. The credibility of U.S. coercion is also impugned so long as the United States must cooperate with Pakistan on counterterrorism or seek Pakistani help to promote reconciliation and stability in Afghanistan ahead of the U.S. military withdrawal. In addition, the United States will likely rely on Pakistan for retrograde transit to withdraw U.S. war materiel from the Afghan theater. This fundamental logic explains why conditions imposed on U.S. aid have so far failed to alter Pakistan's behavior: Pakistani leaders calculate that the risks of sanctions being imposed are manageable given the diversity of other U.S. interests. Even if the United States were to determine that a condition of aid has not been met, they assess that Washington would waive the requirement rather than execute the threat.[69]

In practice, U.S. strategy toward Pakistan, including on nuclear matters, appears to be headed toward continued engagement in the hopes of buttressing the new Sharif government, without offering so much support as to embolden Sharif into being too aggressive in consolidating power. Sharif's earlier efforts to weaken the presidency, supreme court, and army chief led to his downfall in 1999 after a military coup. If he can slowly consolidate his position and avoid naked power grabs, his government has the potential to move Pakistan toward more normal democratic governance and greater civilian control of the military. Greater civilian control of the military is the most likely pathway toward moderating Pakistani nuclear developments, given the country's resource constraints. Additionally, in recent decades civilians have proved less interested in Indo-Pakistani enmity than their uniformed colleagues. As the above analysis has shown, fears of India are the dominant driver for the expansion of Pakistan's nuclear arsenal. If an empowered decision-maker determines that bilateral relations have improved, then that expansion could slow, stop, or perhaps be partially reversed.

If nurturing civilian rule in Pakistan is the appropriate strategy for the United States, this further complicates coercive efforts. Most U.S. coercion would harm the civilian government as much as, if not more than, the Pakistan military. To be sure, defense sales and training could be modulated to express U.S. concern. But if these items are targeted because the United States is afraid of Pakistan's nuclear buildup, the denial of military equipment might have the perverse effect of leading Pakistan to compensate for the worsening conventional balance with India by developing its nuclear arsenal. Even if

---

[69] In the last year, the Obama administration, citing national security interests, elected to waive several requirements for aid and defense sales to Pakistan. Susan B. Epstein and K. Alan Kronstadt, "Pakistan: U.S. Foreign Assistance," CRS Report for Congress no. R41856, July 1, 2013, 33–34, http://www.fas.org/sgp/crs/row/R41856.pdf.

this outcome is unlikely, Pakistan's increasing reliance on Chinese equipment for many of its India-focused military missions diminishes U.S. leverage via weapons transfers. Additionally, most U.S. defense sales to Pakistan involve equipment with utility for counterinsurgency or counterterrorism missions, so in many cases those U.S. objectives would have to be sacrificed for coercion to succeed.

The preceding analysis suggests that the United States will continue to muddle through its Pakistan policy, attempting to nurture civilian rule but remaining fearful of unmitigated efforts at coercion or engagement. The success of the Sharif government in consolidating civilian rule will be outside U.S. control. It is by no means definite that civilians will support calmer policies toward India, but it is probable, and as a result support for civilian consolidation of power remains the least worst of several bad options available for U.S. decision-makers.

Conclusion

From the modest capabilities of May 1998 to today, Pakistan has acquired an impressive array of capabilities to deter India from being able to achieve conventional military success in a campaign against Pakistan. It has done so despite considerable resource constraints. Pakistan, however, is increasingly reliant on its nuclear arsenal for deterrence, despite the fact that India's conventional-force advantages are not yet dire. Although nuclear risks in South Asia are not large in absolute terms, they are worrisome in relative terms. Pakistan remains one of the most likely sources of nuclear risk globally—be that through theft of nuclear material, unauthorized use during a conflict, or intentional use in war. This is not a normative critique of Pakistan's decisions, which have frequently been explicable given the challenges faced by its leaders. Rather it is an acknowledgement that the country is home to many dangerous groups, that it is situated in a dangerous neighborhood, and that the Pakistan military faces serious difficulties in maintaining conventional parity with India over the long term. The future of Pakistan's nuclear weapons program is likely a larger arsenal, with more types of delivery means and an expanding role in warfighting. All of this entails growing nuclear risk for Pakistan, its neighbors, and the world.

STRATEGIC ASIA 2013–14

LATENT
NUCLEAR POWERS

EXECUTIVE SUMMARY

This chapter presents a new framework of analysis to explore North Korea's evolving use of its nuclear arsenal and implications for both the Korean Peninsula and U.S. policy.

MAIN ARGUMENT:
With origins dating back to the late 1960s, North Korea's nuclear weapons program has evolved to be a multipurpose instrument of the regime's security strategy. The regime's goals include deterring adversaries with its nuclear arsenal, generating revenue from nuclear commerce, and creating a North Korean version of President Dwight Eisenhower's New Look policy. In particular, given internal constraints related to a domestic economy that lacks basic infrastructure, the regime appears to be improving its nuclear arsenal as one means to compensate for a rapidly deteriorating conventional military. If North Korea stays on this course, then it will likely conduct more nuclear tests to miniaturize a warhead design, as well as launch more ballistic missiles to increase range and payload, with grave regional and global consequences.

POLICY IMPLICATIONS:
- Future nuclear tests by North Korea have the potential to destabilize the region by increasing public pressure in South Korea and Japan to explore a nuclear deterrent. These countries' well-developed but latent nuclear capabilities make a decision to pursue a nuclear deterrent more a political than a technical matter.

- If the U.S. is determined to preserve the regional stability resulting from its provision of extended deterrence to South Korea and Japan, it will need to devote more resources and effort to disrupting the North Korean regime's channels for generating revenue and procuring sensitive components for WMD programs.

- Washington's inability to disrupt these channels could eventually result in a North Korean regime with a nuclear deterrent that could threaten the security of the U.S. homeland, as well as in a regime with strategic procurement partnerships with other regimes.

Nuclear Ambition and Tension on the Korean Peninsula

John S. Park

Despite a steady stream of high-level U.S. efforts to demonstrate the United States' long-term commitment to the East Asia region, a key challenge has been dealing with the nuclear weapons advancements of the Democratic People's Republic of Korea (DPRK). In a region with extensive latent nuclear weapon capabilities, the stakes are high as Washington seeks to reassure allies and make progress in peacefully rolling back North Korea's nuclear program.

As the DPRK expands its nuclear capabilities, the prospects rise for further nuclear proliferation on the Korean Peninsula. Even non-nuclear states such as the Republic of Korea (ROK)—which enjoys a comprehensive security alliance with Washington that includes protection under the U.S. nuclear umbrella—are not immune to the significant improvements demonstrated by North Korea's nuclear and ballistic missile tests. South Korea's considerable latent capabilities could facilitate rapid nuclear weaponization following a political decision to do so. The country's opinion leaders have been using this potential to increase pressure on Beijing and Washington to rein in Pyongyang—especially after the apparent recent progress by the North toward the operationalization of its nuclear arsenal. Frustrated with the seemingly endless coordinating meetings and exploratory talks with the regime while it moves ahead with nuclear weapons development, the South Korean public has

John S. Park is an Associate with the Project on Managing the Atom at the Harvard Kennedy School's Belfer Center for Science and International Affairs. He can be reached at <john_park@hks.harvard.edu>.

called for an indigenous nuclear deterrent in recent opinion polls. Following North Korea's third nuclear test in February 2013, 66% of the South Korean public supported a domestic nuclear weapons program.[1]

Despite a bipartisan consensus, South Korea is severely constrained by its awareness of the likely direct consequences of a decision to develop a nuclear arsenal of its own. Moving beyond emotions and rhetoric is a stark choice for South Koreans. In addition to an intertwined comprehensive security alliance, Seoul is heavily dependent on assistance from the United States in running an extensive civilian nuclear energy industry and launching an ambitious nuclear power plant export program. Nuclear energy currently provides 13% of South Korea's domestic energy use, and this percentage is expected to grow.[2] South Korea's nuclear export business is projected to be a multi-billion dollar endeavor, with it already securing a $40-billion contract with the United Arab Emirates in 2009 to construct and manage four nuclear power plants.[3] Most importantly, South Korea is a member of the elite club of countries with $1 trillion in annual GDP and was ranked as the world's twelfth-largest economy in 2012.[4] Thus, unlike North Korea, South Korea is acutely vulnerable to sanctions should it violate its responsibilities under the Nuclear Non-Proliferation Treaty (NPT).

The first part of this chapter explores the drivers of North Korea's nuclear weapons program and how the country's arsenal has evolved into a multipurpose instrument that is central to the regime's security strategy. The second part examines North Korea's ongoing efforts to miniaturize a nuclear warhead and mate it to a long-range ballistic missile with proven range and payload. The third part assesses how these growing nuclear capabilities constitute one factor emboldening the regime to carry out conventional provocations against South Korea. These capabilities also constitute a trigger that is influencing South Korean and Japanese debates about whether these countries should follow suit and develop nuclear deterrents of their own. The final part highlights the implications of a potential South Korean decision to convert the ROK's latent capabilities into a viable nuclear weapons program,

---

[1] Jiyoon Kim, Karl Friedhoff, and Chungku Kang, "The Fallout: South Korean Public Opinion Following North Korea's Third Nuclear Test," Asan Institute for Policy Studies, Issue Brief, no. 46, February 25, 2013, 7.

[2] Meeyoung Cho, "South Korea to Expand Nuclear Energy Despite Growing Safety Fears," Reuters, January 8, 2013, http://in.reuters.com/article/2013/01/08/nuclear-south-korea-idINDEE90702420130108.

[3] Troy Stangarone, "Why South Korea Won't Develop Nuclear Weapons," Korea Economic Institute of America, Peninsula web log, May 13, 2013, http://blog.keia.org/2013/05/why-south-korea-wont-develop-nuclear-weapons.

[4] Central Intelligence Agency, "South Korea," in World Factbook 2012 (New York: Skyhorse Publishing, 2011), available at https://www.cia.gov/library/publications/the-world-factbook/geos/ks.html; and "Facts & Figures," U.S. Korea Connect, http://www.uskoreaconnect.org/facts-figures.

as well as the implications of North Korea's current and future approach to nuclear weapons for U.S. policy. The chapter concludes by outlining steps that Washington could take to delay and disrupt North Korea's march toward a fully operational nuclear arsenal.

North Korea's Nuclear Program

North Korea represents the leading threat to the stability of East Asia and to the viability of the international nonproliferation regime. For decades, Pyongyang has chosen to pursue the development of a nuclear weapons program in the face of increasingly stringent targeted sanctions and diplomatic isolation. (**Table 1** summarizes key negotiations and results.) This section describes how North Korea initiated its nuclear program and how the program has evolved over time. It will also describe how the purposes of this program evolved into what they are today—critical elements of North Korea's domestic and international security strategies for ensuring the survival of the Kim regime.

The History of North Korea's Nuclear Program

The origins of North Korea's nuclear program remain fairly mysterious to outside analysts.[5] While much is known about the capabilities the DPRK developed and acquired over time, little is definitively known about the strategic motivations that inspired these activities. The purposes that nuclear capabilities serve for Pyongyang seem to have evolved with North Korea's external security environment and its domestic politics, yet the exact dynamics of this evolution remain unclear.

While North Korea's nuclear program has deep roots, it was officially born in 1952 when Pyongyang established the Atomic Energy Research Institute and the Academy of Sciences. In its early years, the program was entirely dependent on scientists, technicians, and technologies from the Soviet Union. In 1959, North Korea and the Soviet Union signed an agreement on the peaceful use of nuclear energy, under which Moscow agreed to help establish a nuclear research complex in Yongbyon, North Pyongan Province. This cooperation continued through the early 1960s, when Moscow constructed the Yongbyon Nuclear Research Center and provided an IRT-2000 nuclear

---

[5] Several sources are particularly valuable in highlighting the history of North Korea and its nuclear program. See Bradley K. Martin, *Under the Loving Care of the Fatherly Leader: North Korea and the Kim Dynasty* (New York: St. Martin's Press, 2004); Don Oberdorfer, *The Two Koreas: A Contemporary History* (New York: Basic Books, 2001); Jonathan D. Pollack, *No Exit: North Korea, Nuclear Weapons and International Security* (London: Routledge, 2011); and the Nuclear Threat Initiative (NTI), "Country Profile: North Korea," May 2013, http://www.nti.org/country-profiles/north-korea/nuclear.

TABLE 1 Nuclear negotiations with North Korea

Date	Agreement	Terms and commitments	Sources of deterioration	Deterioration date
December 12, 1985	North Korea ratifies the NPT.	Beyond the five recognized nuclear powers, all parties to the NPT agree never to acquire nuclear weapons.	With the collapse of the Agreed Framework in 2002–3, North Korea makes good on a decade-old threat to withdraw.	Pyongyang withdraws from the NPT on January 11, 2003.
December 31, 1991	North and South Korea sign the Joint Declaration on the Denuclearization of the Korean Peninsula.	Both sides agree not to test, make, buy, or use nuclear weapons, or to possess reprocessing or uranium-enrichment facilities.	North Korea never agrees to inspections by the Joint Nuclear Control Commission pursuant to the deal; in 2002, it admits to uranium-enrichment efforts.	In October 2002, the U.S. determines that North Korea is in breach of the Joint Declaration.
April 9, 1992	Six years after entering the NPT, North Korea ratifies the required IAEA Safeguards Agreement.	The IAEA will be allowed to inspect North Korean nuclear facilities to ensure Pyongyang's compliance with its obligations under the NPT.	As early as April 1993, the IAEA finds North Korea in violation of the NPT. In June 1994, North Korea expels the IAEA, although the Safeguards Agreement remains in effect as per the NPT.	North Korea's withdrawal from the NPT in January 2003 effectively terminates the agreement.
February 15, 1994	North Korea agrees to allow IAEA inspectors to visit seven atomic sites.	Pyongyang averts a likely trade embargo and UN Security Council sanctions by finalizing a deal with the IAEA to allow inspections.	IAEA inspectors are initially barred from taking samples at the Yongbyon nuclear facility and subsequently find that North Korea is destroying key evidence.	The agreement deteriorates soon after it is negotiated in spring 1994.
October 21, 1994	The U.S. and North Korea sign the Agreed Framework in Geneva, Switzerland.	North Korea agrees to shut down its nuclear facilities and remain in the NPT; in exchange, it will obtain light-water reactors and fuel oil from the U.S., South Korea, and Japan.	The North complains of delays in funding light-water reactors and fuel-oil deliveries; Pyongyang acknowledges its uranium-enrichment program in 2002.	In December 2002, the North announces it will restart frozen facilities and expels IAEA inspectors.

Table 1 continued.

September 12, 1999	The U.S. and North Korea negotiate the Berlin Accords, which address long-range missile testing.	North Korea agrees to a moratorium on long-range missile tests during negotiation of a permanent ballistic missile pact with the U.S., which reduces sanctions.	Pyongyang agrees to extend its moratorium beyond 2003 but begins threatening to resume long-range missile tests as early as 2002.	On July 5, 2006, North Korea tests a long-range ballistic missile (Taepodong-2).
September 19, 2005	During the fourth round of the six-party talks, the parties agree on a joint statement of six articles.	All parties agree that the goal of the talks is the "verifiable denuclearization of the Korean Peninsula" in exchange for aid and diplomatic relations.	A dispute over frozen funds in Macao is resolved, but Pyongyang continues secret work on nuclear weapons. It detonates its first device on October 9, 2006, and also fires additional long-range rockets.	In April and May 2009 respectively, North Korea withdraws from the talks and conducts a second nuclear test.
February 13, 2007	During the fifth round of the six-party talks, North Korea agrees to shut down its Yongbyon nuclear facility.	In exchange for North Korea's promise to close Yongbyon, the U.S., South Korea, China, Japan, and Russia agree to provide North Korea with fuel oil.	In July 2007, the IAEA verifies that Yongbyon has been shut down. Yet after the UN condemns the April 5, 2009, rocket launch, North Korea expels foreign monitors.	North Korea resumes reprocessing to separate plutonium on April 25, 2009.
October 11, 2008	North Korea agrees to allow inspectors to "verify" its nuclear programs.	After the North promises to provide access to a set of key sites, the U.S. removes North Korea from its list of state sponsors of terrorism.	Even as the U.S. removes North Korea from the terrorism list and continues fuel-oil shipments, North Korea backs away from its October 11 commitments.	On December 11, 2008, negotiations on verification end in a stalemate.
February 29, 2012	North Korea again agrees to suspend operations at its Yongbyon facility, as well as all long-range missile tests.	In exchange for a North Korean promise to allow IAEA inspections and halt all nuclear and long-range missile tests, the U.S. offers 240,000 metric tons of food aid.	In March 2012, Pyongyang announces that it will launch a "satellite" in April to mark the centennial of Kim Il-sung's birth.	On April 13, 2012, North Korea fires an Unha-3 rocket, which constitutes a breach of its pledge.

SOURCE: Arms Control Association, "Chronology of U.S.-North Korean Nuclear and Missile Diplomacy," Fact Sheet, April 2013, http://www.armscontrol.org/factsheets/dprkchron; National Committee on North Korea, "A Short History of U.S. Relations with North Korea," Issue Brief, August 2011, http://www.ncnk.org/resources/briefing-papers/all-briefing-papers/dprk-security-and-non-proliferation-key-events; and "Timeline of North Korea's Nuclear Program," *New York Times*, August 6, 2013, http://www.nytimes.com/interactive/2013/02/05/world/asia/northkorea-timeline.html.

research reactor, which produced radioisotopes and helped train North Korean personnel. As North Korea's domestic nuclear expertise took root, its dependence on the Soviet Union diminished. North Korea also began to expand the IRT-2000 nuclear reactor with indigenous technologies.

The motivations during these early stages of the DPRK's nuclear program remain unclear. While there may have been a genuine interest in the peaceful use of nuclear energy in order to build the North Korean economy, Kim Il-sung may also have been motivated by a sense of isolation. Pyongyang's relations with Moscow had soured as a result of a series of North Korean provocations aimed at destabilizing the South, and China's Cultural Revolution had soured relations with Beijing. Indeed, Kim feared the outbreak of a "two-front war" during this time, which suggests that military considerations played some role in the regime's nuclear efforts.[6] Still, attempts to definitively ascribe motivations to North Korea's nuclear program during this period are speculative at best.

In the 1970s, North Korea explicitly began to expand its nuclear capabilities while at the same time attempting to present a reasonable, responsible diplomatic face to the international community. In July 1977, it signed an agreement with the International Atomic Energy Agency (IAEA) and the Soviet Union, which imposed IAEA safeguards on the IRT-2000 research reactor and a critical assembly facility in Yongbyon.

During the 1980s, North Korea achieved substantial progress toward developing the technical capacity to produce nuclear weapons by building fuel-rod fabrication and uranium-milling facilities and by completing construction of the 5 megawatt-electric (MWe) experimental nuclear reactor at Yongbyon. This period also saw the DPRK begin working on non-nuclear components of atomic weaponry, such as a triggering mechanism. It also commenced building a 50 MWe reactor at the Yongbyon complex and negotiated Soviet assistance in acquiring light-water reactor technology. As part of the agreement with Moscow, Pyongyang acquiesced to long-standing international demands that it sign the NPT as a non–nuclear weapons signatory. However, given the regime's contemporaneous work on the military applications of nuclear power, it would appear that North Korea did not intend to abide by its NPT commitments.

It is unclear what strategic calculations motivated Kim Il-sung's nuclear behavior during this period of time. In all likelihood, Pyongyang accelerated its nuclear program because of several factors, including the perceived need to establish deterrence against external threats—a concern that was likely intensified by revelations about an indigenous South Korean nuclear program

---

[6] Pollack, *No Exit*, 69.

and by the regime's deepening strategic isolation. This sense of isolation was further heightened by South Korea's implementing its *nordpolitik* policy, whereby Seoul negotiated the establishment of diplomatic relations with Moscow and Beijing. As North Korea's economic and diplomatic isolation grew, its nuclear weapons development program increasingly provided a critical element of existential deterrence against the rising Asian tiger across the 38th parallel, particularly in the context of an ever more hostile regional neighborhood. This deterrent enabled North Korea to restore a semblance of balance on the peninsula after the enormous effectiveness of South Korea's nordpolitik initially skewed inter-Korean power dynamics heavily in Seoul's favor.

Following announcements in 1991 by Washington and Seoul about the withdrawal of U.S. tactical nuclear weapons from South Korea, North and South Korea signed a Joint Declaration on the Denuclearization of the Korean Peninsula. Under the terms of the declaration, both sides pledged that they would "not test, manufacture, produce, receive, possess, store, deploy, or use nuclear weapons." In addition, the agreement bound the two sides to forgo the possession of "nuclear reprocessing and uranium enrichment facilities."[7]

North Korea also signed an IAEA safeguards agreement in January 1992, under which it was required to make an "initial declaration" of its nuclear facilities and materials and provide access so that IAEA inspectors could verify the completeness and correctness of its declaration. Six rounds of inspections occurred from May 1992 through February 1993. Pyongyang's initial declaration included a small plutonium sample of less than one hundred grams, which it claimed was reprocessed from damaged spent-fuel rods that had been removed from the 5 MWe Yongbyon reactor. IAEA analysis, however, indicated that DPRK technicians had previously reprocessed plutonium in 1989, 1990, and 1991. When the IAEA requested access to two nuclear waste sites that it suspected had been used to process plutonium, North Korea declared them off-limits because they were military sites.

As a result, the IAEA asked the UN Security Council (UNSC) to authorize special inspections (for an overview of this and other relevant UNSC resolutions, see **Table 2**). North Korea responded to this move by declaring its intention to withdraw from the NPT on March 12, 1993. The terms of the treaty stipulate that a state's withdrawal takes effect 90 days after it has given notice. North Korea suspended its withdrawal from the

---

[7] "Joint Declaration of South and North Korea on the Denuclearization of the Korean Peninsula," February 19, 1992, available from the Center for Nonproliferation Studies, Inventory of International Nonproliferation Organizations and Regimes, http://cns.miis.edu/inventory/pdfs/aptkoreanuc.pdf.

TABLE 2 UN Security Council resolutions on North Korea

Resolution	Date enacted	Provocation	Measures adopted	Vote
UNSCR 825	May 11, 1993	North Korea announces its intent to withdraw from the NPT; IAEA Board of Governors later finds North Korea in noncompliance with Safeguards Agreement.	• Calls on North Korea to reconsider its decision to withdraw from the NPT and instead adhere to its commitments as an NPT signatory nation • Does not implement sanctions	13-0 in favor, with China and Pakistan abstaining
UNSCR 1695	July 15, 2006	North Korea launches a series of missiles on July 4, 2006.	• Prohibits UN member states from transferring technologies or materials to North Korea that would aid its missile and WMD programs • Prohibits member states from acquiring missiles or associated technologies from North Korea • Requires member states to prevent the transfer of financial resources to North Korea that would aid its missile or WMD programs	15-0 in favor
UNSCR 1718	October 14, 2006	North Korea conducts a nuclear test on October 9, 2006.	• Reaffirms and expands sanctions imposed by UNSCR 1695 • Prohibits the sale or transfer of certain luxury goods to North Korea • Enforces the inspection of cargo to and from North Korea for illicit materials related to WMDs • Bans the import and export of arms and related items to and from North Korea • Bans travel for select individuals associated with North Korea missile and WMD programs • Establishes a committee of the UN Security Council to review compliance with the resolution	15-0 in favor

Table 2 continued.

UNSCR 1874	June 12, 2009	North Korea conducts a second nuclear test on May 25, 2009.	• Reaffirms and expands sanctions imposed under UNSCR 1718 • Prohibits member states from extending financial assistance to North Korea, except on humanitarian grounds • Establishes a panel of experts to analyze member compliance with the resolution and recommend improvements	15-0 in favor
UNSCR 2087	January 22, 2013	North Korea conducts a long-range rocket launch on December 12, 2012.	• Reaffirms and expands sanctions imposed by UNSCRs 1718 and 1874 • Freezes the assets of several entities associated with providing financial support to North Korea • Broadens the travel ban to include additional individuals associated with North Korean missile and WMD programs • Encourages member states to enhance enforcement of existing sanctions	15-0 in favor
UNSCR 2094	March 7, 2013	North Korea conducts a third nuclear test on February 12, 2013.	• Reaffirms and expands sanctions, including financial sanctions, imposed by UNSCRs 1718, 1874, and 2087 • Imposes sanctions to block financial transactions or the transfer of bulk cash and to limit North Korean access to international financial institutions • Calls on member states to deny permission to any aircraft wishing to take off from, land in, or overfly their territory if the aircraft is suspected of transporting prohibited items • Extends the panel of experts' mandate an additional year • Strengthens member states' authority to inspect suspicious cargo emanating from or traveling to North Korea • Requires member states to deny port access to any North Korean vessel refusing inspection	15-0 in favor

SOURCE: UN Security Council Resolutions 825, 1695, 1718, 1874, 2087, and 2094, available at http://www.un.org/en/sc/documents/resolutions/index.shtml.

NPT a day before the withdrawal was to take effect. Although the regime agreed to suspend its withdrawal as long as negotiations continued with Washington, it claimed to have a special status under which North Korea agreed to safeguards on its present activities but refused to allow inspections to assess past nuclear activities.

By this time, it was clear that the purpose of North Korea's nuclear weapons program had evolved. While it remained an essential element of the regime's national security strategy, Pyongyang also had grown to see its nascent program as an important bargaining chip in negotiations with the United States and the rest of the world, with which it was able to extract a series of significant concessions while never completely abandoning its nuclear ambitions.[8]

In May 1994 the international crisis over North Korea's nuclear weapons program escalated when DPRK technicians began removing spent fuel rods from the Yongbyon 5 MWe reactor without being supervised by IAEA inspectors. This action undermined the ability of inspectors to verify the country's production of nuclear materials.

With the intervention of former president Jimmy Carter, the United States and the DPRK established a denuclearization process that became known as the Agreed Framework. The Agreed Framework stipulated that in exchange for North Korea consenting to certain measures—a freeze on its nuclear program, movement toward the requirements of the 1992 Joint Declaration, and maintenance of its status as a NPT non-nuclear signatory—the United States would offer security assurances and significant energy assistance. This included the construction of two light-water reactors and the provision of heavy fuel oil until the reactors could be completed in 2003.

Although the Agreed Framework remained in place for nearly a decade, North Korea chafed under what it saw as delays in the United States implementing its side of the bargain. Washington, meanwhile, continued to push for more stringent inspections. The situation almost broke down entirely over the 1998 launch of a Taepodong long-range rocket over Japan, which resulted in the adoption of UNSC Resolution 1695 and an eventual self-imposed moratorium on missile launches by North Korea in exchange for the loosening of some U.S. sanctions.

The new millennium brought with it new challenges regarding North Korea's nuclear program. Soon after the start of its first term, the George W. Bush administration launched a review of U.S. policy toward

---

[8] Victor Cha has extensively addressed North Korea's use of its nuclear weapons program as a bargaining chip. See Victor D. Cha, "Hawk Engagement and Preventive Defense on the Korean Peninsula," *International Security* 27, no. 1 (2002): 40–78; and Victor D. Cha, *The Impossible State: North Korea, Past and Future* (New York: Ecco, 2012). See also David C. Kang and Victor D. Cha, "Think Again: North Korea," *Foreign Policy*, March 25, 2013.

North Korea, which was completed in early June 2001. The review concluded that the United States should seek "improved implementation of the Agreed Framework, verifiable constraints on North Korea's missile program, a ban on missile exports, and a less threatening North Korean conventional military posture."[9] Subsequent references to North Korea as a member of the "axis of evil" in President Bush's 2002 State of the Union address, along with the labeling of North Korea as a "rogue state," raised concerns in Pyongyang about U.S. intentions and its commitment to the Agreed Framework.

North Korea had long been suspected of benefitting from the black market nuclear activities of Pakistani scientist A.Q. Khan and was thought to have received over twenty gas centrifuges—and the associated technology, materials, and data—to produce enriched uranium for nuclear weapons in the early to mid-1990s. More contemporary intelligence suggested that North Korea was in the process of developing an industrial uranium-enrichment capability.[10] The existence of a North Korean uranium-enrichment program was revealed by then U.S. assistant secretary of state for East Asian and Pacific affairs James Kelly during a visit to Pyongyang in 2002—a revelation that Pyongyang subsequently denied for years. Although North Korean officials later amended the admission, this episode confirmed U.S. suspicions about the regime's continued clandestine nuclear activities. Consequently, the United States declared North Korea to be in violation of the terms of the Agreed Framework and duly suspended further shipments of heavy fuel oil. North Korea responded by restarting nuclear activities at its Yongbyon complex, ejecting IAEA inspectors from the country, and withdrawing from the NPT. The Agreed Framework subsequently collapsed.

The U.S. invasion of Iraq in March 2003, for the purported reason of preventing Saddam Hussein from developing or using WMDs, served to place Pyongyang on notice that it might suffer a similar fate. This realization appears to have provided additional impetus for the development of a nuclear deterrent. A common refrain from North Korean officials is that if Saddam Hussein had developed nuclear weapons, he would still be in power today.[11] Relations between the United States and North Korea continued to deteriorate throughout 2003. U.S. intelligence reporting on North Korea's ongoing efforts to reprocess spent fuel rods only served to push relations between the two nations to a new nadir. During this period, North Korea is estimated to have

---

[9] See NTI, "Country Profile: North Korea."

[10] Pollack, *No Exit*, 123.

[11] Author's meetings with senior North Korean diplomats during Track 2 dialogues in summer 2011.

reprocessed 8,000 spent fuel rods (its entire spent-fuel stockpile), yielding enough weapons-grade plutonium for four to six weapons.[12]

International dialogue on North Korea's nuclear program resumed with Beijing's initiation of a trilateral dialogue among North Korea, the United States, and China aimed at easing tension on the peninsula. South Korea, Japan, and Russia were subsequently included in the discussion, opening the first round of the six-party talks in August 2003. Despite their ambitious agenda, the participants held largely divergent views on many issues. Consequently, progress was not forthcoming, and the talks themselves were intermittent. The six-party talks continued in an on-again, off-again pattern until February 2005, when North Korea announced that it would no longer participate in the dialogue. At this juncture, the regime also disclosed for the first time that it had built a nuclear device, with intelligence assessments indicating that North Korea intended to carry out a nuclear test in the near term.

North Korea conducted its first nuclear test at the Punggye-ri test site on October 9, 2006. Despite the apparent failure of the device to detonate as expected, the test was swiftly condemned by the international community, with the UNSC imposing sanctions on North Korea through the adoption of Resolution 1718. The United States and North Korea engaged in serious bilateral discussions shortly thereafter and convened again in Berlin in early 2007. Although progress was slow and relatively minor, the bilateral forum appeared to be more conducive to building forward momentum. When the six-party talks reconvened in February 2007, a denuclearization action plan—Initial Actions for the Implementation of the Joint Statement—was announced under which North Korea would allow the return of IAEA inspectors, "shut down and seal" and eventually "disable all nuclear facilities," and disclose "a complete and correct declaration of all its nuclear programs" by the end of the year. The agreement also prohibited North Korea from transferring "nuclear materials, nuclear technology, or nuclear know-how" to other actors. In return for the regime's completion of these steps, the other members of the talks would fulfill their obligations under earlier agreements. In addition, the United States would remove North Korea from the "state sponsors of terrorism" list and lift restrictions placed on it under the Trading with the Enemy Act.

Despite some progress, most notably the shuttering of the Yongbyon facility and the destruction of the iconic cooling tower in June 2008, the agreement suffered numerous setbacks. When North Korea submitted the required declaration of its full nuclear activities, the United States raised issues

---

[12] Mary Beth Nikitin, "North Korea's Nuclear Weapons: Technical Issues," Congressional Research Service, CRS Report for Congress, RL34256, April 3, 2013, 5.

relating to the DPRK's suspected clandestine enriched-uranium program. North Korea's alleged cooperation in building a nuclear facility in Syria also proved to be a source of friction. The DPRK meanwhile complained about delays in being removed from the list of state sponsors of terrorism. Negotiations moved forward at a snail's pace, suggesting that the regime was intent on simply waiting out the Bush administration in the hope that the next president would prove more pliable.

President Barack Obama faced a test from North Korea early in his administration. In April 2009, North Korea conducted a second long-range rocket launch that prompted the UNSC to issue a statement condemning the test. In response, North Korea once again expelled IAEA inspectors and announced that it intended to restart the Yongbyon reactor to "weaponize its entire inventory of plutonium," conduct additional missile tests, and begin uranium-enrichment experiments.[13] The regime's reversion to belligerence was no accident. Indeed, the response appears to have been carefully calibrated to coincide with the impending succession of Kim Jong-il's third son and heir, Kim Jong-un. On May 25, 2009, North Korea conducted a second nuclear test, also at the Punggye-ri test site. The international response was once again predictable, with the UNSC imposing additional sanctions on North Korea.

The situation on the Korean Peninsula continued to deteriorate over the next two years as a result of several low-level incursions by the North against the South. A North Korean submarine torpedoed the South Korean corvette *Cheonan* in March 2010, killing 46 sailors. Several months later, a North Korean artillery detachment shelled a South Korean island in response to an ROK live-fire exercise, killing two marines and two civilians. Tensions remained high on the peninsula, and several attempts to restart the six-party talks were unsuccessful. In 2010, a U.S. delegation led by Siegfried Hecker was shown what appeared to be an operational gas-centrifuge uranium-enrichment facility located within the Yongbyon nuclear complex. This revelation confirmed suspicions that North Korea was in possession of a clandestine enrichment program and thus had a potential alternative pathway to the bomb.

The death of Kim Jong-il in December 2011 prompted many to hope that under the new leadership of Kim Jong-un North Korea might be finally willing to abandon its provocative international stance and come in from the cold. These expectations were to prove short-lived. U.S. negotiators attempted to complete a bilateral agreement in February 2012 (the "leap day deal") that would have seen the United States provide North Korea with food assistance in exchange for the regime's moratoria on nuclear and missile tests,

---

[13] Pollack, *No Exit*, 158.

as well as on further uranium enrichment. Unfortunately, North Korea soon launched a third long-range rocket, thereby breaking the deal. Although this rocket—like the previous two—failed in mid-flight, North Korea launched a fourth long-range rocket several months later in December 2012, which successfully delivered a satellite into orbit. International condemnation of these launches was harsh, with additional sanctions being imposed upon North Korea in each instance.

In defiance of the subsequent round of sanctions, North Korea conducted a third nuclear test on February 12, 2013, its largest to date, which it claimed was a successful test of a "lighter, miniaturized atomic bomb."[14] Later, in April 2013, North Korean state media outlets announced that Pyongyang was restarting its 5 MWe reactor and uranium-enrichment plant at Yongbyon.

After Pyongyang's third nuclear test, the UNSC passed Resolution 2094 condemning yet another North Korean threat to international peace and security. Susan Rice, then U.S. ambassador to the United Nations, argued that the new measures under this resolution would have teeth in significantly impeding "North Korea's ability to develop further its illicit nuclear and ballistic missile programs, as well as its proliferation activities."[15] In response, North Korea made threats in early March 2013 to launch a preemptive nuclear strike against the United States. During annually scheduled U.S.-ROK joint military exercises, the United States added a new feature. It flew nuclear-capable long-range bombers from bases in Guam and Missouri to South Korea as a demonstration of its extended capabilities, both to reassure its South Korean ally and deter North Korea. Alarmed by the sudden escalation of tensions on the Korean Peninsula and the elevated danger of destabilizing the region, the new Chinese leader Xi Jinping reportedly sent clear messages for Pyongyang to de-escalate and return to the six-party talks. Soon after, North Korea initiated a cooling-off period.

Current and Potential Nuclear Capabilities

As of this writing, North Korea is thought to possess fewer than a dozen nuclear devices. Whether it also possesses credible delivery systems is unclear, although in 2011 Lieutenant General Ronald Burgess, then director of the Defense Intelligence Agency (DIA), testified that North Korea "may now have several plutonium-based nuclear warheads that it can deliver by ballistic

---

[14] Choe Sang-hun, "North Korea Threatens to Attack U.S. with 'Lighter and Smaller Nukes,'" *New York Times*, March 5, 2013.

[15] U.S. Mission to the United Nations, "UN Security Council Resolution 2094 on North Korea," Fact Sheet, March 7, 2013.

missiles and aircraft as well as unconventional means."[16] Additionally, Hecker's 2010 confirmation of the existence of a uranium-enrichment plant within the Yongbyon nuclear complex elevated concern that Pyongyang possessed the means to pursue a nuclear device utilizing a highly enriched uranium (HEU) core.

To date, Pyongyang has conducted three nuclear tests—in 2006, 2009, and 2013—to demonstrate its capability. These tests were all carried out underground at the Punggye-ri test site and demonstrated progressive improvement in terms of successful detonation and weapon yield. The first test in October 2006 is widely considered by U.S. technical experts to have failed, producing a "fizzle" with an estimated yield of less than one kiloton.[17] The two subsequent tests, however, were more successful. The second test, conducted in May 2009, was estimated to have had a yield of "a few kilotons," demonstrating an improvement from the first attempt.[18] The third device, tested in February 2013, possessed an estimated yield of between six and seven kilotons. When it became clear that North Korea intended to conduct a third nuclear test, there was speculation over whether the test would be of a uranium- or plutonium-based device, given North Korea's development of a uranium-enrichment capability. Unfortunately, it appears that the DPRK was able to successfully cap the test site, thereby preventing the release of radioactive particles that would indicate, among other things, the type of fissile material used in the weapon.[19]

In its most recent test, Pyongyang claims to have detonated a smaller and lighter warhead, which, if true, would be a major step toward developing a deployable warhead. Given North Korea's proven short- and medium-range ballistic missile capability and improving aptitude with long-range rocket technology, it appears that the regime is moving toward an operational nuclear capability.

---

[16] Ronald L. Burgess, "World Wide Threat Assessment," statement before the Senate Committee on Armed Services, March 10, 2011, http://www.armed-services.senate.gov/statemnt/2011/03%20 March/Burgess%2003-10-11.pdf.

[17] North Korea informed China beforehand that it intended for the test to be about four kilotons. See Mark Mazzetti, "Preliminary Samples Hint at North Korean Nuclear Test," New York Times, October 14, 2006, http://www.nytimes.com/2006/10/14/world/asia/14nuke.html.

[18] "Statement by the Office of the Director of National Intelligence on North Korea's Declared Nuclear Test on May 25, 2009," DNI, no. 23-09, June 15, 2009, http://www.dni.gov/files/documents/ Newsroom/Press%20Releases/2009%20Press%20Releases/20090615_release.pdf.

[19] The Preparatory Commission for the Comprehensive Nuclear-Test-Ban Treaty Organization (CTBTO) stated that "no radioactive noble gases attributable to the 12 February event have been detected by CTBTO radionuclide stations so far. While an on-site inspection could still potentially locate evidence of a nuclear explosion, this option will only become available after the CTBT's entry into force." See "Update on CTBTO Findings Related to the Announced Nuclear Test by North Korea," Preparatory Commission for CTBTO, March 12, 2013, http://www.ctbto.org/press-centre/ highlights/2013/update-on-ctbto-findings-related-to-the-announced-nuclear-test-by-north-korea.

Plutonium production. Although North Korea is not suspected of currently producing weapons-grade plutonium (WGP), it has a proven capability of doing so. To date, it has carried out four major rounds of plutonium reprocessing at its Yongbyon nuclear complex, beginning in the late 1980s. Estimates for North Korea's separated plutonium stockpile vary, although the range tends to be between 30 and 50 kilograms (kg). The South Korean Ministry of Defense's calculation that North Korea has fabricated approximately 40 kg of WGP since 1989 falls in the middle of this range.[20] The U.S. Department of Defense estimates that North Korea possesses around 50 kg of WGP.[21] North Korea declared in 2008 that it possessed 37 kg of WGP and subsequently claimed in 2009 to have weaponized 30.8 kg of its stockpile.[22] These claims have never been independently verified, and North Korea's true WGP stockpile remains a mystery, although it has likely decreased, perhaps significantly, as a result of its 2006 and 2009 nuclear tests.[23] (As stated above, at the time of writing, it remains unclear if the February 2013 detonation was of a plutonium device or marked the first test of a uranium device.) David Albright and Christina Walrond estimate in a 2012 report that the existing North Korean stockpile of WGP would be enough for 12–23 weapons.[24] Consequently, the regime's announcement in early April 2013 that it intended to restart the Yongbyon reactor to increase the "quantity and quality" of its nuclear arsenal would seem to indicate that Pyongyang may be concerned about its diminishing plutonium stockpile. Once North Korea restarts the Yongbyon reactor—a process that will likely take between 3 and 6 months[25]—Hecker estimates that it would be able to produce approximately one bomb's worth of plutonium per year.[26]

Uranium production. Growing evidence of a clandestine uranium-enrichment program has overshadowed earlier concerns about North

---

[20] Ministry of Defense (ROK), *2012 Defense White Paper* (Seoul, December 2012), 34.

[21] "Unclassified Report to Congress on Nuclear and Missile Programs of North Korea," Office of the DNI, August 8, 2007. More recent estimates from the U.S. intelligence community regarding North Korean stockpiles of fissile material remain classified.

[22] Larry A. Niksch, "North Korea's Nuclear Weapons Development and Diplomacy," Congressional Research Service, CRS Report for Congress, RL33590, January 5, 2010, 7.

[23] Nikitin, "North Korea's Nuclear Weapons: Technical Issues," 4–5.

[24] David Albright and Christina Walrond, "North Korea's Estimated Stocks of Plutonium and Weapon-Grade Uranium," Institute for Science and International Security, August 16, 2012, http://isis-online.org/uploads/isis-reports/documents/dprk_fissile_material_production_16Aug2012.pdf.

[25] For a three-month estimate, see ibid., 11. For an estimate of six to twelve months, see Samuel Burke, "Expert: North Korea Could Restart Yongbyon Nuclear Plant in Six Months to a Year," CNN, April 2, 2013, http://amanpour.blogs.cnn.com/2013/04/02/expert-north-korea-could-restart-yongbyon-nuclear-plant-in-six-months-to-a-year.

[26] Burke, "Expert: North Korea Could Restart Yongbyon."

Korea's plutonium program.[27] After years of vociferous denials regarding such a secret program, North Korea announced in 2009 that it had been successful in "developing uranium enrichment technology to provide fuel" for a new experimental light-water reactor.[28] Although Pyongyang initially reaffirmed its earlier assertion that the enrichment facility, which it had shown to Hecker's delegation in November 2010, would only produce 3.5% low-enriched uranium for use in an experimental light-water reactor currently under construction, Pyongyang stated in April 2013 that it would "use the uranium plant to make nuclear weapons."[29]

If the recent third nuclear test is verified to have been of a uranium device, it raises the prospect of a new source of weapons-grade nuclear material that North Korea could use for additional tests in a concerted effort to miniaturize a nuclear warhead and mate it to a reliable long-range delivery system. An active uranium-enrichment program would thus provide North Korea with a second pathway to such a weapon and remove a key constraint on conducting more nuclear tests—namely the country's small existing stockpile of fissile material.

The Yongbyon uranium-enrichment facility is estimated to possess 2,000 centrifuges (thought to be variants of the P-2 centrifuge) arrayed in six cascades.[30] Estimates regarding production rates or stockpiles of HEU are highly speculative due to uncertainties regarding the configuration, efficiency, and consistency with which the regime has operated the centrifuge cascades at the plant. Additional uncertainty arises from the potential existence of other clandestine uranium-enrichment facilities in North Korea, long regarded as a serious possibility given the country's apparent aptitude with the technology involved, as well as its previous acquisition of resources and components sufficient to build 10,000 centrifuges. Based on his observations of the Yongbyon uranium-enrichment plant, Hecker estimated that if the cascades were reconfigured, the facility could yield approximately 40 kg of HEU per year (see **Table 3** for an overview of North Korea's nuclear facilities).[31]

---

[27] Siegfried S. Hecker, "A Return Trip to North Korea's Yongbyon Nuclear Complex," Center for International Security and Cooperation, Stanford University, November 20, 2010, http://cisac.stanford.edu/publications/north_koreas_yongbyon_nuclear_complex_a_report_by_siegfried_s_hecker.

[28] "North Korea Sees Light-Water Reactor This Decade," Associated Press, March 30, 2010.

[29] Choe Sang-hun and Mark Landler, "North Korea Says It Will Restart Reactor to Expand Arsenal," *New York Times*, April 2, 2013, http://www.nytimes.com/2013/04/03/world/asia/north-korea-threatens-to-restart-nuclear-reactor.html.

[30] Hecker, "A Return Trip to North Korea's Yongbyon Nuclear Complex," 4.

[31] Ibid., 7.

TABLE 3   North Korean nuclear facilities

Location	Type/power capacity	Status	Production purpose
Yongbyon	• Graphite-moderated heavy-water experimental reactor • 5 MWe	Currently shut down, with the cooling tower destroyed in June 2009; restart announced in April 2013	Weapons-grade plutonium
Yongbyon	• Graphite-moderated heavy-water power reactor • 50 MWe	Never fully constructed; project halted since 1994	Stated to be electricity production; potentially could have been for weapons-grade plutonium
Yongbyon	• Experimental light-water reactor • 25–30 MWe	U.S. observers saw basic construction in November 2010; reactor dome in place on top of containment structure in summer 2012	Stated to be electricity production; potentially could have been for weapons-grade plutonium
Yongbyon	• Uranium-enrichment plant; approximately 2,000 P-2 centrifuges arrayed in six cascades*	Unknown/operational; facility revealed to a U.S. delegation in 2010	Weapons-grade uranium; reactor-fuel fabrication
Taechon	• Graphite-moderated heavy-water power reactor • 200 MWe	Never fully constructed; project halted since 1994	Stated to be electricity; potentially could have been for weapons-grade plutonium
Kumho District, Sinpo	• Four light-water reactors • 440 MWe	Part of the 1985 NPT deal with the Soviet Union but never fully constructed; Russia cancelled in 1992	Stated to be electricity; potentially could have been for weapons-grade plutonium
Kumho District, Sinpo	• Two light-water reactors • 1,000 MWe	Part of a reactor agreement in 1999 but never fully constructed; based on the Agreed Framework in 1994	Electricity

SOURCE: This table is derived from Mary Beth Nikitin, "North Korea's Nuclear Weapons: Technical Issues," Congressional Research Service (CRS), CRS Report for Congress, RL34256, April 3, 2013, 7; and David Albright and Christina Walrond, "North Korea's Estimated Stocks of Plutonium and Weapon-Grade Uranium," Institute for Science and International Security (ISIS), ISIS Report, August 16, 2012.

NOTE: Asterisk indicates that North Korea appears to have recently doubled the size of its uranium-enrichment facility, which would provide sufficient space to operate approximately 4,000 centrifuges.

Means of Delivery

According to an unclassified report submitted to Congress by the U.S. intelligence community, North Korea possesses "short- and medium-range missiles that could be fitted with nuclear weapons, but we do not know whether it has in fact done so."[32] Despite North Korea's threats in March 2013 to carry out a nuclear attack on the United States, there is still no definitive evidence that it has successfully mated a nuclear warhead to a proven long-range ballistic missile. The DPRK's missile arsenal includes several variants from the short-range Scud family, as well as the medium-range Nodong ballistic missile (see **Table 4**). North Korea has also deployed, but not yet tested, the Musudan medium-range ballistic missile that is estimated to have sufficient range to reach Guam (see **Figure 1**).

North Korea's efforts to develop a ballistic missile capable of striking targets at intercontinental range go back to the late 1990s. After a series of failed long-range Taepodong missile tests by the DPRK beginning in 1998, many U.S. analysts deemed the country to be many years away from mastering long-range rocket technology.[33] While North Korea still has to develop advanced guidance and re-entry capabilities for weapons purposes, the successful satellite launch in December 2012 marked the beginning of a new phase in its ongoing efforts to deploy an operational nuclear warhead capable of striking at intercontinental ranges. In addition to its continued development of the Taepodong intercontinental ballistic missile (ICBM), North Korea is thought to be developing a second road-mobile ICBM, dubbed the KN-08, which made its first appearance in a military parade celebrating the one hundredth anniversary of Kim Il-sung's birth. However, there is an ongoing debate over whether the KN-08 is a real system in development, as it appears that the mobile missiles on display in the parade were either mock-ups or at the very early stages of being operationalized. The U.S. director of national intelligence James Clapper stated in his testimony before a Senate panel in March 2013 that North Korea "displayed what appears to be a road-mobile ICBM…. We believe North Korea has already taken initial steps towards fielding this system, although it remains untested."[34]

While North Korea has achieved progress with its most recent nuclear test and long-range missile launch, a dominant view in the U.S. intelligence

---

[32] "Unclassified Report to Congress on Nuclear and Missile Programs of North Korea." See also Steven A. Hildreth, "North Korean Ballistic Missile Threat to the United States," Congressional Research Service, CRS Report for Congress, RS21473, February 24, 2009.

[33] Nikitin, "North Korea's Nuclear Weapons: Technical Issues."

[34] James R. Clapper, "Worldwide Threat Assessment of the U.S. Intelligence Community," testimony before the Senate Select Committee on Intelligence, March 12, 2013, available at http://www.intelligence.senate.gov/130312/clapper.pdf.

TABLE 4   North Korea's ballistic missile arsenal

Type	Range (km)	Number of launchers	Status
Toksa/KN-02	120	Fewer than 100	Operational
Hwasong-5/ SCUD-B	300		Operational
Hwasong-6/ SCUD-C	500		Operational
SCUD-ER	700–1,000		Operational
Rodong-1/ Nodong-1	1,300	Fewer than 50	Operational
Taepodong-1	2,500	–	In testing
Musudan/ Taepodong-X	2,500–4,000	Fewer than 50	Operational (yet to be tested)
Taepodong-2/ Unha-2/Unha-3	5,500+	–	Under development
KN-08	Unknown*	Unknown	Unknown

SOURCE: Office of the Secretary of Defense, *Annual Report to Congress: Military and Security Developments Involving the Democratic People's Republic of Korea 2012* (Washington, D.C., 2013), 15; ROK Ministry of Defense, *2012 Defense White Paper* (Seoul, December 2012), 356; "DOD News Briefing on Missile Defense from the Pentagon," U.S. Department of Defense, News Transcript, March 15, 2013, http://www.defense.gov/transcripts/transcript.aspx?transcriptid=5205; Duyeon Kim, "North Korea's Nuclear and Ballistic Missile Programs," Center for Arms Control and Non-Proliferation, Fact Sheet, July 18, 2013, http://armscontrolcenter.org/publications/factsheets/fact_sheet_north_korea_nuclear_and_missile_programs; and Charles P. Vick "North Korean Missiles: Taep'o-dong 1 (TD-1) Paeutudan-1," Federation of American Scientists, July 18, 2013, http://www.fas.org/nuke/guide/dprk/missile/td-1.htm.

NOTE: Asterisk indicates that the U.S. Department of Defense estimates that the KN-08 potentially possesses an intercontinental range.

community is that the regime is still some ways off from developing an operational nuclear capability. Responding to a report by the DIA that assessed with "moderate confidence" that North Korea was capable of mounting a nuclear warhead on a missile, Clapper issued a clarifying statement in which

FIGURE 1   Ranges of North Korean missiles

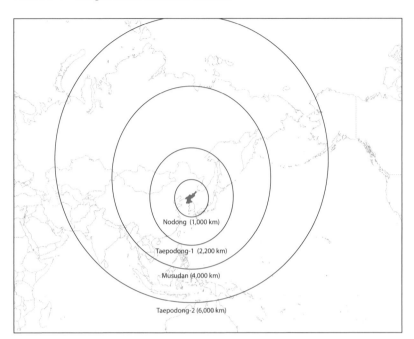

SOURCE: Data from Council on Foreign Relations.

he insisted that North Korea had "not yet demonstrated the full range of capabilities necessary for a nuclear-armed missile."[35]

In terms of other means of delivery, North Korea possesses around 80 Hong-5 light bombers (Chinese variants of the Ilyushin Il-28), which could conceivably be retrofitted to carry nuclear ordnance. However, these legacy aircrafts from the late 1940s would be highly vulnerable to modern aerial and ground-based air-defense systems.[36] It therefore seems unlikely that North Korea would choose to use bombers as a means of delivery. A more plausible tactical delivery method would be using radiological material in munitions for some of the more than 11,000 long-rang artillery tubes trained on Seoul.

North Korea's successful long-range missile test in December 2012 and third nuclear test in February 2013 dramatically elevated the status of its

---

[35] Clapper, "Worldwide Threat Assessment."

[36] Bruce E. Bechtol Jr., "Planning for the Unthinkable: Countering a North Korean Nuclear Attack and Management of Post-Attack Scenarios," *Korean Journal of Defense Analysis* 23, no. 1 (2011): 6.

nuclear program to a clear and direct danger to the U.S. homeland. The most visible trigger for this change in assessment was the dramatic improvement in North Korea's long-range ballistic missile capabilities following the high-profile failure of its previous test in April 2012. This leap in the test performance of the Unha-3 rocket raises questions about the regime's cooperation on advanced missile development with Iran. A major area of interest is the extent to which Iran may have shared the lessons it learned from the Russian company that helped develop its satellite launch capabilities. These commercially gained insights could provide critical assistance to North Korea as it seeks to address the next major hurdles to increasing the payload of its long-range missiles, improving its guidance system, and developing the re-entry capability necessary for a miniaturized nuclear warhead to reach its target.[37]

North Korea is also seeking to use each nuclear test as a means to miniaturize a warhead. Intelligence estimates on this endeavor vary widely due to a number of key factors, including uncertainty regarding the accuracy of the warhead designs the regime may have procured and the sealing of nuclear test tunnels. The latter factor has prevented the U.S. military from gathering isotope samples that would enable it to ascertain more details about the type of fissile material North Korea used.[38]

Although North Korea still must complete critical steps—miniaturizing a nuclear warhead that can survive re-entry into the atmosphere and mating it to a ballistic missile with expanded range, guidance, and payload capabilities—its successful satellite launch in December 2012 and nuclear test in February 2013 (the largest to date) have resulted in the international community regarding it as a de facto nuclear weapons state. Although the United States, South Korea, and Japan have reiterated that they will not accept such an outcome, in practice they have responded to the tests in a manner that is commensurate with a nuclear-capable North Korea. Until recently, Washington's primary threat concern was not North Korea's direct nuclear-strike capability but rather the prospect of the regime selling or transferring nuclear material to a party that could use it in a terrorist attack on the U.S. homeland. In light of recent developments, however, the focus of U.S. threat perceptions is likely to change further.

---

[37] John S. Park, "The Leap in North Korea's Ballistic Missile Program: The Iran Factor," National Bureau of Asian Research, NBR Analysis Brief, December 19, 2012, http://www.nbr.org/publications/issue. aspx?id=276.

[38] See "Update on CTBTO Findings."

The Role of Nuclear Weapons in North Korea's National Security Strategy

The purpose of nuclear weapons in North Korea's national security strategy has evolved drastically since the program's inception. Officially, North Korea's nuclear doctrine is to counter the United States' "hostile policy" with a nuclear deterrent. Pyongyang previously stated that it has a "no first use" policy, but that precedent was called into question when North Korea made an explicit threat in March 2013 to carry out a preemptive nuclear strike against the United States in response to the passage of UNSC Resolution 2094.[39] Setting aside the regime's rhetoric, however, North Korea appears to be continuing to employ a nuclear doctrine of minimal deterrence.[40] Indeed, given the apparent centrality of nuclear weapons to the regime's survival and the small size and highly vulnerable nature of the arsenal, it is unlikely that North Korea has developed a nuclear doctrine beyond that of limited reprisal, in the hopes that a retributive nuclear threat will be enough to safeguard the regime from "imperialist aggression."

As a pivotal instrument central to the North Korean regime's security strategy, the nuclear weapons program today serves the following key purposes:

- Deterring adversaries

- Creating a North Korean version of President Dwight Eisenhower's New Look policy

- Generating revenue for the regime from nuclear commerce

Deterring adversaries. As stated above, a common refrain from North Korean officials is that Saddam Hussein would still be in power today if he had developed nuclear weapons.[41] Although North Korea has cited the United States' "hostile policy" as justification for its nuclear arsenal, it has increasingly invoked its self-declared status as a nuclear weapons state in an effort to deter South Korea from retaliating in response to recent military provocations.

North Korea began to specifically reference the goal of leveraging its nuclear arsenal as a deterrent in the early 2000s, claiming that it was prompted to do so by the George W. Bush administration's designation of North Korea

---

[39] "Security Council Strengthens Sanctions on Democratic People's Republic of Korea, in Response to 12 February Nuclear Test, Security Council," UN Security Council, Press Release, March 7, 2013, http://www.un.org/News/Press/docs/2013/sc10934.doc.htm.

[40] John S. Park and Dong-Sun Lee, "North Korea's Nuclear Policy Behavior: Deterrence and Leverage," in *The Long Shadow: Nuclear Weapons and Security in 21st Century Asia*, ed. Muthiah Alagappa (Stanford: Stanford University Press, 2008), 278–79.

[41] Author's meetings with senior North Korean diplomats during Track 2 dialogues in summer 2011.

as a member of the "axis of evil."[42] Despite multilateral efforts to negotiate a comprehensive deal leading to peaceful nuclear rollback, North Korea conducted its first nuclear test in October 2006. As noted above, technical experts deemed the test unsuccessful due to its explosive yield of under one kiloton.[43] The DPRK appeared to dispel doubts about its nuclear capabilities, however, when its second nuclear test in May 2009 produced an estimated explosive yield of a few kilotons.[44]

These advancements in its nuclear capabilities have translated into emboldened rhetoric vis-à-vis South Korea. Following a limited artillery exchange between the two Koreas in November 2010, Pyongyang issued a striking statement as South Korean marines completed their unfinished live-fire artillery exercise in December.[45] It claimed that no country would dare retaliate against a nuclear-armed state.[46] In this instance, North Korea invoked its nuclear capability in an attempt to negate South Korea's superiority in technologically advanced conventional armaments.[47] Subsequently, the regime internally lauded its nuclear weapons advantage over South Korea during an escalation of tensions following the third nuclear test in February 2013.[48]

Creating a North Korean version of the New Look policy. A key aspect of Eisenhower's New Look policy was diverting funding from the military to the civilian economy during the post–World War II period in the United States.[49] Reliance on a massive conventional military force for deterrence was deemed to be extravagant in its use of valuable resources. This perspective informed the military dimension of Eisenhower's New Look policy, which stressed strategic nuclear weapons.[50] In the process, the United States sought

---

[42] Author's meetings with senior North Korean diplomats, 2011.

[43] Mary Beth Nikitin, Mark E. Manyin, Emma Chanlett-Avery, and Dick K. Nano, "North Korea's Second Nuclear Test: Implications of UN Security Council Resolution 1874," Congressional Research Service, CRS Report for Congress, R40684, April 15, 2010.

[44] "Statement by the Office of the Director of National Intelligence."

[45] Van Jackson, "Beyond Tailoring: North Korea and the Promise of Managed Deterrence," *Contemporary Security Policy* 33, no. 2 (2012): 299.

[46] Author's interview with a North Korean defector who previously served as a senior manager of a state trading company linked to the Korean People's Army (KPA), Seoul, February 20, 2013.

[47] The high degree of interoperability between the militaries of South Korea and the United States is an indicator of the advanced weapons capabilities of the ROK armed forces. Most of the major advanced military assets of the two allies were either patrolling or on standby as the ROK Marines completed their live-fire exercise in December 2010. See Kurt M. Campbell, "U.S. Policy Toward North Korea," testimony before the Senate Foreign Relations Committee, Washington, D.C., March 1, 2011, http://www.state.gov/p/eap/rls/rm/2011/03/157472.htm.

[48] Author's interview with a North Korean defector who previously directed a procurement unit of a KPA-linked state trading company, Seoul, February 22, 2013.

[49] Steven Metz, *Eisenhower as Strategist: The Coherent Use of Military Power in War and Peace* (Carlisle: Strategic Studies Institute, 1993), http://www.strategicstudiesinstitute.army.mil/pubs/summary.cfm?q=359.

[50] Ibid.

to maximize the strength of its deterrent while minimizing costs.[51] With a deteriorating conventional military force of over one million in uniform, North Korea derives a significant benefit from using its nuclear deterrent as an equalizer on the Korean Peninsula. With the sunk costs of the nuclear program committed decades ago, the regime's acceleration of efforts to increase the payload of its long-range ballistic missiles and miniaturize a nuclear warhead provides a cost-effective way to build the country's military strength and get more bang for its buck.[52] The North Korean regime appears to be focused on maintaining a minimal nuclear deterrent, but one with a mobile launch capability.[53] In this respect, current and projected North Korean nuclear and missile tests in the near term are likely to increase the quality rather than the quantity of its nascent arsenal.

Generating revenue for the regime from nuclear commerce. Pyongyang has also begun to use its nuclear expertise to generate revenue through illicit nuclear cooperation with other rogue states. In the mid-2000s, North Korean nuclear engineers and construction workers in Syria were closely monitored by Israel. The Pyongyang regime was essentially monetizing its experience in developing a nuclear program with an old, but durable, reactor design. The scale of North Korea's involvement in the Syrian nuclear program was staggering. In addition to supplying components, Pyongyang also provided a sizeable contingent of North Korean workers and technicians. Nuclear proliferation experts were alarmed by the comprehensive nature of the clandestine cooperation between the two pariah regimes given that it took place during a period of heightened monitoring of North Korea's activities.[54] In September 2007 the threat level became sufficient to trigger an Israeli surgical air strike that destroyed this Syrian reactor site.[55]

The precedent set by nuclear cooperation between North Korea and Syria, which is largely overlooked now, raises concerns about the potential for similar cooperation between North Korea and Iran. Pyongyang and Tehran's

---

[51] Jean Edward Smith, *Eisenhower in War and Peace* (New York: Random House, 2012).

[52] The North Korean people lost faith in their national currency, the won, following a sudden redenomination of the currency in November 2009 that essentially wiped out any savings. U.S. dollars and euros are the primary currencies used by regime elites. John S. Park, "North Korea's Currency Redenomination: A Tipping Point?" United States Institute of Peace (USIP), Briefing Memo, December 2009, http://www-previous.usip.org/publications/north-korea-s-currency-revaluation-tipping-point.

[53] The China Aerospace Science and Industry Corporation completed a sale of transporter erector launchers to the DPRK, which were prominently displayed during the April 2012 military parade in Pyongyang. "Final Report of the Panel of Experts Established Pursuant to Resolution 2050 (2012)," UN Security Council, S/2013/337, June 11, 2013, 80–84.

[54] "Background Briefing with Senior U.S. Officials on Syria's Covert Nuclear Reactor and North Korea's Involvement," Office of the DNI, April 24, 2008, http://www.dni.gov/files/documents/Newsroom/Speeches%20and%20Interviews/20080424_interview.pdf.

[55] Ibid.

long-established track record of cooperation on ballistic missile commerce and development represents a set of proven capabilities that could be quickly applied in the nuclear sphere—if the two sides have not already done so.[56] In many respects, the major considerations for the North Korean and Iranian leaderships would be political rather than technical. One feature that is unique to potential North Korea–Iran nuclear cooperation is the opportunity for Iran to pay in the form of stockpiled oil. The country's oil stockpiles have grown as a result of U.S.-led efforts to pressure Tehran to resume nuclear talks.[57]

In terms of domestic constraints on North Korea's nuclear weapons development activities, the most significant has been resources. In order to finance its nuclear weapons development program, the regime primarily focused on generating funds by operating North Korean state trading companies. Despite increasing financial sanctions on North Korea, analysts have not been able to discern any major disruption to its nuclear programs.[58] North Korea's booming bilateral trade with China has overshadowed targeted sanctions efforts by the United States and the international community—particularly in North Korea's mineral-extraction sector. The coal trade with China started increasing significantly in the mid-2000s after a delegation led by then premier Wu Yi signed mining-sector deals intended to help stabilize the North Korean economy and aid economic development efforts in the Chinese provinces bordering the DPRK.[59] After a series of initial setbacks, including Chinese companies exiting agreements due to sudden changes in terms by the North Korean side, new business partnerships eventually began to gain traction in the late 2000s. The clearest sign of this improvement was the growing transport of coal across the border into China.

The coal trade disproportionately benefits the elites in North Korea. In instances where it does not directly boost regime coffers for WMD programs, it frees up other resources for this purpose. In many respects, the coal trade has characteristics akin to the diamond trade in conflict zones in Africa, where key groups have exchanged diamonds for weapons and ammunition. In the North Korean case, the phenomenon could be called "conflict coal."[60]

---

[56] Park, "The Leap in North Korea's Ballistic Missile Program."

[57] "North Korea Seeking Iran Oil, Oil Minister," Islamic Republic News Agency, April 20, 2013.

[58] Leon V. Sigal, "How North Korea Evades Financial Sanctions," 38 North, May 3, 2013, http://38north. org/2013/05/lsigal050313/#_edn7.

[59] Dick K. Nanto and Mark E. Manyin, "China-North Korea Relations," Congressional Research Service, CRS Report for Congress, R41043, December 28, 2010, 10–18, http://www.fas.org/sgp/crs/row/ R41043.pdf.

[60] In response to a question about how the North Korean regime arranged and ran the coal trade with Chinese partners, as well as about how it used proceeds from this trade to procure specific components for WMD programs, a defector explained a transactional pattern that mirrored how "conflict diamonds" funded the acquisition of weapons in war-torn areas in western Africa. Author's interview with a North Korean defector, Seoul, February 20, 2013.

Revenues generated from this trading pattern constitute a key driver of further development of North Korea's nuclear weapons program.

The Global and Regional Impact of North Korea's Nuclear Capabilities

The Elusive Nature of Deterrence Strategy

British deterrence expert Lawrence Freedman observed that deterrence strategy "is a gift to strategists in that its nature and workings remain so elusive and so imperfectly understood as to permit endless speculation with little danger of empirical refutation."[61] North Korea traditionally made the perfect gift to strategists for these same reasons. For policymakers, on the other hand, the application of deterrence strategy to North Korea presents an increasingly complex dilemma, particularly after the regime's belligerence turned kinetic during two provocations against South Korea in 2010. What makes an analysis of deterrence strategy more challenging in the North Korean case is the fact that in many respects the DPRK does not function like a nation-state. The entity that the international community refers to as North Korea is in practice a regime that constitutes 1% of the population and exists to preserve the Kim family's rule.[62] The nuclear weapons program is a direct extension of the Kim family, resulting in significant differences when evaluating the calculus related to the various forms of stability.[63]

At its core, North Korea has shifted from using its plutonium-based weapons program as a bargaining chip for a grand deal containing concessions in return for peaceful nuclear rollback. By further developing its uranium-enrichment program, the regime has made strides in launching a second pathway to miniaturizing a nuclear warhead. As a self-declared nuclear weapons state, North Korea announced its willingness in April 2013 to engage in negotiations to give up its nuclear weapons if the United States

---

[61] Keith Payne, "Deterrence and Stability Beyond 'New START'" (paper delivered at the Symposium on "21st Century Deterrence Challenges" at the U.S. Strategic Command, Omaha, August 3, 2011), available at http://www.newparadigmsforum.com/NPFtestsite/?p=1029.

[62] The 99% of North Koreans who constitute the general population are carving out an existence through expanding commercial interactions in previously banned informal markets. USIP conference on "Informal Markets and Peacebuilding in North Korea," July 19, 2011, http://www.usip.org/events/informal-markets-and-peacebuilding-in-north-korea.

[63] In terms of potential internal threats to the regime, Daniel Byman and Jennifer Lind argue that the Kim family has utilized three tools of authoritarian control in North Korea: "restrictive social policies that prevent potentially hostile social classes from forming and create society's dependence on the state; manipulation of ideas and information to increase the regime's legitimacy and weaken that of potential opponents; and the heavy use of force to deter or crush potential resistance." See Daniel L. Byman and Jennifer Lind, "Pyongyang's Survival Strategy: Tools of Authoritarian Control in North Korea," International Security 35, no. 1 (2010): 47.

reciprocated. Although Washington did not treat this offer seriously, the announcement revealed a core priority for Pyongyang—initiating nuclear arms control talks with the United States. This North Korean pivot in nuclear policy—from using the nuclear weapons program as a bargaining chip in negotiating a grand deal centered on denuclearization to leveraging it as the basis of nuclear arms control talks—significantly alters the dynamics of deterrence stability, crisis stability, arms-race stability, and political stability.

With respect to deterrence stability, the regime continues to justify its nuclear weapons development activities as a means to counter the United States' alleged long-standing "hostile policy." In further assessing the regional impact of North Korea's nuclear capabilities, it is important to first address the lingering shadow cast by North Korea's two provocations against South Korea in 2010. Did these acts denote the failure of deterrence?[64] Although the progress of the DPRK's nuclear weapons development activities may have emboldened it to carry out provocations against South Korea, a larger factor was Pyongyang's enhanced confidence at the time resulting from closer party-to-party ties between the Workers' Party of Korea (WPK) and the Communist Party of China (CPC). A clear manifestation of this relationship is the increasing bilateral trade between North Korea and China, which in 2011 reached $6 billion.[65] As a result, North Korea has noted that China has called on all parties—particularly South Korea—to exercise restraint following recent periods of rising tensions triggered by North Korean behavior. China's priority is to prevent a larger escalation, which it believes the involved parties will not be able to control or manage. In practice, the result is a situation where North Korea evades retaliation by South Korea. China's priority focus on preventing escalation is, in effect, unintentionally contributing to a situation where the credibility of South Korean deterrence is eroded and North Korea's view of its own deterrence capability is inflated.

The Global Impact of North Korea's Nuclear Capabilities

The primary global impact of North Korea's nuclear program has been the increased likelihood of the regime proliferating nuclear weapons material or technology to other state and nonstate actors. How do we evaluate this impact in terms of deterrence stability, crisis stability, arms-race stability, and political stability? For nuclear aspirants, North Korea's path to nuclear weapons development provides a blueprint of sorts for structuring a program,

---

[64] For further discussion of this question, see Ken Jimbo, "Did Deterrence Against North Korea Fail in 2010?" Center for U.S.-Korea Policy, Asia Foundation, Newsletter, July 2011, http://www.asiafoundation.org/resources/pdfs/CUSKPNewsletter37July2011.pdf.

[65] "2011 PRC-DPRK Trade Figures," PRC Ministry of Commerce, available at http://english.mofcom.gov.cn/article/statistic.

devising drawn-out negotiation tactics that buy time, and utilizing highly effective techniques to evade sanctions.[66] Two aspects of the North Korean regime's activities, in particular, do not bode well for nonproliferation and counterproliferation efforts.

The first is the regime's management of smuggling networks. Sheena Chestnut has identified a "major shift in North Korean smuggling during the 1990s from a state-operated network to one that relies on criminal networks over which the DPRK has decreased control."[67] During the current period of power consolidation in Pyongyang, these smuggling networks provide different groups an opportunity to increase their coffers amid intense competition for access and influence with the inner circle of the Kim family.[68] How this tension between power-consolidation efforts (centralization) and the growth of different elite groups' smuggling networks (decentralization) plays out will have serious implications in terms of potential proliferation patterns.

The second aspect is the North Korean regime's transmission of tacit knowledge. Alexander Montgomery defines tacit knowledge as "knowledge that cannot be formulated in words or symbols, but must be learned through trial and error, potentially under the direct tutelage of someone who has already learned it; nuclear weapons design and production in particular depends heavily on such knowledge."[69] The collaboration between North Korea and Syria is a clear example of the transmission of tacit knowledge. Given the regime's documented track record of having supplied and assisted Syria in constructing a nuclear reactor under suspect conditions, North Korea's relations with Iran are now the focus of increased scrutiny by nuclear experts. In light of the two countries' established missile cooperation, there is strong concern about possible cooperation through coping mechanisms between two national nuclear programs that are targets of extensive sanctions.

---

[66] "Final Report of the Panel of Experts Submitted Pursuant to Resolution 1985 (2011)," UN Security Council, S/2012/422, June 2012.

[67] Sheena Chestnut, "Illicit Activity and Proliferation: North Korean Smuggling Networks," *International Security* 32, no. 1 (2007): 83.

[68] John S. Park, "North Korea, Inc.: Gaining Insights into North Korean Regime Stability from Recent Commercial Activities," USIP, Working Paper, April 22, 2009, 8–11, http://www.usip.org/publications/north-korea-inc-gaining-insights-north-korean-regime-stability-recent-commercial-activitie.

[69] Alexander H. Montgomery, "Ringing in Proliferation: How to Dismantle an Atomic Bomb Network," *International Security* 30, no. 2 (2005): 176–77.

The Regional Impact on South Korea's Latent Nuclear Capabilities

The primary regional impact of North Korea's nascent nuclear weapons capabilities is growing adventurism vis-à-vis South Korea.[70] During the two provocations against South Korea in 2010, North Korean military actions led to the deaths of 50 South Korean nationals—46 sailors, 2 marines, and 2 civilians. Pyongyang's forward march to developing a nuclear weapons arsenal with fixed and mobile launchers raises U.S. concerns about the prospects of South Korea turning its latent nuclear capabilities into a nuclear deterrent in response.[71]

There are two main factors behind these concerns. First, South Korea under President Park Chung-hee launched a nascent nuclear weapons program in the early 1970s after facing growing uncertainty about the U.S. security commitment. In an effort to bring U.S. involvement in the war in Vietnam to an "honorable" conclusion, President Richard Nixon unveiled the Nixon Doctrine in July 1969. While the United States would keep all its treaty commitments with allies and provide a nuclear shield for them, allies had to assume primary responsibility for providing troops for their own defense.[72] Washington's announcement of drastic reductions to the levels of U.S. troops stationed in South Korea sowed insecurity among senior members of the Park government. Ultimately, the U.S. threat to completely withdraw its troops and cut off development aid to the fledgling South Korean economy proved to be effective in rolling back South Korea's nuclear ambitions.[73] However, President Park Chung-hee's nascent nuclear weapons program continues to cast a lingering shadow on the Korean Peninsula.[74]

---

[70] This subsection draws on NTI, "Country Profiles: South Korea," July 2013, http://www.nti.org/country-profiles/south-korea.

[71] Complex U.S.-ROK nuclear negotiations—related to the confluence of Seoul's push for a closed nuclear fuel cycle, a bilateral nuclear cooperation agreement pending renewal, and the credibility of the U.S. extended deterrence guarantee in Seoul—have placed South Korea's latent nuclear capabilities in a different light in Washington. Senior U.S. policymakers are giving these latent capabilities serious consideration. Mark Holt, for example, argues that "the United States is concerned about the nuclear weapons proliferation implications of such an expansion of enrichment and reprocessing, along with its potential impact on other security issues on the Korean peninsula." See Mark Holt, "U.S. and South Korean Cooperation in the World Nuclear Energy Market: Major Policy Considerations," Congressional Research Service, CRS Report for Congress, R41032, June 25, 2013, 1.

[72] Robert Litwak, *Détente and the Nixon Doctrine: American Foreign Policy and the Pursuit of Stability, 1969–1976* (Cambridge: Cambridge University Press, 1984), 122.

[73] Rebecca K.C. Hersman and Robert Peters, "Nuclear U-Turns: Learning from South Korean and Taiwanese Rollback," *Nonproliferation Review* 13, no. 3 (2006): 540–41.

[74] Recent publications explore President Park's nuclear weapons development program in more detail. See, for example, Byung-Kook Kim and Ezra F. Vogel, eds., *The Park Chung Hee Era: The Transformation of South Korea* (Cambridge: Harvard University Press, 2011); and Peter Hayes, Chung-in Moon, and Scott Bruce, "Park Chung Hee, the U.S.-ROK Strategic Relationship, and the Bomb," *Asia-Pacific Journal*, October 31, 2011.

Second, lacking indigenous sources of energy, South Korea began construction of its first power plant in 1970 as part of an extensive civilian nuclear energy industry designed to help fuel rapid economic development. Since 1974, South Korea has been bound by a bilateral accord with the United States banning the reprocessing of spent nuclear fuel. With the March 2014 expiration of this accord looming, South Korea has sought to lift this ban.[75] Despite the 1992 Joint Declaration on the Denuclearization of the Korean Peninsula, whereby Seoul and Pyongyang agreed neither "to manufacture, possess, store, deploy, or use nuclear weapons" nor to "possess nuclear reprocessing and uranium enrichment facilities," many nuclear experts assert that the fact that South Korea never officially renounced its obligations under the declaration following North Korea's nuclear weapons tests in 2006, 2009, and 2013 does not necessarily constitute an ironclad guarantee of South Korea's non–nuclear weapons status.[76]

After decades of running 23 civilian nuclear power plants that have accounted for over a third of the country's annual electricity production in recent years, South Korea has accumulated considerable stockpiles of nuclear waste. In proliferation terms, these stockpiles underpin South Korea's advanced latent capabilities to develop nuclear weapons.[77] Given these stockpiles and the country's ambition to become a global power in the civilian nuclear industry, South Korea is seeking the United States' consent to use pyroprocessing technology. South Korea's primary position is that this new technology would enable it to deal with its more than 10,000 tons of nuclear waste, currently housed in storage facilities that are expected to reach capacity by 2016. Nonproliferation experts, however, assert that pyroprocessing is not significantly different from reprocessing and that South Korea could use this technology to quickly convert nuclear waste into weapons-grade plutonium.[78]

External and domestic factors informing South Korea's future approach to nuclear weapons. One external factor that could contribute to a transformation of South Korea's latent capabilities into a nuclear deterrent is North Korea's sudden and remarkable progress with both the launch of a long-range ballistic missile and the third nuclear test. Although South Korea has faced the threat of a large-scale North Korean conventional attack for decades, its advanced conventional weapons systems and the U.S. guarantee of extended deterrence have underwritten a strong sense of confidence that the ROK has the means

---

[75] "United States–Republic of Korea Agreement for Peaceful Nuclear Cooperation Extension," U.S. Department of State, Press Release, April 24, 2013.

[76] NTI, "Country Profiles: South Korea."

[77] Ibid.

[78] "S. Korea Renews 'Firm Commitment' to Enriching Uranium in Talks with U.S.," Yonhap News Agency, June 3, 2013.

to deter North Korea. However, the North's recent and unexpected leaps in its nuclear weapons and delivery capabilities have created the perception in South Korea of a security gap.

A domestic factor influencing Seoul's nuclear strategy is the early-stage but growing public support for the idea that South Korea should develop its own nuclear weapons to counterbalance North Korea's advancements. In annual surveys conducted by the Asan Institute for Policy Studies, South Korean public support for a domestic nuclear weapons program increased from 56% in 2010 to 66% in 2013, following North Korea's third nuclear test.[79] What is remarkable is that among South Korea's deeply partisan political groups, there is broad support for such a program grounded in "sovereignty-based arguments."[80]

While the possibility that South Korea will actually embark on the path of nuclear proliferation is remote, the robust debate on the acquisition of nuclear weapons initially seemed to raise larger questions about the South Korean public's view of the credibility of U.S. extended deterrence.[81] However, as former South Korean political leaders explained at international conferences convened in Seoul, the thrust of these views was actually aimed at China. Frustrated with North Korea's cycle of broken agreements followed by increasingly frequent provocations against the South, ROK public opinion leaders wanted to send a clear message to Chinese policymakers. The possibility of a South Korean nuclear deterrent was intended to pressure China to take Seoul's concerns seriously and use its leverage with North Korea to effect peaceful denuclearization and secure an end to attacks on South Korea.[82]

Implications of a future decision by South Korea to develop its latent nuclear capabilities. Should South Korea decide to develop a nuclear deterrent, there are two major implications. First, such a decision by South Korea would trigger a host of sanctions and punitive measures from the United States and the international community for its violation of NPT commitments and IAEA safeguards agreements. The alliance with the United States would be fundamentally altered, and the future status of U.S. military personnel on the Korean Peninsula would be uncertain. Moreover, for an economic powerhouse tightly integrated with the global financial and trading systems, such measures

---

[79] Kim, Friedhoff, and Kang, "The Fallout: South Korean Public Opinion," 7.

[80] Ibid., 8.

[81] Jackson, "Tailored Deterrence," 292.

[82] Remarks made by Han Sung-joo, the former ROK minister of foreign affairs and trade, and Lee Hong-koo, the former ROK prime minister, at "Plenary Session 1: A World Free of Nuclear Weapons—A Bold Dream vs. A Reality in the Making" (Asan Plenum 2011 on "Our Nuclear Future," Seoul, June 13–15, 2011).

would present a major shock to the South Korean economy. Second, South Korea's nuclearization could trigger Japan to also pursue nuclear weapons, given that Japan would then be the sole country without nuclear weapons in Northeast Asia. Domestic pressure to respond to the situation would put Japanese political leaders in a difficult position. Despite Tokyo's security alliance with Washington—which includes coverage under U.S. extended deterrence—internal calls to acquire nuclear weapons for defensive purposes would grow rapidly. Current efforts by the Abe government to revise the Japanese constitution to permit preemption in self-defense—inspired by ongoing disputes with China over islands in the East China Sea and North Korea's expanding nuclear and missile capabilities—could create the initial opening that provides domestic political logic for adopting a nuclear deterrent.

U.S. Policy Implications

South Korea Goes Nuclear

For the United States, a South Korean decision to convert the country's latent nuclear capabilities into a nuclear deterrent would largely undermine Washington's long-standing effort to achieve peaceful denuclearization in North Korea. The collapse of this pillar of U.S. policy in Northeast Asia would also undermine coordination among member countries of the dormant six-party talks. With two nuclear Koreas, the United States would be closely scrutinized for how it dealt with both proliferants on the peninsula. An *ad hoc* and inconsistent U.S. approach regarding sanctions relief would adversely affect U.S. credibility in a rapidly evolving region, thereby complicating delicate negotiations with Beijing on rolling back North Korea's minimal nuclear deterrent. The Chinese government's stance would likely be more uniform, expressing clear and unqualified opposition to both Koreas' nuclear weapons arsenals.

These nuclear dynamics on the Korean Peninsula would frame a policy debate in Japan on the acquisition of nuclear weapons in terms of a legitimate self-defense posture. In doing so, Japan's decades-old nuclear weapons allergy would likely dissipate.[83] South Korea's efforts to find security through nuclearization would thus trigger an increasingly complex process whereby neighboring countries recalibrated and adjusted their positions. As a result, the United States would find itself at the center of policy responses that would significantly complicate efforts to manage its relationships in the region.

---

[83] Michael J. Green and Katsuhisa Furukawa, "New Ambitions, Old Obstacles: Japan and Its Search for an Arms Control Strategy," *Arms Control Today*, July/August 2000, http://www.armscontrol.org/act/2000_07-08/japanjulaug.

The North Korea Variable

During the current process of power consolidation in Pyongyang, the regime's approach to nuclear weapons provides an insight into what is likely to continue in the near term. Increasingly dependent on a variety of Chinese partners—ranging from the central and provincial CPC leadership groups to provincial state-owned mining companies and private commercial firms—the Kim Jong-un regime now has the opportunity to further pursue a North Korean version of Eisenhower's New Look policy. At its core, the regime's strategic policy focuses on the self-proclaimed potency of North Korea's minimal nuclear deterrent—irrespective of the fact that the regime still has significant technical hurdles to overcome before realizing a fully operational nuclear arsenal. By doing so, North Korea achieves two important tactical goals. The first goal—an external one—is to compensate for a rapidly deteriorating conventional military force that, although a massive size, chronically lacks spare parts and fuel. In North Korean propaganda, South Korea is not deemed to be in the same advanced military category as the North—that is, a member of the elite club of nuclear weapons states. South Korea's technologically advanced weaponry is merely labeled as conventional armaments. Lacking nuclear weapons, South Korea is viewed by the North as being increasingly dependent on the U.S. nuclear umbrella.[84]

The second tactical goal—an internal one—is to free scarce resources to stabilize the decrepit national economy. Rather than economic reform, the initial step would be rudimentary economic stabilization. The primary motivation is not to improve the lives of the general population. Instead, the plan appears to be directed at creating more opportunities for elite North Korean state trading companies to trade and invest with different partners—first from China and then from other countries—to gradually reduce North Korea's dependence on its Chinese neighbor. A key prerequisite for such basic economic stabilization is diverting substantial resources away from the military, which has enjoyed the benefits of the military-first (*songun*) policy launched and managed by Kim Jong-il during his seventeen-year rule, and redistributing them to the WPK. The unique discernible feature of the Kim Jong-un regime's ongoing power consolidation is the redistribution of military-held economic concessions to the party, as well as the removal of Kim Jong-il's generals and the installment of WPK-linked senior officials in

---

[84] Author's interview with a North Korean defector, February 20, 2013.

top military posts.[85] In a concerted effort to restore the WPK to the central role in the power structure that it had occupied during the rule of Kim Il-sung, the Kim Jong-un leadership group will need to achieve an operational minimal nuclear deterrent. By doing so, it could then fully shift to economic stabilization activities. The priority of this goal translates into a greater likelihood of more nuclear and long-range missile tests.

In this environment, the strategic patience and financial sanctions that provide the basis for the current U.S. policy represent different pathways to the same destination—the sidelines. In order to change the calculus for North Korea in terms of seeking substantive denuclearization negotiations with the United States and other members of the six-party talks, Washington needs to actively explore and implement programs aimed at disrupting the activities of elite North Korean state trading companies engaged in generating critical revenues through the coal trade and procuring sensitive components for the WMD programs. An urgent undertaking for policymakers and analysts is to develop a better understanding of how "North Korea, Inc." operates.[86] While leadership dynamics in Pyongyang were once a black box, analysts can now discern much more by reading the barometer of state trading-company activities in commercial hubs in China. The regime, which comprises only 1% of the overall North Korean population, is increasingly operating within the Chinese national economy and using its gateways to access busy ports in Southeast Asia.[87]

As the resource needs of the regime grow, the probability of lucrative nuclear cooperation reoccurring between North Korea and other rogue states rises significantly. The next likely candidate partner is Iran. With already well-established routes and modalities for facilitating cooperation on ballistic missile development, North Korea and Iran have the building blocks to replicate that pattern of interaction in nuclear cooperation. Should this transpire, Washington would then be faced with the prospect of the two states' nuclear endeavors fusing into one. The nonproliferation and counterproliferation efforts of the United States and the international community would fall farther behind should Pyongyang and Tehran apply their respective technical expertise, components, and resources to form an effective coping mechanism through which they could advance their nuclear ambitions.

---

[85] The removal of Kim Jong-il's general, Vice Marshal Ri Yong-ho, and the appointment of Vice Marshal Choe Ryong-hae as head of the KPA's General Political Bureau and vice-chair of the WPK's Central Military Commission supports this analysis. Vice Marshal Choe is not a career military officer but rather is a senior WPK official. Author's interview with a North Korean defector, February 21, 2013.

[86] For more on this point, see Park, "North Korea, Inc."

[87] Author's interview with a North Korean defector, February 23, 2013.

Conclusion

North Korea's nuclear weapons program has evolved to be a multipurpose instrument of the regime's security strategy. The regime has employed this instrument to deter adversaries, generate revenue for itself from nuclear commerce, and create a North Korean version of Eisenhower's New Look policy. With respect to the latter purpose, Pyongyang appears to be improving its nuclear arsenal as a means to compensate for a rapidly deteriorating conventional military resulting from chronic internal constraints related to a domestic economy that lacks basic infrastructure. Should North Korea continue on this course, the likely outcome will be more nuclear tests to miniaturize a warhead design, as well as additional ballistic missile launches to increase range and payload. The regional and global consequences of such developments would be grave.

Of particular concern is growing public support in South Korea for a domestic nuclear weapons program. South Korea's well-developed latent capabilities make a decision to pursue a nuclear deterrent more a political than a technical matter. Rising public support for the nuclear option implicitly raises difficult questions about the credibility of U.S. extended deterrence guarantees to South Korea. If the South Korean public were satisfied with these guarantees, why would polls and surveys reveal increasing support for an indigenous nuclear deterrent?

Washington could bridge this gap by going back to the source of recent security re-evaluations in Seoul—North Korea's proliferation activity. If the United States is determined to preserve regional stability rooted in its provision of extended deterrence to South Korea and Japan, it will need to do more to disrupt the regime's channels for generating revenue and procuring sensitive components for its WMD programs. Washington's inability to significantly disrupt these channels could result in a North Korean regime that possesses strategic procurement partnerships with other regimes and a nuclear deterrent capable of reaching and threatening the security of the U.S. homeland.

A deeper understanding of the activities of North Korean state trading companies would provide operational insights that the United States could then use to fashion new policy tools aimed specifically at disrupting procurement channels for North Korea's WMD programs. In particular, incentivizing private companies that serve as middlemen in procurement transactions—most of which are based in China—is a starting point. A program offering monetary rewards in return for information leading to the interdiction of North Korea–bound components transiting busy ports in Southeast Asia would present these companies with the opportunity to earn a double payment: a commission fee from their North Korean client and a monetary reward from the counterproliferation program. Such a U.S.-led multilateral effort could significantly delay—and potentially prevent—further advancements by North Korea toward fully operationalizing its nuclear arsenal and thus create significant setbacks in the Kim Jong-un regime's bid to create its version of the New Look.

EXECUTIVE SUMMARY

This chapter assesses Iran's potential to develop nuclear weapons, the nature of its nuclear decision-making, and the possible consequences and policy implications of Iran's nuclear choices.

MAIN ARGUMENT:
Iran may already possess the ability to produce nuclear weapons, but for the time being Tehran appears content to continue gradually advancing its nuclear program while remaining within the Nuclear Non-Proliferation Treaty. Iran's nuclear decision-makers are guided by three principal considerations: the security of the regime, Iranian international prestige and influence, and their own particular interests. The U.S. and its partners will need to address all three of these factors to convince Iranian leaders to agree to verifiable limitations on Iran's nuclear program.

POLICY IMPLICATIONS:
- Any successful negotiating offer by the P5+1 countries will have to accept Iran's limited possession of the fuel cycle and provide a clear path to lifting sanctions.

- Iranian leaders are unlikely to support any deal unless the U.S. can effectively reassure them that it does not seek regime change. As a result, military threats and covert attacks can reduce the chances for a negotiated settlement.

- Air strikes can set back Iran's program by years but cannot destroy it. An attack against Iran's nuclear facilities could provoke retaliation, trigger regional unrest, and convince the regime to double down on its nuclear efforts.

- A nuclear-armed Iran would be most likely to use nuclear weapons if the leadership were to believe a direct attack against the regime is imminent.

- Major Asian states, especially China and India, have interests in Iran that diverge from those of the U.S. and complicate nonproliferation efforts. The U.S. must work to address the security concerns of these states, specifically over energy security, to maintain their support for U.S. policies.

Iran's Nuclear Ambitions: Motivations, Trajectory, and Global Implications

Robert Reardon

This chapter assesses Iran's potential to develop a nuclear weapons arsenal, the factors that shape its nuclear decision-making process, and the likely regional and global consequences of Iran's nuclear choices. Tehran likely already possesses the technical wherewithal to produce nuclear weapons if it chose to do so. Over the long term, the central issue is not whether Iran can develop nuclear weapons but whether it will opt to do so.

For the next year, and possibly longer, it is unlikely that Iran will develop a nuclear arsenal.[1] But although currently limited by the inability to produce uranium fuel for a bomb quickly enough to avoid detection, Iran is working steadily to shorten the time it would need for a nuclear "breakout." For the time being, Tehran appears content to slowly advance its nuclear capabilities while remaining within the Nuclear Non-Proliferation Treaty (NPT). However, it is unclear what the regime's ultimate intentions are—that is, whether Tehran intends to acquire weapons or would be content to remain just below the threshold of weaponization. It is additionally unclear what the

Robert Reardon is a Research Fellow with the Project on Managing the Atom and the International Security Program in the Belfer Center for Science and International Affairs at the Harvard Kennedy School. He can be reached at <robert.reardon@hks.harvard.edu>.

[1] President Barack Obama recently stated, "We think it would take over a year or so for Iran to actually develop a nuclear weapon." See Michael D. Shear and David E. Sanger, "Iran Nuclear Weapon to Take Year or More, Obama Says," *New York Times*, March 14, 2013. This statement is consistent with the 2007 and 2010 National Intelligence Estimates. See "Iran: Nuclear Intentions and Capabilities," Office of the Director of National Intelligence, National Intelligence Estimate, November 2007; and James R. Clapper, "Unclassified Statement for the Record on the Worldwide Threat Assessment of the U.S. Intelligence Community," statement presented before the Senate Select Committee on Intelligence, January 31, 2012.

capabilities and force posture of Iran's arsenal would be if the country were to acquire nuclear weapons.

Iran faces complex strategic trade-offs in any nuclear future it may choose to pursue. Over the long term, its nuclear status will depend on how Iranian decision-makers view the nuclear program in the context of the country's regional and global interests, and even more importantly its security and domestic stability. If Iran is intent on acquiring nuclear weapons, the United States and its allies may delay but likely cannot permanently prevent Iran from doing so.

The Iranian nuclear issue therefore presents more a long-term problem than a short-term crisis and will require effective policymaking on the part of the United States. Even if Iran forgoes nuclear weapons, it will likely retain the knowledge and technical base to make them. Long-term confidence about Tehran's nuclear intentions will require comprehensive safeguards and assurances, likely more than the regime is currently willing to provide. If Iran develops either nuclear weapons or a virtual nuclear capability, an international effort will be required to maintain regional stability, prevent further proliferation, uphold the integrity of the international nonproliferation regime, avoid miscalculation and unintended conflict, and contain Iranian regional ambitions.

This chapter proceeds as follows. The first section outlines Iran's nuclear decision-making process and identifies the principal drivers of its nuclear choices. The next section describes the history of the Iranian nuclear program, its major elements and achievements to date, and the conditions that could convince Iran to remain below the weapons threshold. The subsequent two sections look, first, at the potential regional and global impact if Iran were to acquire nuclear weapons and, second, at how the United States and its allies might either prevent Iran from acquiring nuclear weapons or, failing to do so, effectively contain a nuclear-armed Iran and maintain regional stability. The final section concludes by arguing that regardless of the nuclear path Iran takes, the United States and its allies will be faced with long-term challenges to their efforts to promote regional stability and maintain the international nonproliferation regime.

Iran's Nuclear Decision-making

Iran's nuclear decisions are driven by a rational consideration of costs and benefits in the context of the broader interests of the regime.[2] Iranian

---

[2] The U.S. intelligence community has assessed that "Iran's nuclear decisionmaking is guided by a cost-benefit approach." See Clapper, "Unclassified Statement for the Record on the Worldwide Threat Assessment of the U.S. Intelligence Community."

decision-makers face a number of complex incentives and disincentives to pursuing nuclear weapons. The strategic context is an important driver, but it is not the only one. Iraq's nonconventional weapons programs likely inspired Iran's revival of its nuclear efforts in the 1980s. Since that time, however, the strategic environment has changed considerably, and the Iranian nuclear program has become more closely tied to other regime interests such as international prestige and domestic legitimacy. There are a number of important costs to the country's nuclear development, not least because the regime's efforts to acquire the means to produce nuclear weapons have been met with hard-hitting economic sanctions, diplomatic and political isolation, and military threats. The following discussion analyzes both the external and internal influences on Iran's nuclear decision-making.

External Influences

Iran's leaders likely believe that nuclear weapons can enhance the country's security against conventionally superior adversaries like the United States and deter an attack on Iranian territory or an attempt to overthrow the regime by force. Iran considers U.S. forces in the region to be a potential threat to the regime. A small nuclear arsenal with relatively poor delivery capabilities, or perhaps even a virtual or ambiguous nuclear capability, could deter a U.S. attack on Iran under most circumstances in which U.S. vital interests were not at stake. Tehran may also see nuclear weapons as potential leverage for increasing its regional influence. Iran has long considered itself the natural hegemon of the Persian Gulf and has consistently demanded both more input in regional security and the withdrawal of U.S. forces. Conversely, the United States and its allies in the Gulf Cooperation Council (GCC) have worked to marginalize Iran and deny it any role in regional security arrangements. Confronted with the possibility of a nuclear-armed Iran, the GCC states would have a greater incentive to accommodate Iranian security interests in order to promote stability and mitigate potential sources of conflict. Yet Iran must weigh these benefits against the potential strategic costs and risks of developing nuclear weapons. A nascent nuclear program risks inviting a preventive military attack; encouraging other balancing behavior by regional competitors, including the development of their own nuclear weapons; or leading the United States to deploy greater forces in the region.

The nuclear program is also a source of international prestige for the regime. Iran's nuclear advances resonate with popular attitudes and resentment toward the West in the region and within the Non-Aligned Movement (NAM) by demonstrating the country's technical prowess, its resoluteness and independence in the face of Western opposition, and its championship of the rights of weaker states. Arab populations have expressed a far more positive view of Iran's nuclear program than have regional political elites.[3] Similarly, members of the NAM have shown considerable sympathy for the regime's claims that Iran has a right to enrich uranium. Tehran's attempt to portray itself as the victim of Western neocolonialism likewise appears to carry some legitimacy among publics and elites in NAM states.[4] Nonetheless, it is uncertain whether the development of actual weapons would enhance Iran's prestige beyond what it already receives from its civilian program. Iran might benefit from playing the role of challenger to Israel's nuclear monopoly, but a declared nuclear status could also prompt regional balancing and an arms race that could highlight Iran's strategic vulnerability. In addition, support from populations in NAM states likely depends on whether Iran continues to maintain at least the pretense of a peaceful, civilian nuclear program. Crossing the nuclear threshold, or even continuing to defy the United Nations and international law, may lead more people in the region and within the NAM to view Iran as a dangerous source of instability and a risky business partner.

Internal Influences

Although Iran's nuclear calculus is a rational one, the values and preferences that inform that calculus are shaped by the regime's ideology and by the assumptions and beliefs of Iranian elites. Iranian elites are unified in their support for the nuclear program and possession of the fuel cycle, but they disagree over the relative costs and benefits of acquiring nuclear weapons or accepting limitations on the program through a negotiated settlement.[5] It is unlikely that any Iranian leader would agree to give up the nuclear program entirely, but support for a compromise agreement will depend to a large degree on the domestic political balance in Tehran. The recent election of Hassan Rouhani to the presidency has brought greater reason for optimism that a negotiated settlement can be reached. However, it remains to be seen whether Rouhani will be both willing and able to pursue a markedly different

---

[3] In a survey conducted in five Arab countries, 64% of responders supported Iran's right to a nuclear program, while 35% (a plurality) opposed Iranian nuclear weapons. Sibley Telhami, "The 2011 Arab Public Opinion Poll," Brookings Institution, November 21, 2011, http://www.brookings.edu/research/reports/2011/11/21-arab-public-opinion-telhami.

[4] Thomas Erdbrink, "Nonaligned Nations Back Iran's Nuclear Bid, but Not Syria," *New York Times*, August 31, 2012.

[5] Sharam Chubin, "The Domestic Politics of the Nuclear Question in Iran," in *The Strategic Implications of the Iranian Nuclear Program*, ed. Joachim Krause and Charles King Mallory IV (Berlin: Aspen Institute, 2010), 84–93.

course for Iran in its dealings with the P5+1, and if the members of the P5+1 can offer Iran a realistic path toward the lifting of financial and oil sanctions.[6]

Iranian domestic politics is notoriously complex in its mixture of formal and informal institutions and personal networks. Although Iran's supreme leader, Ayatollah Ali Khamenei, is the ultimate arbiter of Iranian policy, political elites can influence the decision-making process through both formal and informal levers. In broad terms, it is useful to group Iranian elites according to loosely defined political networks or factions: conservatives (which include traditional conservatives and "principlists"), pragmatic conservatives, and reformists.[7] These political factions are fluid networks and not formal groups. The factions compete for power within the country's byzantine formal political structure and informally through the control of political networks, business interests, and access to the supreme leader's inner circle.

All factions share a common ideology that considers the Islamic Republic of Iran to be the vanguard of an international movement to overturn an illegitimate and oppressive world order backed by U.S. hegemony and extend the influence of Iran's system of *velayat-e faqih* (rule of the jurisprudent), based on Islamic principles. However, Iranian elites are divided on the question of the appropriate role of these revolutionary imperatives, on the one hand, and the need for a pragmatic foreign policy and economic and political liberalization to provide greater security and legitimacy to the regime, on the other.[8] Conservatives are more likely to view the world in terms of a zero-sum competition between Iran and the West (and especially the United States). At the extreme, this view makes greater openness toward the United States undesirable and even threatening, inasmuch as U.S. influence could have an insidious effect on Iran domestically.

These domestic political differences extend to the nuclear dispute. The different factions are united in their support of the nuclear program but disagree over the merits of acquiring nuclear weapons and the costs Iran should be willing to pay to do so. Conservatives place a greater value on nuclear weapons and are more willing to incur the costs of sanctions and diplomatic isolation than are pragmatists and reformists.[9] Conservatives

---

[6] The P5+1 are the five permanent members of the UN Security Council plus Germany.

[7] Alireza Nader, David E. Thaler, and S.R. Bohandy, *The Next Supreme Leader: Succession in the Islamic Republic of Iran* (Santa Monica: RAND Corporation, 2011). "Principlist" is a broad term used to describe the most conservative faction within Iran's Islamist Right. Principlists share a rejection of political and social reform, an ideologically rigid view of the Iranian Revolution, and a commitment to resist Western influence. They enjoy a strong support base among the Iranian Revolutionary Guard Corps and Basiji.

[8] David E. Thaler et al., *Mullahs, Guards, and Bonyads: An Exploration of Iranian Leadership Dynamics* (Santa Monica: RAND Corporation, 2010).

[9] Chubin, "The Domestic Politics."

understand opposition to the nuclear program as a U.S.-led effort to keep Iran down and deny it a capability that could both enhance the state's self-sufficiency and give it the regional influence it rightly deserves. Pragmatists and reformists also often understand the nuclear issue in terms of broader themes of self-sufficiency and independence. However, they do not see compromise as a fundamental rejection of the revolution's principles but as a way to advance them. These factions are also more sensitive to the costs of sanctions and diplomatic isolation and place a higher value on resolving the nuclear dispute in order to improve Iran's relations with the West and better integrate the country into the global economy.

The nuclear issue takes on an important symbolism within Iranian society and is often used instrumentally for political advantage in domestic debates. Iranian conservatives—and in particular Khamenei, who is best considered a traditional conservative—have made the nuclear program a core element of the regime's legitimacy narrative. Themes of Western aggression and unfairness resonate with the Iranian public, and there is broad support for continuing the nuclear program and efforts toward possession of the fuel cycle. Conservatives may therefore benefit from the nuclear dispute insofar as open defiance of Western pressure reinforces their legitimizing narrative. Elites likely also perceive a substantial domestic political cost in yielding to Western demands for Iran to suspend its enrichment program. Nonetheless, public support for the nuclear program does not extend to the acquisition of nuclear weapons. Nor does it mean that there is broad opposition in principle to negotiating with the P5+1 group a settlement in which Iran agrees to place limits on its enrichment program.[10] In this sense, the general public's views are more in line with the pragmatic conservative and reformist factions. As the 2013 election demonstrated, pragmatists are able to use public opinion on this issue to their political advantage.

Although conservative factions have been dominant for the past decade, they have been split by bitter divisions. The election of Mahmoud Ahmadinejad as president in 2005, with the support of Khamenei, elevated hard-line principlists and pushed Iranian politics rightward. Khamenei again backed Ahmadinejad in the 2009 election, and conservatives were united in suppressing the Green Movement in the months after the election, which resulted in the political marginalization of reformists and, to a lesser degree, pragmatists. However, Ahmadinejad's efforts to develop an independent power base and to challenge the authority of the clerics and the supreme

---

[10] A 2011 survey found that 87% of Iranians support a civilian nuclear energy program, but only 32% strongly favor developing nuclear weapons. See Sarah Beth Elson and Alireza Nader, "What Do Iranians Think? A Survey of Attitudes on the United States, the Nuclear Program, and the Economy," RAND Corporation, 2011.

leader created deep rifts among conservatives and divided principlists between those loyal to Khamenei and those who backed Ahmadinejad. The resulting political feud erupted in unusually public confrontations.[11]

Rouhani's unexpected victory in the 2013 presidential election demonstrated how divisions among conservatives, and between conservatives and the general public, can make them electorally vulnerable and suggests that Iranian politics could undergo a significant shift. Rouhani, who was Iran's nuclear negotiator under President Mohammad Khatami, is a pragmatic conservative who has been highly critical of Iran's nuclear policies under Ahmadinejad. His candidacy was supported by former presidents Rafsanjani and Khatami, and he won a slight majority of the vote in the first round of the election. Rouhani made the nuclear stand-off and economic sanctions against Iran central issues in his campaign and repeatedly signaled that he would adopt a more conciliatory approach in negotiations with the P5+1.[12]

However, the election of Rouhani may lead to greater changes in Iran's bargaining style than in the substance of its negotiating position. Rouhani, like his predecessors, is committed to Iran's nuclear program and is unlikely to agree to any deal that would require Iran to suspend enrichment.[13] His control over Iran's nuclear policy will also be limited, given that he will need to contend with the more conservative preferences of the supreme leader and navigate the many veto points in the Iranian political system, which aside from the presidency is still dominated by the conservatives. The election of Rouhani presents the United States and its partners with an opportunity, but they still must capitalize on that opportunity. It is not clear whether the Obama administration has the domestic and international backing necessary to put forward a proposal that is valuable enough to Iran to reach an agreement. At a minimum, such a deal would have to provide Iran with a clear and realistic path to the lifting of financial and oil sanctions, something the P5+1 has yet to do.

---

[11] Thomas Erdbink, "Presidential Aide Freed, Reports Say, as Top Iranian Politicians Trade Accusations," *New York Times*, February 6, 2013; and Mehran Kamrava, "The 2009 Elections and Iran's Changing Political Landscape," *Orbis* 54, no. 3 (2010): 400–412.

[12] Rouhani's last public statement before the election focused on Iran's foreign relations and struck a very different note than Ahmadinejad's foreign policy statements: "My administration's first priority will be to maintain and protect our national interests by building confidence and easing tension with the outside world." Mustafa al-Labbad, "Iran's Presidential Candidates Make Closing Arguments," *Al-Monitor*, June 14, 2013.

[13] Barbara Slavin, "Chances for Nuclear Deal Rise with Rouhani," *Al-Monitor*, June 15, 2013.

Iran's Nuclear Program

History of the Program

Under the last shah, Mohammad Reza, Iran was the beneficiary of U.S. nuclear assistance and an original signatory of the NPT. It was during this period that Iran first sought to master the nuclear fuel cycle, and there is evidence that the shah also sought to acquire the ability to produce nuclear weapons.[14] The 1979 revolution brought Iran's nuclear program to a temporary halt, as Ayatollah Ruhollah Khomeini believed the nuclear program violated the teachings of Islam. Many of Iran's top scientists fled the country, and foreign nuclear suppliers became increasingly unwilling to cooperate with the new regime. However, Iran's nuclear interests were rekindled during the Iran-Iraq War, possibly as a result of Iraq's nuclear and chemical weapons and ballistic missile programs, as well as the West's failure to condemn Iran's use of chemical weapons and missile attacks.[15] In 1987, Iran began to purchase the key elements of its uranium-enrichment program from A.Q. Khan's black market network. Khan may also have given Iran the design of a nuclear warhead.

After Iran's enrichment-related activities—some in contravention of its safeguards agreement with the International Atomic Energy Agency (IAEA)—were revealed publicly in 2002 by an Iranian opposition group in exile, the United Kingdom, France, and Germany (the "EU-3") began a series of negotiations that resulted in Iran's agreement to enhance safeguards and temporarily suspend fuel cycle–related activities during these talks. However, despite offers of security assurances and civilian nuclear assistance, negotiations deadlocked over the EU-3's insistence that Iran permanently give up enrichment, which Tehran vowed it would "never do."[16] Shortly after the election of Ahmadinejad as president in 2005, Iran began to enrich uranium at Natanz. In response, the IAEA board of governors voted to report Iran's nuclear dossier to the UN Security Council.

In 2006 the United States, along with Russia and China, joined the EU-3 countries' diplomatic efforts with Iran and formed what has been termed the P5+1. The P5+1 group has engaged in repeated rounds of negotiations with Iran without success. Between 2006 and 2008 the UN Security Council passed three sanctions resolutions that imposed restrictions on Iranian arms imports and exports, as well as civilian nuclear assistance to Iran (the Bushehr

---

[14] Seyed Hossein Mousavian, *The Iranian Nuclear Crisis: A Memoir* (Washington, D.C.: Carnegie Endowment for International Peace, 2012), 48–50.

[15] Shahram Chubin, *Iran's Nuclear Ambitions* (Washington, D.C.: Carnegie Endowment for International Peace, 2006), 7–10.

[16] "Iran Vows to Resist Pressure to Drop Nuclear Fuel Program," Reuters, March 13, 2005.

facility was exempted), and placed financial sanctions on a number of Iranian entities tied to the nuclear program. The sanctions implemented during this period caused only minor economic pain in Iran but still may have played an important role in slowing its nuclear progress by limiting access to foreign materials and assistance.[17]

Upon taking office, President Barack Obama signaled his intention to pursue greater engagement with Iran as part of a dual-track strategy that combined inducements with sanctions and the threat of military force. However, the 2009 Iranian presidential election, the resulting Green Movement protests, and the continued progress of Iran's nuclear program—including the revelation in fall 2009 that a secret and heavily fortified enrichment facility was being constructed at Fordo—pushed the Obama administration toward a more coercive approach.[18]

Also in 2009, the Obama administration proposed a confidence-building "fuel swap" agreement under which Iran would ship its stocks of enriched uranium out of the country in return for the 20%-enriched fuel Iran needed for the Tehran Research Reactor (built by the United States in 1960). The deal aimed to ease tensions and create space for negotiations by reducing Iran's stock of enriched uranium, which had recently passed the mark believed sufficient for a bomb (if further enriched), and removing any Iranian justification for enriching uranium to higher levels. The deal, however, unraveled after failing to win support among Tehran's divided political factions, with even reformists objecting to the agreement because it could hand Ahmadinejad a political victory.[19] In February 2010, Iran began to enrich uranium to the 20% level at Natanz.

In response, the UN Security Council passed Resolution 1929 in June 2010, which tightened the ban on arms imports by Iran and provided a legal justification for tougher unilateral sanctions on its financial and energy sectors. The resolution opened the door to U.S. and EU financial sanctions and an EU oil embargo against Iran in late 2011 and early 2012. The result of these sanctions was to almost entirely isolate Iran from the international banking system and embargo roughly 40% of the country's oil trade. The United States also passed sanctions aimed at foreign purchasers of Iranian

[17] UN Security Council, "Final Report of the Panel of Experts Established Pursuant to Resolution 1929 (2010)," S/2012/395, June 12, 2012, 3.

[18] Trita Parsi, *A Single Roll of the Dice: Obama's Diplomacy with Iran* (New Haven: Yale University Press, 2012).

[19] Mark Fitzpatrick, "Iran: The Fragile Promise of the Fuel-Swap Plan," *Survival* 52, no. 3 (2010): 67–94.

energy exports.[20] Yet despite their substantial effect on Iran's economy, these measures have not yet convinced the regime to make concessions. The P5+1 continues to pursue a confidence-building agreement with Iran under which the country would freeze its production of 20% low-enriched uranium (LEU), including all of its enrichment activities at Fordo, and reduce its existing stocks of 20% LEU by either shipping material abroad or converting it to fuel. In return, the P5+1 would provide needed parts for civilian aircraft and lift some minor economic sanctions. Iran continues to assert its right to enrich uranium but has signaled a willingness to limit enrichment to the 3.5% level. However, it has demanded that an end to the EU's oil embargo be part of any deal.[21] It is possible that the P5+1 will present a new bargaining offer to Iran after Rouhani assumes the presidency in early August 2013 that provides a clearer path to the lifting of financial and oil sanctions.

Nuclear Program Status and Potential

Iran not only possesses an enrichment capability that could be used to produce weapons-grade uranium to fuel a bomb but has developed most of the elements of the nuclear fuel cycle, including uranium mining and milling, a conversion facility at Isfahan, and a fuel-fabrication facility.[22] Iran's stated goal is to master the nuclear fuel cycle for energy and medical-isotope production without having to rely on a foreign nuclear supplier. Iran's lone power reactor at Bushehr requires 3.5% LEU fuel, and its research reactor at Tehran requires 20% LEU fuel.[23] Iran currently produces and stockpiles uranium at both levels of enrichment and has not enriched beyond 20%. However, the same technology used to produce reactor-grade fuel can also further enrich uranium to weapons grade. Iran could also use its existing stocks of LEU as starting material for further enrichment, greatly shortening the time needed to produce weapons-grade uranium (roughly 90% or higher).

The program has significantly expanded since Iran first began to produce 3.5% LEU in 2007. It took the country until the end of 2009 to produce enough 3.5% LEU for a single weapon (if further enriched). By summer

---

[20] In December 2011 the U.S. Congress enacted sanctions against foreign banks that process oil-related payments through Iran's Central Bank. See Kenneth Katzman, "Iran Sanctions," Congressional Research Service, CRS Report for Congress, RS20871, April 24, 2013, 16–18.

[21] David M. Herszenhorn, "Nuclear Talks with Iran End without Accord or Plans for Another Round," *New York Times*, April 6, 2013.

[22] Iran is also constructing a heavy-water reactor at Arak that, once in operation, could provide Iran with a plutonium route to a weapon.

[23] Russia currently provides fuel for the Bushehr reactor, with the provision that Iran return the spent fuel to Russia.

2010, however, Iran had produced twice that amount, and by early 2013 its stock of 3.5% LEU had increased by sixfold. During this time, it also produced nearly enough 20% LEU for an additional weapon.[24] Yet even as Iran's enrichment program has progressed, it has suffered technical setbacks. Many of these stem from the inferior design of the IR-1 centrifuge, which is based on a 1970s-era European design that was never deployed and that Iran has failed to improve.[25] Iran's program has also been set back by sabotage, most notably the Stuxnet cyberattack that resulted in the loss of about 1,000 centrifuges at Natanz.[26] Although it is impossible to determine definitively how many of Iran's technical problems were the result of cyberattacks rather than endogenous factors, it is unlikely that cyberattacks have succeeded in causing more than a temporary setback to the enrichment program. Iran's LEU production rate stagnated over most of 2010 and 2011, but it did not significantly decline, and the country's stocks of enriched uranium have steadily grown.[27]

Tehran has announced plans to greatly expand its enrichment capacity, both by constructing new facilities and by increasing the quantity and quality of its centrifuges. In 2010, Iran stated its intent to construct ten new enrichment facilities, although it has not provided any details to the IAEA.[28] It has installed thousands of new IR-1 centrifuges at Fordo but has not yet (as of May 2013) begun to enrich with them.[29] Iran has also experimented with more advanced centrifuge designs than the IR-1 and by May 2013 had installed 689 IR-2m centrifuges (including empty centrifuge casings) in the production hall at Natanz used for producing 3.5% LEU.[30] As of May 2013, none of these centrifuges had been used for enrichment, but if they

---

[24] This analysis assumes that producing a single weapon would require 1,000 kilograms (kg) of 3.5% LEU (in the form of uranium hexafluoride gas, or UF6) or 250 kg of 20% LEU (UF6). These are lower-bound estimates presented as a rough benchmark.

[25] After early gains, the effective separative power of Iran's centrifuges quickly plateaued at roughly 0.8 separative work units per machine per year.

[26] David Albright, Paul Brannan, and Christina Walrond, "Stuxnet Malware and Natanz: Update of ISIS December 22, 2010 Report," Institute for Science and International Security, February 15, 2011, http://isis-online.org/isis-reports/detail/stuxnet-malware-and-natanz-update-of-isis-december-22-2010-reportsupa-href1.

[27] International Atomic Energy Agency (IAEA), "Implementation of the NPT Safeguards Agreement and Relevant Provisions of Security Council Resolutions in the Islamic Republic of Iran," GOV/2012/37, August 30, 2012.

[28] IAEA, "Implementation of the NPT Safeguards Agreement and Relevant Provisions of Security Council Resolutions in the Islamic Republic of Iran," GOV/2013/6, February 21, 2013, par. 29; and "Iran Specifies Location for 10 New Enrichment Sites," Fars News Agency, August 16, 2010, http://english.farsnews.com/newstext.php?nn=8905251308.

[29] As of February 2013, there were 2,710 centrifuges installed at Fordo, 696 of which were enriching uranium. See IAEA, GOV/2013/6, par. 23–24.

[30] IAEA, "Implementation of the NPT Safeguards Agreement and Relevant Provisions of Security Council Resolutions in the Islamic Republic of Iran," GOV/2013/27, May 22, 2013, par. 13.

were successfully deployed in greater numbers, they could shorten the time needed to enrich uranium to weapons grade. Overall, however, Iran has appeared content to slowly and steadily advance its enrichment capabilities and complete its acquisition of the elements of the fuel cycle, while largely avoiding far more provocative steps, such as enriching uranium above the 20% level or removing its facilities from IAEA safeguards.

Iran is also constructing a heavy-water reactor at Arak, the IR-40, which could be used to produce plutonium, providing Iran with an alternative path to a nuclear bomb. Iran has told the IAEA that it intends to bring the IR-40 reactor online in the third quarter of 2014. However, international sanctions and export controls may complicate its ability to complete the reactor.[31] Iran also has no known reprocessing facility, which would be required to separate weapons-usable plutonium from the reactor's spent fuel. In addition, the Arak reactor would be more difficult for Iran to replace if it were destroyed by an air strike.[32]

The U.S. intelligence community has assessed that Iran is seeking to acquire the knowledge and technology to quickly develop nuclear weapons if it were to choose to do so, but that it has not yet made such a decision.[33] Iran steadfastly maintains its intentions are peaceful and points to a *fatwa* (legal judgment) issued by the supreme leader that forbids the construction, stockpiling, and use of nuclear weapons.[34] However, there is considerable evidence available to support the intelligence community's conclusion that Iran seeks at least the means to make nuclear weapons if it were to choose to do so. According to the IAEA, Iran had been running an organized weapons program until 2003, when the program was halted for reasons possibly related to the U.S. invasion of Iraq and the end of any concern about an Iraqi nuclear weapons program. This evidence suggests that Iran has conducted research on nearly every step required to produce a deliverable nuclear weapon, including the conversion of uranium gas to metal, the design of a re-entry vehicle for a warhead, and the use of high explosives to implode the uranium pit.[35] Until 2003, this work appears to have taken place as part of a single, coordinated effort within a centralized organization tied to the Iranian Revolutionary Guard Corps. Most of this work appears to have stopped in 2003, although

---

[31] IAEA, GOV/2013/27, par. 28–37.

[32] An air strike would need to be conducted before the reactor is fueled to avoid a potential environmental and health catastrophe from radiation release.

[33] Clapper, "Unclassified Statement for the Record."

[34] IAEA, "Communication Dated 12 September 2005 from the Permanent Mission of the Islamic Republic of Iran to the Agency," INFCIRC/657, September 15, 2005, 121–2.

[35] IAEA, "Implementation of the NPT Safeguards Agreement and Relevant Provisions of Security Council Resolutions in the Islamic Republic of Iran," GOV/2011/65, November 8, 2011.

there is some evidence that less coordinated, smaller-scale research has continued since that time.[36] Although Iran denies the existence of these programs, it has not satisfactorily explained the available evidence, nor has it provided international inspectors with the access to the facilities they have requested, despite repeated rounds of negotiation between Iran and the IAEA to arrange such access.

Iran has also pursued an advanced ballistic missile capability, which it could use to deliver nuclear weapons. This missile development effort has focused on acquiring short- and medium-range missiles that can hit targets anywhere in the region, including Israel. Iran currently has deployed several hundred short-range missiles (the Shahab-1 and Shahab-2), based on Soviet SCUD designs, that could target both neighboring states and U.S. military assets in the Persian Gulf.[37] Iran has also developed medium-range missiles, including the Shahab-3, which may have a range of up to 1,000 kilometers and a payload capacity of 1,000 kilograms, and the solid-fueled Sejil-2, which may have a 2,000-kilometer range with a similar payload. In theory, these weapons could reach targets in Israel, but their reliability is questionable given the low number of flight tests. There is no evidence to indicate that Iran is nearing an ability to develop an intercontinental ballistic missile, although the U.S. Department of Defense estimated in 2010 that Iran could do so by 2015 if it were to receive foreign assistance.[38]

Potential Tipping Points and Restraints

Iran's breakout potential is currently limited by both the time it would take to enrich weapons-grade uranium and the risk of detection. According to U.S. government estimates, it would likely take at least several months to produce enough highly enriched uranium (HEU) for a weapon and a year or more to make a bomb. Iran would risk detection before it could finish either task, as IAEA inspectors conduct inspections once every two weeks on average, half of them unannounced. Iran would also assume a number of additional risks. Enrichment of weapons-grade uranium is a highly uncertain process—and, for the country's nuclear scientists and engineers, an untested one. Iran would not know beforehand exactly how long the process would take, how much HEU would be needed for a weapon, how much LEU feedstock would be needed to produce sufficient HEU, or whether technical

[36] International Institute for Strategic Studies (IISS), *Iran's Nuclear, Chemical and Biological Capabilities: A Net Assessment* (London: IISS, 2011), 86–88.

[37] U.S. Department of Defense, "Unclassified Report on Military Power in Iran," April 2010, http://www.fas.org/man/eprint/dod_iran_2010.pdf.

[38] IISS, *Iran's Ballistic Missile Capabilities: A Net Assessment* (London: IISS, 2010).

problems would be encountered along the way. If the United States detected such enrichment activity, it could destroy the facility before the process was complete. Given these risks, Iran appears content to forgo a breakout, at least until it has an unobstructed path to a bomb.

Nonetheless, Iran could improve its breakout potential in several ways. For example, it could divert existing stocks of LEU to a secret facility for further enrichment. Because these stocks are under electronic seal, such a diversion would be quickly detected, but they could be hidden quickly enough to deny the United States an opportunity to intervene. Tehran may have considered this route, as both Natanz and Fordo were originally secret and were not revealed to the IAEA until their existence had already been discovered. Iran could also improve its breakout potential by stockpiling greater quantities of 20% LEU or even HEU. Iranian officials have already publicly raised the possibility of enrichment to the 50% level (HEU) for naval reactors.[39] However, Iran has so far kept its stocks of 20% LEU below what would likely be required for a bomb by converting much of this LEU to oxide for fuel plates.[40] Iran could also deploy more advanced centrifuge designs. Although it has long been developing new centrifuge designs, Iran had not deployed any for LEU production until early 2013, when it began to install IR-2m centrifuges in the production hall at Natanz. As of May 2013, these machines had not begun to enrich uranium, and it is unknown whether they could be deployed in sufficient numbers to greatly speed up the enrichment process.[41]

While, as discussed above, it is unlikely that Tehran would agree to give up the uranium fuel cycle entirely, an agreement with the P5+1 could keep Iran from breaking out over the long term by imposing strict limits on its enrichment capacity and providing for more stringent safeguards and reporting requirements. Limits on Iran's enrichment program would have to address the location and number of enrichment facilities, the number and quality of centrifuges, the enrichment level, and the size of LEU stockpiles. Enhanced safeguards would have to include implementation of both the IAEA's Additional Protocol and the modified Code 3.1 of Iran's safeguards agreement. The former would expand Iran's reporting requirements to include

---

[39] "AEOI Head: Iran to Enrich to 50% If Nuclear Powered Vessels Needed," Fars News Agency, April 16, 2013, http://english.farsnews.com/newstext.php?nn=9107161520.

[40] IAEA, GOV/2013/27, par. 243–25. The conversion of UF6 to oxide can, however, be reversed within a relatively short time. See Mark Hibbs, "Reconverting Iran's U3O8 to UF6," Arms Control Wonk, web log, April 27, 2013, http://hibbs.armscontrolwonk.com/archive/1748/reconverting-irans-u3o8-to-uf6.

[41] IAEA, GOV/2013/6, par. 13; and David Albright and Christina Walrond, "Iran's Advanced Centrifuges," Institute for Science and International Security, ISIS Report, October 18, 2011, http://isis-online.org/uploads/isis-reports/documents/Iran_Advanced_Centrifuges_18October2011.pdf.

any activities that could further the development of nuclear weapons and give IAEA inspectors broader access to sites. The latter would require Iran to declare any new nuclear facilities during the planning stage rather than merely notify the IAEA 180 days before it intends to introduce nuclear materials at a site. Together, these measures would improve the IAEA's ability to verify both the accuracy and the completeness of Iran's declaration.[42]

Even if Iran were to have an unobstructed path to a nuclear breakout, there are a number of different choices it could make. Iranian leaders might decide to remain below the weaponization threshold and be content with a virtual capability if they conclude that the net gains of weaponization are not greater. This option could allow Iran to remain within the NPT. Alternatively, Iran might choose to maintain nuclear ambiguity about whether it possessed a virtual capability or extant weapons. Tehran could see such a step as a way to maintain a deterrent without triggering an arms race or leading Israel to openly declare itself as a nuclear-armed state. Iran might also choose to become a formally declared nuclear weapons state and test a weapon. Tehran would likely choose this route if it believed that such a move was the only credible way to establish a nuclear deterrent or that doing so would enhance its prestige and influence.

Iran is more likely to pursue nuclear weapons if the regime were to conclude that it faces a greater near-term strategic threat. A preventive attack on the country's nuclear facilities by the United States or Israel would thus likely lead Iran to redouble its nuclear effort and seek to acquire nuclear weapons. As discussed later in this chapter, such an attack could set Iran's program back by several years but over the longer term could make it more likely for Iran to acquire weapons by providing an incentive to withdraw from the NPT and expel IAEA inspectors. These developments would enable Iran to reconstitute its nuclear program and pursue weaponization with fewer restraints. Economic sanctions could also push Iran to move more quickly toward nuclear weapons.[43] Admittedly, Iran is already subject to tough international sanctions, and it is unlikely that sanctions alone will lead the country to attempt a breakout in the near future. However, Tehran has responded to sanctions with escalatory measures that could set off an unintended conflict and trigger a breakout dash.

Paradoxically, the unwillingness of China and other major oil importers in Asia to fully back the U.S. sanctions effort and eliminate oil imports and other ties to the Iranian energy sector could have a moderating influence

---

[42] See David Cliff, "Nuclear Verification Issues and Priorities in Iran," VERTIC, web log, February 3, 2012, http://www.vertic.org/pages/posts/nuclear-verification-issues-and-priorities-in-iran-243.php.

[43] Zachary Keck, "Asia Is Purchasing Nearly All of Iran's Oil," *Diplomat*, January 5, 2013, http://thediplomat.com/pacific-money/2013/01/05/asia-is-purchasing-nearly-all-of-irans-oil/.

on Iran's nuclear decision-making. China, India, Japan, and South Korea are all major importers of Iranian oil and would suffer economically if they were to cease imports. Japan and South Korea, as major U.S. allies, have been more susceptible to U.S. pressure and more willing to cut oil imports. India has also been forced to make steep cuts in its oil imports from Iran because of Europe's July 2012 ban on insurance for Iranian oil shipments.[44] China, however, has been less willing to follow suit and has sought to balance competing interests by playing a key role in UN nonproliferation deliberations, maintaining stability in the world's major oil-producing region, establishing good relations with a Persian Gulf oil and gas producer that is outside the U.S. orbit, and keeping good relations with the West. This approach has led China to reluctantly support sanctions while seeking to preserve its access to Iranian energy resources and maintain good relations with Iran.[45] The oil embargo may have increased China's influence in Tehran by making Iran more dependent on the Chinese export market. Iranian leaders are likely aware that a breakout attempt or a military conflict would jeopardize this relationship by putting China under greater pressure to distance itself from Iran and further back U.S. sanctions efforts. The regime's current policies appear to reflect this view: Iran is slowly advancing its capabilities while carefully seeking to justify its actions as part of a civilian nuclear effort.

Regional and Global Implications

Containing a Nuclear-Armed Iran

The consequences of Iran acquiring nuclear weapons would depend on the characteristics of its arsenal, the policy choices of major states both in the region and globally, and how Iranian leaders perceive the utility of nuclear weapons. Overall, it is likely that a nuclear-armed Iran could be contained. Iran is not an irrational actor and has historically adopted a pragmatic foreign policy when regime security required one. The regime places a high value on its survival, and after maintaining power for more than three decades is unlikely to behave in a suicidal manner. It is therefore unlikely that Iran would launch a first strike against Israel or U.S. interests in the region. Doing so would guarantee massive retaliation, and in the case of Israel almost certainly nuclear retaliation.

---

[44] European insurers underwrite roughly 95% of all policies for tankers worldwide. See Nidhi Verma, "India's Iran Oil Imports Plunge 26.5 pct in FY13—Trade," Reuters, April 24, 2013.

[45] Min-Jeong Lee, "South Korea's Iran Imports Fall While China's Increase," Wall Street Journal, March 22, 2013; and Manochehr Dorraj and James E. English, "China's Strategy for Energy Acquisition in the Middle East: Potential for Conflict and Cooperation with the United States," Asian Politics & Policy 4, no. 2 (2012): 173–91.

Furthermore, Iran's nuclear capabilities would likely be limited. Its arsenal would at first be small—likely only a handful of weapons—and barring radical advances in its nuclear program, the regime would require many years to develop an arsenal with warhead numbers comparable to the arsenals of more established nuclear powers like Israel, India, and Pakistan. The reliability of its weapons and delivery systems would also likely remain low unless Iran were to conduct repeated tests, which would take time, consume precious fissile material, and likely incur international rebuke. Moreover, if sanctions were to remain in place, Iran would have difficulty importing the materials and equipment necessary to continue to develop its nuclear and ballistic missile capabilities. Procuring foreign assistance would be equally difficult.

The threat of overwhelming U.S. and Israeli retaliation in response to an Iranian nuclear first strike would be credible and would likely deter Iran from using nuclear weapons under most circumstances. A U.S. threat to retaliate in response to the transfer of nuclear weapons to Hezbollah or other regional proxies would be similarly credible, and Iran would have strong incentives not to do so. Nor would it wish to surrender control of precious nuclear assets, particularly if its arsenal were to remain small.

The danger of an Iranian nuclear attack would be greatest during a crisis, especially if the regime were to feel threatened. Any major U.S. force buildup in the region, and particularly any attack on Iranian territory, could be misinterpreted by Tehran as a prelude to regime change. Likewise, an attack that disrupted Iran's command and control of its nuclear forces could lead to an unintended use of a weapon if local commanders with launch authority were to conclude that a decapitation of the leadership had occurred.

Iran could also seek to use its nuclear arsenal as a shield to cover conventional aggression or to deter retaliation against terrorist attacks. Although possession of a nuclear arsenal would likely deter the United States and U.S. allies from attacking Iranian territory, it would be unlikely to deter the use of force against offensive actions taken by Iran in the Persian Gulf or elsewhere, nor would it prevent Israel and other allies from taking military action against proxy groups such as Hezbollah. Both the United States and Israel possess substantial nuclear forces of their own, making an Iranian nuclear first strike suicidal and undermining the credibility of any threat of nuclear coercion. At present, the United States and its allies can successfully protect their interests in the region without needing to attack Iranian territory, and they could continue to do so even if Iran possessed nuclear weapons.

Some missions might be more difficult or require greater caution if undertaken against a nuclear-armed Iran, such as if Iran were to mine the Strait of Hormuz. The United States might also be more reluctant to target missile batteries on Iran's southern coast to prevent attacks on mine-clearing operations. This would not, however, prevent the United States from clearing the Strait of Hormuz, nor would nuclear weapons change the fact that Tehran has a strong interest in keeping the strait open for its own economic interests. Iran's acquisition of nuclear weapons would also not necessarily prevent the United States from retaliating against missile sites that attacked U.S. forces in the strait, as the regime would still have an enormous incentive to exercise nuclear restraint unless it believed it was under imminent threat. Nonetheless, even if a nuclear arsenal would not give Iran the ability to more successfully project military power in the region, the regime could still adopt more adventurous policies if it believed nuclear weapons would deter reprisals on Iranian territory. This by itself could be destabilizing, given that even low-level conflict has the potential to escalate, and it is unclear how Iran's leaders would perceive this risk or how much risk they would be willing to accept.

Israel and the Middle East

Israeli leaders have adopted a more forceful stance toward Iran's nuclear program than Washington has and have identified it as an "existential threat." Israel has also consistently pushed for clearer red lines that would trigger the use of military force and has expressed impatience with both the P5+1 negotiations and the Obama administration's reluctance to commit itself to specific triggers for a military response. Furthermore, Israel has suggested that it is willing to carry out an attack on Iranian nuclear sites on its own if it believes that the United States is unwilling to take action to forestall Iran's acquisition of nuclear weapons.[46]

Although Israeli rhetoric is likely aimed at least in part at influencing Washington, it also likely reflects genuine differences in threat perceptions between the two allies.[47] Israel's vulnerability to a nuclear-armed Iran is much greater than that of the United States. Even if Iran were successfully deterred from using its nuclear weapons, the very possession of such weapons—or even a virtual capability—could threaten Israel by triggering regional instability, leading other states in the region to pursue nuclear weapons of their own and deterring U.S. power projection in the region. Israeli leaders have also expressed concern that a nuclear competition with Iran could encourage some Israelis to emigrate or force Israel to become a permanent garrison state. These views are informed and strengthened by the country's historical experiences and traditional reliance on superior military capabilities to defend against threatening neighbors.

---

[46] Jeffrey Goldberg, "The Point of No Return," *Atlantic Monthly*, September 2010, 56–69.

[47] Dana H. Allin and Steven Simon, *The Sixth Crisis: Iran, Israel, America, and the Rumors of War* (Oxford: Oxford University Press, 2010).

Many Israeli leaders see the country's nuclear arsenal in a similar light and believe the country's regional nuclear monopoly is an important guarantor of Israeli security. Under the "Begin doctrine," Israel has proved itself willing to use preventive military force against nascent nuclear weapons programs in the region—first against Iraq in 1981 and then against Syria in 2007. Nonetheless, a central concern for Israel is its relationship with the United States, and it is likely Israel will defer to U.S. policy initiatives with Iran unless Israeli leaders become convinced the United States is unwilling or unable to prevent Iran from acquiring nuclear weapons. Additionally, Israel may lack the military capabilities to substantially set back the Iranian program through air strikes against Iran's nuclear facilities.[48]

Iran's acquisition of nuclear weapons could also trigger a cascade of regional proliferation. Saudi officials have suggested that Saudi Arabia would seek nuclear weapons if Iran were to acquire them.[49] Also, Israel has suggested that it might respond to Iran's acquisition of nuclear weapons by openly declaring itself a nuclear power.[50] However, nuclear proliferation is historically rare, and there is no historical evidence that the emergence of a new nuclear power would trigger a cascade of proliferation.[51] The most likely candidates in the region for additional proliferation—Saudi Arabia, Turkey, and Egypt—have significant technical limitations that would prevent them from achieving a nuclear capability in the near term and face a number of important disincentives to acquiring nuclear weapons.

Turkey is a NATO member that is not only under the U.S. nuclear umbrella but has U.S. nonstrategic weapons stationed on its territory. Egypt's nuclear infrastructure is old and in poor repair, and the government lacks the economic capacity, and likely the organization, to mount an effective crash nuclear program. Saudi Arabia is the least technically advanced of the three and lacks the technical base to develop nuclear weapons over the near or medium term. Saudi leaders may seek to purchase weapons from Pakistan or elsewhere or have weapons stationed on Saudi territory. However, doing so would invite international opprobrium and risk creating a rupture in U.S.-Saudi relations, which could leave Riyadh less secure as a result. The United States also has considerable leverage with Saudi Arabia, far more than it does with Iran. At the same time, Pakistan and other nuclear-armed states have

---

[48] Jonathan Marcus, "Analysis: How Israel Might Strike at Iran," BBC, February 27, 2012, http://www.bbc.co.uk/news/world-middle-east-17115643.

[49] Jason Burke, "Riyadh Will Build Nuclear Weapons If Iran Gets Them, Saudi Prince Warns," *Guardian*, June 29, 2011.

[50] Paul Bracken, *The Second Nuclear Age: Strategy, Danger, and the New Power Politics* (New York: Times Books, 2012), 151–56.

[51] Colin H. Kahl, Melissa G. Dalton, and Matthew Irvine, *Atomic Kingdom: If Iran Builds the Bomb, Will Saudi Arabia Be Next?* (Washington, D.C.: Center for a New American Security, 2013).

few reasons to provide Saudi Arabia with nuclear arms and many reasons not to, not least to avoid rupturing their own relations with the United States. If Iran were to acquire nuclear weapons, it is more likely that Saudi Arabia would seek greater U.S. defense guarantees or even the protection of the U.S. nuclear umbrella.

Impact beyond the Middle East

Beyond the implications for the United States and for states in the Middle East, Iranian nuclear advances and the potential acquisition of nuclear weapons would affect a number of important states in Asia, especially China and India. China has both economic and strategic interests in Iran that would be affected by any major changes in its nuclear status. Iran is an important source of energy resources for China and is the country's third-largest oil supplier. China's energy security thus could be put at risk if Iran's nuclear behavior were to provoke a crisis or military conflict that disrupted regional oil shipments or led to even tighter international sanctions on Iranian oil.[52]

At the same time, U.S. tensions with Iran are a potential source of distraction for Washington that consume military and diplomatic resources that might otherwise be deployed in East Asia. Also, Iran's dependence on China and the relatively close relationship between the two countries give Beijing an important foothold in a strategically significant region where most of the major energy players are U.S. allies.[53] Yet these interests present China with a set of conflicting policy choices. On the one hand, China's access to Persian Gulf energy resources depends on stability in the Middle East, and the country's overall economic well-being depends on continued stable relations with the United States. On the other hand, Beijing can reap strategic benefits from tensions between the United States and Iran and stands to lose from any major political change in Tehran that would greatly improve U.S.-Iranian relations.[54] Regardless of whether China may benefit from a continued stand-off, it would face considerable risks to its regional and global interests if Iran were to acquire nuclear weapons.

India's policy toward Iran is also strongly influenced by the need for energy security, which could also be threatened by any change in Iran's nuclear status that disrupts the flow of Persian Gulf oil or creates a spike in oil prices. India must balance its interest in Iranian energy security with its

---

[52] China's trade and investment with Iran have already been negatively affected by international sanctions. See John Lee, "China's Geostrategic Search for Oil," *Washington Quarterly* 35, no. 3 (2012): 75–92.

[53] John W. Garver, "Is China Playing a Dual Game in Iran?" *Washington Quarterly* 34, no. 1 (2011): 75–88.

[54] Carrie Liu Currier and Manochehr Dorraj, "In Arms We Trust: The Economic and Strategic Factors Motivating China-Iran Relations," *Journal of Chinese Political Science* 15, no. 1 (2010): 49–69.

need to maintain good relations with U.S. leaders, who are exerting significant diplomatic pressure on New Delhi to support UN sanctions. India sees China as a competitor in this regard, and many Indian leaders are concerned that close relations with the United States restrain India's ability to effectively compete with China for market share.[55]

Iran's acquisition of nuclear weapons could also have an impact on the broader strategic balance in South Asia. Pakistan and Iran have had tense relations in the past and compete for influence in Afghanistan and elsewhere in the region.[56] Although the two states have more recently engaged in greater cooperation, ties remain strained, and Pakistan would likely consider a nuclear-armed Iran to be a security threat. Pakistan's close ties with Saudi Arabia could also influence Islamabad's reaction to a nuclear-armed Iran. Pakistan could seek to extend its nuclear umbrella to Saudi Arabia or even provide the Saudis with nuclear weapons or the means to make them. Such a development, although unlikely, would upset the current nuclear balance in South Asia and could provoke an arms race.[57]

The International Nonproliferation Regime

Iran's acquisition of nuclear weapons could weaken the international nonproliferation regime. Iran is an original signatory of the NPT and would join North Korea as the only two NPT members to develop nuclear weapons. An Iranian withdrawal from the NPT might not, by itself, weaken other states' adherence to the treaty, but the failure of the UN Security Council to enforce the treaty could undermine the credibility of both the Security Council and the United States, which has been the principal sponsor of sanctions. Economic and diplomatic sanctions against Iran are designed, in part, to address this concern. Even if they fail to coerce Iran into changing its behavior, they can signal to other potential proliferators that the pursuit of nuclear weapons will carry steep costs. Nonetheless, a nuclear Iran could signal to other states that it is possible to develop nuclear weapons even in the face of strong international opposition and tough sanctions. This could present the international community with a dilemma. To uphold the credibility of the nonproliferation regime, it would make sense for the UN Security Council to maintain tough sanctions against a nuclear-armed Iran. However, such sanctions could also be regionally destabilizing by leading

---

[55] Harsh V. Pant and Julie M. Super, "Balancing Rivals: India's Tightrope between Iran and the United States," *Asia Policy*, no. 15 (2013): 69–88.

[56] Harsh V. Pant, "Pakistan and Iran's Dysfunctional Relationship," *Middle East Quarterly* 16, no. 2 (2009): 43–50.

[57] Shashank Joshi, "The Implications of a Nuclear Iran," *Whitehall Papers* 79, no. 1 (2012): 75–129.

Iran to adopt more aggressive policies, while a more strategically pragmatic path might be to better enmesh a nuclear-armed Iran in regional and global security and economic institutions.

A negotiated settlement with Iran to keep it below the nuclear weapons threshold also presents challenges for the international nonproliferation regime. Although the NPT does not forbid possession of the fuel cycle, and a member state can remain in compliance with the treaty while advancing nearly the entire way to a weapon, the United States and many of its allies see this as a weakness of the treaty. Formal recognition of Iran's right to the fuel cycle, which Iran has set as a firm condition for any agreement, would set an undesirable precedent, particularly as the United States seeks to persuade close allies like South Korea to forgo sensitive fuel-cycle technologies.[58]

U.S. Policy Implications

The United States has military, economic, and diplomatic tools at its disposal to influence Iran's nuclear decisions. Militarily, the United States can use air strikes to destroy key Iranian nuclear facilities, and the threat that it will do so may have an important deterrent effect on an Iranian breakout. The United States has been the primary sponsor of multilateral economic sanctions and has used its global diplomatic and economic leverage to convince key partners to support sanctions and sever or reduce trade with Iran. The United States is also the major player in negotiations with Iran through the P5+1. Despite possessing these levers of influence, Washington has nonetheless failed to make significant progress in convincing Tehran to give up or adopt limits on its nuclear program. This failure results from the limited overall effectiveness of coercive policies, the unwillingness of the United States and many of its allies to compromise on their demands for either an end to or long-term suspension of Iran's enrichment activities, and unfavorable conditions in Iranian domestic politics. At the same time, the failure to change the trajectory of Iran's nuclear program likely masks the success of the United States and its allies in slowing (but not reversing) the program's progress, particularly through sanctions.

Military Force

In the absence of clear provocation—for example, an attack on U.S. forces in the Persian Gulf or a blatant attempt at nuclear breakout—it is unlikely that the United States would use military force to try to destroy Iran's nuclear

---

[58] Choe Sang-Hun, "South Korea and U.S. Fail to Reach Deal on Nuclear Energy," *New York Times*, April 24, 2013.

program. On an operational level, the United States would probably be able to destroy Iran's main nuclear facilities, including its enrichment plants at Natanz and Fordo, its uranium conversion facility at Isfahan, and the heavy-water reactor under construction at Arak and the heavy-water production plant that is already there. Although an attack could set Iran's program back by several years, it would likely not prevent the country from reconstituting the program and ultimately acquiring nuclear weapons. In the first place, Iran would retain much of the knowledge and expertise it has developed. It is also unlikely that the United States would be able to destroy key facilities that Iran would use to reconstitute its program, such as small factories to produce centrifuge components hidden and dispersed within dense urban areas.

Because it is unclear whether or when Iran will acquire nuclear weapons, air strikes could possibly lead the country to develop a nuclear capability sooner than it otherwise would. Not only would Tehran be more motivated to acquire nuclear weapons, but given the likelihood that after an attack Iran would expel IAEA inspectors and withdraw from the NPT, its path to nuclear weapons could be more open. Either way, the United States and its allies would be less able to monitor Iranian activities and have less confidence that Iran had not begun to pursue weapons in secret, making future U.S. policy choices more difficult. In the absence of a provocation, it is also likely that an attack would lead to the breakdown of the current sanctions regime, further complicating U.S. efforts to keep Iran below the nuclear threshold over the long term.

The threat of U.S. air strikes likely deters Iran from attempting a breakout dash, and Iran appears content to slowly advance its program instead. U.S. air strikes to stop an Iranian breakout would carry the lowest risk of triggering a nationalist backlash within Iran and command the greatest international legitimacy and support if the United States could present convincing evidence that the breakout was taking place and limit the scope of the attack to targets directly involved in the breakout attempt. However, limiting the scope of air strikes would be difficult. U.S. military forces, for example, could destroy the Natanz or Fordo enrichment facility but would face incentives to expand the mission to a broader set of targets, particularly if a breakout were to occur at Fordo, which could require many sorties to destroy. In that case, the United States would want to destroy air defenses and other military targets in the country that could put U.S. forces at risk. This would present an opportunity to attack additional targets related to the nuclear program and potentially additional military and regime targets. However, the broader the attack and the more expansive its goals, the greater the likelihood that it would trigger negative strategic consequences for the United States and its allies.

UN Sanctions

Although the United States has maintained sanctions against Iran for decades, as has the UN Security Council since 2006, the economic effects of these measures have been relatively minor until recently. Their impact has increased dramatically since the passage of tough financial and oil sanctions at the end of 2011. Particularly since the EU oil embargo began in 2012, Iran's monthly oil exports have plummeted, falling by two-thirds over the twelve months prior to May 2013.[59] In addition, U.S.-led financial sanctions have effectively cut Iran off from the global banking system and severed Iran's access to foreign-exchange markets. This has imposed sizable limits on Iran's ability to conduct business abroad, contributing to a huge drop in the value of the Iranian rial and a rise in inflation, which is now over 30% and continues to rise.[60]

However, this economic pain has thus far not led Iran to make concessions, and P5+1 negotiators have been unsuccessful in using sanctions to increase their bargaining leverage. Without a clear path to lifting sanctions beyond complete capitulation, it is unlikely that Iran will yield to economic coercion: successful coercion is difficult under most circumstances and particularly so with an authoritarian regime.[61] Increased sanctions have also raised the prospect of escalation. Iran has often timed significant advances in its program, such as the addition of new centrifuges, to respond to new sanctions and has made repeated threats to retaliate by closing the Strait of Hormuz and taking other actions.[62]

Iran's economic and diplomatic isolation has not been total, and the country could gradually adapt to sanctions if it can shift its trade toward states that are less willing to sever ties. While the United States and its allies in Europe have imposed tight financial and trade sanctions, Asian states in particular have been less willing to follow suit. The majority of Iran's energy exports now flow to South and East Asia, with four states—China, India, Japan, and South Korea—representing the bulk of Iran's foreign oil and gas sales.[63] In response, the United States and the EU have begun to use a creative

---

[59] Alex Lawler and Nidhi Verma, "Sanctions Push Iran's Oil Exports to Lowest in Decades," Reuters, June 5, 2013.

[60] Between April 2011 and April 2013, the rial declined 80% in value. See Kambiz Foroohar, "Iran Moves Away from Oil to Withstand Sanctions, Minister Says," Bloomberg, April 23, 2013, http://www.bloomberg.com/news/2013-04-23/iran-moves-away-from-oil-to-withstand-sanctions-minister-says.html.

[61] One influential study finds a 30% chance of success for economic sanctions overall. See Gary C. Hufbauer et al., *Economic Sanctions Reconsidered*, 3rd ed. (Washington, D.C.: Peterson Institute for International Economics, 2007).

[62] Scott Peterson, "Sanctions May Be Speeding Iran's Nuclear Advancement," *Christian Science Monitor*, March 26, 2013.

[63] "Asia to Deepen Iran Oil Import Cuts in 2013 As Sanctions Bite," Reuters, January 31, 2013.

set of policy tools to put pressure on Asian importers of Iranian oil. They have banned insurance underwriters from covering oil shipments, sanctioned banks that transfer oil payments, and have convinced Saudi Arabia and other Gulf oil producers to ramp up production to offset the loss of Iranian oil sales.[64] However, it is unclear whether the United States can convince these states to maintain this policy over the long term, given their dependence on foreign energy suppliers. U.S. allies like Japan and South Korea have cut purchases in order to win U.S. sanctions waivers but have not been willing to sever trade completely. China has been less willing to bow to U.S. pressure. Given these realities, the long-term sustainability of sanctions is uncertain.

Sanctions have been most effective at denying Iran much of the materials, equipment, and assistance it requires for its nuclear program. Iran's nuclear technology is the result of foreign assistance from both the A.Q. Khan black market network and major states like China, Russia, and—before 1979—the United States. Sanctions have already slowed Iran's progress, and could prevent (or delay) Iran from deploying large numbers of more advanced centrifuge designs, bringing its heavy-water reactor online, and making other critical advances. This success, however, is based on sanctions that have specifically targeted the nuclear program rather than on broader sanctions on the energy and financial sectors.

Iran's domestic political conditions, with conservative hard-liners in power and reformists politically marginalized, have been unreceptive to pressure. This may change after Hassan Rouhani, who has signaled an eagerness to negotiate a lifting of sanctions, assumes the presidency in August 2013. The popular resonance of Rouhani's campaign, which made sanctions and their effect on the economy a central theme, suggests that the Iranian public does not share the resolve of conservative elites to continue to incur the economic pain of increasing international sanctions and isolation. The regime leadership has been able to insulate many key supporters from the effects of sanctions by selectively passing on their costs to groups it does not depend on for political support and providing rents to those it does, such as the Revolutionary Guard.[65] The Iranian public has more greatly experienced the brunt of sanctions in the form of shortages, inflation, and unemployment. This situation has not led to an open challenge of the authority of the regime, and the public continues to support Iran's enrichment of uranium. Yet it has facilitated the election of a moderate president and has opened the

---

[64] Katzman, *Iran Sanctions*; and Javier Blas, "Saudis Offer Extra Oil to Offset Price Rises," *Financial Times*, September 18, 2012.

[65] Mohammad Sadeghi Esfahlani and Jamal Abdi, "Sanctions Cripple Iran's Middle Class, Not the Regime," *Foreign Policy*, August 2, 2012, http://mideast.foreignpolicy.com/posts/2012/08/02/sanctions_cripple_irans_middle_class_not_the_regime.

possibility of greater negotiating flexibility, however limited. Whether or not this translates into greater flexibility at the negotiating table will depend on whether the P5+1 is willing to offer Iran a credible path to the lifting of the toughest sanctions—those on oil and the country's financial system—and recognition of Iran's right to an enrichment program, at least in a limited form and under strict safeguards.

P5+1 Negotiations

The United States and its partners in the P5+1 group have been working unsuccessfully for nearly a decade to negotiate a solution to the dispute over Iran's nuclear program. Several factors have worked to prevent the two sides from reaching a negotiated agreement. Iran's domestic political conditions have not been fortuitous, as regime conservatives are suspicious of the intentions of the United States and its partners in the West and likely do not value greater economic and political ties with the West (or see such ties as potentially threatening). Moreover, Washington faces political pressure—both domestically and from Israel—to drive a hard bargain with Iran and will likely continue to insist on a suspension of enrichment as a precondition to any lifting of sanctions or other major inducements. Finally, many decision-makers in Washington are convinced that Iran's supreme leader has committed himself to eventually acquiring weapons or, at a minimum, is uninterested in any deal that could foreclose that option. Although the election of a moderate president, Rouhani, to replace the hard-liner Ahmadinejad could improve the chances of a settlement, many of the central barriers to an agreement are likely to remain. Iranian conservatives continue to control all the major organs of government besides the presidency and count the supreme leader, whose support will be essential to any deal, among their ranks. The White House will also continue to face domestic pressure to adopt a hard line toward Iran despite the election of Rouhani.

While the chances of a deal may not be high, there is a risk of this outcome becoming a self-fulfilling prophecy, as each side becomes increasingly convinced that the other is uninterested in bargaining in good faith. To improve the chances that diplomacy will succeed, there are two changes the P5+1 can make to its bargaining posture. One would be to give Iran a clear picture of the steps it must take for sanctions to be lifted. Iran's leaders—not unreasonably—may fear that sanctions are as much motivated by the West's overall animosity toward the regime as they are by the nuclear program and that U.S. policy in particular is motivated by Washington's desire to effect regime change. At the same time, the P5+1 has not offered Iran any clear path to the lifting of sanctions beyond what likely appears to Tehran as full capitulation: the indefinite suspension of enrichment activities and permanent acquiescence to more invasive safeguards. Moreover, the U.S. Congress has linked U.S. sanctions to issues entirely beyond the nuclear question, such as Iran's human rights record, and Congress's control over sanctions legislation prevents the Obama administration from credibly committing to lift sanctions. The reluctance of the United States and its allies to offer to lift sanctions in the absence of considerable upfront concessions by Iran is understandable, given the difficulty of organizing and maintaining the sanctions regime. To lift sanctions, the P5+1 will need reassurances that Iran will not renege on a deal, as the reinstitution of sanctions would be difficult and perhaps impossible. Furthermore, if significant concessions on sanctions were made as part of a confidence-building agreement, the P5+1 would greatly reduce its leverage in future negotiations. At the same time, Iranian leaders have little incentive to agree to any deal, including a confidence-building agreement, that does not provide significant sanctions relief.

Second, the P5+1 could drop its insistence on a suspension of enrichment activities, lift sanctions, and provide other inducements if Iran agrees to strict and verifiable limits on its program. This would involve both placing limits on the size and characteristics of the program—including the number of centrifuges, location of enrichment facilities, centrifuge designs, and stockpile amounts and enrichment levels—and implementing tougher safeguards that expand reporting requirements and allow for inspections of suspected sites without advance notice. At a minimum, this agreement would require Iran to implement the IAEA's Additional Protocol and the modified Code 3.1.

An agreement would also have to cover the Arak reactor and contain strong provisions to prevent Iran from acquiring plutonium for a bomb. Iran would need to pledge not to reprocess plutonium or acquire the facilities to do so. In addition, it would need to provide detailed plans of the Arak reactor to the IAEA and agree to strict safeguards that would allow IAEA inspectors to detect the diversion of spent fuel from the facility. However, given the already late stage of the reactor's construction, the lack of existing safeguards, and the possibility that diversion pathways were built deliberately into the structure, it would be reasonable for the P5+1 to insist that Iran close the facility.

Whether or not Iran acquires nuclear weapons, the United States will continue to play an important role in maintaining stability and security in the Middle East. In particular, the United States will continue to act as a guarantor of free passage through the Persian Gulf and the Strait of Hormuz and provide positive security assurances to its Gulf allies and to Israel. The latter assurances will be especially important both to convince Israel to forgo a unilateral attack on Iran's nuclear facilities and to prevent follow-on proliferation in the region if Iran does manage to acquire nuclear weapons.

Conclusion

Iran's nuclear future is uncertain. Iran likely has the technical wherewithal to produce a nuclear weapon if it chooses. Over the long term, the course of its nuclear development will depend more on political and strategic factors than technical ones. Three of these factors are paramount to Iran's decision-makers: the security of the regime, Iran's international prestige and influence, and the particular interests of Iranian decision-makers within a domestic political context. Iranian leaders can be expected to weigh any nuclear decisions according to how well they advance these values.

That being said, Iran has strong disincentives to acquiring nuclear weapons in the near term. Not only is the regime unlikely to produce a weapon quickly enough to avoid detection and interdiction, but even a successful breakout would give Iran only a single, untested weapon and a questionable means of delivering it. In the absence of an unobstructed path to nuclear breakout, regime security is maximized by the slow improvement of Iran's program while remaining within the NPT, a path that Iran appears content to follow.

Iran is also unlikely to ever agree to give up the fuel cycle entirely. Its enrichment program is an important bargaining chip in its relations with the West, a potential source of international prestige, and a potent domestic political symbol that is now strongly linked to the regime's ideology and legitimizing narrative. Possession of the fuel cycle commands broad support among Iranian political elites and the public alike, across all political factions. However, such support does not translate into support for acquiring nuclear weapons or for incurring any cost to continue on the country's present course.

The policy choices of the United States and its allies can have an important effect on Iran's nuclear decision-making. The best chance for preventing Iran from acquiring nuclear weapons (or even a virtual capability) is through continued negotiations. A successful deal must address the three factors of greatest importance to Iranian leaders. Specifically, it must recognize the legitimacy of the regime and foreswear efforts at regime change, provide a face-saving path under which Iran will not sacrifice the status and prestige it incurs from its nuclear program, and recognize the legitimacy of Iranian strategic interests. To do this, the P5+1 must drop its insistence that Iran suspend or give up uranium enrichment. More promising is an agreement under which Iran could continue to enrich uranium but would agree to limits on the number, design, and location of centrifuges, as well as a cap on enrichment levels and stockpile quantities. Iran would also have to agree to implement enhanced safeguards and inspections, including the additional protocol and the supplemental code 3.1. In return, the P5+1 would need to offer Iran a clear and obtainable path to the lifting of financial and oil sanctions. The regime is unlikely to agree to any arrangement that does not include these concessions.

Both sides involved in the current negotiations harbor suspicions of the other's intent that undermine diplomacy. Iran's domestic political conditions have not been conducive to reaching an agreement. Iran's conservatives, who have been dominant within the regime, are skeptical of rapprochement with the West. Iran's pragmatists and reformists are more sensitive to the costs of sanctions and the benefits of improved relations—and also place a lower value on possessing nuclear weapons—but they have not been able to play a major role in Iran's decision-making process on the nuclear issue. At the same time, U.S. domestic politics have also been unfavorable to negotiations, and domestic pressure for the administration to adopt a tougher stance toward Iran has made it difficult to put the sort of inducements on the table that Iran would value sufficiently to give up its nuclear ambitions.

This could change, however, with the recent election of Rouhani to the presidency. His surprise victory will likely give Iranian pragmatists and reformists a more potent voice in nuclear decisions, and could weaken the role of conservatives, especially the principlist hard-liners who had until the election been the dominant force in Iran's politics. Rouhani's identity as a moderate and his more conciliatory tone toward the West may also provide Washington with greater political space to put forward a negotiating offer that the Tehran could accept. However, Iran's new president is committed to the country's enrichment program and is unlikely to agree to give it up in negotiations. Washington must decide whether it is able and willing to make the concessions likely required to reach a deal: security assurances, regime acceptance, a clear path to the lifting of sanctions and the normalization of relations, and acceptance of an Iranian nuclear fuel cycle under international safeguards.

As difficult as successfully negotiating an agreement may appear, other options are much less promising. In particular, preventive air strikes against Iranian nuclear facilities are unlikely to accomplish more than merely delaying Iran's progress. An attack could in fact convince Iran of the need to acquire a nuclear deterrent, leading the regime to redouble its nuclear efforts and commit itself to reconstituting the program. An attack could also undermine international support for the current nonproliferation effort and make it easier for Iran to withdraw from the NPT and expel IAEA inspectors.

A nuclear-armed Iran would present a major security challenge to the region and the world, and the United States and its allies should seek to prevent Iran from acquiring nuclear weapons. Nonetheless, if Iran were to acquire nuclear arms, there are a number of steps that the United States and its regional allies could take to ensure stability. U.S. and Israeli conventional and nuclear forces would likely deter an Iranian nuclear first strike unless Iranian leaders believed the regime was under imminent threat. More concerning would be the threat of the use of nuclear weapons in a crisis. The United States would have to meet Iranian aggression with firmness and resolve, while reassuring Iran that regime change is not imminent. The United States would also need to provide sufficient security assurances to its allies in the region to prevent additional nuclear proliferation and to persuade Israel to maintain its existing nuclear posture and declaratory policy. Managing regional and global stability with a nuclear-armed Iran would be a significant challenge for policymakers, but would not be beyond the military and diplomatic capabilities of the United States.

EXECUTIVE SUMMARY

This chapter examines the future of Japan's hedged dependence on U.S. extended deterrence and encourages more imaginative thinking about potential outcomes and strategic implications as the second nuclear age unfolds.

MAIN ARGUMENT:

- With the U.S. nuclear umbrella shrinking and nuclear threats in Asia becoming greater and more complex, analysts cannot dismiss a nuclear-armed Japan as a purely academic exercise.

- While we do not expect a Japanese nuclear breakout in the near term, Washington's traditional reassurances—massive numbers of weapons deployed in theater and a robust regional presence—have given way to a less convincing reliance on specific weapon systems amid a diminishing conventional military advantage.

- Enhanced bilateral dialogue has been used to strengthen the alliance, but Japan's neighborhood is more dangerous than ever, and the many domestic constraints on Japanese nuclear breakout—cultural, political, and institutional—could become less restrictive than before.

POLICY IMPLICATIONS:

- A U.S. decision to sustain extended deterrence will require significantly more resources and attention than heretofore assigned.

- A more integrated, alliance-based approach to deterrence might therefore become attractive.

- Alternatives to Japan's long-practiced nuclear hedge may come to have appeal in Tokyo or Washington.

- Coordinated regional action to limit North Korea's nuclear development remains critical.

Japan's Nuclear Hedge: Beyond "Allergy" and Breakout

Richard J. Samuels and James L. Schoff

Japanese strategists have long been ambivalent about nuclear weapons. On the one hand, memories of horrific nuclear attacks on Hiroshima and Nagasaki have sustained anti-nuclear sentiment and helped justify national policies championing nonproliferation and forgoing an indigenous nuclear arsenal. This "nuclear allergy" has been diagnosed as a genetic condition, and associated institutional and diplomatic constraints on nuclear breakout have been invoked to predict that Japan will find it virtually impossible to reverse course on nuclear weapons.

Japan's non-nuclear bona fides are well established. Until its revision in 2012, Article 2 of Japan's Atomic Energy Basic Law (1955) stated clearly that research, development, and utilization of atomic energy was limited to peaceful purposes.[1] Japan joined the International Atomic Energy Agency (IAEA) in 1957 and has generously supported the agency's work. After

Richard J. Samuels is Ford International Professor of Political Science and Director of the Center for International Studies at the Massachusetts Institute of Technology. He can be reached at <samuels@mit.edu>.

James L. Schoff is a Senior Associate in the Asia Program at the Carnegie Endowment for International Peace. He can be reached at <jschoff@ceip.org>.

The authors are grateful to Mark Bell, Alison Chang, and Kuni Shimoji for their research assistance and to colleagues James Acton, Vipin Narang, and Christopher Twomey for their review of an early draft.

[1] The 2012 amendment to the law adds "national security" as one of several reasons why nuclear safety should be guaranteed. Although the government and individual lawmakers claim this addition does not conflict with the "peaceful use" of nuclear energy, the revised law is arguably less clear on this point. See, for example, "'National Security' Amendment to Nuclear Law Raises Fears of Military Use," *Asahi Shimbun*, June 21, 2012.

considerable debate and delay—and the receipt from the United States of much greater latitude for nuclear fuel handling and reprocessing—Japan ratified the Nuclear Non-Proliferation Treaty (NPT) in 1976 and supported the treaty's indefinite extension in 1995. Japan also ratified the Comprehensive Nuclear Test Ban Treaty in 1997 and was the first to sign the IAEA's Additional Protocol in 1998, allowing a stricter regimen for IAEA inspections of Japanese nuclear facilities.

Consequently, it was surprising to some in 2013 when Japan declined to join 74 other nations and sign a statement in advance of the next NPT review stating that nuclear weapons are inhumane and should not be used under any circumstance.[2] This illuminates the other, more realistic side of Japan's approach to nuclear weapons. The Japanese government does indeed believe that some circumstances might warrant the acquisition and use of nuclear weapons, and the fact that Japan's ability to act on this belief rests solely in U.S. hands is unnerving for certain politicians and bureaucrats in Tokyo.

Amid periodic reviews of the nuclear option in Japan, national policy has consistently depended on the "full range" of U.S. military might to deter nuclear attacks. This policy has been accompanied by frequent reminders to nuclear-armed rivals, as well as to Washington, that preemptive strikes and the use of nuclear weapons can be valid forms of self-defense. Japan has made it clear since the 1950s that it reserves the right (and will maintain the capacity) to develop a nuclear arsenal of its own. This strategy—"lying between nuclear pursuit and nuclear rollback"—is the essence of "the most salient example of nuclear hedging" among global powers.[3] One Japanese analyst has framed Japan's position on nuclear weapons as a balancing act between nuclear approval and nuclear denial.[4]

Over the past four decades, Japan has maintained viable—and unconcealed—options for the relatively rapid acquisition of nuclear weapons and has justified its decision not to pursue nuclear breakout in many ways. But each time the regional security environment has shifted—such as after China's first nuclear test in 1964, the end of the Cold War, North Korea's nuclear

---

[2] "Japan Refuses to Back Statement against A-bombs," *Japan Times*, April 26, 2013.

[3] This concept is introduced and developed in Ariel E. Levite, "Never Say Never Again: Nuclear Reversal Revisited," *International Security* 27, no. 3 (2002/3): 59–88, 59, 71. Mike M. Mochizuki calls it "pragmatic pacifism" and argues that "it made sense [for Japan] to retain at least a latent capability to exercise the nuclear option." See Mike M. Mochizuki, "Japan Tests the Nuclear Taboo," *Nonproliferation Review* 14, no. 2 (2007): 311. Llewelyn Hughes rejects the term "nuclear hedging" but acknowledges that "the door to independent nuclearization [by Japan] remains ajar" and that "formal barriers to nuclearization are surmountable." See Llewelyn Hughes, "Why Japan Will Not Go Nuclear (Yet): International and Domestic Constraints on the Nuclearization of Japan," *International Security* 31, no. 4 (2007): 67–96, 69, 91.

[4] Yuri Kase, "The Costs and Benefits of Japan's Nuclearization: An Insight into the 1968/70 Internal Report," *Nonproliferation Review* 8, no. 2 (2001): 55.

breakout in the 2000s, or the 2010 U.S.-Russia New Strategic Arms Reduction Treaty (START) agreement limiting warheads and launchers—Tokyo has re-examined its policy before signaling for (and accepting) U.S. reassurance on extended deterrence.

Early on, U.S. reassurances were a straightforward matter. In the 1960s, U.S. nuclear weapons were dispersed widely around the world. In addition to thousands of nuclear-tipped missiles back home and patrolling the seas, the United States kept nearly 3,000 nuclear weapons "on shore" in the Asia-Pacific, including some 1,200 in Okinawa, where U.S. strategic bombers were based.[5] This nuclear deterrent cost Japan relatively little: hosting U.S. military bases and providing for its own basic defense. The combination of Japan's unwillingness to contribute fully to its own defense or to the defense of its U.S. ally and Japanese expressions of concern about the reliability of the U.S. nuclear umbrella accentuated Japan's cheap ride on national security.[6]

Reassuring Japan is more challenging today, however, and how Tokyo sorts through its strategic choices is more pertinent than ever. Japan faces new nuclear threats and relative shifts in the regional balance of power. Although more accurate and more potent, the U.S. nuclear arsenal is now smaller and less visible, and the "second nuclear age" is ushering in a multipolar and less predictable nuclear landscape.[7] The United States withdrew the last of its land-based nuclear weapons from Asia in 1991 and reduced its overall nuclear stockpile by about 75% since then, with further reductions being considered.[8] More recently, U.S. reassurance has focused on the capability and flexibility of specific systems, but this has been undercut by Washington's retirement of some that were earlier touted as being mission-critical.[9] Bilateral dialogue and closer policy coordination have become more important aspects

---

[5] Robert S. Norris, William M. Arkin, and William Burr, "Where They Were: How Much Did Japan Know?" *Bulletin of the Atomic Scientists* 56, no. 1 (1999): 30. Okinawa was under U.S. administrative control at the time.

[6] On U.S. concerns about a Japanese nuclear breakout in the 1960s, see Francis J. Gavin, *Nuclear Statecraft: History and Strategy in America's Atomic Age* (Ithaca: Cornell University Press, 2012). For an analysis of Japan's "cheap ride," see Richard J. Samuels, *Securing Japan: Tokyo's Grand Strategy and the Future of East Asia,* (Ithaca: Cornell University Press, 2007). On the connection between extended deterrence and the "irony" of the imbalanced commitments to the alliance, see Barry R. Posen, *U.S. Grand Strategy: The Case for Restraint* (Ithaca: Cornell University Press, forthcoming).

[7] Keith B. Payne, *Deterrence in the Second Nuclear Age* (Lexington: University Press of Kentucky, 1996).

[8] "Fact Sheet: Increasing Transparency in the U.S. Nuclear Weapons Stockpile," U.S. Department of Defense, May 3, 2010, http://www.defense.gov/npr/docs/10-05-03_fact_sheet_us_nuclear_transparency__final_w_date.pdf; and Scott Wilson, "Obama, in Berlin, Calls for U.S., Russia to Cut Nuclear Warheads," *Washington Post*, June 19, 2013.

[9] For example, the retirement of nuclear-tipped Tomahawk land attack cruise missiles (TLAM/N) was announced in 2010. See Wade L. Huntley, "Speed Bump on the Road to Global Zero: U.S. Nuclear Reductions and Extended Deterrence in East Asia," *Nonproliferation Review* 20, no. 2 (2013): 311–12.

of reassurance and deterrence for the alliance, but the degree to which this can mitigate rising Japanese concerns about North Korea and China is uncertain.

Japanese public opinion remains staunchly anti-nuclear, and Japan would likely be the last country in Northeast Asia to opt for nuclear arms. But while there are many domestic and international constraints on nuclear breakout, there are also signs of a more sophisticated debate in Japan about these issues as the demand for reassurance has escalated. The key questions are how Japan perceives its options, whether and how its calculus could change, and what this would mean for the region and the U.S.-Japan alliance.

To address these questions, this chapter examines the origins and current state of Japan's nuclear hedge and considers how deterrence and reassurance dynamics are evolving in the region. It then explores the prospects and implications for a nuclear breakout by Japan, as well as alternative strategic paths that Japan and the alliance can take. Although Japan's nuclear hedging strategy is likely to continue in the near future, U.S. policymakers (and those throughout the region) should not be sanguine about this strategy continuing indefinitely. Japan's choices will be determined ultimately by how well potential threats can be managed and by the strength of the U.S. commitment to extended deterrence.

Japan's Current Posture

The evolution of Japan's nuclear posture owes as much to political circumstances as to a realistic assessment of U.S. capabilities and commitment. Japanese leaders have understood that the pursuit of nuclear weapons is politically, diplomatically, and economically impracticable, but they also recognize that an independent nuclear deterrent is unnecessary as long as U.S. guarantees remain credible to potential adversaries. As a result, Japan decided early on to deny itself nuclear weapons and instead hedge against changing circumstances.

Japan's nuclear hedge has two elements. The first involves confirming (and serially reconfirming) the U.S. commitment and capability to use nuclear weapons in defense of Japan. In 1965, for example, Prime Minister Eisaku Sato asked Defense Secretary Robert McNamara to pledge to deploy nuclear weapons against China in the event of war. McNamara and President Lyndon Johnson gave that assurance. Similar conversations have followed at various levels of government and the military, always backed by reassuring public statements from Washington. In addition, for decades the Japanese government turned a blind eye to the possible introduction of U.S. ship- and aircraft-based nuclear weapons during port and base visits in Japan, despite its public pledge to forbid such practices.[10] Beginning in 1976, each of Japan's National Defense Program Outlines has stated that Japan will depend on U.S. extended deterrence.

The second element involves Japan's maintenance of the foundation for its own nuclear weapons program, should the country ever make that choice. Former prime minister Nobusuke Kishi believed that nuclear weapons were absolutely necessary if Japan were to have influence in world affairs, and he instructed his Cabinet Legislation Bureau in 1957 to formally pronounce that Japan's constitution allowed the country to possess nuclear weapons for self-defense.[11] An original member of Japan's Atomic Energy Commission recalled how "we were pressured repeatedly to do basic research on how to make an atomic bomb."[12] Leading politicians have reasserted the constitutionality of nuclear weapons throughout the years, including current and former prime ministers Shinzo Abe and Taro Aso.[13] In addition, an important policy study by Japan's Ministry of Foreign Affairs (MOFA) noted in 1969 that "regardless of joining the NPT or not, we will keep the economic and technical potential for the production of nuclear weapons, while seeing to it that Japan will not be interfered with in this regard."[14]

Toward this latter end, and despite considerable opposition from within Japan and from the international community, Japan has never wavered from its early commitment to completing the nuclear fuel cycle. This commitment entails the maintenance of vigorous enrichment and reprocessing capabilities, the stockpiling of separated plutonium, and the development of a fast breeder reactor (FBR) that other nations—most prominently the United States—have long since abandoned as too costly and dangerous. In fact, Japan has the largest nuclear power program of any non-weapons state and is the only one

---

[10] Martin Fackler, "Japan Says It Allowed U.S. Nuclear Ships to Port," *New York Times,* March 9, 2010; and Norris, Arkin, and Burr, "Where They Were," 31.

[11] Samuels, *Securing Japan,* 176. Kishi and then foreign minister Hisanori Yamada reportedly told Ambassador MacArthur in 1958 that their government was exploring the nuclear weapons option. See "Japan Discussed Acquisition of 'Defensive' Nuclear Weapons in 1958," *Japan Times,* March 17, 2013.

[12] Jacques E.C. Hymans, "Veto Players, Nuclear Energy, and Nonproliferation: Domestic Institutional Barriers to a Japanese Bomb," *International Security* 36, no. 2 (2011): 167.

[13] Abe made his comment in a speech at Waseda University in May 2002 when he was deputy chief cabinet secretary, and Aso made the comment in November 2006 when he was foreign minister. The first Abe administration officially clarified this stance in a 2006 statement before the Diet, saying that "even with nuclear weapons, we've understood that possessing them would not necessarily violate the constitution as long as it is kept within [the limits of minimum capabilities necessary for self-defense]." See, for example, "Japan Can Hold Nuclear Arms for Self-Defense: Govt.," Reuters, November 14, 2006.

[14] See Taka Daitoku, "The Kishi Doctrine and the Construction of a Virtual Nuclear State in Postwar Japan" (paper presented to the Annual Meeting of the American Historical Association, New Orleans, January 5, 2013); and *Mainichi Daily News,* August 2, 1994.

with full-spectrum fuel cycle capabilities.[15] Of course, Japan's nuclear power industry suffered a major blow after the 2011 tsunami-induced meltdowns at plants in Fukushima, and there are many legal, political, and technical restrictions that would make a Japanese nuclear breakout extremely difficult. Nonetheless, it has always been important for Japan to keep that option open.

Opening the Nuclear Umbrella

Nestling under the U.S. "nuclear umbrella" was never uncontroversial. Left-wing politicians argued in the mid-1960s that this policy was part of Washington's plan for global domination, and much of the public feared becoming entangled in a nuclear war between superpowers.[16] Some on the political right, seeing reliance on U.S. nuclear weapons as a symbol of Japan's second-tier status, worried about national prestige and pushed for a more overt hedge.[17] Conservative political leaders—including Shigeru Yoshida and Hayato Ikeda in the pragmatic wing of the Liberal Democratic Party (LDP) and revisionists such as Ichiro Hatoyama and Yasuhiro Nakasone—repeatedly called in private for an indigenous nuclear capability.[18]

Inside the bureaucracy, opinions were mixed. MOFA warned in 1959 that Japan should not rule out the possibility of developing nuclear weapons, lest the country lose flexibility in pursuing national security.[19] Later, in 1966, a vice minister of foreign affairs stated publicly that Japan was not protected under the U.S. nuclear umbrella. MOFA immediately issued a "unified viewpoint," introducing one of many awkward locutions the Japanese government uses to describe its national security strategy: it was not accurate to say that Japan was not covered by the nuclear umbrella.[20]

Sato, initially a supporter of Japanese nuclear armament, reversed course when confronted with Washington's strong nonproliferation policy

---

[15] Nobumasa Akiyama and Kenta Horio, "Can Japan Remain Committed to Nonproliferation?" *Washington Quarterly* 36, no. 2 (2013): 152. For more on the domestic disputes about Japan's "nuclear back end," see Richard J. Samuels, *3.11: Disaster and Change in Japan* (Ithaca: Cornell University Press, 2013).

[16] *Nikkan Joyaku nado Tokubetsu Iinkai: Nipponkoku to Dai Kan Minkoku to no aida no Kihon Kankei ni Kansuru Joyaku nado no Teiketsu ni tsuite Shonin wo Motomeru no Ken* [Proceedings of the Special Committee Considering the Proposed Japan-Korea Treaty], House of Councillors, National Diet of Japan, December 3, 1965.

[17] Daitoku, "Kishi Doctrine," 2.

[18] See Ayako Kusunoki, "The Sato Cabinet and the Making of Japan's Non-Nuclear Policy," *Journal of American–East Asian Relations* 15, nos. 1–2 (2008): 28–29; and Daitoku, "Kishi Doctrine," 3.

[19] "No-Nuke Policy Ruled Out Years before Declaration," *Kyodo News*, December 22, 2008.

[20] Nobumasa Akiyama, "The Socio-Political Roots of Japan's Non-Nuclear Posture," in *Japan's Nuclear Option: Security, Politics, and Policy in the 21st Century*, ed. Benjamin L. Self and Jeffrey W. Thompson (Washington, D.C.: Henry L. Stimson Center), 86. For similar rhetorical gymnastics on defense policy, see Samuels, *Securing Japan*.

and his own government's internal studies concluding that reliance on extended deterrence was the best way forward.[21] None of the conceivable alternatives—i.e., domestic nuclear weapons production, nuclear sharing with the United States, or overtly denying U.S. nuclear protection—was considered viable at that time by most Japanese strategists. Understanding this reality, and provided with high-level U.S. assurances, in 1967 Sato announced three non-nuclear principles: non-possession, non-manufacture, and non-introduction. A year later he articulated the "four pillars" policy, and in 1970 the government signed the NPT, leaving no doubt about Japan's reliance on the U.S. nuclear umbrella.[22]

One of the four pillars is the three non-nuclear principles, and this pillar is accompanied by three more: (1) promoting nuclear power for peaceful purposes, (2) promoting global nuclear disarmament, and (3) relying on the U.S. nuclear deterrent for protection from the international nuclear threat. The four pillars policy officially opened the nuclear umbrella, and even if it is perceived as leaky by some, this umbrella has remained open ever since. Although he privately called the three principles "nonsense," Sato was awarded the Nobel Peace Prize in 1974.

Japan's "Basic Defense" Rationale and Its Latent Nuclear Deterrent

Around this time in the early 1970s, Japanese defense officials moved away from ambitious plans for a robust Self-Defense Force (SDF) and adjusted to the political and economic realities of the time. A bellwether document penned in 1971 by Takuya Kubo, the director of the Defense Bureau of the Japan Defense Agency (JDA), outlined a new direction toward basic defense. Kubo saw "no probable threats" to Japan and rationalized a small defense establishment and close alliance with the United States.[23] Kubo agreed with other leading strategic thinkers that nuclear weapons had limited military utility for Japan. The country was too dense and too small and would always

---

[21] Some suggest that it is also possible that rather than seriously advocating for nuclear weapons, Sato was instead taking that position in order to extract security guarantees from Washington. See Kusunoki, "Sato Cabinet," 31; and Michael J. Green and Katsuhisa Furukawa, "Japan: New Nuclear Realism," in *The Long Shadow: Nuclear Weapons and Security in 21st Century Asia*, ed. Muthiah Alagappa (Singapore: National University of Singapore Press, 2009), 357. Others are less certain. See Kurt M. Campbell and Tsuyoshi Sunohara, "Japan: Thinking the Unthinkable," in *The Nuclear Tipping Point: Why States Reconsider Their Nuclear Choices*, ed. Kurt M. Campbell, Robert J. Einhorn, and Mitchell B. Reiss (Washington, D.C.: Brookings Institution Press, 2004), 218–53; and Etel Solingen, *Nuclear Logics: Contrasting Paths in East Asia and the Middle East* (Princeton: Princeton University Press, 2007), 73.

[22] For more on the Sato turnaround, the three principles, and the four pillars, see Green and Furukawa, "Japan: New Nuclear Realism"; Kusunoki, "Sato Cabinet"; and Solingen, *Nuclear Logics*.

[23] Kubo's memo was titled "A Framework to Consider the Arrangement of Japan's Defense Capabilities," available at World and Japan database, University of Tokyo Institute of Oriental Culture, February 20, 1971, http://www.ioc.u-tokyo.ac.jp/~worldjpn/documents/texts/JPSC/19710220.O1J.html.

lose more than it gained in a nuclear exchange. Moreover, adversaries were unlikely to believe that Japan would actually use its nuclear weapons—a lack of credibility that, according to Kubo, undermined their deterrent effect. "There is no choice but to rely on U.S. extended deterrence," he concluded.[24]

Japan's basic defense concept became the centerpiece of the country's first National Defense Program Outline in 1976 and continued to shape Japan's defense strategy until it was superseded in 2010 by a "dynamic defense" concept.[25] Although for Kubo nuclear breakout was off the table, his memo clearly articulated Japan's nuclear hedge, positioning the hedge more as a signal to Japan's U.S. ally than to its adversaries: "[Japan should] establish a structure to develop considerable nuclear armament capability at any time… [so] the United States will get worried about unstable international relations due to nuclear proliferation and will desire to maintain the U.S.-Japan security regime including extended deterrence."[26]

The most prominent and credible element of Japan's latent weapons capability is its sophisticated nuclear energy program and, in particular, its decades-long national commitment to completing the nuclear fuel cycle in the name of energy independence. This goal justifies reprocessing spent fuel and accumulating separated plutonium for use in a "pluthermal" mixed-oxide (MOX) product. Extracting more energy from spent fuel by reusing it and operating FBRs that produce more fissile material than they consume can release Japan from its dependence on imported fuels. In theory, this energy strategy sounds sensible. The problem, however, is that the economics and engineering behind this MOX/FBR strategy are not working, and the plutonium continues to accumulate.[27] Japan's stocks of plutonium now vastly outweigh the amount needed for any plausible nuclear power or nuclear

---

[24] Kubo, "A Framework to Consider the Arrangement of Japan's Defense Capabilities."

[25] See "Summary of National Defense Program Guidelines for FY 2011 and Beyond," Japan Cabinet Secretariat, 3, http://www.kantei.go.jp/foreign/policy/decisions/2010/__icsFiles/afieldfile/2012/01/27/summary_ndpg_e.pdf.

[26] Kubo, "A Framework to Consider the Arrangement of Japan's Defense Capabilities."

[27] See "The Current Situation of Plutonium Management in Japan," Atomic Energy Commission of Japan, September 20, 2011, http://www.aec.go.jp/jicst/NC/iinkai/teirei/siryo2011/siryo36/110920e.pdf. At the end of 2011, Japan had 44.3 metric tons of separated reactor-grade plutonium. Of this, 9.3 metric tons are in Japan. The remaining 35 metric tons are in reprocessing plants in France (La Hague) and the United Kingdom (Sellafield). See "Communication Received from Japan Concerning Its Policies Regarding the Management of Plutonium," International Atomic Energy Agency (IAEA), October 3, 2012, http://www.iaea.org/Publications/Documents/Infcircs/2012/infcirc549a1-15.pdf.

weapons program. One leading American expert suggests that today there is "enough plutonium in Japan to make 1,000 nuclear weapons."[28]

Japan's nuclear hedge requires that the connection between nuclear power and nuclear arms not be hidden. When the Japanese nuclear power industry faced elimination after the March 2011 catastrophe in northeastern Japan, senior leaders—including Satoshi Morimoto, the incumbent defense minister in 2012—argued that nuclear power was the basis for a "latent deterrent" and must be preserved. Likewise, former defense minister Shigeru Ishiba said that it was "important to maintain our commercial reactors because it would allow us to produce a nuclear warhead in a short amount of time."[29]

A second element of Japan's nuclear hedge is the expertise in potential weapon-delivery platforms that the country has gained through its space program.[30] Although its primary space-launch vehicle, the H-II series, is poorly suited as a missile—given its liquid-fuel composition—Japan has consistently pursued solid-fuel rocket technology, starting with the Kappa in 1956 and eventually leading to the 1.8-ton payload M-V in 1989.[31] The decision to discontinue the M-V in 2006 over cost concerns was opposed by some members of the Diet who believed the government should maintain such technology for its potential military utility.[32] The M-V's successor, the Epsilon-1, failed to launch in its first attempt but should fly later in 2013.

Although Japanese rockets are not designed to re-enter the atmosphere or hit a specific target, the Japan Aerospace Exploration Agency has been experimenting with re-entry technology since at least 1994 and accomplished its first controlled re-entry for the upper stage of the H-IIB rocket in 2011.[33] Japan has had access to U.S. ballistic missile defense technologies at both the

---

[28] Frank von Hippel, "Should the U.S. Encourage South Korea and Japan to Make Plutonium-based Nuclear Fuels?" (presentation at the Nonproliferation Policy Education Center, Washington, D.C., April 4, 2013). Ichiro Ozawa, a senior Japanese politician, has suggested that the number of potential warheads is closer to three or four times von Hippel's estimate. A decade ago, Self and Thompson estimated that number to be in the hundreds. See Benjamin L. Self and Jeffrey W. Thompson, "Nuclear Energy, Space Launch Vehicles, and Advanced Technology: Japan's Prospects for Nuclear Breakout," in Self and Thompson, *Japan's Nuclear Options*, 163.

[29] Samuels, *3.11: Disaster and Change*, 124. For their part, American officials rushed to support the beleaguered Japanese nuclear power program after the disasters of March 11, 2011. Some report that this was due to U.S. concerns about the effect of a shutdown on excessive plutonium stockpiles, but others suggest that U.S. dependence on Japanese nuclear technology requires a robust nuclear power industry. Author interview with a former senior Japanese intelligence official, Tokyo, March 26, 2013.

[30] For an optimistic assessment of the military capabilities of Japan's space program, see Saadia M. Pekkanen and Paul Kallender-Umezu, *In Defense of Japan: From the Market to the Military in Space Policy* (Stanford: Stanford University Press, 2010); and for an opposing view, see Thompson and Self, "Nuclear Energy."

[31] Katsuhisa Furukawa, "Making Sense of Japan's Nuclear Policy: Arms Control, Extended Deterrence, and the Nuclear Option," in Self and Thompson, *Japan's Nuclear Option*, 114.

[32] Author interview with a Japanese defense analyst, February 8, 2008.

[33] See "Successful Execution of Controlled Re-entry of Launch Vehicle Upper Stage," *JAXA Today*, August 2012, 22–23.

upper (mid-course) and lower (terminal phase) tiers, and has been developing space technologies to assist with precision targeting, including high-precision time control and orbital estimation.[34]

Studies of Japan's nuclear options do not agree on how quickly the country could establish a robust, survivable, independent nuclear deterrent—a much more challenging task than building a few bombs. Some conclude that Japan is technically capable of developing a nuclear weapon within a year (some studies even suggest six months or less), whereas others argue that it would take at least a decade.[35] It is widely acknowledged that Japan lacks expertise on bomb and warhead design, reliable delivery vehicles, intelligence and counterintelligence capabilities designed to protect and hide assets from a potential first strike, a comprehensive command-and-control system, and infrastructure to safely test weapons.[36] These are not trivial constraints that could be overcome immediately. For example, if Japan wanted a sea-based deterrent—an attractive option given its greater survivability—it would have to develop ballistic missile submarines and possibly nuclear-powered ones. Likewise, the use of reactor-grade plutonium, though not impossible (and not likely Japan's first choice), would create new difficulties and take additional time.

There is, of course, an alternative and more likely route—using highly enriched uranium (HEU). The controversial Rokkasho nuclear enrichment plant has sophisticated centrifuges that provide Japan with a uranium-enrichment capability. Another, less likely path to producing weapons-grade HEU could be through a process of laser isotope separation, which Japan dabbled in for years before inefficiencies led to a cutback on implementation plans in 2001. Although laser enrichment is not commercially attractive, the know-how and equipment remain in Japan, and as we learned

---

[34] Pekkanen and Kallender-Umezu, *In Defense of Japan*, 36–37; and Narushige Michishita, "Japan's Response to Nuclear North Korea," *Joint U.S.-Korea Academic Studies* 23 (2012): 99–112.

[35] These comparisons are imperfect. Some refer to building a single bomb, others to building a robust, survivable arsenal. For a range of estimates, see Federation of American Scientists, "Japan's Nuclear Weapons Program," April 16, 2000, http://www.fas.org/nuke/guide/japan/nuke; Matake Kamiya, "Nuclear Japan: Oxymoron or Coming Soon?" *Washington Quarterly* 26, no. 1 (2002–3): 63–75; Toshi Yoshihara and James R. Holms, eds., *Strategy in the Second Nuclear Age: Power, Ambition, and the Ultimate Weapon* (Washington, D.C.: Georgetown University Press, 2012); Kusunoki, "The Sato Cabinet"; and National Intelligence Estimate, "The Likelihood of Further Nuclear Proliferation," no. 4-66, January 20, 1966, available from George Washington University's National Security Archive, Electronic Briefing Book, no. 155, June 1, 2005, http://www.gwu.edu/~nsarchiv/NSAEBB/NSAEBB155/prolif-12.pdf. A secret government-requested study in 2006 estimated that it would take "at least 3 to 5 years until Japan can go into trial production of a miniaturized warhead." See *Sankei Shimbun*, December 25, 2006.

[36] See Jeffrey Lewis, "How Long for Japan to Build a Deterrent?" Arms Control Wonk, web log, December 28, 2006, "http://lewis.armscontrolwonk.com/archive/1339/japans-nuclear-status; and Hajime Izumi and Katsuhisa Furukawa, "Not Going Nuclear: Japan's Response to North Korea's Nuclear Test," *Arms Control Today* 37, no. 5 (2007), http://www.armscontrol.org/act/2007_06/coverstory.

in the case of South Korea in 2004, experiments to produce HEU in small doses can be difficult for IAEA inspectors to detect.[37]

There are other skills in which Japanese researchers excel that are often neglected in discussions of Japan's latent deterrent. These include high-speed framing radiography, heavy-metal shock physics, radiation hydrodynamics, and explosive shaping. Knowledge in these areas and others that are basic for development of a thermonuclear device is scattered throughout Japan's industrial and research communities. It is not uncommon for Japanese research scientists to attend and present papers on shock compression or high-speed photonics at international conferences also attended by nuclear weapons scientists from the United States, Russia, and China.[38] These research activities have practical application in a wide range of non-military areas and are not necessarily telltale signs of a secret nuclear weapons research program. Indeed, while some policymakers in Tokyo would like to foster closer ties between Japan's scientists and defense planners, a wide gulf remains between the two communities.[39] It also appears that Japan lacks deep experience with other activities relevant to a weapons program such as plutonium metallurgy or beryllium machining, which could be helpful depending on what path it chooses.

Still, Japan clearly has mature capabilities in certain areas, capabilities that are as relevant to its nuclear hedge as the country's plutonium stockpile. It is also evident that national policy recognizes the value of these programs in preventing both the United States and potential adversaries from taking Japan's non-nuclear status for granted. In short, given Japan's level of technological sophistication, stable civil-military relations, accessible and plentiful plutonium stockpiles, self-contained nuclear fuel cycle, and history of success in "spinning on" commercial technologies, the country's nuclear hedge remains intact and credible.[40]

---

[37] In 2004, South Korean officials admitted to the IAEA that government scientists conducted HEU experiments in 2000 (without authorization) using laser isotope separation, successfully producing small amounts of nearly weapons-grade uranium.

[38] For a more detailed assessment of Japan's technical and scientific capacity to produce nuclear weapons, see James L. Schoff, "Realigning Priorities: The U.S.-Japan Alliance and the Future of Extended Deterrence," Institute for Foreign Policy Analysis, March 2009, 44–49, http://www.ifpa.org/pdf/RealignPriorities.pdf.

[39] Katsuhisa Furukawa, "Japan's Policy and Views on Nuclear Weapon: A Historical Perspective," *Jebat: Malaysian Journal of History, Politics, & Strategic Studies* 37 (2010): 21–22.

[40] The U.S. Department of Energy reports that reactor-grade plutonium could be used to produce reliable weapons comparable to those produced using weapons-grade plutonium. See Marvin Miller, "Japan, Nuclear Weapons, and Reactor-Grade Plutonium" (paper presented at a seminar at the Nuclear Control Institute, Washington, D.C., March 27, 2002), http://www.nci.org/02NCI/04/mm-jpu-paper.htm. For a history of Japan's technological "spin on" from commercial to military applications, see Richard J. Samuels, *"Rich Nation, Strong Army": National Security and the Technological Transformation of Japan* (Ithaca: Cornell University Press, 1994).

Extended Deterrence 2.0

The U.S.-Japan alliance and its extended deterrent have enabled the nonproliferation policies that help Tokyo signal its intention to refrain from breaking out with its own nuclear arsenal. Another vital factor has been the absence of a consistent existential threat to Japan. Whenever one or both of these factors seems to shift, signs of reconsideration in Tokyo become apparent and subtle reminders that Japan has other nuclear options are issued to Washington. Japan has long understood how important the nonproliferation objective is to the United States, and how to use it for policy leverage.[41]

The Primacy of Reassurance

Japanese policymakers often remind their U.S. and regional counterparts (both privately and publicly) about the importance of the U.S. nuclear umbrella and Japan's own ability to go nuclear if necessary. As we have noted, then prime minister Sato made such a statement in 1964 and 1965, as did former prime minister Morihiro Hosokawa in 1998, opposition leader Ichiro Ozawa in Beijing in 2002, and then foreign minister Aso after North Korea's 2006 nuclear test.[42] Additional signals have been sent through Diet interpellations, as well as through unofficial channels and provocative political commentary.[43]

Washington's response to these signals has been consistent. In 2006, then U.S. secretary of state Condoleezza Rice visited Japan and reaffirmed the United States' "will and capability" to meet the "full range of its deterrence and security commitments" in an attempt to reassure Japan that it is still well protected under the U.S. nuclear umbrella.[44] President Barack Obama offered similar public assurances after North Korea's subsequent tests in 2009 and

---

[41] See Green and Furukawa, "Japan: New Nuclear Realism." See also Steven Pifer, Richard C. Bush, Vanda Felbab-Brown, Martin S. Indyk, Michael O'Hanlon, and Kenneth M. Pollack, "U.S. Nuclear and Extended Deterrence: Considerations and Challenges," *Arms Control Series,* no. 3, June 2010.

[42] One could also speculate that Japan's December 2008 declassification of the Sato-McNamara notes was another subtle reminder, coming as it did on the heels of the U.S. delisting of North Korea as a state sponsor of terrorism, despite the lack of progress on verifying North Korean denuclearization promises.

[43] Although there were no mentions of "extended deterrence" in Diet hearings in 2008, there were 68 in 2009 and 58 in 2010. See http://kokkai.ndl.go.jp. There is also a long history of comments by "autonomists" outside government, such as Ikutaro Shimizu, Nishihachi Hyodo, Tadae Takubo, and Terumasa Nakanishi, who have pressed Japan to break away from U.S. security guarantees and develop its own nuclear arsenal. See Kamiya, "Nuclear Japan," 66–67; and Furukawa Katsuhisa, "Making Sense of Japan's Nuclear Policy: Arms Control, Extended Deterrence, and the Nuclear Option," in Self and Thompson, *Japan's Nuclear Option,* 111.

[44] "Remarks with Japanese Foreign Minister Taro Aso after Their Meeting," U.S. Department of State, October 18, 2006.

2013 when Prime Minister Abe asked him to reconfirm the U.S. commitment to defend Japan with "an unshakeable nuclear umbrella."[45]

For now, reliance on U.S. extended deterrence persists even if discomfort with the status quo is growing. This discomfort stems from different sources. Some Japanese politicians and analysts are worried that a policy designed for a bipolar world order will become less reliable in a multipolar environment filled with regional nuclear powers. Japan could, in this formulation, become "detached" from U.S. strategic thinking.[46] While some seek to prevent this through closer ties with Washington, others chafe under the postwar legal and diplomatic restraints that Japan agreed to live with for the sake of economic development; they would pursue a different postwar relationship with the United States by taking more security and diplomatic matters into their own hands.

Yet the Japanese express concern about extended deterrence in contradictory ways. Whereas once they worried about the U.S. commitment when North Korean nuclear weapons could not reach the continental United States—i.e., that Washington might prioritize proliferation over the medium-range missile threat—now that the prospect has become more realistic, they express concerns because North Korea's nuclear weapons could target the U.S. homeland. For example, a *Sankei Shimbun* editorial suggested that Washington could be "intimidated," quoting a former defense ministry official who opined that "we cannot completely rule out the possibility of Japan's being cut off from U.S. nuclear strategy."[47]

In the case of China, the allies' superiority in conventional forces appears more important than the nuclear balance for now, especially as the U.S. arsenal shrinks. This comes in part from a core challenge of extended deterrence, wherein a deterrence provider seeks to limit a conflict to the region it is protecting in order to avoid an all-out war that might entangle its homeland. Based on this logic, while Washington will do everything it can to prevent the escalation or expansion of an East Asian regional conflict, if the U.S. military cannot dominate conventionally, Washington might default to accommodation rather than resort to nuclear weapons. As one former diplomat explained, "the conventional superiority advantage is critical, because it obviates the whole debate about whether or not Washington would 'sacrifice Los Angeles to save Tokyo' in a nuclear exchange."[48] Consequently, even though nuclear weapons are a major psychological component of

---

[45] *Sankei Shimbun,* February 22, 2013.

[46] Yukio Satoh, "Agenda for Japan-U.S. Strategic Consultations" (article adapted from a presentation made at the International Symposium on Security Affairs, Tokyo, November 18, 2009).

[47] *Sankei Shimbun,* February 22, 2013.

[48] Author interview with a former MOFA official, August 1, 2007.

extended deterrence (and certainly the most talked about), Japan is also focused on the U.S. projection of conventional power, which is under strain from U.S. budget politics, Chinese military developments, and Japan's unwillingness to invest in its own defense.

The United States' budget problems, coupled with its efforts to reduce nuclear weapons globally, exacerbate a concern some have in Japan over the long-term durability of the U.S. nuclear infrastructure. By some measures, U.S. nuclear capabilities have atrophied over time. The United States has not developed a new warhead in over 25 years, and it has not tested a weapon since 1992. The U.S. Departments of Defense and Energy stated in 2008 that the United States "is now the *only* nuclear weapons state party to the NPT that does not have the ability to produce a new nuclear warhead."[49] The Obama administration is making some investments to upgrade existing nuclear infrastructure, but Washington will soon face tough and expensive choices about what kind of nuclear deterrent the United States (and its allies) should have in the future.

Some U.S. defense planners believe that when modern security problems are pushed to the higher rungs of a conflict-escalation ladder, the nuclear arsenal inherited from the Cold War will prove to be inappropriate for uses beyond deterring a large-scale nuclear attack against the United States or a close ally. As former deputy secretary of defense John Hamre observed, "the Cold War left us with a massive inventory of [nuclear] weapons we no longer need...[and] a shrinking community of nuclear experts hold on [to it] as a security blanket for a future they cannot define."[50]

Recent U.S. administrations have believed that deterrence through conventional weapons is decisively more credible than deterrence through any existing nuclear alternative. The challenge, however, is that continued U.S. investment in conventional military superiority is precisely what drives weaker states to pursue asymmetric solutions with nuclear weapons (e.g., North Korea and Iran) and prompts other major powers to keep pace with their own military investments (e.g., China), further worrying regional allies like Japan. There is no easy balance that truly guarantees security through strength without feeding into a broader security dilemma.

Given the rising profile of these challenges since 2001, the United States and Japan began bilateral consultations in 2009 on strategic issues raised by

---

[49] "National Security and Nuclear Weapons in the 21st Century," U.S. Department of Energy and U.S. Department of Defense, September 2008 (emphasis in the original). Some argue that since the United States has no need to develop a new warhead or, given the size of its database, to test one, the term "atrophied" is hyperbolic. Others highlight U.S. investments in expensive testing tools—such as the National Ignition Facility—that bolster the United States' confidence in the reliability of its arsenal. Authors' personal communication with Vipin Narang, June 9, 2013, and James Acton, July 8, 2013.

[50] John J. Hamre, "Toward a Nuclear Strategy," *Washington Post*, May 2, 2005.

the impending U.S. Nuclear Posture Review (NPR) and Quadrennial Defense Review (QDR). For the first time, Japan moved onto the path of officially discussing and even influencing U.S. nuclear strategy and force planning, something to which the United States' NATO partners had long become accustomed. Japan had been unsettled by prior NPRs that unilaterally shifted the U.S. force posture with little consultation.[51] It was concerned that the United States might reach a decision to accommodate North Korea, move toward a "no first use" policy on nuclear arms, or retire nuclear weapons systems, particularly the nuclear Tomahawk cruise missile (TLAM/N), without deploying compensating capabilities.[52]

During this time, Japanese officials reportedly gave American interlocutors a "non-paper" that described key criteria for sustaining extended deterrence. The paper highlighted reliability (i.e., confidence that warheads will function properly), flexibility (holding different targets at risk), responsiveness, discrimination (keeping low-yield options), and the ability to be either stealthy or visible, as warranted by the situation.[53] While there was some doubt at the time about how high up this paper had been approved within the Japanese government, aspects of these criteria continue to be raised by Japanese officials, and the continuation of bilateral consultations on extended deterrence suggests that the allies have plenty to discuss.[54] These criteria appear to reflect real concerns in Japan that require continued alliance attention.

The success of the bilateral NPR consultations led both sides to want to continue talks, and in March 2011 they "regularized" the Extended Deterrence Dialogue (EDD). The EDD is now a biannual event, with one of the meetings often involving a visit to a deterrence-infrastructure site. In 2013, for example, this included a tour of Naval Base Kitsap in Washington State to see the submarine leg of the nuclear triad and Trident missile facilities.[55] These discussions are not trivial conversations or mere photo opportunities. They

---

[51] For similar reasons, the United States initiated a dialogue with South Korea at around the same time.

[52] For Japanese concerns about no first use, see Satoh, "Agenda"; and Yukio Satoh, "Kakugunshuku jidai no Nihon no anzen hosho" [Japanese National Security in an Age of Nuclear Arms Reduction], *Gaiko Forum* (2009): 46–49. For concerns about the TLAM/N, see Hans M. Kristensen, "U.S. Navy Instruction Confirms Retirement of Nuclear Tomahawk Cruise Missile," FAS Strategic Security Blog, web log, March 18, 2013, http://blogs.fas.org/security/2013/03/tomahawk.

[53] Hans M. Kristensen, "Japan's Nuclear Secrets," *Sekai,* October 2009, http://www.fas.org/programs/ssp/nukes/publications1/Sekai2009.pdf.

[54] For suggestions that these criteria are not representative of government or citizen views, see Gregory Kulacki, "Japan and America's Nuclear Posture," Union of Concerned Scientists, March 2010, http://www.ucsusa.org/assets/documents/nwgs/japan-american-nuclear-posture.pdf. Japanese officials mentioned these criteria in numerous author interviews between 2010 and 2013.

[55] Kevin Baron, "U.S., Japan Met to Talk Nuclear Deterrence," Foreign Policy, E-Ring, web log, April 12, 2013, http://e-ring.foreignpolicy.com/posts/2013/04/12/us_japan_met_to_talk_nuclear_deterrence.

are a joint exploration by knowledgeable officials of current and emerging nuclear threats to the alliance, along with possible deterrence strategies.[56]

The site visits are thorough and underscore the fact that U.S. declaratory statements are backed by demonstrable capabilities, with the human capital being among the most important. Site visits make the U.S. nuclear umbrella visible and tangible for Japanese officials, and they highlight the significant investments that support it. Both countries' principals hope that, over time, the EDD will also enhance deterrence by better integrating nuclear and conventional capabilities within the alliance for a tailored deterrence strategy, especially vis-à-vis North Korea. The EDD also provides Japan with an official channel to share its perceptions about extended deterrence with the United States, which makes the dialogue a useful bellwether for how the Japanese government feels about its nuclear hedge.

The U.S. side reportedly is pleased that the EDD has deepened Japan's understanding of extended deterrence and provided a better appreciation of the role played by conventional forces and missile defense, including high-end missile-tracking radar deployments in Japan.[57] Still, the Japanese side appears to have an appetite for continued dialogue. Security planners in Tokyo acknowledge that discussions are "far deeper than before," but some express concern that Washington will continue to surprise them.[58] Reaffirmation of U.S. commitments and reliability alone is no longer sufficient. The EDD portends a more collaborative form of deterrence that encompasses the full spectrum of conventional and nuclear capabilities possessed by the allies. Japanese strategists who once expressed little more than "sheer and total dependence upon the American deterrent" now understand that assuaging their abandonment fear requires more Japanese involvement in lower (conventional) thresholds of potential conflict, and they seek greater input into Washington's nuclear doctrine and priorities. The EDD will have to balance this carefully.[59]

---

[56] This information is based on interviews with participating U.S. and Japanese officials and military officers in April 2013. The two sides are led by officials from the Japanese Foreign and Defense Ministries and the U.S. State and Defense Departments at the deputy director general and deputy assistant secretary levels, respectively.

[57] Huntley, "Speed Bump on the Road to Global Zero," 16, 21.

[58] Author interview with a senior defense planner in Japan's Ministry of Defense, Tokyo, March 25, 2013.

[59] Paul J. Saunders, "Extended Deterrence and Security in East Asia: A U.S.-Japan-South Korea Dialogue," Center for the National Interest, January 2012, http://www.cftni.org/2012-Extended-Deterence-In-East-Asia.pdf.

External Threats

While Washington has some control in addressing the reassurance factor, it faces limits when it comes to threats and threat perceptions. North Korea is a primary concern for Japan, largely because Pyongyang appears to care little about its people and invests heavily in nuclear and missile programs. North Korea's nuclear capability could make the leadership even more reckless. Should the regime face imminent collapse or preemptive attack, it might judge that it has little to lose (and could even forestall outside interference) by striking Japan with a nuclear weapon. There are also questions about whether Pyongyang can maintain effective command and control over these weapons.

Washington's official assessments of North Korea's nuclear capability are written vaguely but express confidence that the North will be able to produce nuclear-tipped missiles in the not-too-distant future and that their accuracy will improve.[60] To strike Japan, North Korea could use some of its estimated two hundred Nodong medium-range ballistic missiles, which have a range of 1,500 kilometers and a payload of one ton. North Korea is also developing a land-based intermediate-range missile (Musudan) that might be able to reach Okinawa and Guam. Although the accuracy of these missiles has been derided in the past, a battery of test launches in July 2006 suggested that North Korea had improved their performance, and in December 2012 it put a satellite into orbit for the first time using a three-stage rocket.[61]

A key problem for extended deterrence is the allies' limited understanding of Pyongyang's strategic calculus and Washington's unexpressed preference to deal with North Korean nuclear threats by conventional methods. There could come a point where Japanese leaders feel that they need more control over the means of response. A 1995 JDA report made this point while otherwise dismissing the value of a nuclear option for Japan: "North Korean nuclearization…is not an issue that cannot be a condition for discussing the possibility of Japan going nuclear in the future."[62] In other words, the JDA identified North Korea as a threat that could cause Japan to go nuclear.

Compared with North Korea, China's nuclear arsenal and conventional capabilities are much larger and weigh heavily on the minds of Japanese defense planners. The main worry is not simply that China's defense budget

---

[60] Bradley Klapper and Lara Jakes, "North Korea Tension Puts Pressure on China, U.S.," *Christian Science Monitor*, April 13, 2013. Note, though, that inaccuracy can be an even greater threat—for example, if an adversary targets the Sea of Japan but hits an urban center.

[61] Yossef Bodansky, "DPRK Strategic Command and Control, Missile Launch Exercise Marks Operational Watershed," *Defense & Foreign Affairs Special Analysis* 24, no. 42 (2006).

[62] Japan Defense Agency, "Concerning the Problem of the Proliferation of Weapons of Mass Destruction," 1995, 34, http://www.ucsusa.org/assets/documents/nwgs/1995jdastudy.pdf.

has almost tripled since 2001 to become the world's second largest.[63] Rather, it is the nature of China's military modernization and the relatively quick and substantial investments in capabilities that are aimed at the allies' ability to dominate the skies and seas around East Asia. This strategic force modernization raises the potential costs that U.S. policymakers would need to weigh when considering the option of intervening against Chinese interests on behalf of Japan or Taiwan.

Another long-term problem is that China keeps building new nuclear warheads (up to ten in 2012). Although official Chinese policy states that China will not use nuclear weapons first—or ever against a non–nuclear weapon state—its intimidation tactics in the maritime and cyber domains have worried some in Japan that these tactics could someday spread to the nuclear realm.[64] The People's Liberation Army (PLA), after all, manages one of the world's most active ballistic missile programs. Many of its tactical weapons have enhanced ranges, accuracies, and payloads, and some put Okinawa within range when forward-deployed. Upgrades to Chinese missile warheads—including multiple independently targeted re-entry vehicles—are enhancing Beijing's deterrent and strategic-strike capabilities vis-à-vis Japanese and U.S. missile defenses.[65] These slow-moving upgrades to the quality and quantity of Chinese nuclear weapons have some in Tokyo wondering whether Beijing will eventually seek nuclear parity with the United States, something that would require considerable time and investment given that the U.S. arsenal is significantly larger.

Japanese strategists have to ask how much vulnerability the United States is willing to tolerate amid China's strategic modernization and what it is prepared to do on Japan's behalf, if anything, in response to China's moves.[66] Some prominent Japanese analysts suggest that a national nuclear deterrent, even if it were insufficient to deter a force as big as China's in all circumstances, could complicate strategic calculations in Beijing to the extent that China would think twice before threatening to use (or actually using)

---

[63] U.S. officials estimate that China's actual defense spending was roughly $60 billion in 2001 and that it could have been as high as $215 billion in 2012. See Office of the Secretary of Defense, *Annual Report to Congress: Military and Security Developments Involving the People's Republic of China 2013* (Washington, D.C., 2013), 45.

[64] For China's warhead increase, see the press release for the *2013 SIPRI Yearbook*, Stockholm International Peace Research Institute (2013), June 3, 2013, http://www.sipri.org/media/pressreleases/2013/YBlaunch_2013.

[65] Office of the Secretary of Defense, *Annual Report to Congress: Military and Security Developments Involving the People's Republic of China 2011* (Washington, D.C., 2011), 34.

[66] Brad Roberts, "Nuclear Minimalism," *Arms Control Today* 37, no. 4 (2007).

its own nuclear forces in a regional crisis or conflict.[67] In short, Japan faces its own threats and has its own interests. As Kurt Campbell and Tsuyoshi Sunohara suggest, "the persistence of a Japanese-American alliance so robust that it can indefinitely persuade Japanese leaders from acquiring nuclear weapons cannot be guaranteed."[68]

Prospects and Implications for a Nuclear Weapons Breakout by Japan

At the moment, the likelihood that Japan would build its own nuclear weapons is low. Constraints are multiple and significant. But they are not fixed, and it is worthwhile to examine the conditions, both internal and external, under which these constraints could loosen and Japan might change course.

Internal Factors

Public opinion. The "nuclear allergy" metaphor was coined in part to describe the Japanese public's aversion to visits by U.S. Navy vessels that might be carrying nuclear weapons.[69] Japanese perceptions were colored not only by the bombs dropped on Hiroshima and Nagasaki in 1945 but also by other incidents, such as in 1954 when a U.S. nuclear test at Bikini Atoll exposed 23 Japanese fishermen to high levels of radiation, eventually killing one and inspiring the *Godzilla* film series that sensationalized the potential danger and unpredictable nature of nuclear weapons.[70]

It was against this backdrop that then prime minister Sato announced the three non-nuclear principles, a policy that maintains strong public support. As the Cold War wound down, polls showed that more than 75% of Japanese respondents still agreed with the three principles, and similar polls in 2006 and 2013 produced the same result. A 1998 Gallup poll found that only 16% of the nation was afraid of being attacked by another country using nuclear weapons and 89% felt no need for Japan to have nuclear

---

[67] See the arguments by Hisahiko Okazaki, "Mazu gijutsutekina men wo tsumeyo" [First, We Need to Examine the Technical Feasibility of a Nuclear Option], *Shokun!* August 2003; and Group Ichigaya, "Kakubuso naki Nippon ni asu wa nai" [There Is No Tomorrow for a Japan without Nuclear Weapons], *Shokun!* February 2007.

[68] Campbell and Sunohara, "Japan: Thinking the Unthinkable," 237.

[69] Glenn D. Hook, "The Nuclearization of Language: Nuclear Allergy as Political Metaphor," *Journal of Peace Research* 21, no. 3 (1984): 259–75.

[70] Michael Schaller, *Altered States: The United States and Japan since the Occupation* (New York: Oxford University Press, 1997): 71–75.

weapons.[71] Being a non–nuclear weapons state had, it seemed, become part of Japanese national identity.[72]

The rise of China and the belligerency of North Korea, however, have raised awareness about the U.S. nuclear umbrella: only about 20% of the Japanese public thought the umbrella was "necessary" in 1995, but almost half thought so in 2010.[73] In addition, when candidates for the national Diet were polled in 2012 and 2013 on the issue of Japan developing its own nuclear weapons, the number believing such an option should never be considered dropped 26 percentage points to the 60% level for the first time, while a new high of nearly a third favored keeping this option open for the future, depending on the international situation.[74]

The 2011 Fukushima nuclear accident hardened popular opinion against all things nuclear in Japan and led the government to shut down Japan's nuclear power infrastructure.[75] Yet despite public opinion, a more independent regulatory system, and the disturbing news of water contamination in Fukushima, the current Abe administration and private industry are pushing to revive and sustain the nuclear sector. With little organized political opposition to the conservative, business-friendly LDP government, we have seen Japan's nuclear industry begin to regain its footing. It is already aggressively pursuing development opportunities in Asia, Europe, and the Middle East.

The return to power of the LDP in 2012 is a reminder that overwhelming majorities can vote against their polled preferences and that even democratic governments can act independently of public opinion. The connection of public opinion to policymaking is particularly tenuous with respect to national security. For example, there was considerable opposition to the NPT from the media, business community, and public when Japan signed the treaty in 1970.[76] As we have seen, the decision to forgo an independent nuclear arsenal was based on realist calculations amid U.S. pressure, not on

---

[71] "Shitsumon to kaito—Boei mondai, *Asahi Shimbun* seron chosa shoho" [Questions and Answers on Defense Issues: Report on *Asahi Shimbun* Opinion Survey], *Asahi Shimbun,* November 6, 1988; "Hikaku sangensoku 'mamorubeki' 8 wari, 'kakuhoyu giron' wa sanpi nibun, *Yomiuri Shimbun* seron chosa" [80% Want to Keep the Three Non-nuclear Principles: *Yomiuri* Opinion Poll], *Yomiuri Shimbun,* November 21, 2006; "*Asahi Shimbun* sha yusou seron chosa, shitsumon to kaito" [Questions and Answers for *Asahi* Mail-in Survey], *Asahi Shimbun,* May 2, 2013; and "Gallup Japan Poll on the Ownership of Nuclear Weapons and the Threat of Nuclear War," Gallup News Service, June 5, 1999.

[72] Pifer et al., "U.S. Nuclear and Extended Deterrence," 33.

[73] "Towareru anpo, Nichibei kankei" [Issues and the U.S.-Japan Alliance], *Asahi Shimbun,* November 11, 1995; and "Genbaku tōka kara 65 nen, kienu kaku no kyoi" [65 Years since the Atomic Bomb Was Dropped, the Nuclear Threat Remains], NHK Reporting Research and Surveys, October 2010.

[74] "More Lawmakers Want Japan to Consider Nuclear Arms Option," *Mainichi Shimbun,* August 8, 2013.

[75] See Samuels, *3.11: Disaster and Change,* chap. 5.

[76] George H. Quester, "Japan and the Nuclear Non-Proliferation Treaty," *Asian Survey* 10, no. 9 (1970): 766.

polling data. Campbell and Sunohara's conclusion is correct that "although public sentiment against nuclear weapons remains strong, its ability to fully inhibit the decisions of Japanese leaders should not be exaggerated."[77]

Institutional opposition. Japanese political leaders considering nuclear breakout will face other obstacles besides public opinion, including opposition from an expanding variety of political, bureaucratic, and economic actors. For decades, bureaucratic responsibility for nuclear strategy resided solely in the Cabinet, with support from MOFA. Over time, however, the JDA—renamed the Ministry of Defense (MOD) in 2007—assumed a greater policy role. Nuclear power research and development, which is critical for any potential dual use, was split between the Ministry of International Trade and Industry (MITI)—now the Ministry of Economy, Trade and Industry (METI)—and the Science and Technology Agency, which is now part of the Ministry of Education. Each ministry had its own preferences.[78]

In the economic realm, there are those whose interests lie in preserving a purely commercial exploitation of nuclear power.[79] Japan's utilities, the wider business community, bureaucrats charged with promoting economic growth, and politicians with ties to these interests are all powerful actors who would likely oppose a nuclear weapons program. In the event of a nuclear breakout, Japan's electric-power industry could be crippled by a loss of access to nuclear fuel and would possibly be required to return current fuel stocks, given that their purchase was predicated on peaceful use. Moreover, large manufacturers such as Hitachi and Mitsubishi could be shut out of overseas nuclear development projects, and there might be a wider economic backlash against Japanese firms in key markets like China and South Korea, as their governments hype the fear of a remilitarized Japan.[80]

Prefectural governors also have an important vote on what kinds of nuclear-related activities can occur within their jurisdictions. In addition, some influential nonprofit organizations dedicated to preserving Japan's non-nuclear status gained strength following the Fukushima crisis.[81] Proponents of changing the nuclear status quo in Japan would likely face numerous legal and bureaucratic hurdles, including the certainty of drawn-out legal challenges.

---

[77] Campbell and Sunohara, "Japan: Thinking the Unthinkable," 242. See also Paul Midford, *Rethinking Japanese Public Opinion and Security* (Stanford: Stanford University Press, 2011).

[78] According to one study, each policy silo acquired an independent veto on nuclear breakout. See Hymans, "Veto Players."

[79] Hughes, "Why Japan Will Not Go Nuclear (Yet)."

[80] For further analysis of how nuclear plant exports have been central to Japan's "new growth strategy," see Samuels, *3.11: Disaster and Change.*

[81] Ibid., chap. 6–7.

Although there is no question that weaponization would be difficult in Japan's contested political system, circumstances can change over time. Japan's robust democratic politics and its determined leadership have repeatedly demonstrated that opposition and veto power are not the same. The Japan-U.S. Security Treaty was ratified in 1960 over violent protests and widespread opposition and now is widely embraced. Japan's Self-Defense Forces, which began as the National Police Reserve during the Korean War, became a robust and lethal military force despite Japan's pacifist constitution and early public opposition. The SDF has never been more widely embraced by the Japanese public than it is at present.

The postwar history of the Japanese military is filled with examples of government restrictions applied, only to be loosened at a later date. This was the case with Japan's acquisition of fighter jets (first denied, then allowed), as well as its acquisition of mid-air refueling capabilities, legislating an ability to deploy overseas, use of outer space for defense purposes, and now the possible development of a long-range strike capability.[82] Moreover, while approval for a weapons-related program surely would be even harder to obtain from local officials than approval for nuclear power reactors, it is worth noting that some prefectural governors, such as Issei Nishikawa from Fukui, support nuclear power as the leading employment vehicle in their prefectures. And some governors, such as Shintaro Ishihara of Tokyo, have openly argued for acquiring nuclear weapons. Weaponization work could be done in prefectures with supportive leaders, even if they hosted no reactors.

Finally, even if Japan's plutonium stockpile in Europe is out of reach and much of the separated fuel is controlled by private firms worried about repercussions in international markets, more than enough is held domestically under the aegis of the Japan Atomic Energy Agency (JAEA), a governmental unit. The rest is held by Japan Nuclear Fuel Limited, which is nominally a private firm, but one that performs public functions under close government supervision. Even allowing that only two tons of Japan's plutonium stocks are both owned by the state (through the JAEA) and present in Japan, and that this might be the only plutonium available for Japanese weapons, this amount alone would be enough to build a large nuclear arsenal of several hundred weapons. In short, it is not clear how much of a constraint contending interests, private ownership of weapons materiel, and the overseas location of much of Japan's plutonium would actually place on Japan if it were

---

[82] The Japanese government has studied and considered acquisition of a long-range conventional strike capability in the past, most notably during the National Defense Program Guideline review of 2004. A similar study is underway in 2013. For a list of the "salami slicing" of restrictions on the Japanese military, see Samuels, *Securing Japan*.

to decide to move from being a latent to an open nuclear weapons state. The motivation, not the obstacles, is the critical factor.

Discount Factors

There are four additional constraints that would require Japan's leaders to discount the costs of dramatic policy change: (1) the vulnerability of the Japanese population to a first strike, (2) the undermining of Japanese diplomacy, (3) regional instability, and (4) damage to bilateral relations with the United States.

Japan's central vulnerability is its lack of strategic depth. The argument here is straightforward and has often been repeated. The majority of the Japanese population is clustered in a small number of densely populated urban centers. Because a first strike against Tokyo, Osaka, or Nagoya would cripple Japan, nuclear weapons have little military utility.[83] While superficially compelling, this argument is hardly dispositive. It did not prevent Great Britain or Israel, with their similar geo-demographic profiles and same primary ally, from developing nuclear arsenals. The Israeli case, in fact, impressed some Japanese with how vulnerability can be discounted in the face of an existential threat.[84] Nor would we expect a strike on New York or Los Angeles to be any less crippling to the U.S. national economy. Moreover, Japan's population density and vulnerability to a first strike—particularly when its arsenal is still limited—could provide a strong motivation to deploy an independent ability to wipe out North Korea's nuclear arsenal preemptively.

Second, there is the loss of benefits derived from Japan's diplomatic posture as a non–nuclear weapons state. Legal withdrawal from the NPT is technically very easy—it requires only a 90-day notice to the other parties to the treaty and the United Nations Security Council—but the costs associated with the repudiation of decades of Japanese diplomacy and the nullification of many of the bilateral agreements that undergird the Japanese nuclear power program would require a steep discount by the country's decision-makers. Still, many of these leaders are concerned that the nonproliferation regime has been eroding, and Japanese diplomacy is already less strident on this point. Additionally, whether one agrees with this logic or not, supporters of a Japanese indigenous nuclear program have long argued that Japan neutered itself diplomatically by opting out of the nuclear club and that, from a realist perspective, Japan would fortify its diplomacy over the long run by changing its stance.

---

[83] This was a central argument in every official study of the nuclear weapons option. See, for example, Hughes, "Why Japan Will Not Go Nuclear (Yet)"; and Mochizuki, "Japan Tests the Nuclear Taboo."

[84] Group Ichigaya, "Kakubuso naki Nippon ni asu wa nai," 2007.

Third, a nuclear breakout would certainly trigger or accelerate a regional arms race—one that would require a considerably greater investment in defense than postwar Japan has heretofore accepted. If South Korea had not yet broken out, it surely would after a Japanese decision to do so. South Koreans have long been suspicious of Japan's nuclear hedging, and the South Korean media and its "unnamed" government sources regularly feed the perception that Japan is just a "few screwdriver turns" from a functioning weapon.[85] Even the former ambassador to Japan, Chul-hyun Kwon, explained on the record that "Japan didn't declare having nuclear weapons but they made the raw materials, and they…are in fact getting rid of the obstacles one by one as the opportunity offers. In the long term, I guess they are preparing for a nuclear weapon."[86] A Japanese nuclear breakout would not surprise South Korea, but neither would it be met with sympathetic understanding.

China and Russia would likewise respond by repositioning and possibly strengthening their strategic forces, and China in particular would push to isolate Japan diplomatically. Additionally, North Korea could be convinced that its reckless behavior has been rewarded with new alignments in the region. It is understandable, then, that many in Japan see no military benefit to be gained from breakout; instead, they worry that a new, higher-cost round in the extant security dilemma would detract from Japanese national security.[87] But if Japan acted in response to a breakout by South Korea or to significant provocation by other states, then, as Nobumasa Akiyama suggests, "nuclear proliferation in Asia…might lower the threshold even for Japan to violate international agreements and treaties."[88]

Fourth, the United States has worked ceaselessly since the 1960s to keep Japan from becoming a nuclear weapons state, arguing that extended deterrence is a nonproliferation tool. According to one confident former Japanese diplomat, "the United States would never allow Japanese nuclear weapons."[89] But what if the drawdown in U.S. budgets and Washington's desire to balance China collide on the Japanese archipelago? What if they meet in the form of a reversal of U.S. policy toward Japanese nuclear armament, especially against a backdrop of an even more dangerous North Korea that threatens to draw the United States into a nuclear war? Given current U.S.

---

[85] See, for example, Tae-Ho Kang and Park Jung-Won, "Ilbon haekmujang hamyeon Hankookdo 'mat dae eung'" [Korean Counter-action, If Japan Seeks Nuclear Armament], *Hankyoreh,* October 19, 2006.

[86] Sang-Moo Hwang, "Ilbon eui haekmujang chujinkwah Dongbukah jungsae" [Japan's Nuclear Armament and the Political Conditions on Northeast Asia], *KBS News,* July 1, 2012.

[87] Kitaoka Shinichi, "Kita no kaku o yokushi suru tame no itsutsu no sentakushi" [Five Options to Deter North Korea's Nuclear Weapons], *Chuo Koron,* December 2006.

[88] Akiyama, "Socio-political Roots," 90.

[89] Author interview with a retired ambassador, Tokyo, March 27, 2013.

budgetary trends, exhaustion from more than a decade of war, and the United States' refusal to act alone during the Arab Spring, it is not far-fetched to imagine Washington determining that it can no longer provide regional, much less global, strategic public goods on its own. In other words, it is hardly inconceivable that economic need and existential threat could trump vulnerability in nuclear strategy and overcome political constraint.

The Durability of the U.S. Security Umbrella amid New Threats

Despite shifting threat perceptions among Japanese policymakers, Tokyo's level of confidence in U.S. security guarantees remains high due to the Obama administration's emphasis on diplomatic and military investments in Asia, Washington's bipartisan emphasis on the importance of alliances, and robust U.S. support for Japan during the tsunami and nuclear disaster in 2011. In the medium term, however, Japanese strategists are closely watching the U.S. response to Sino-Japanese confrontation in the East China Sea over the Senkaku/Diaoyu Islands. For many, this is a representative or test case of the United States' capacity and determination to deter Chinese aggression.[90] Moreover, an anticipated one-third drop in U.S. defense spending from 2010 to 2015 and congressional resistance to funding base realignment plans in the Asia-Pacific raise doubts for some in Japan about U.S. staying power in the region over the long term.[91] Thus, while there is no imminent loss of confidence, certain trends are unsettling to the leadership in Tokyo.

One of these trends is the decline in the qualitative advantage that the allies have traditionally held over China's armed forces. As one analyst opined, "if the U.S.-China military balance in East Asia reaches parity, then the credibility of the U.S. nuclear umbrella will be gravely shaken."[92] On this view, Chinese and North Korean nuclear-force modernization programs will exacerbate the decoupling problem for Japan. But such modernization could also accelerate U.S. rethinking of a possible Japanese breakout. Although a decision by Japan to acquire nuclear weapons may not be in the United States' current interest, Washington's ability and willingness to prevent it would wane over time if China's capabilities were to continue to expand and especially

---

[90] Author interviews with an LDP Diet representative, a retired ambassador, a former senior intelligence official, and an adviser to the prime minister's office, Tokyo, March 26–27, 2013.

[91] Clark A. Murdock, Kelley Sayler, and Ryan A. Crotty, "The Defense Budget's Double Whammy: Drawing Down while Hollowing Out from Within," Center for Strategic and International Studies (CSIS), October 18, 2012, http://csis.org/files/publication/121018_Murdoch_DefenseBudget_Commentary.pdf.

[92] Nakanishi Terumasa, "'Nippon kakubuso' no giron wo hajimeru toki" [The Start of Japan's "Nuclear Debates"], in "'Nippon kakubuso' no ronten: Kokka sonritsu no kiki wo ikinuku michi" [Debates on "Japan's Nuclear Armament": How to Survive This Critical Moment in National Existence], ed. Nakanishi Terumasa (Tokyo: PHP, 2006).

if North Korea's status as a nuclear power were to become a normal part of the strategic environment in Asia. Under such conditions, Japan's desire for nuclear weapons would appear more reasonable and harder to counter.[93]

The United States is taking steps to reassure Japan and shore up deterrence through close consultation and efforts to update plans and capabilities. But if Washington decides to sustain extended deterrence, it will have a tougher time demonstrating consistency and endurance. In years past, the United States' reassurance methods fluctuated, beginning with significant forward presence in the region (both conventional and nuclear) that paved the way for Japan's low-cost strategy of basic defense. When the Cold War ended and U.S. reliance on Japan seemed more equivocal, symbols of the United States' presence and commitment became important, such as the maintenance of force levels in the region above 100,000 personnel.[94] When U.S. force levels eventually dropped, Washington emphasized underlying capabilities as the critical factor, and this was also true on the nuclear front—for example, touting the TLAM/N to compensate for lower numbers and then conventional strength and dual-capable aircraft when the TLAM/N was retired.[95] If the allies' conventional advantage over China declines, however, and U.S. defense planners decide that U.S.-based strategic bombers can address nuclear threats more efficiently than introducing dual-capable aircraft into the theater, then Washington's "reassurance story" will no doubt need to change again.

Alternative Strategic Paths

To this point, our review of Japan's nuclear weapons options has elided at least four alternative paths to more independent nuclear deterrence for Japan within the alliance framework. The first three involve sharing nuclear weapons that are not of indigenous design and over which Japan would have less than full control. The fourth involves significant enhancement of Japan's conventional strike capabilities. All these options would require major changes to Japanese defense policy and possibly constitutional reinterpretation or revision.

In the first of the three acquisition scenarios, Japan could opt to buy or lease U.S. weapons. Japanese analysts have raised the possibility of a lease

---

[93] Author communication with Thomas Christensen, February 15, 2013.

[94] See "Japan-U.S. Joint Declaration on Security: Alliance for the 21st Century," Ministry of Foreign Affairs of Japan, April 17, 1996, http://www.mofa.go.jp/region/n-america/us/security/security.html.

[95] For repeated emphasis of the role of "unrivaled" U.S. conventional military "preeminence," as well as mention of the option to forward deploy dual-capable aircraft and the potential value of a conventional "prompt global strike" weapon, see "Nuclear Posture Review Report," U.S. Department of Defense, April 2010, 6, 7, 20, 28, http://www.defense.gov/npr/docs/2010%20nuclear%20posture%20review%20report.pdf.

deal with a sunset provision for up to two hundred nuclear warheads with cruise missiles. Under the agreement, the United States would retain control over the electronic maps loaded onto the warheads and a right of launch refusal.[96] Although such an approach would still require Japan to cross many of the same legal and diplomatic hurdles that it would face in building its own deterrent, while adding new hurdles for the United States, it would be the quickest and cheapest way for Japan to acquire and maintain nuclear weapons and could be easily reversed if desired. For example, in the event of Korean unification and denuclearization, Japan could simply terminate the lease and return the weapons and infrastructure. Among the many complicating factors, it is hard to imagine the U.S. government providing active support to a Japanese nuclear weapons program if South Korea is emphatically opposed. Presumably, Seoul would have taken a nuclear step first (with some sympathetic understanding from Washington) and would grudgingly accept a Japanese nuclear lease.

The second option could be modeled on the extant arrangement between the United States and the United Kingdom, whereby Britain leases U.S.-made Trident II missiles, co-develops aspects of the submarine platform, and manufactures its own nuclear warhead according to certain U.S. specifications, including the use of some U.S.-made non-nuclear components.[97] This approach would be less reversible and more expensive than the "turn key" lease method described above, but it would allow Japan to scale up its nuclear program more quickly and somewhat more affordably compared with homegrown options. Either of these approaches, however, assumes a U.S. attitude toward the NPT and the Missile Technology Control Regime that is fundamentally different from its current stance, and would be feasible only in the context of a collapse of the global nonproliferation regime. Still, one can imagine how U.S. policymakers could view this kind of approach as preferable to a purely indigenous Japanese effort, not only because it would maintain alliance ties but also because it would provide for a coordinated means of rollback if future conditions permitted.

A third alliance-based option could follow the NATO model of nuclear burden-sharing, by which U.S. nuclear weapons are deployed on allied territory under U.S. control until a crisis erupts. At that point, following U.S. authorization, responsibility for the delivery of the weapons

---

[96] Masahiro Matsumura, "Prudence and Realism in Japan's Nuclear Options," Brookings Institution, November 10, 2006, http://www.brookings.edu/opinions/2006/1110japan_matsumura.aspx.

[97] See Jenifer Mackby and Paul Cornish, eds., *U.S.-UK Nuclear Cooperation after 50 Years* (Washington, D.C.: CSIS Press, 2008).

devolves to the allied host state.[98] Before then, the ally would participate in command-and-control arrangements and its pilots would be trained in nuclear warfighting doctrine. Although such burden-sharing arrangements were more widespread during the Cold War, there remain approximately 150 B-61s deployed at bases controlled by the allied host nations Turkey, Italy, Belgium, the Netherlands, and Germany for delivery by their F-16s or Tornados. The legality of these arrangements, however, has long been disputed under Articles 1 and 2 of the NPT.[99]

Each of these options goes beyond Japan possessing a few bombs but falls short of a fully independent and survivable Japanese nuclear force. All three would, of course, require relaxation of Japan's three non-nuclear principles and the reintroduction of U.S. nuclear weapons to bases on the archipelago. Each would allow more rapid deployment than a purely indigenous deterrent, and each requires U.S. cooperation. Many Japanese analysts who write on nuclear issues, however, advocate greater autonomy. Nisohachi Hyodo, for example, has argued for a force of two submarines roaming separate seas with one missile each, while Kan Ito and Yasuhiro Nakasone recommend "small size" Japanese nuclear weapons.[100] Mitsuo Takai argues, however, that a reliably survivable Japanese nuclear strategy to deal with China or North Korea would require a much larger force—up to six nuclear submarines with three hundred high-yield nuclear warheads—while Takayuki Nishi has suggested that even this might be too small a force to deal with a foe like China.[101] Either way, this level of militarization would contradict the Japanese Constitution's prohibition of "war potential," as currently interpreted by the government, which makes a distinction based on scale of destructive power.[102] Ultimately, Nishi's consideration of nuclear strategy convinces him that the best approach for Japan remains nuclear abstention coupled with missile defenses, as long as the growth of China's nuclear missile force levels off.

---

[98] See Catherine McArdle Kelleher, "NATO Nuclear Operations," in *Managing Nuclear Operations*, ed. Ashton B. Carter, John D. Steinbruner, and Charles A. Zraket (Washington, D.C.: Brookings Institution, 1987); Hans M. Kristensen, "U.S. Nuclear Weapons in Europe: A Review of Post-Cold War Policy, Force Levels, and War Planning," Natural Resources Defense Council, February 2005, http://www.nrdc.org/nuclear/euro/euro.pdf; and Thomas Maettig, "Tactical Nuclear Weapons in Germany: Time for Withdrawal?" Nuclear Threat Initiative, March 1, 2008, http://www.nti.org/analysis/articles/tactical-nuclear-weapons-germany.

[99] Author communication with Owen Cote, June 10, 2013. On the legal questions, see Otfried Nassauer, "Nuclear Sharing in NATO: Is It Legal?" Berlin Information-Center for Transatlantic Security, April 2001, http://www.bits.de/public/articles/sda-05-01.htm.

[100] Yoshihara and Holms, *Second Nuclear Age*, 124–25.

[101] Takayuki Nishi, "Nuclear Strategy as a Constraint on Japanese Nuclear Armament" (paper presented at the 52nd annual convention of the International Studies Association, Montreal, March 17, 2011).

[102] Japan Ministry of Defense, *Defense of Japan 2013* (Tokyo, 2013), 143, http://www.mod.go.jp/e/publ/w_paper/pdf/2013/22_Part2_Chapter1_Sec2.pdf.

This raises the fourth alternative deterrence strategy, a much discussed non-nuclear one that would maintain Japan's nuclear hedge but entail a considerable enhancement of its conventional offensive capabilities. As one defense planner has explained, there is much more Japan can do to augment its deterrent short of nuclear weapons breakout.[103] Although Japan's self-imposed ban on the acquisition of long-range strike capabilities has been thinned by successive reinterpretations of the constitution, the MOD budget has remained static, and the military has been slow to acquire the carriers, bombers, strike fighters, and ballistic or cruise missiles that would expand Japan's capacity to punish adversaries at a distance.[104] But some Japanese leaders are seriously considering the need to augment U.S. capabilities. One senior military officer invoked a common metaphor: "we have been at our parents' knee [*oya no sune ni kajiru*], but U.S. shins have become thin."[105] He joins a chorus of defense planners who advocate changing the extant alliance model in which the United States is the "sword" and Japan is the "shield" to one in which both countries have offensive capabilities sufficient to deter regional aggression.[106] As Narushige Michishita has reported, "the most widely debated" military option for Japan going forward is the acquisition of strike capabilities for preemptive counterforce operations against hostile bases.[107]

This "strike capability" movement reached a climax during the drafting of the National Defense Program Guidelines in 2004, when the JDA sought funds to develop long-range, surface-to-surface missile technology.[108] But the LDP's coalition partner, the New Komeito Party, vetoed that proposal and the plan was dropped. The Abe administration put this issue back on the table for consideration in 2013 after South Korea's decision in 2012 to extend the range of its ballistic missile forces to eight hundred kilometers

---

[103] Author interview with a National Institute for Defense Studies official, Tokyo, March 25, 2013. See also Mochizuki, "Japan Tests the Nuclear Taboo," 314. This is consistent with the plans of the Obama administration. See *Washington Post*, June 19, 2013.

[104] The Self-Defense Forces have acquired the basics for counterforce conventional strike, including attack fighters, airborne refueling, and joint direct-attack munitions that convert gravity bombs into precision-guided munitions. See Michishita, "Japan's Response," 108.

[105] Author interview with Japanese military officer, Tokyo, March 27, 2013.

[106] This converging sentiment was heard in multiple interviews with senior officials at the Ministry of Defense and with former MOFA and intelligence officials in Tokyo, March 25–27, 2013.

[107] Michishita, "Japan's Response," 107. He adds that some (unnamed) security specialists think that acquisition of these capabilities could actually undermine the alliance by giving Washington the option of not defending Japan. For a 2006 study on this issue by an influential Japanese analyst, see Sugio Takahashi, "Dealing with the Ballistic Missile Threat: Whether Japan Should Have a Strike Capability under Its Exclusively Defense-Oriented Policy," *NIDS Security Reports*, no. 7 (2006): 79–94.

[108] "Draft of Next Midterm Defense Buildup Plan Seeks Missile Research," *Kyodo News*, December 3, 2004.

provided diplomatic cover. Such a shift could enhance Japan's deterrence posture, whether or not it were integrated with U.S. military doctrine in ways that would make deterrence more effective and credible; however, it also risks complicating the regional security dilemma and engendering domestic political blowback. Washington has long pushed for a more militarily capable Japan but is reluctant to weigh in publicly on this sensitive issue, lest the United States be viewed as either encouraging or restraining Japan. On this latter point, in particular, the U.S. side is aware that efforts to dissuade Tokyo from adding strike capacity could be unsuccessful and might accelerate the loss of Japanese confidence in its ally, thereby prompting an even quicker development of independent capabilities.

Conclusion

Henry Kissinger has suggested that the logic of war shifted with the introduction of nuclear weapons in ways that are connected directly to issues examined in this chapter. He stated that before the nuclear age "the consequences of abandoning an ally were deemed to be more risky than fulfilling one's obligations. In the Nuclear Age, this rule no longer necessarily held true; abandoning an ally risked *eventual* disaster, but resorting to war at the side of an ally guaranteed *immediate* catastrophe."[109] It is of no little significance that this passage is well known among Japan's strategic elites, many of whom point to the declining credibility of extended deterrence and the fact that nonproliferation norms have also withered.

Campbell and Sunokawa, who insist that a Japanese nuclear breakout "would be potentially catastrophic," have warned U.S. leaders and public commentators against raising questions about extended deterrence or encouraging Japan to consider alternatives to its nuclear hedged status quo: "American leaders and influential commentators both within and outside the government should never signal to the Japanese, even inadvertently, that they actually favor Japan's acquisition of nuclear weapons."[110] But as we have seen, thoughtful Japanese security specialists have not needed encouragement to cast an unsentimental and realistic eye on the future of extended deterrence. They have needed no prompting to raise questions about Japan's strategic defense and to interrogate U.S. overextension.

Equally thoughtful international security specialists in the United States have begun asking similar questions. Michael J. Mazarr, a professor

---

[109] Henry Kissinger, *Diplomacy* (New York: Simon and Schuster, 1994), 608. Note that as secretary of state Kissinger managed alliance relations successfully and assured allies that Washington would come to their aid.

[110] Campbell and Sunohara, "Japan: Thinking the Unthinkable," 219, 246.

of national security strategy at the U.S. National War College, is concerned about U.S. "strategic insolvency"—the pursuit of "yesterday's strategy under today's constraints" and the United States' growing inability to manage the gap between its strategic commitments and its national objectives.[111] Barry Posen argues that

> extended deterrence is a very risky business, and the United States ought to have been glad to shed such commitments after the Cold War ended. Instead, the United States retains extended deterrence commitments in Europe and Asia…. Extended deterrence remains a plausible path to one or more nuclear weapons being used either against U.S. forces or the U.S. homeland.[112]

Posen lays out four options for Japan beyond its alliance with the United States. Two are low-probability courses of action: that Japan could find a new nuclear protector or that it could bandwagon with China or other rivals. Echoing some of the strategists explored in this chapter, Posen observes that a third option is for Japan to persist with its nuclear hedge, which he says is tantamount to "ignoring the problem" and which one Diet representative called "closing our eyes and whistling past the graveyard."[113] The fourth option, nuclear breakout, is the one that has been explored in this chapter in its several possible forms.

Like Israel, which has climbed much higher up the nuclear weapons ladder, Japan has assumed what Vipin Narang labels a "catalytic posture," one that "relies on an ambiguous nuclear capability aimed at 'catalyzing' third-party—often U.S.—military or diplomatic assistance to defend the state by threatening to unsheathe its nuclear weapons."[114] To assume this posture, having assembled nuclear weapons is not even strictly necessary—one simply requires the "ability to assemble a handful of nuclear weapons." Given the availability of a superpower patron and other constraints on more overt change, this posture may continue to serve Japanese security interests well and is Tokyo's most likely choice should it opt to follow Israel. Manipulating the threat of breakout remains a mechanism to keep Washington in the game in East Asia.

Still, as this chapter has shown, much remains uncertain in the changing East Asian security environment. North Korea, in particular, is an unpredictable actor and a growing threat to alter Tokyo's calculus. At present, few voices in the Japanese or U.S. strategic communities openly

---

[111] Michael J. Mazarr, "The Risks of Ignoring Strategic Insolvency," *Washington Quarterly* 35, no. 4 (2012): 8.

[112] Posen, *U.S. Grand Strategy*, 97.

[113] Ibid., 102; and author interview with an LDP Diet member, Tokyo, March 27, 2013.

[114] Vipin Narang, "Posturing for Peace? Pakistan's Nuclear Postures and South Asian Stability," *International Security* 34, no. 3 (2009/10): 41.

advocate a Japanese nuclear breakout. But given questions about how the emergence of a multipolar nuclear Asia will complicate national and alliance strategies, the possibility cannot be dismissed. Both communities should be aware that extant constraints on such a dramatic shift can be stretched, that threat perceptions can change, and that a range of once unthinkable alternatives is available.

STRATEGIC ASIA 2013–14

SPECIAL STUDY

EXECUTIVE SUMMARY

This chapter analyzes the complex relationships that exist around the extended deterrence of China and North Korea, the assurance of U.S. allies in Asia of the reliability of U.S. security guarantees, and the reassurance of China that the U.S. does not seek to thwart its peaceful rise.

MAIN ARGUMENT:
The need to simultaneously deter China and North Korea, assure multiple allies, and reassure China, combined with regional nuclear dynamics, makes extended deterrence more complex now than during the Cold War. Particularly challenging is deterring low-level confrontations in the maritime sphere and, in the future, the cyber domain. The Asia-Pacific region is subject to a "security trilemma," where U.S. actions to deter North Korea can have negative consequences for U.S. and allied security relations with China, making both assurance and reassurance much more difficult. Japan and South Korea have unique assurance requirements and need separate consideration. Reassuring China is particularly important but particularly difficult.

POLICY IMPLICATIONS:
- Because both China and U.S. allies (especially Japan) are concerned about extended-deterrence commitments below the nuclear threshold, the U.S. should review the management of those commitments and use the results of that review to expand dialogue with allies and China.

- Because assuring its allies is inherently difficult, the U.S. should continue extensive consultations on extended deterrence, especially with Japan and South Korea, should make no major changes in declaratory policy on nuclear use, and should maintain rough strategic nuclear parity with Russia to avoid allied perceptions of U.S. inferiority.

- Because China believes the U.S. seeks to deny it an effective deterrent, U.S. leaders should reassure China by privately conveying Washington's acceptance of mutual vulnerability as a fact of life and by working to implement modest confidence-building measures.

Extended Deterrence, Assurance, and Reassurance in the Pacific during the Second Nuclear Age

Linton Brooks and Mira Rapp-Hooper

Former British defense minister Denis Healey once observed that "it takes only five percent credibility of American retaliation to deter the Russians but ninety-five percent credibility to reassure the Europeans."[1] He was referring to the Cold War–era difficulty of convincing NATO allies of the credibility of U.S. extended-deterrence commitments, but his words continue to ring true. An abundance of new challenges accompany extended deterrence, assurance, and reassurance in the second nuclear age, as the United States continues to guarantee the sovereignty of more than 30 countries worldwide. Nowhere are these challenges more pronounced than in Northeast Asia, where assuring allies of the United States' willingness and ability to defend them must be an integral part of U.S. foreign policy. Given that the U.S.-China relationship will be the most important geopolitical dynamic of the next several decades, what are the tasks of and challenges to U.S. extended deterrence in the Pacific?

Linton Brooks is an independent consultant on national security issues and a former government official with extensive experience in positions associated with nuclear weapons. He can be reached at <linton.brooks@cox.net>.

Mira Rapp-Hooper is a PhD candidate in Political Science at Columbia University and a 2013–14 Stanton Nuclear Fellow at the Council on Foreign Relations. She can be reached at <mrh2149@columbia.edu>.

We wish to thank Brad Roberts and two anonymous reviewers for their helpful comments on earlier drafts of this chapter. We alone are responsible for the final version.

[1] Denis Healey, *Time of My Life* (London: Michael Joseph, 1989), 243, quoted in David Yost, "Assurance and U.S. Extended Deterrence in NATO," *International Affairs* 85, no. 4 (2009): 768.

This chapter begins by defining key terms, including extended deterrence, assurance, and reassurance. It then briefly reviews the requirements of and challenges to extended deterrence during the Cold War before moving on to demonstrate why extended deterrence in the Pacific during the second nuclear age is a unique task. After summarizing current nuclear policy, we identify and analyze five specific challenges to extended deterrence in the Pacific. The chapter then analyzes the implications of these challenges for U.S. nuclear force structure, as well as for nuclear declaratory policy and allied consultation efforts. On the basis of these implications, we offer a number of policy recommendations on how the United States should approach its extended deterrence, assurance, and reassurance efforts in this crucial region over the coming decades.

Extended Deterrence, Assurance, and Reassurance Defined

Extended deterrence, assurance, and reassurance are all strategies of influence that states can direct at adversaries and allies.[2] These three terms are often used interchangeably or given a variety of meanings, so we begin by defining them for the purposes of this analysis. "Extended deterrence" aims to affect the cost calculations of adversaries, specifically dissuading them from attacking a U.S. ally.[3] Extended deterrence is related to, but not synonymous with, assurance. "Assurance" is a strategy directed at allies that seeks to convince them of the United States' commitment to their defense.[4] "Reassurance," on the other hand, is a strategy that endeavors to convince adversaries that they are not going to be the target of serious harm. Reassurance may complement extended deterrence, or it may be employed as an entirely distinct strategy.[5] It seeks, in part, to convince an adversary that the military component of extended deterrence is intended to protect the U.S. ally and not to threaten or destabilize the potential aggressor if it refrains from aggression. The target of both extended deterrence and reassurance is an adversary or potential adversary, whereas the target of assurance is an ally.[6]

---

[2] Jeffrey W. Knopf, "Varieties of Assurance," *Journal of Strategic Studies* 35, no. 3 (2012): 378.

[3] Jeffrey W. Knopf, "Security Assurances: Initial Hypotheses," in *Security Assurances and Nuclear Nonproliferation,* ed. Jeffrey W. Knopf (Stanford: Stanford University Press, 2012), 14.

[4] "Exploring the Nuclear Posture Implications of Extended Deterrence and Assurance: Workshop Proceedings and Key Takeaways," Center for Strategic and International Studies (CSIS), November 2009, 8.

[5] Knopf, "Security Assurances: Initial Hypotheses," 16.

[6] "Exploring the Nuclear Posture Implications," 12.

Although both concepts are associated with security guarantees, neither assurance nor extended deterrence is a subset of the other. An adversary may be deterred from attacking, without an ally being convinced of U.S. commitment; likewise, it is possible (though less likely) that an ally could be assured while an adversary is still willing to attack.[7] Extended deterrence and assurance are positive promises—they each rest on a commitment of military aid in case of attack by a third party.

Like deterrence generally, extended deterrence can take the form of deterrence by punishment or deterrence by denial. Extended deterrence by punishment is an effort to convince adversaries that if they attack a U.S. ally, they will face retaliation from the United States. The prospect of such retaliation is intended to convince an adversary not to attack in the first place. Extended deterrence by punishment can be practiced through the use of a variety of tools. These include security guarantees to allies, public statements by U.S. leaders that reaffirm defense commitments, nuclear declaratory policy, and the demonstration of U.S. retaliatory capabilities through military exercises and other overt displays of force. All these signals suggest that if an adversary attacks an ally under U.S. protection, serious consequences will be forthcoming.

By contrast, extended deterrence by denial aims to convince an adversary that, if it attacks, it will not achieve its military goals. Extended deterrence by denial has become an important alliance strategy in the 21st century through the use of ballistic missile defense (BMD). In addition to deploying a ground-based BMD system to intercept missiles directed at the U.S. homeland, the United States engages in missile defense cooperation with allies in Europe, Northeast Asia, and the Middle East. Other tools of denial include the hardening of military installations and the potential to employ preemptive strikes against an adversary's military capabilities to prevent them from being used.

For the purposes of this chapter, U.S. extended-deterrence commitments are defined by the presence of positive, formal treaties providing security guarantees to allies. These include the U.S. guarantee to NATO, as well as bilateral treaty commitments to Japan, South Korea, Australia, and the Philippines. This chapter also considers the U.S. relationship with Taiwan,

---

[7] "Exploring the Nuclear Posture Implications," 1.

which approaches the status of a formal security guarantee because of the 1979 Taiwan Relations Act.[8]

Many nuclear analysts use the phrase "the second nuclear age" to distinguish the current era of multiple nuclear powers and potential regional conflicts from the essentially bipolar, large-scale nuclear confrontation of the Cold War.[9] This term has been adopted—without attempting a formal definition—to emphasize the degree to which the current situation differs from the Cold War.

With key terms and the scope of this chapter's analysis defined, we now turn to an assessment of extended deterrence, assurance, and reassurance during the Cold War.

Extended Deterrence in the Cold War

Unlike most other nuclear states, the United States has consistently viewed its nuclear weapons as deterring attacks against its allies as well as against the United States itself. For example, the Carter administration's Presidential Directive 59 (PD-59), which formed the basis for a similar policy document under the Reagan administration, reads: "Our strategic nuclear forces must be able to deter nuclear attacks not only on our own country but also on our forces overseas, as well as on our friends and allies, and to contribute to deterrence of non-nuclear attacks."[10]

During the Cold War, extended deterrence and its companion, assurance of allies, were conceptually straightforward.[11] While the United States did extend deterrence to its Asian allies, as a practical matter extended deterrence, like Cold War deterrence generally, was almost entirely about the Soviet Union and its potential to invade Western Europe. China was

---

[8] The 1979 Taiwan Relations Act considers "any effort to determine the future of Taiwan by other than peaceful means, including by boycotts or embargoes, a threat to the peace and security of the Western Pacific area and of grave concern to the United States" and requires "the United States to resist any resort to force or other forms of coercion that would jeopardize the security, or the social or economic system, of the people on Taiwan." See "Taiwan Relations Act, January 1, 1979," American Institute in Taiwan, http://www.ait.org.tw/en/taiwan-relations-act.html.

[9] For a lengthier discussion of the concept and its application to Asia, see Paul Bracken, "The Second Nuclear Age," Foreign Affairs 79, no. 1 (2000): 146–56.

[10] PD-59 did not establish any new policy; similar statements appear in the Nixon administration's nuclear employment guidance designated NSDM-242. Both documents were originally classified as top secret, but redacted versions are available from George Washington University's National Security Archives, http://www.gwu.edu/~nsarchiv.

[11] Our discussion of the Cold War refers primarily to the latter half of that decades-long confrontation, which is the period that shaped the experience of today's senior policymakers. For insights into the earlier stages, see, among others, John Lewis Gaddis, The Cold War: A New History (New York: Penguin Press, 2005).

treated as a lesser included case.[12] The United States and its European allies were bound together by a common alliance against a single common adversary. The United States maintained hundreds of thousands of troops in Western Europe.[13] It also maintained thousands of tactical nuclear weapons designed to compensate for any imbalance in conventional forces. This strong deterrent force was recognized and reinforced by Article V of the North Atlantic Treaty, which embodied the principle that an attack on one NATO member was an attack on all members. Thus both legally and as a practical matter, it was impossible for the Soviet Union to attack European allies without effectively attacking the United States. Further, it was widely believed that Soviet domination of Western Europe would so fundamentally alter the international strategic situation that it would put the United States in a permanent position of geopolitical inferiority. As a result, there was little doubt that the United States would meet its treaty obligations to NATO allies. U.S. involvement in a potential conflict was inherently credible.

What was less credible was the belief that the United States would put its homeland at risk of nuclear devastation in order to defend its European allies. In essence, while extended deterrence was relatively easy, assurance was not. In particular, the United States believed it had to go to great lengths to convince its NATO allies that the nuclear component of extended deterrence was credible. Allied concern was embodied in the catchphrase, "Would the United States trade New York for Bonn?" Enormous effort was required to make U.S. assurances credible. Extensive consultation through bodies like the Nuclear Planning Group (consisting of defense ministers) and the High-Level Group (at the assistant secretary level) kept the allies involved in nuclear issues. Nuclear weapons in Europe, in addition to their military role of compensating for Soviet conventional superiority, served the political role of linking the war in Europe to U.S. strategic forces. By the end of the Cold War, practitioners

---

[12] The declassified version of PD-59 does not mention China explicitly, although there are three redacted lines that, in context, almost certainly discuss China.

[13] For example, in the year that PD-59 was signed, the United States maintained four army divisions, four army independent brigades, two armored cavalry regiments, and eight fighter/attack wings in Europe. In very rough terms, this was about a third of the total force structure of the army and air force. Harold Brown, *Department of Defense Annual Report Fiscal Year 1980* (Washington, D.C., 1979), 140, 178.

and academics had a good concept of how extended deterrence and the assurance of allies worked.[14]

Extended Deterrence in the Pacific during the Second Nuclear Age

The end of the Cold War did not mean the end of either extended deterrence or assurance, both of which have remained integral to U.S. nuclear policy. For example, the 2010 Nuclear Posture Review (NPR) states: "The fundamental role of U.S. nuclear weapons, which will continue as long as nuclear weapons exist, is to deter nuclear attack on the United States, our allies, and partners."[15] As China's nuclear modernization has accelerated and its foreign policy has become more assertive, and as North Korea's nuclear program has resulted in a series of nuclear tests, the United States has focused increasingly on extended deterrence in the Pacific. It is natural for practitioners to draw on Cold War concepts. Extended deterrence in the Pacific today, however, is different in many respects from that practiced during the Cold War.

The first difference is geopolitical. Unlike the single nuclear threat of the Cold War, there are multiple threats in the Pacific, with the primary threat varying from country to country. For most states, the perceived primary threat comes from China, but the Democratic People's Republic of Korea (DPRK) is also a significant threat, particularly to the Republic of Korea (ROK). Additionally, there remains residual concern in the region over the Russian nuclear threat, given the authoritarian turn of Russian foreign policy.

Another important difference concerns alliance structure: the United States extends deterrence on an individual basis to allies in the Pacific through a "hub and spoke" system rather than through one single cohesive multilateral alliance. As is illustrated in **Table 1**, the degree of military ties varies widely among these allies, as does the nature and strength of the

---

[14] An extensive set of post–Cold War interviews with senior Soviet military and defense officials reveals that Western understanding was not perfect, "overestimating Soviet aggressiveness" and underestimating "the extent to which the Soviet leadership was deterred from using nuclear weapons." William Burr and Svetlana Savranskaya, eds., "Previously Classified Interviews with Former Soviet Officials Reveal U.S. Strategic Intelligence Failure Over Decades," National Security Archive, George Washington University, September 11, 2009, http://www.gwu.edu/~nsarchiv/nukevault/ebb285. See also Document 2 by John G. Hines, Ellis M. Mishulovich, and John F. Shulle, "Soviet Intentions 1965–1985, Volume I: An Analytical Comparison of U.S.-Soviet Assessments During the Cold War," BDM Federal, Inc., September 22, 1995, http://www.gwu.edu/~nsarchiv/nukevault/ebb285.

[15] U.S. Department of Defense, *Nuclear Posture Review Report* (Washington, D.C., April 2010), vii, http://www.defense.gov/npr.

TABLE 1 U.S. extended deterrence commitments in Asia

	Japan	South Korea	Philippines	Australia*	Taiwan
Extended deterrence commitment	U.S.-Japan Treaty of Mutual Security and Cooperation (1951, revised 1960–present)	U.S.-ROK Mutual Defense Treaty (1953–present)	U.S.-Philippines Mutual Defense Treaty (1951–present)	ANZUS (1951–present)	Taiwan Relations Act (1979–present); U.S.-ROC Mutual Defense Treaty (1954–79)
Major U.S. military installations	26 total (army, navy, air force, and marines)	28 total (army, navy, air force, and marines)	None	1 communications station (navy)	None
Total U.S. military personnel	52,692	28,500	131	183	9
Regular joint military exercises	Keen Sword/Keen Edge, Orient Shield, Rim of the Pacific, Tempo Brave, Yama Sakura	Foal Eagle, Key Resolve, Max Thunder, Rim of the Pacific, Ulchi-Freedom Guardian	Balikatan, PHIBLEX, Philippine Interoperability Exchange	Rim of the Pacific, Talisman Saber	None
Ballistic missile defense	BMD Framework partner; AN/TPY-2 radar host; X-band radar host; PAC-3 and Aegis/SM-3 deployed; cooperative BMD research program	BMD Framework partner; PAC-3 deployed; developing independent KAMD system	Potential host of U.S. X-band radar	BMD Framework partner; acquiring Aegis capability	PAC-2 and PAC-3 deployed (not part of integrated framework)

SOURCE: "Total Military Personnel and Dependent End Strength by Service, Regional Area, and Country," U.S. Department of Defense, December 31, 2012, available at http://siadapp.dmdc.osd.mil/personnel/MILITARY/miltop.htm; and "U.S.–South Korea Relations," Congressional Research Service, CRS Report for Congress, R41481, April 26, 2013, 9, http://www.fas.org/sgp/crs/row/R41481.pdf.

NOTE: Asterisk indicates the following notes about data for Australia. At its founding, ANZUS included the United States, Australia, and New Zealand. However, the U.S.–New Zealand leg of the alliance is no longer active. The total U.S. military personnel value for Australia does not reflect the rotational assignment of U.S. marines to Darwin. The initial deployment of approximately 200 marines arrived in April 2012 and left in September 2012; the second rotation of approximately 200 marines arrived in April 2013 and will also serve a six-month tour. The end strength of these deployments will increase to approximately 2,500 marines by 2017.

formal U.S. commitment. Further, the allies do not all have the same threat perceptions nor do some of them routinely cooperate with one another militarily. Japan and the ROK, for example, despite having common interests, have found cooperation difficult because of the historical legacy of enmity between them.

Unlike in Cold War Europe, the nature of U.S. commitments to East Asian allies varies significantly. Most U.S. alliances are codified in formal treaty commitments, but the United States also maintains close relations with Taiwan, with whom it formally ended its treaty ties in 1979. Although it does not deploy troops there, the United States is obligated by the 1979 Taiwan Relations Act to sell Taiwan sufficient arms to provide for its own defense. The legislation also states that any efforts to determine Taiwan's future by nonpeaceful means will be considered a threat to the security of the region and of "grave concern" to the United States. Past presidents have made clear that the United States would come to Taiwan's aid if it were the victim of an unprovoked attack by China.[16]

Today's military situation in the Pacific differs significantly from the Cold War situation in Europe. With the exception of South Korea, the threat to the United States' Pacific allies is from naval, missile, or cyber attack rather than land attack. As will be discussed in greater detail below, the most likely military threat to the region is not a major conventional or nuclear war but a variety of lower-level conflicts. It is hard to envision a single contingency in which all of Asia is engaged. Thus, the U.S. position as a major international actor is not dependent on responding to any specific regional conflict, nor does the United States' survival depend on the survival of any specific ally. Given that some allies have relatively limited U.S. military forces stationed on their territory, that the United States does not routinely base nuclear weapons in the region, and that distances are greater and historical ties are weaker, the geopolitical incentives for the United States to come to the defense of its allies are less clear than in Europe during the Cold War. This makes assurance both more important and more difficult.

The military situation is also influenced by the development and deployment of a limited national BMD.[17] Missile defense is important to extended deterrence and assurance in the Pacific in a way that has no Cold

---

[16] Shirley A. Kan, "China/Taiwan: Evolution of the 'One China' Policy—Key Statements from Washington, Beijing, and Taipei," Congressional Research Service, CRS Report for Congress, RL30341, June 24, 2011.

[17] National missile defense is designed to defend the United States against missiles of intercontinental range, while theater defenses deal with shorter-range missiles aimed at allies or deployed U.S. forces. Theater defenses are technically easier, although the effectiveness of any specific missile defense system is a matter of debate within the U.S. defense analytic community.

War analog. The United States is deploying national BMD so that even if North Korea or Iran develops an effective intercontinental ballistic missile (ICBM) in the future, North Korea (or Iran) cannot credibly threaten the U.S. homeland. Limiting the risk to the homeland enhances U.S. willingness to take military action to protect its allies. Further, theater BMD clearly reduces North Korea's ability to threaten U.S. allies; U.S. willingness to provide such defenses, either directly or through defense cooperation agreements, is an important element of assurance. In contrast, with existing technology the United States cannot prevent China from inflicting significant damage on at least a few U.S. cities. The current U.S. policy is to not seek to alter this situation.[18] As will be discussed in more detail below, this dichotomy significantly complicates relations with China.

A third difference involves reassurance. The nuclear situation between the two superpowers was stable for the second half of the Cold War. The U.S. policy of containment (rather than rollback) was well understood by the Soviets. Neither superpower threatened the core interests of the other after the Berlin and Cuban missile crises of the early 1960s.[19] Reassuring the Soviet Union that the United States did not intend to threaten its vital interests came to be an inherent element of the international system and was perceived as requiring little direct action by the United States.

The need for reassurance in the Pacific today is different because of the complicated U.S. relationship with China. Reassurance of the Soviet Union was an adjunct to deterrence, making a deterrence relationship acceptable by making it clear that the United States had no plans to attack. Reassurance of China has a broader purpose. While it is probable that the geopolitical competition between the United States and China will be the dominant feature of the 21st century, it is not inevitable that this competition will degenerate into a new Cold War. The United States, therefore, has a strong incentive to reassure China that it does not seek to threaten its peaceful rise. Among other things, this requires convincing Beijing that U.S. security guarantees to Asian allies are not an attempt at containing China, while simultaneously not weakening allies' perceptions of U.S. reliability. As will be discussed later in this chapter, efforts to reassure China are complicated by the challenges to U.S. security posed by the DPRK. U.S. actions to counter North Korean threats, particularly the deployment of ballistic missile defenses, risk being interpreted by China as directed at it.

Yet another difference between contemporary extended deterrence in the Pacific and extended deterrence during the closing decades of the

---

[18] U.S. Department of Defense, *Ballistic Missile Defense Review Report* (Washington, D.C., February 2010), 13.

[19] Gaddis, *The Cold War.*

Cold War involves the proliferation of nuclear weapons. During the Cold War, the United States and the Soviet Union shared a common interest in preventing the emergence of new nuclear weapons states. Even when tension between the two superpowers was high, they were often able to cooperate on nonproliferation. After France (1960) and China (1964) successfully tested nuclear weapons and the United States convinced South Korea to abandon its own nuclear ambitions (1970), no Soviet or U.S. ally seriously contemplated developing nuclear weapons.[20] In contrast, it is widely assumed (including by the Chinese) that if Japan lost confidence in the U.S. nuclear deterrent, it might elect to develop its own nuclear weapons and could do so in a relatively short time.[21] While not as advanced technically, the ROK could take a similar step if it lost confidence. Indeed, there is already strong public (though not government) support for acquiring an indigenous nuclear capability, with recent opinion polls showing that two-thirds of South Koreans favor such a step.[22] However remote the possibility of Japan or South Korea acquiring nuclear weapons is (and we judge it highly unlikely), it heightens the importance of allied assurance.

The final difference between the contemporary Pacific and Cold War Europe involves intellectual understanding. By the later stages of the Cold War, U.S. academics and practitioners believed that, through extensive study and intelligence collection, they had developed a good understanding of how the Soviets thought and thus what was necessary to deter them. Through multiple discussions of arms control, the two sides had a common (or at least similar) set of terms and concepts concerning nuclear war. But these understandings are not necessarily universal. Specifically, they may not apply to states like North Korea with different value systems, risk tolerances, and methods of gathering and processing information.[23] A separate intellectual problem arises from differences in nuclear concepts in the United States and China. One commonly cited example is that the

---

[20] Indeed, there was substantial U.S.-Soviet discussion during negotiation of the Limited Test Ban Treaty—barring nuclear tests in the atmosphere, underwater, or in outer space—as to whether the treaty could be used to get both France and China out of the nuclear business. William Burr and Jeffrey T. Richelson, "Whether to 'Strangle the Baby in the Cradle': The United States and the Chinese Nuclear Program, 1960–64," *International Security* 25, no. 3 (2001): 54–99.

[21] In response to the October 2006 North Korean nuclear test, then secretary of state Condoleezza Rice traveled to Japan, South Korea, and China. In Tokyo, she stressed the United States' extended-deterrence commitment to Japan. When she arrived in Beijing, the Chinese thanked her for that action, clearly demonstrating that they understood the nonproliferation benefits of U.S. extended deterrence. Author discussion with a senior U.S. State Department official, Washington, D.C., June 2011.

[22] Martin Fackler and Choe Sang-Hun, "As North Korea Blusters, South Flirts with Talk of Nuclear Arms," *New York Times*, March 11, 2013.

[23] For an amplification of this point, see Keith Payne, *Deterrence in the Second Nuclear Age* (Lexington: University Press of Kentucky, 1996).

Chinese translation of the Western term "deterrence" has overtones of coercion not found in the English word. To help mitigate these problems, unofficial dialogues, most prominently one organized by the National Academies of Science, are seeking to develop a common lexicon.[24]

The Essential Backdrop: U.S. Nuclear Policy

Those seeking to understand and manage the nuclear aspects of extended deterrence, assurance, and reassurance in the Pacific region must do so against the backdrop of U.S. nuclear policy. The Obama administration has crafted a coherent, ambitious, and nuanced nuclear policy, beginning with President Obama's April 2009 speech in Prague, which committed the United States to "seek the security of a world without nuclear weapons."[25] This is more than rhetoric; not since Ronald Reagan has there been a president as deeply and personally committed to abolishing nuclear weapons as President Obama.

The administration followed by issuing its 2010 NPR, which among other things called for a strategic stability dialogue with China:

> [T]he purpose of a dialogue on strategic stability is to provide a venue and mechanism for each side to communicate its views about the other's strategies, policies, and programs on nuclear weapons and other strategic capabilities. The goal of such a dialogue is to enhance confidence, improve transparency, and reduce mistrust. As stated in the 2010 Ballistic Missile Defense Review Report, "maintaining strategic stability in the U.S.-China relationship is as important to this Administration as maintaining strategic stability with other major powers."[26]

The report also committed the United States to "pursue high-level dialogues with Russia and China to promote more stable, transparent, and non-threatening strategic relationships between those countries and the United States."[27] Reaction to these developments among U.S. allies— including those in the Pacific—was generally favorable, in part because of the extensive consultations the administration undertook in conducting

---

[24] Committee on the U.S.-Chinese Glossary of Nuclear Security Terms, National Research Council, *English-Chinese, Chinese-English Nuclear Security Glossary* (Washington, D.C.: National Academies Press, 2008).

[25] Barack Obama, "Remarks by President Barack Obama" (remarks at Hradčany Square, Prague, April 5, 2009).

[26] U.S. Department of Defense, *Nuclear Posture Review Report,* 29.

[27] Ibid., 46.

the NPR. The reaction in China, however, was decidedly mixed.[28] Formally, China welcomed the call for disarmament in the Prague speech but made it clear that until the total arsenals of Russia and the United States were each reduced to near China's size (a reduction of nearly 90% in each case), China would not be involved in arms reduction discussions.

With regard to the NPR itself, Chinese analysts generally applauded the U.S. reduction in inventories and in reliance on nuclear weapons, the bans on new weapons and nuclear testing, the narrowing of situations in which the United States would contemplate nuclear use, and the fact that "China is not grouped with rogue states hostile to the United States or included on a list of states that might be attacked by the United States with nuclear weapons." In contrast, Chinese analysts were concerned with the emphasis on missile defense and advanced conventional capabilities, especially so-called prompt global strike; the continuation of extended deterrence; and statements about China's lack of transparency.[29]

An unexpected problem arose from the extensive discussion of "strategic stability," a term used in half the references to China in the NPR. One analyst surveying the Chinese literature found that

> between 1981 and 2010, the vast majority of Chinese studies emphasized "strategic stability" as a Cold War, U.S.-Soviet construct. This term is generally reserved for describing the balance between two roughly equivalent or balanced nuclear powers…. China has long insisted that it does not fit into the paradigms of competitive power and nuclear relations that characterized the Cold War.[30]

The United States had intended the term "strategic stability" to convey an equality of interest between Russia and China. When challenged, however, it was and remains unable to reach a common understanding with China on exactly how the term applies to Sino-U.S. relations, an issue this chapter addresses below.

---

[28] In addition to the specific sources cited, the insights on China in this section are based on several years of participation in Track 1.5/Track 2 dialogues sponsored by the Pacific Forum CSIS, National Academies of Science Committee on International Security and Arms Control, Naval Postgraduate School, and Science Applications International Corporation.

[29] Thomas Fingar, "Worrying about Washington: China's Views on the U.S. Nuclear Posture," *Nonproliferation Review* 18, no. 1 (2011): 62. See also Lora Saalman, "China and the U.S. Nuclear Posture Review," Carnegie Endowment for International Peace, Washington, D.C., February 2011.

[30] Saalman, "China and the U.S. Nuclear Posture Review," 4.

Five Challenges

The complex situation we have described poses multiple unique challenges for the U.S. leadership in maintaining a regime of extended deterrence and providing assurance to allies, while simultaneously reassuring China that the United States is not seeking to thwart its rise. This section considers the most important of those challenges.

Challenge 1: Regional Nuclear Dynamics

Nuclear dynamics in the Asia-Pacific region are complex. While U.S. nuclear policy concentrates on China, there are several other nuclear relationships that complicate the situation. China has had uneasy relations in the past with both Russia and India and can be expected to respond to nuclear developments in those countries, thus complicating U.S. attempts at reassurance. In unofficial dialogues (not contradicted to our knowledge by any official statements) Chinese experts and officials routinely assert that because it has "no first use" agreements with both India and Russia and because all territorial disputes with those states have been resolved, there are no nuclear issues with either state. The reality may be more complex.

One analysis suggests that China's Second Artillery Force maintains roughly the same number of nuclear-armed ballistic missiles with regional and intercontinental ranges (around 75 missiles in each case).[31] These weapons would have clear military utility in confrontations with Russia or India. A separate analysis of admittedly opaque Chinese doctrine concludes that China's nuclear forces have missions beyond that of deterring the United States in a confrontation over Taiwan:

> That China's strategic posture seems now well suited to the requirements of deterrence in the cross strait contingency does not mean that it has been tailored solely for this purpose.… China's leaders expect nuclear deterrence to play a role in many high tech local wars under modern conditions—because of the possession of nuclear weapons by some of its neighbors, or their protection under a nuclear shield extended from elsewhere. As one PLA expert has argued: "What, then, are the targets of the nuclear deterrence of China? The targets are countries with nuclear weapons." And what countries other than the United States have nuclear weapons that are also a source of potential conflict with China? At the very least, Russia and India.[32]

---

[31] Hans M. Kristensen and Robert S. Norris, "Chinese Nuclear Forces, 2011" *Bulletin of the Atomic Scientists* 67, no. 6 (2011): 81. Official Department of Defense figures in annual reports to Congress confirm the large-scale deployment of ballistic missiles of less than intercontinental ranges but make no estimates of the fraction of these missiles equipped with nuclear weapons.

[32] Brad Roberts, "Strategic Deterrence Beyond Taiwan," in *Beyond the Strait: PLA Missions Other Than Taiwan*, ed. Roy Kamphausen, David Lai, and Andrew Scobell (Carlisle: Strategic Studies Institute, 2009), 190.

In managing relations with China, it will thus be necessary to recognize that the country's nuclear posture may in the future be driven by these regional pressures, although the Chinese government is unlikely to say so. The relationship with India is less likely to spill over into the Sino-American dynamic both because the U.S. nuclear relationship with India is benign and because there is a significant convergence in policy approaches between India and China that lessens the chance of major perturbations.[33]

Russia, however, is another matter. Russian experts privately acknowledge that their nonstrategic nuclear weapons are intended to counter Chinese conventional superiority, as well as that of NATO. Russia also appears to believe that Chinese nuclear forces are far larger than U.S. analysts assume. A former Strategic Rocket Forces chief of staff recently estimated that the tunnel complex known as the "underground Great Wall" may contain three thousand warheads.[34] Two of the most respected nuclear experts in Russia recently stated that "if China's nuclear forces are as limited as they are believed to be, they would be unable to deliver a retaliatory strike and are operationally most likely oriented toward a preemptive attack. The Chinese second-strike capability is only viable if China has hidden missile reserves."[35]

We do not share the assessment of these experts. Further, this Russian belief—if it is reflected in official thinking—will probably have more impact on U.S.-Russian arms control than on nuclear dynamics in the Pacific region. But in addition to a major modernization of its strategic offensive forces, to which the Chinese probably will not react, Russia plans substantial improvements in strategic defenses. If China came to believe that those defense improvements were aimed at it, the result could be an increase in the incentives for a qualitative or even quantitative arms race.

An entirely separate regional dynamic arises from the relationship between China and North Korea. A July 1961 treaty between the two states provides that "in the event of one of the Contracting Parties being subjected to the armed attack by any state or several states jointly and thus being involved in a state of war, the other Contracting Party shall immediately render military and other assistance by all means at its disposal."[36] Given China's no-first-use policy, "all means" probably does not include the use

---

[33] Lora Saalman, ed., *The China-India Nuclear Crossroads* (Washington, D.C.: Carnegie Endowment for International Peace, 2012), especially 171–90.

[34] Author conversation, Moscow, December 2012.

[35] Alexei Arbatov and Vladimir Dvorkin, "The Great Strategic Triangle," Carnegie Endowment for International Peace, Washington, D.C., April 2013, 1.

[36] Treaty of Friendship, Co-operation and Mutual Assistance between the People's Republic of China and the Democratic People's Republic of Korea, Article II, July 11, 1967, http://www.marxists.org/subject/china/documents/china_dprk.htm.

of nuclear weapons, but the obligations otherwise look remarkably like extended deterrence.

The treaty symbolizes an important difference between the United States and China with regard to North Korea. Eliminating North Korea's nuclear capability is not a high priority for China. Rather, Chinese leaders seek to preserve stability in North Korea, retain it as a buffer, and prevent U.S. hegemony. A recent survey of 825 articles by Chinese experts reveals a perception that U.S. interests are to control the Korean Peninsula, secure regime change, and contain China and Russia in order to maintain U.S. hegemony.[37] These attitudes do not imply that China will tolerate North Korea's use of nuclear weapons, but they could embolden other forms of reckless behavior by Kim Jong-un.

Challenge 2: Extended Deterrence at Lower Levels of Escalation

Although extended deterrence in East Asia is backstopped by the United States' nuclear capability, aggression against U.S. allies in the Pacific is more likely to take the form of lower-level, non-nuclear attacks than a major conventional or nuclear war. The most probable lower-level conflicts include conventional disputes over contested territory and cyberattacks. With these new conflict domains come new credibility problems: lower-level incursions are not a challenge that the U.S. nuclear umbrella is designed to deter. As two prominent theorists have noted, conceptualizing deterrence is "more difficult…for deterrence of limited conflicts than for strategic deterrence."[38] This section discusses the challenges of extended deterrence in the cases of both maritime disputes and cyberattacks.

Effective extended deterrence requires credible threats of retaliation, but this is a tall task when stakes are limited. It is difficult for the United States to threaten to seriously escalate a limited conventional or sub-conventional conflict on behalf of its allies if vital U.S. interests are not obviously engaged.[39] Unlike during the Cold War, in which U.S. interests in the integrity of Western Europe were congruent with those of its allies, it is much harder for the United States to make the case that its security or reputation is inextricably bound to the outcome of a lower-level conflict involving an ally. Moreover,

---

[37] Lora Saalman, "Balancing Chinese Interests on North Korea and Iran," Carnegie Endowment for International Peace, Washington, D.C., April 1, 2013, 20–21.

[38] Alexander L. George and Richard Smoke, *Deterrence in American Foreign Policy: Theory and Practice* (New York: Columbia University Press, 1974), 2.

[39] Patrick M. Morgan, "Applicability of Traditional Deterrence Concepts and Theory to the Cyber Realm," in *Proceedings of a Workshop on Deterring Cyberattacks: Informing Strategies and Developing Options for U.S. Policy,* ed. National Research Council (Washington, D.C.: National Academies Press, 2010), 67.

in cyber engagements and conflicts over disputed territory, red lines are far from clear. It is not obvious what transgression against an ally will invite U.S. retaliation. As Thomas Schelling remarked, "There is always some threshold below which [a] commitment is just not operative, and even that threshold itself is usually unclear."[40]

Extended deterrence and maritime disputes. One major extended-deterrence challenge in Northeast Asia is the numerous regional maritime conflicts that include U.S. allies. Although many of these disputes have been outstanding for decades, China's recent increase in power-projection capabilities has made it a more assertive claimant. For the most part, however, the United States has not clamored to unreservedly back its allies in these disputes. This is understandable: although the United States clearly remains committed to the security of its allies and partners, U.S. national interests are not necessarily at stake everywhere an ally lays claim to an uninhabited offshore island. It is therefore difficult for the United States to credibly declare that it is willing to escalate a serious conventional or nuclear war with China over an uninhabited atoll.[41] The nature of territorial disputes makes strong deterrent threats even more difficult; the United States is less able to issue clear deterrent threats when claimants disagree about where red lines lie.

The United States' involvement in its allies' territorial disputes varies widely, which may contribute to the perception that there are few clear red lines. The United States has been the most vocal in the Senkaku/Diaoyu Islands dispute between China and Japan, stating that the U.S.-Japan mutual security treaty applies to the islands, and that it would oppose a change in status except as a result of negotiation among all the parties involved.[42] The United States has reaffirmed its defense commitment to the Philippines in that country's dispute with China over the Scarborough Islands but has not expressly said that the mutual defense treaty covers the territory.[43] The United States has had little involvement in the Russo-Japanese dispute over the Sakhalin/North Kuril Islands and has called for ASEAN mediation for

[40] Thomas C. Schelling, *Arms and Influence* (New Haven: Yale University Press, 2008), 67.

[41] For more on this point, see Mira Rapp-Hooper, "An Ominous Pledge," *Diplomat*, September 26, 2012, http://thediplomat.com/china-power/uncharted-waters-for-extended-deterrence-in-east-china-sea.

[42] Stephen Harner, "Hillary's 'Parting Gift' to Japan in the Senkaku/Diaoyu Dispute Should Be Left Unopened; Obama and Kerry May Ask for It Back," *Forbes*, February 7, 2012, http://www.forbes.com/sites/stephenharner/2013/02/07/hillarys-parting-gift-to-japan-in-the-senkakudiaoyu-dispute-should-be-left-unopened-obama-and-kerry-may-ask-for-it-back.

[43] Floyd Whaley, "U.S. Reaffirms Defense of Philippines in Standoff with China," *New York Times*, May 1, 2012, http://www.nytimes.com/2012/05/02/world/asia/us-reaffirms-defense-of-philippines-in-standoff-with-china.html.

disputes in the South China Sea, some of which involve the Philippines.[44] Finally, in a dispute between two allies, South Korea and Japan, over the Dokdo/Takeshima Islands, the United States has called upon both to resolve the dispute peacefully.[45]

Another important maritime border dispute exists between North and South Korea. The North disputes the Northern Limit Line, the western maritime boundary of military control established by the United Nations in 1953.[46] It has challenged South Korean control of waters around this line on several occasions, including by shelling Yeonpyeong Island and sinking the South Korean corvette *Cheonan* in 2010, resulting in the death of 46 crew members. One reason that the DPRK may choose this area as a target for provocations is precisely because deterrence is so difficult here.[47] A limited U.S. national interest in these peripheral waters combines with a disputed maritime border to create a lack of clear red lines. It is far more difficult for the United States to threaten retaliation in advance for incursions like these than it is to promise an overwhelming response to an attack on Seoul.

Extending deterrence to cyberspace. Current debates over cyber deterrence in some ways mirror the early Cold War: conversations about what a true cyberwar would look like and what it would take to deter one are largely hypothetical.[48] Some analysts argue that cyber deterrence is impossible. The difficulty of attributing attacks and the prospect of inflicting collateral damage if a state retaliates erroneously make deterrence ineffective in cyberspace, especially because many cyberattackers are not states.[49] Others assert that deterrence of the most serious cyberattacks should be possible if states can impose costs for or reduce the benefits of waging them.[50] The United States has not yet adopted a clear cyber deterrence posture, but there are obvious obstacles to deterring cyberattacks against

---

[44] Patrick Ventrell, "South China Sea," U.S. Department of State, Press Release, August 3, 2012, http://www.state.gov/r/pa/prs/ps/2012/08/196022.htm.

[45] "U.S. 'Uncomfortable' on Japan-Korea Dokdo Spat," *Korea JoongAng Daily,* August 25, 2012, http://koreajoongangdaily.joinsmsn.com/news/article/article.aspx?aid=2958414.

[46] Dick K. Nanto, "North Korea: Chronology of Provocations, 1950–2003," Congressional Research Service, CRS Report for Congress, RL30004, March 18, 2003, 19.

[47] For more on why a lack of clarity on red lines invites deterrence challenges, see Daniel Altman, "Red Lines and the Fait Accompli: A Theory of Bargaining, Coercion, and Crisis Among Nations" (paper presented at the International Studies Association Annual Meeting, San Francisco, April 3–6, 2013).

[48] Morgan, "Applicability of Traditional Deterrence Concepts," 62.

[49] James A. Lewis, "The 'Korean' Cyber Attacks and Their Implications for Cyber Conflict," CSIS, October 2009, 4; and David C. Gompert and Phillip C. Saunders, *The Paradox of Power: Sino-American Strategic Restraint in an Age of Vulnerability* (Washington, D.C.: National Defense University, 2011), 117.

[50] Scott W. Beidleman, "Defining and Deterring Cyber War," U.S. Army War College, 2010, 17.

allies.[51] In some important respects, these are similar to the challenges of extended deterrence in the realm of maritime disputes.

One obstacle for the United States in setting red lines in the cyber domain is determining what actions against allies might qualify as acts of war and invite a serious response. Most cyberattacks are classified as crimes or espionage and do not constitute a use of force.[52] The United States may, however, decide that it is appropriate to adopt a declaratory policy that promises retaliation for attacks on allies above a certain level. There are at least three specific scenarios in which the United States might respond to a cyberattack on an ally that holds a U.S. security guarantee. The first is a cyberattack accompanied by a conventional attack.[53] The second is a cyberattack that does serious damage to civilian targets or to critical infrastructure, causing destruction comparable to a kinetic attack.[54] The third is a cyberattack that poses a fundamental danger to U.S. or allied military targets by jeopardizing C4ISR (command, control, communications, computers, intelligence, surveillance, and reconnaissance) and, in turn, obstructing the ability to use conventional capabilities.[55]

Even if the United States can locate the threshold above which cyberattacks qualify as acts of war, there are credibility problems involved in any effort to provide extended cyber deterrence. First, as with deterrence and disputed territories, it is difficult to extend deterrence if the deterrer does not make an advanced claim that an ally's cyber integrity is among its vital interests. Second, extended deterrence of cyberattacks rests on the threat of retaliation being displayed at all times, even though few attacks will rise to the level where an overwhelming response is necessary.[56] If extended deterrence is to include cyber retaliation, the United States will need to draw clear red lines on what kind of damage to what targets will provoke a serious response.

Challenge 3: Assuring Japan

Japan's pressing security concerns include the nuclear and missile threat posed by the DPRK in the near term and China's rise and military

---

[51] Patrick Morgan argues that the United States should not rush to articulate a cyber deterrence posture, lest it formulate a doctrine before fully understanding the threat at hand. See Morgan, "Applicability of Traditional Deterrence Concepts," 60.

[52] Ibid., 65.

[53] This occurred during the Russian invasion of Georgia in 2008. See Beidleman, "Defining and Deterring Cyber War," 6.

[54] Lewis, "The 'Korean' Cyber Attacks," 5.

[55] Gompert and Saunders, The Paradox of Power, 129.

[56] Morgan, "Applicability of Traditional Deterrence Concepts," 64–65.

modernization in the longer term. Additionally, Japan is broadly concerned with the United States' defense commitment. While North Korea poses the most immediate threat to South Korea (as discussed in more detail below), three nuclear detonations and many more missile tests give Tokyo reason to worry that it could become the victim of a devastating attack by North Korea. Indeed, some of Tokyo's recent military developments are direct responses to North Korean, rather than Chinese, threats.

China's ascendance in the region and its expanding military capabilities are of great concern to Tokyo in a longer-term, strategic sense. China's naval modernization, active missile program, and the impending development of the Jin-class ballistic missile submarine mean not only that China may continue to be assertive in maritime disputes but that it may soon possess a robust second-strike capability. The condition of U.S.-China mutual vulnerability may increase Tokyo's fears of abandonment: if Beijing's nuclear arsenal is highly survivable, the Japanese may believe that the United States will be deterred from defending its ally.[57] Because of this, Japanese assurance may be hard to come by if the U.S. nuclear arsenal does not remain second-to-none. Although a survivable U.S. second-strike capability may technically be all that is necessary to deter adversaries, according to some experts, Japanese concerns about U.S. willingness to engage in conflict with China result in more exacting nuclear requirements.[58] Moreover, if the United States and Russia continue to reduce the size of their nuclear arsenals, Japan worries that China may be tempted to seek parity.[59] Additionally, China's focus on an anti-access/area-denial strategy, which aims to prevent rapid U.S. military assistance to allies in the region, gives Tokyo cause for concern.

Beyond any specific Chinese development, Tokyo also has broader fears about U.S. abandonment.[60] Since the end of the Cold War, Japan's value to the United States is perceived to have diminished, yet the United States is Japan's only real ally. If U.S.-China relations improve considerably, or the United States makes concessions to China in the security realm, officials in Tokyo worry that the U.S. commitment to Japan may weaken.[61] This concern is all the more acute given the country's historically low defense

---

[57] Clark A. Murdoch and Jessica M. Yeats, "Exploring the Nuclear Posture Implications of Extended Deterrence and Assurance," CSIS, November 2009, 32–33.

[58] Nobuyasu Abe and Hirofumi Tosaki, "Untangling Japan's Nuclear Dilemma: Deterrence before Disarmament," in "Disarming Doubt: The Future of Extended Deterrence in East Asia," ed. Rory Medcalf and Fiona Cunningham, Lowy Institute for International Policy, April 11, 2012, 25, 34.

[59] Ralph A. Cossa and Brad Glosserman "Extended Deterrence and Disarmament: Japan and the New U.S. Nuclear Posture," *Nonproliferation Review* 18, no. 1 (2011): 133.

[60] Abe and Tosaki, "Untangling Japan's Nuclear Dilemma," 23.

[61] Murdoch and Yeats, "Exploring the Nuclear Posture Implications," 82.

spending and Article 9 of the Japanese constitution, which prevents Japan from maintaining a military for purposes other than self-defense.

Japan's concerns about China's rise and U.S. abandonment have, in recent years, been mitigated somewhat through an important new initiative, the Extended Deterrence Dialogue (EDD). Following the 2010 NPR, the EDD was established as a bilateral U.S.-Japanese consultation mechanism that is focused on enhancing regional stability.[62] The EDD is a welcome addition as far as extended deterrence and assurance are concerned because it allows U.S. defense officials to communicate with their Japanese counterparts about how exactly the United States plans for the defense of Japan. Although NATO has included this kind of information-sharing since the establishing of the Nuclear Planning Group in 1967, no such mechanism previously existed in any East Asian alliances.

The recent nuclear policy context also provides some cause for optimism where Japan's fears of abandonment are concerned. Tokyo is generally supportive of the stated U.S. goal of eventual nuclear disarmament, although there is some tension between this objective and Japan's continued reliance on extended deterrence.[63] The recent retirement of the Tomahawk land attack missile-nuclear (TLAM-N), however, suggests that this alliance tension may be manageable. The TLAM-N cruise missile has been in storage since the early 1990s but continued to have value to Japan as a visible symbol of extended deterrence that could be redeployed if necessary.[64] The retirement of the aging TLAM-N system was announced in the 2010 NPR. Despite fears to the contrary, the United States' decision to retire the TLAM-N appears to have resulted in relatively little backlash and has been managed through close consultations. The United States has emphasized the fact that other weapons systems such as heavy bombers and dual-capable aircraft can be used to signal alliance resolve in a crisis, and Japanese assurance does not appear to have hinged on one particular capability.[65]

Because of the emerging nuclear and missile threats from China and North Korea, the United States' changing emphasis on nuclear weapons, and its own domestic military constraints, Tokyo has embraced BMD capabilities in recent years. Japan has partnered with the United States to deploy a multilayered system that relies on the sea-based Aegis/SM-3 and

---

[62] "Joint Statement of the U.S.-Japan Security Consultative Committee," U.S. Department of State, Press Release, June 21, 2011, http://www.state.gov/r/pa/prs/ps/2011/06/166597.htm.

[63] Abe and Tosaki, "Untangling Japan's Nuclear Dilemma," 26.

[64] Murdoch and Yeats, "Exploring the Nuclear Posture Implications," 26, 50–51.

[65] Ibid., 31.

the land-based PAC-3 system.[66] Japan initially became interested in BMD because of the North Korean missile threat, but the capability has obvious uses against China's substantial missile arsenal.

Challenge 4: Assuring South Korea

In the past two decades, the nuclear balance on the Korean Peninsula has shifted in ways that are unnerving for Seoul. The U.S. withdrew its nonstrategic nuclear weapons from South Korea in 1991. This action was intended to pave the way for a denuclearized Korean Peninsula.[67] Instead, North Korea now has a small arsenal of plutonium devices, a uranium program, and a significant ballistic missile capability. These developments, coupled with the changing nuclear policy environment, mean that some in Seoul have concerns about the credibility and efficacy of the U.S. nuclear umbrella. These concerns will only be aggravated if North Korea's arsenal continues to expand, as we assess that it will.

In the wake of the North's recent missile and nuclear tests, South Korean officials and the general public have expressed mixed sentiments about U.S. extended deterrence. A June 2012 poll showed that less than half of the South Korean public believed that the United States would respond with nuclear weapons if the South became the victim of a nuclear attack by the North. Overall support for the U.S.-ROK alliance is at an all-time high, however, with 94% of the public approving. A February 2013 poll found that 67% of respondents favored the return of U.S. nonstrategic nuclear weapons to the peninsula.[68] About two-thirds of the public also supports an indigenous South Korean nuclear weapons program.[69] Prominent officials have echoed these sentiments, although, to date, the government has not.[70] While confidence in the alliance could scarcely be

---

[66] Japan decided to begin missile defense R&D following North Korea's 1998 test of a Taepodong-1 missile and decided to acquire the capability in 2003. The Aegis/SM-3 system is a three-stage missile designed to intercept short- to intermediate-range missiles in space at intermediate phases of flight. The PAC-3 system intercepts short-range missiles and cruise missiles at later phases of flight. See "Elements: Aegis Ballistic Missile Defense," Missile Defense Agency, http://www.mda.mil/system/aegis_bmd.html; and "Elements: Patriot Advanced Capability-3 (PAC-3)," Military Defense Agency, http://www.mda.mil/system/pac_3.html.

[67] The ROK and DPRK signed the Joint Declaration on the Denuclearization of the Korean Peninsula in 1991.

[68] The government does not share this view. See "PM Opposes U.S. Tactical Nuke Weapons Redeployment," Yonhap News Agency, April 25, 2013, http://english.yonhapnews.co.kr/northkorea/2013/04/25/5/0401000000AEN20130425008551315F.HTML.

[69] Kim Jiyoon, Karl Friedhoff, and Kang Chungku, "The Fallout: South Korean Public Opinion Following North Korea's Third Nuclear Test," Asan Institute for Public Policy Studies, February 25, 2013.

[70] David E. Sanger, "In U.S., South Korean Makes Case for Nuclear Arms," New York Times, April 9, 2013, http://www.nytimes.com/2013/04/10/world/asia/in-us-south-korean-makes-case-for-nuclear-arms.html.

better, South Koreans are clearly concerned about the adequacy of the nuclear dimension of the U.S. security guarantee.

These concerns stem from the fear that North Korea may be able to use its nuclear weapons for blackmail, and that its nuclear arsenal increases its ability and willingness to launch conventional attacks. In the South, some believe that the return of U.S. nonstrategic nuclear weapons or an independent nuclear capability would strengthen strategic stability on the Korean Peninsula.[71]

In addition to the North's nuclear and missile capability, Seoul also has concerns about the changing nuclear policy environment. The 2010 NPR declared that the United States would not use or threaten the use of nuclear weapons against non-nuclear states, as long as those states were in compliance with the Nuclear Non-Proliferation Treaty (NPT). During the late Cold War, a similar declaratory policy was in place, but it included an exception for states that were allied with other nuclear powers and attacked the United States or its allies. This meant that despite the DPRK's non-nuclear status, the United States reserved the right to retaliate against a North Korean invasion of the South using nuclear weapons. North Korea is, of course, not compliant with the NPT, so the United States retains this same right (and indeed, this caveat was carved out with Seoul in mind). In the eyes of some in South Korea, however, the contingencies in which the United States would be willing to use nuclear weapons against the North are narrowing, despite the fact that the DPRK only recently acquired a nuclear arsenal.[72] During the NPR process, these fears about the reduced role of U.S. nuclear weapons in extended deterrence led some officials in Seoul to oppose the adoption of a "sole purpose" doctrine. Such a doctrine would have stated that the exclusive mission of the U.S. nuclear arsenal was to deter or respond to a nuclear attack—a formulation that is more restrictive than the "fundamental role" statement that was ultimately adopted.[73]

As in the U.S.-Japan alliance, a new consultation mechanism, the Extended Deterrence Policy Committee (EDPC), was formed to manage some of Seoul's concerns about changes to nuclear policy. Also established in 2010, the EDPC serves a similar function to the EDD with Japan and aims to strengthen extended deterrence.[74] As with the EDD, the EDPC's

---

[71] Hyun-Wook Kim, "U.S. Extended Deterrence and the Korean Peninsula," in Medcalf and Cunningham, "Disarming Doubt," 80.

[72] U.S. Department of Defense, *Nuclear Posture Review Report,* vii; and Kim, "U.S. Extended Deterrence," 77.

[73] U.S. Department of Defense, *Nuclear Posture Review Report,* viii.

[74] U.S. Department of Defense, "Joint Communiqué: The 42nd U.S.-ROK Security Consultative Meeting," October 8, 2010, http://www.defense.gov/news/d20101008usrok.pdf.

most important contribution is information provision to Seoul about the strategy and means the United States uses to plan for South Korea's defense.

Outside of the nuclear context, Seoul harbors some concerns about the increasing U.S. emphasis on conventional deterrence. Operational control of Combined Forces Command will transfer from the United States to South Korea in 2015. At that time, troops that are currently deployed on the Korean Peninsula may be transferred to operations elsewhere. The drawdown of troops in Iraq and Afghanistan means that the United States will maintain fewer ground troops overall, and the 2012 Defense Strategic Guidance suggests that U.S. forces will no longer be able to undertake large-scale operations in two regions simultaneously.[75] Some in Seoul worry that this means that the United States would not be able to muster a forceful response to North Korean aggression if it were already engaged in another war. A second consequence of the transfer of operational control could be that the United States will be less able to moderate South Korea's "proactive deterrence" posture, which could increase the risks of escalation.[76]

As is true for Japan, the threat from the North has increased Seoul's interest in missile defense, although the South opted to develop an independent BMD capability rather than join the U.S.-led system. The Korea Air and Missile Defense System is a lower-tier system that will be deployed in summer 2013.[77] In late 2012 the United States and South Korea also reached an agreement that allows the South to extend the range of its ballistic missiles to eight hundred kilometers to counter the threat from the North.[78]

Although the alliances are unique, both the U.S.-Japan and U.S.-ROK partnerships face some similar challenges. These include deterring North Korea, dissuading China from aggression while also reassuring it, and assuring both allies while putting less emphasis on nuclear weapons.

Challenge 5: Reassuring China

Since Richard Nixon, every U.S. president has called for good relations with China. For example, in welcoming the Chinese president to

---

[75] U.S. Department of Defense, *Sustaining U.S. Global Leadership: Priorities for 21st Century Defense* (Washington, D.C., January 2012), 4, http://www.defense.gov/news/Defense_Strategic_Guidance.pdf.

[76] We are indebted to Joel Wit for this insight.

[77] Kim Eun-jung, "South Korea to Deploy Indigenous Missile Defense System in July," Yonhap News Agency, April 10, 2013, http://english.yonhapnews.co.kr/news/2013/04/10/17/0200000000AEN20130410010900315F.HTML.

[78] South Korean ballistic missiles were previously capped at three hundred kilometers. Kelsey Davenport, "South Korea Extends Missile Range," Arms Control Association, November 2012, http://www.armscontrol.org/act/2012_11/South-Korea-Extends-Missile-Range.

Washington in 2011, President Obama said, "We have an enormous stake in each other's success…. The United States welcomes China's rise as a strong, prosperous and successful member of the community of nations."[79] Despite these statements, there is a strong view within China—and especially within the Chinese military—that the United States seeks to contain China and prevent its rise, as well as to transform and "Westernize" China's political system under the guise of support for human rights.[80] The recent Chinese defense white paper noted that "some country [i.e., the United States] has strengthened its Asia-Pacific military alliances, expanded its military presence in the region, and frequently makes the situation there tenser."[81] Chinese political and military concerns are extensive; this chapter, however, will limit its discussion to broad strategic and nuclear aspects.

The Chinese often assert, at least in unofficial dialogues, that the ultimate reassurance would be for the United States to adopt a no-first-use policy. The United States is unlikely to do so because such a declaration could cause its allies to lose confidence in U.S. protection. What other reassurance options might be available? Although the Chinese use the disparity between their force structure and those of the United States and Russia to justify remaining aloof from arms control, they appear to be relatively indifferent to the size of the U.S. nuclear arsenal. Instead, they are concerned primarily with threats to their own deterrent, including U.S. development of new nuclear or conventional capabilities, and are fearful that the U.S. extended deterrent will give U.S. allies a blank check for reckless behavior.

On the first point, the Chinese fear that the United States seeks to deny them the ability to conduct a retaliatory strike, primarily through the deployment of national missile defense but also through deployment of conventional precision-strike systems. Indeed, a recent article by a normally authoritative Chinese expert suggested that these two developments could threaten the continuation of China's no-first-use policy.[82]

The Chinese solution to their concerns on national missile defense is for the United States to formally accept mutual vulnerability. Dealing with

[79] "Remarks by President Obama and President Hu of the People's Republic of China at Official Arrival Ceremony," Office of the Press Secretary, White House, January 19, 2011.

[80] Andrew J. Nathan and Andrew Scobell, "How China Sees America," *Foreign Affairs* 91, no. 5 (2012): 32–47; Michael Pillsbury, "The Sixteen Fears: China's Strategic Psychology," *Survival* 54 (October 2012): 149–82; and "How China Deals with the U.S. Strategy to Contain China," trans. Chinascope, *Qiushi Journal,* December 10, 2010, http://www.chinascope.org/main/content/view/3291/92.

[81] Information Office of the State Council of the People's Republic of China, *The Diversified Employment of China's Armed Forces* (Beijing, April 2013), Section I, http://news.xinhuanet.com/english/china/2013-04/16/c_132312681.htm.

[82] Yao Yunzhu, "China Will Not Change Its Nuclear Policy," *China-US Focus,* April 22, 2013, http://www.chinausfocus.com/peace-security/china-will-not-change-its-no-first-use-policy/.

this concern raises two problems, one practical and one conceptual. The practical problem is that U.S. national missile defense is sized to deal with the Iranian and North Korean threats, as illustrated by the recent decision to increase the number of interceptors from 30 to 44.[83] The United States took this action as a signal to North Korea and on behalf of U.S. allies in the region. Yet the Chinese, who consider U.S. alliances as aimed at containment, often see such steps as directed at them.

The conceptual problem concerns the nature of mutual vulnerability. Some believe accepting mutual vulnerability (that is, accepting that China can deliver an effective nuclear attack on the U.S. homeland) is a policy choice rather than a recognition of reality. Those who believe this assert that the United States could construct a national missile defense system that could essentially deny China the ability to conduct a successful ballistic missile attack if it chose to do so. In this view, opting for mutual vulnerability is a dangerous and irresponsible choice that the United States should not accept.[84] Others assert that mutual vulnerability is a fact of life that the United States cannot alter—a condition to be acknowledged and managed. Those who favor this view believe that China has the resources and technical ability to overcome any U.S. national missile defense that is technically and fiscally feasible. This second view appears to be the Obama administration's position, although it has been unwilling to say so explicitly, presumably for a combination of domestic political reasons and concern over allied reactions.

A related Chinese concern is with U.S. "prompt global strike," a limited capability for conventional strike at intercontinental ranges that is now in the early stages of development. Beijing fears that such a system, when deployed, could "have the capability to strike China's nuclear arsenal and make China's [no first use] policy redundant."[85] Other than the United States canceling development, it is not clear how the Chinese might be reassured. As an interim confidence-building measure, the United States and China could develop a set of procedures for notifying China of future launches of prompt-global-strike systems. These procedures should be used during future development launches and should ultimately be available for operational launches. Once developed, the procedures could be exercised through a joint U.S.-China tabletop exercise involving the military staffs of

---

[83] Amaani Lyle, "Hagel: U.S. Bolstering Missile Defense," American Forces Press Service, March 15, 2013.

[84] For a forceful defense of this view, see "China's Strategic Modernization," International Security Advisory Board, draft report, 2008. The draft was leaked to the Washington Times and is available at Bill Gertz, "China Report Urges Missile Shield," Washington Times, October 1, 2008, http://www.washingtontimes.com/news/2008/oct/01/new-us-defenses-sought-to-counter-beijing-buildup/.

[85] Yao, "China Will Not Change Its Nuclear Policy."

both countries. China generally objects to calls for transparency with respect to its own forces but urges transparency about U.S. strategic intentions. Beijing thus might welcome such a proposal.

Confidence-building measures can apply in other areas as well. To help China understand the U.S. national BMD system, government technical experts from both China and the United States could conduct a joint technical analysis of the U.S. program and its capabilities against Chinese systems, as well as a joint threat analysis of the North Korean missile threat. China might also be given the opportunity to observe U.S. national BMD testing in order to gain confidence that it understands the performance parameters of the system.[86]

The second area where the Chinese desire reassurance is their fear that the U.S. extended deterrent will give U.S. allies a blank check for reckless behavior. The argument—which the Chinese particularly apply to Japan—is that an open-ended, "ambiguous U.S. extended deterrence commitment could embolden Japan to take a more escalatory response" during low-level confrontations. China could perceive this as an example of nuclear coercion that it needs to resist. In contrast, if the United States were to "explicitly remove its nuclear extended deterrent from small conflicts…its allies [would] be more cautious," thus reducing China's anxiety. Therefore, the United States should "publicly limit…extended nuclear deterrence to existential threats: that is…conventional attacks that threaten the survival of one of its allies."[87]

This chapter discussed earlier the problems of extended deterrence at lower levels of conflict. In this area, it is more important for the United States to assure its allies than reassure China. Thus, Washington should not issue any public statements that appear to limit its security assurances to those allies. At the same time, it should continue its long-standing policy of not being explicit about the circumstances in which it would use nuclear weapons.

The challenges of reassuring China highlight a broader conundrum— one that we term a "security trilemma." Actions taken by the United States and its allies to deter or defend against North Korea, such as BMD deployments or joint exercises to demonstrate allied cohesion, may have the

---

[86] For additional details, see Linton Brooks, "Building Habits of Cooperation in Pursuit of the Vision: Elements and Roles of Enhanced Dialogue for Strategic Reassurance," in "Building Toward a Stable and Cooperative Long-Term U.S.-China Strategic Relationship," ed. Lewis A. Dunn, Science Applications International Corporation (SAIC), Pacific Forum CSIS, and China Arms Control and Disarmament Association, December 31, 2012, http://csis.org/files/publication/issuesinsights_vol13no2.pdf.

[87] Li Bin and He Yun, "Credible Limitations: U.S. Extended Nuclear Deterrence and Stability in Northeast Asia," in Disarming Doubt: The Future of Extended Nuclear Deterrence in East Asia, ed. Rory Medcalf and Fiona Cunningham (Woollahra: Longueville Media, 2012), 61–68.

effect of making China feel less secure. While China would like the United States to exclude smaller conflicts from its nuclear extended deterrent, the United States must reassure allies who live in an increasingly hostile neighborhood due to the North Korean nuclear and missile threat. North Korean provocations are necessarily met with U.S. efforts to assure South Korea and Japan of the continued U.S. commitment to their security. More military exercises, investments in missile defense, and strong public statements on behalf of South Korea and Japan, however, may undercut efforts to reassure China that the United States is interested primarily in its allies' security rather than regional hegemony.

This security trilemma may also have some stabilizing features. As we have discussed, China generally prioritizes North Korean state stability over denuclearization. It would, however, prefer to see less, not more, U.S. military presence in the region, so efforts to deter and defend against North Korean aggression may also induce China to try to restrain its ally. Nonetheless, the United States cannot be certain how China will interpret its posture against North Korea, making assurance and reassurance in the Pacific far more complex than these strategies of influence were in the past.

Implications for the United States

Implications for U.S. Nuclear Force Structure and Posture

The United States has a number of tools it can use for extended deterrence, assurance, and reassurance. These include force deployments, exercises, public statements, and sanctions, among others. Consistent with the focus of this chapter, the following analysis is limited to nuclear and strategic capabilities.

China appears relatively indifferent to both the size and composition of U.S. nuclear forces, although Chinese experts reacted strongly to suggestions by U.S. academics that the United States should develop (or had already attained) a disarming counterforce capability.[88] Additionally, to the extent that there is an external motivation for North Korea's nuclear program, it is U.S. conventional superiority, not the details of the U.S. nuclear arsenal.

Allies in East Asia have concerns that the dwindling size and availability of the U.S. nuclear arsenal could lead to strategic decoupling. They have a general preference that the United States not be perceived as inferior to any other nuclear state, and Japan in particular worries about

---

[88] Keir A. Lieber and Daryl G. Press, "The Nukes We Need," *Foreign Affairs* 88, no.6 (2009): 39–51; and Keir A. Lieber and Daryl G. Press, "The Rise of U.S. Nuclear Primacy," *Foreign Affairs* 85, no. 2 (2006): 42–54.

a Chinese "sprint to parity" if Russian and U.S. arms control reductions are deep enough. If the U.S. arsenal continues to contract while China's expands, Japan worries that the United States will be less inclined to challenge increased Chinese assertiveness.

Japan and South Korea also have concerns about specific U.S. weapons systems. First, they worry whether the United States would make nonstrategic nuclear weapons available on dual-capable aircraft if allies requested them. They also fear that the United States will not maintain the capability to deploy such weapons in a time of crisis if NATO allies decide to withdraw them from Europe.[89] In essence, they fear strategic decoupling. Related to this is strong public (but not government or military) support in South Korea for reintroducing the U.S. nonstrategic nuclear weapons that were withdrawn in the early 1990s.[90] Additionally, the previous Japanese government saw the TLAM-N as uniquely relevant to Japan's security. Following extensive U.S. consultations, the current government no longer takes that view and posed no objection to the Obama administration's decision to retire the weapon.[91]

Taken in the aggregate, these considerations do not appear to require any major changes in the current U.S. nuclear force structure or posture. In particular, we would reject the suggestions for additional counterforce capability. Provided further reductions are done in parallel with Russia, there should be no concerns about the one-third reduction in deployed strategic forces proposed by President Obama in his June 2013 Berlin speech.[92] The reintroduction of tactical weapons into South Korea, however, would be inconsistent with overall U.S. policy, likely to increase tensions on the peninsula, and unnecessary for assurance given the United States' ability to use nuclear-capable bombers and dual-capable aircraft to send signals.[93] If a future arms control agreement limits U.S. nonstrategic nuclear weapons, however, advanced consideration must be given to Asian allies' concerns.

With respect to mutual vulnerability, we are firmly in the camp that regards such vulnerability as a fact of life and endorse the analysis of the

---

[89] Author conversation with a former government official, Washington, D.C., May 2013.

[90] Ralph Cossa, "U.S. Nuclear Weapons to South Korea?" 38 North, July 13, 2011, http://38north.org/2011/07/rcossa071211.

[91] Cossa and Glosserman, "Extended Deterrence and Disarmament."

[92] Barack Obama, "Remarks by President Obama at the Brandenburg Gate—Berlin, Germany," June 19, 2013.

[93] On March 18, 2013, for example, Deputy Defense Secretary Ashton Carter, speaking in Seoul, said he should "note the presence of strategic bombers taking place in flight training in the Korean peninsula." See "Media Availability with Deputy Secretary Carter at the United States Embassy, Seoul, South Korea," U.S. Department of Defense, News Transcript, March 18, 2013, http://www.defense.gov/Transcripts/Transcript.aspx?TranscriptID=5206.

U.S. State Department's International Security Advisory Board, chaired by former secretary of defense William Perry:

> China's efforts to build a survivable second-generation sea-based and mobile land-based nuclear force are progressing and will over time produce a larger, and less vulnerable, force with more (from 25 to about 100) ICBMs capable of striking the United States. U.S. policymakers should recognize that Chinese perceptions of U.S. intentions, missile defenses, and nuclear and precision conventional strike capabilities will likely shape decisions about China's nuclear force posture. Chinese leaders have been determined to maintain a credible nuclear deterrent regardless of U.S. choices and will almost certainly have the necessary financial and technological resources to continue to do so. Accordingly, mutual nuclear vulnerability should be considered as a fact of life for both sides. However, neither the U.S. ability to use conventional forces to protect our interests in the region nor the U.S. "nuclear umbrella" require the ability to negate China's nuclear forces.[94]

Acknowledging mutual vulnerability as a fact is in the United States' strategic interest. Failing to acknowledge vulnerability makes it easier for China to conclude that it must respond to U.S. actions aimed at North Korea (such as increasing BMD deployments) by changing its current nuclear policy and engaging in a quantitative buildup, which would have adverse consequences in the region. It is important for both the United States and its allies to discourage China from such a course. U.S. allies, especially Japan, can be brought to understand this and to recognize that the United States maintained effective extended deterrence in the Cold War under similar circumstances. Washington should consult with its allies to ensure they understand this rationale but should not make any public acknowledgement of mutual vulnerability in order to avoid placing public pressure on these same allies.

Implications for Non-nuclear Operations

If the United States sends muddled deterrent signals to adversaries on maritime or cyberattacks, allies are unlikely to be assured that their security is provided for in these domains. The fact that the United States maintains massive nuclear and conventional superiority over China and North Korea, the most likely lower-level conventional and cyber adversaries, may be of limited comfort. One way to augment assurance may be to improve coordination with allies in both of these areas. On the

---

[94] International Security Advisory Board, U.S. Department of State, "Report on Maintaining U.S.-China Strategic Stability," October 26, 2012, http://www.state.gov/t/avc/isab/200297.htm. For a similar conclusion reached by a group of rising scholars, see "Nuclear Weapons and U.S.-China Relations: A Way Forward," PONI Working Group on U.S. China Nuclear Dynamics, CSIS, March 2013, 21–23.

maritime front, this could include dialogues to coordinate allied policy for each of the outstanding disputes. On the cyber front, the United States may be able to provide its allies with attribution assistance and can share information about malware threats and specific signatures to bolster deterrence by denial.[95]

Other Implications

Beyond force structure and non-nuclear operations, there are important implications for U.S. declaratory policy, consultation with allies, and public communication on regional nuclear issues more broadly. First, although we see no reason why the United States cannot reduce its nuclear arsenal to 1,000–1,100 deployed strategic warheads, the time has not yet come for further revisions in declaratory policy. The 2010 NPR declared that the United States will "work to establish conditions" under which a "sole purpose" doctrine could be adopted, but our analysis on the requirements of assuring South Korea and Japan suggests that these allies would not favor major changes to U.S. nuclear declaratory policy in the near term. Further narrowing the contingencies in which the United States may use nuclear weapons, without bolstering extended deterrence in other areas, is likely to trigger allies' abandonment fears. Instead, the United States needs to expand the scope of its declaratory policy to send allies and adversaries clearer signals on how it will respond to lower-level conventional provocations and cyberattacks. Both China and Japan have begun to think seriously about how to manage extended-deterrence commitments below the nuclear threshold and may be ahead of the United States in this regard.[96] The United States should join in these conversations and endeavor to set clearer red lines at these lower levels of escalation.

Related are the implications for consultations, both between the United States and its allies and with China. The United States should continue to make use of the Extended Deterrence Dialogue (U.S.-Japan) and Extended Deterrence Policy Committee (U.S.-ROK), as well as similar dialogues with other regional allies such as Australia and the Philippines. These are vital avenues for communicating to allies about how the United States is practicing extended deterrence in a changing nuclear context. Expanding

---

[95] If attribution is possible, this may allow the United States and its allies to threaten the use of more traditional tools of statecraft, such as targeted financial sanctions to deter cyberattacks. Zachary K. Goldman, "Washington's Secret Weapons Against Chinese Hackers: Applying the Lessons of Counterterrorism and Counterproliferation in Cyberspace," *Foreign Affairs*, April 8, 2013, http://www.foreignaffairs.com/articles/139139/zachary-k-goldman/washingtons-secret-weapon-against-chinese-hackers.

[96] Private discussion with a senior Department of Defense official, March 2013.

the purview of these dialogues to explicitly include deterrence below the nuclear threshold would be advisable.

Chinese concerns about prompt global strike and missile defense should also be managed through closer consultation in addition to the confidence-building measure suggested earlier. Dialogues can also be used to communicate to China about how the United States intends to support regional allies in the case of lower-level conventional engagements. Common knowledge about both U.S. capabilities and intentions can only serve to strengthen deterrence and reduce the risk of miscalculation.

On that score, the term "strategic stability" has probably outlived its usefulness. It served an essential purpose in making clear that the United States regards nuclear relations with China as being equally important as those with Russia. But given the difficulty noted earlier in using the term in discussions with China, it may have become an obstacle to deeper dialogue. Rather than continue to seek agreement on a common definition, it is time to acknowledge that the term has served its purpose and move on to a dialogue from which something better can emerge.

A Wild Card: A More Assertive China

An unstated but important presumption of this chapter is that China will seek to manage its rise to what it sees as its rightful international position in a fundamentally peaceful manner. China's primary security challenge is internal insecurity, which it seeks to counter by encouraging national pride and by improving living standards and prosperity. Anti-Western or anti-American rhetoric can assist with internal cohesion and thus may be in the regime's interest, but actual conflict is not. Although China has become more vocal in some of its outstanding regional disputes as its military capabilities have improved, it has not evinced a greater risk tolerance where actual conflict is concerned. Thus, we expect that China will not become appreciably more assertive over time and that its future will be largely like its past.

But what if we are wrong? What if China's extensive non-nuclear military buildup and its aggressive claims and actions in the South China Sea foreshadow a world in which China seeks to use military and economic coercion to establish a visible regional hegemony? How would these recommendations change? In general, these recommendations would remain valid but would be characterized by more urgency and require more effort to implement. The United States would probably need to increase its non-nuclear forces in the region, along with increasing the visibility of its nuclear forces. These steps would be aimed at both assurance and extended deterrence. The most important step would be to continue the emphasis on managing extended deterrence below the nuclear threshold, where the United States might need to be more visible in its response to Chinese provocations, clearer about where red lines exist with respect to situations involving U.S. allies, and more blunt in its private dialogue with China.

Summary and Policy Recommendations

The needs to deter both China and North Korea, to assure multiple allies, and to reassure China that the United States does not seek to contain its peaceful rise all combine to make extended deterrence more complex than its Cold War predecessor. The most conceptually complex aspect of extended deterrence is deterring low-level confrontations in the maritime sphere today and the cyber domain in the future. While this chapter offers some thought on this topic, additional U.S. thinking is required before engaging further.

This analysis suggests the following policy recommendations for the United States:

On extended deterrence:

- Conduct a thorough internal review about how to manage extended deterrence commitments at the conventional and cyber levels. On completion of the review, engage China on the topic, preferably in the context of crisis management.

On assurance:

- Maintain rough strategic nuclear parity with Russia to avoid any perception by U.S. allies, especially Japan, that the United States is no longer "second to none."

- Continue to make extensive use of consultations through the Extended Deterrence Dialogue (U.S.-Japan) and Extended Deterrence Policy Committee (U.S.-ROK), along with similar, though less intensive, consultations with other allies. Use the crisis-management component of these dialogues (or separate forums) to address lower-level deterrence challenges.

- Reject new deployments of nuclear weapons in the Asia-Pacific region.

- Refrain from making further major changes in declaratory policy regarding nuclear use for the time being.

- Despite China's preferences, do not make public statements that would appear to limit U.S. extended deterrence commitments.

On reassurance of China:

- Make it clear to China that the United States accepts mutual vulnerability as a fact of life.[97] Do not, however, go beyond current public statements in order to avoid raising public doubts among U.S. allies.
- Implement modest confidence-building measures with respect to BMD and conventional prompt global strike.
- Drop the term "strategic stability"; the confusion it causes outweighs the signal of importance it was intended to convey to China.

We began this chapter by asserting that the U.S.-China relationship will be the most important geopolitical dynamic of the next several decades. That relationship will inevitably be a blend of cooperation and competition. It is not inevitable that the competition will lead to conflict, but it might if not well-managed. Thus, our most important recommendation—and the premise of this volume—is that academics and practitioners alike must keep this fact firmly in mind as we move deeper into what history may well come to regard as the "Pacific century."

---

[97] For an excellent approach, see the logic set forth in "Nuclear Weapons and U.S.-China Relations."

STRATEGIC ASIA 2013–14

INDICATORS

Strategic Asia
by the Numbers

The strategic dynamics of the Asia-Pacific have evolved significantly in the past year as the global geopolitical center of gravity continues to shift eastward. China's rise still generates concern among neighboring states despite a growing level of regional economic integration. As the United States "rebalances to Asia," a dual regional structure is emerging whereby many Asian nations are increasingly dependent on China economically yet continue to rely on the United States for the maintenance of regional security.

In the second year of the U.S. rebalance, the focus of the strategy has shifted to place greater emphasis on economic and political engagement. Diplomatic and trade initiatives, such as the Trans-Pacific Partnership, have received greater attention, building on the military aspects of the rebalance announced in its first year.

The Asia-Pacific continues to be plagued by several long-term sources of tension, most notably on the Korean Peninsula. Early on in her administration, new South Korean president Park Geun-hye was confronted by North Korean provocations, including nuclear threats. Despite President Park's attempts to recast inter-Korean relations through a policy of *trustpolitik*—aimed at strengthening deterrence while renewing dialogue with the North—progress has been stymied by Pyongyang's belligerence.

Disputes over territorial and historical issues also intensified in 2012 and early 2013, resulting in several armed confrontations. These clashes highlighted the persistent and growing distrust and antagonism among many of Asia's leading powers and may be emblematic of the rising influence of nationalism within the region.

The following pages contain tables and figures drawn from a broad array of sources. These charts cover politics, economics, trade and investment, energy and the environment, security challenges, and nuclear arms and nonproliferation. The data sets summarize the critical trends in Asia and changes underway in the regional balance of power.

The information for "Strategic Asia by the Numbers" was compiled by NBR interns Zane Buckey, Charlie Chung, Miriam D'Onofrio, Christopher Martin, Kuni Shimoji, and Taylor Washburn.

Politics

Late 2012 and early 2013 saw change as well as continuity in the political dynamics of the Asia-Pacific. Discouragingly, a growing strategic distrust has come to characterize many of the bilateral relationships between Asia's most prominent powers over the past year.

- U.S. president Barack Obama hosted visits with leaders from Japan, the Philippines, Afghanistan, Singapore, South Korea, Myanmar, Vietnam, and Brunei in Washington, D.C., and met with Chinese president Xi Jinping in California. In November 2012, Obama took his fifth trip to the Asia-Pacific as president, visiting Bangkok and Rangoon before attending the East Asia Summit in Phnom Penh.

- A number of political transitions took place in the Asia-Pacific in 2012–13. U.S. president Barack Obama was elected to a second term, as was Taiwan president Ma Ying-jeou. In China, South Korea, Japan, Pakistan, Russia, and Iran, new leaders assumed power.

- In Myanmar the military has continued to relinquish political control, creating a platform for improved relations with the United States and the international community.

TABLE 1   Political leadership

	Head of state	Head of government
Australia	Queen Elizabeth II	Prime Minister Kevin Rudd
China	President Xi Jinping	Premier Li Keqiang
India	President Pranab Mukherjee	Prime Minister Manmohan Singh
Indonesia	President Susilo Bambang Yudhoyono	
Iran	Supreme Leader Ali Khamenei	President Hassan Rouhani
Japan	Emperor Akihito	Prime Minister Shinzo Abe
Myanmar	President Thein Sein	
North Korea	Eternal President Kim Il-sung (deceased)	First Chairman Kim Jong-un
Pakistan	President Mamnoon Hussain	Prime Minister Mohammed Nawaz Sharif
Russia	President Vladimir Putin	Premier Dmitri Medvedev
South Korea	President Park Geun-hye	Prime Minister Chung Hong-won
Taiwan	President Ma Ying-jeou	Premier Jiang Yi-huah
Thailand	King Phumiphon Adunyadet	Prime Minister Yingluck Shinawatra
United States	President Barack Obama	
Vietnam	President Truong Tan Sang	Prime Minister Nguyen Tan Dung

SOURCE: Central Intelligence Agency (CIA), *The World Factbook*, 2013; and "North Korea Profile," *BBC*, June 7, 2013.

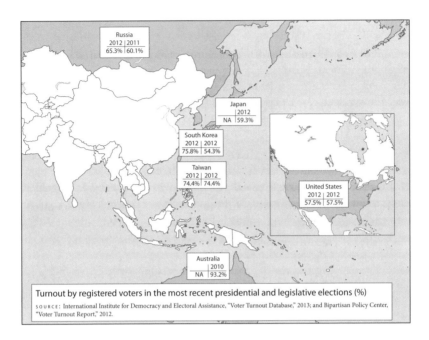

Turnout by registered voters in the most recent presidential and legislative elections (%)

SOURCE: International Institute for Democracy and Electoral Assistance, "Voter Turnout Database," 2013; and Bipartisan Policy Center, "Voter Turnout Report," 2012.

TABLE 2 Political rights, corruption, and democracy

	Political rights score		Corruption index		Democracy index	
	2005	2012	2005	2012	2006	2012
Australia	1	1	8.8	8.5	9.1	9.2
China	7	7	3.2	3.9	3.0	3.0
India	2	2	2.9	3.6	7.7	7.5
Indonesia	2	2	2.2	3.2	6.4	6.8
Iran	6	6	2.9	2.8	2.9	2.0
Japan	1	1	7.3	7.4	8.2	8.1
Myanmar	7	6	1.8	1.5	1.7	2.4
Pakistan	6	4	2.1	2.7	3.9	4.6
Russia	6	6	2.4	2.8	5.0	3.7
Singapore	5	4	9.4	8.7	5.9	5.9
South Korea	1	1	5.0	5.6	7.9	8.1
Taiwan	1	1	5.9	6.1	7.8	7.6
Thailand	3	4	3.8	3.7	5.7	6.6
United States	1	1	7.6	7.3	8.2	8.1

SOURCE: Freedom House, "Freedom in the World," 2006 and 2013; Transparency International, "Corruption Perceptions Index," 2005 and 2012; and Economist Intelligence Unit, "Democracy Index," 2006 and 2012.

NOTE: Political rights score = a people's ability to participate freely in the political process (1 = most free / 7 = least free). Prior to 2011, corruption index = degree to which public official corruption is perceived to exist (1 = most corrupt / 10 = most open); from 2012, corruption index = how corrupt the public sector is perceived to be (0 = highly corrupt / 100 = very clean). NBR has standardized the data for consistency. Democracy index = level of democratization (0 = least democratic / 10 = most democratic).

Economics

GDP growth in the world's developed countries occurred at a rate of about 1.3% in early 2013, compared with a rate of 7.1% in Asia's developing economies. Rising domestic consumption in Southeast Asia was a key driver of GDP growth in East and South Asia and was enough to overcome reduced consumer demand in India, China, the United States, and Europe.

- In the United States, GDP growth continued to improve and unemployment to slowly recede. The International Monetary Fund (IMF) predicts that U.S. GDP will grow 1.7% in 2013 and 2.7% in 2014.

- The IMF forecasts that in 2013 the GDP of Asia's two rising powers, India and China, will grow by 5.7% and 8.0% respectively.

- The Asian Development Bank anticipates that by 2035 Asia's GDP will more than quadruple.

- Improvement in Central Asia's economic performance was largely attributable to growth in the energy sector, with Turkmenistan and Uzbekistan at the front of a boom in oil and natural gas production.

TABLE 3 Gross domestic product

	GDP ($bn)				Rank	
	1990	2000	2012	2012 annual growth (%)	1990	2012
United States	5,800.5	9,951.5	15,684.8	2.1%	1	1
China	390.3	1,198.5	8,227.0	7.8%	3	2
Japan	3,103.7	4,731.2	5,964.0	1.9%	2	3
Russia	516.8	259.7	2,022.0	3.9%	8	4
India	323.5	476.4	1,824.8	3.2%	5	5
Australia	323.8	399.6	1,541.8	3.4%	6	6
South Korea	270.4	533.4	1,155.9	2.0%	4	7
Indonesia	113.8	165.0	878.2	6.2%	9	8
Iran	85.0	96.4	548.9	-1.9%	10	9
Taiwan	165.0	326.2	474.0	1.3%	7	10
Malaysia	43.4	93.8	303.5	5.6%	12	11
Singapore	38.8	94.3	276.5	1.3%	11	12
Pakistan	48.6	74.1	231.9	3.7%	13	13
Kazakhstan	26.9	18.3	196.4	5.0%	15	14
Vietnam	6.5	31.2	138.1	5.0%	14	15
World	22,195.9	32,331.3	71,707.3	2.2%	N/A	N/A

SOURCE: International Monetary Fund (IMF), "World Economic Outlook Database," 2013; and World Bank, "World Development Indicators," 2013.

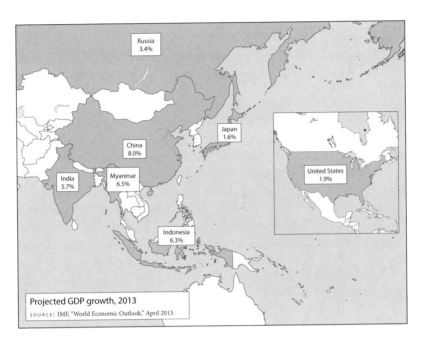

Projected GDP growth, 2013

SOURCE: IMF, "World Economic Outlook," April 2013.

TABLE 4   GDP growth and inflation rates

	Average GDP growth (%)			Average inflation rate (%)		
	2001–5	2006–10	2012	2001–5	2006–10	2012
Australia	3.3	2.8	3.6	2.9	2.9	1.8
China	9.8	11.2	7.8	1.3	2.9	2.7
India	6.4	8.4	4.0	3.9	8.4	9.3
Indonesia	4.7	5.7	6.2	9.2	7.8	4.3
Iran	6.1	4.6	-1.9	13.6	15.7	30.6
Japan	1.2	0.4	2.0	0.0	0.0	0.0
Malaysia	4.8	4.5	5.6	1.7	2.6	1.7
Myanmar	12.9	7.8	6.3	26.4	19.0	6.1
Pakistan	5.3	4.2	3.7	4.8	10.8	11.0
Russia	6.1	3.7	3.4	14.9	10.2	5.1
Singapore	4.8	6.7	1.3	0.7	2.6	4.6
South Korea	4.6	3.8	2.0	3.3	3.0	2.2
Taiwan	3.6	4.2	1.3	0.7	2.9	1.9
United States	2.4	0.7	2.2	2.5	2.2	2.1
Vietnam	7.6	7.0	5.0	4.6	10.9	9.1

SOURCE: IMF, "World Economic Outlook," April 2013.

Trade and Investment

The Trans-Pacific Partnership has become the cornerstone of U.S. trade policy in the region and a key component of the Obama administration's rebalance to Asia. The multilateral free trade agreement has the potential to revolutionize the region's economic architecture, particularly with Japan—whose GDP still exceeds that of ASEAN—joining the negotiations in July 2013.

- In 2012, China surpassed the United States to become the world's largest trading nation, measured by trade volume.

- China accounted for 14% of total U.S. trade and is the world's largest holder of U.S. Treasuries, with $1.2 trillion in U.S. debt, while Japan ranks second with $1.1 trillion.

- Despite FDI outflows from East Asia decreasing by $17 billion dollars from 2011, 24% of world outflows in 2012 originated in the region. FDI inflows to East Asia saw a moderate $4 billion increase from the previous year. Meanwhile, FDI inflows and outflows to South Asia in 2012 decreased by $10 billion and $4 billion, respectively.

TABLE 5   Trade flow and trade partners

	Trade flow ($bn constant 2005)		2010–11 growth (%)	Top export partner, 2012	Top import partner, 2012
	2000	2011			
Australia	210.8	364.4	6.6%	China (29.5%)	China (18.2%)
China	578.1	2,958.8	7.1%	U.S. (17.2%)	Japan (9.8%)
Hong Kong	459.6	918.0	4.3%	China (54.1%)	China (46.9%)
India	158.8	724.8	18.6%	U.S. (12.7%)	China (11.0%)
Indonesia	126.5	275.7	13.5%	Japan (15.9%)	China (15.3%)
Iran	73.4	–	–	China (22.1%)	UAE (32.2%)
Japan	990.1	1,372.7	2.5%	China (18.0%)	China (21.3%)
Malaysia	223.2	352.3	5.1%	Singapore (13.6%)	China (15.1%)
North Korea	–	–	–	China (67.2%)*	China (61.6%)*
Pakistan	24.3	43.5	1.1%	U.S. (13.3%)	China (19.8%)
Russia	246.2	620.2	10.7%	Netherlands (14.4%)	China (15.5%)
South Korea	419.9	1,011.0	8.2%	China (24.4%)*	China (16.5%)*
Thailand	190.4	344.2	11.4%	China (11.7%)	Japan (20.0%)
United States	2,826.1	3,961.8	5.6%	Canada (18.9%)	China (19.0%)
Vietnam	32.9	117.3	7.4%	U.S. (17.0%)	China (27.2%)

SOURCE: World Bank, "World Development Indicators," 1990–2013; and CIA, *The World Factbook*, 2013.
NOTE: A dash indicates that no data is available. An asterisk indicates that data is from 2011.

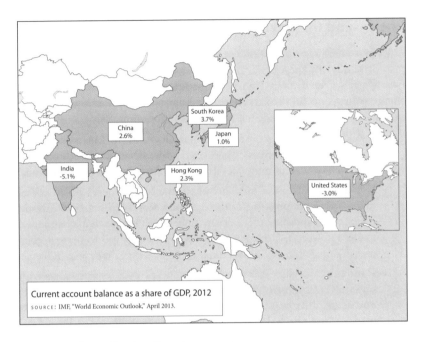

Current account balance as a share of GDP, 2012

SOURCE: IMF, "World Economic Outlook," April 2013.

TABLE 6   Flow of foreign direct investment

	FDI inflows ($bn)			FDI outflows ($bn)		
	2000–2010 annual avg.	2012	2011–12 growth (%)	2000–2010 annual avg.	2012	2011–12 growth (%)
Australia	23.2	57.0	-12.8%	13.0	16.1	13.0%
China	72.8	121.1	-2.3%	23.6	84.2	12.8%
Hong Kong	45.6	74.6	-22.4%	47.2	84.0	-12.4%
India	16.5	25.5	-29.4%	8.7	8.6	-31.1%
Indonesia	3.8	19.9	3.2%	2.3	5.4	-29.7%
Iran	2.3	4.9	17.3%	0.2	0.4	19.4%
Japan	8.4	1.7	198.6%	53.7	122.6	13.9%
Kazakhstan	6.5	14.0	0.9%	1.3	1.6	-65.8%
Malaysia	4.6	10.1	-17.4%	5.8	17.1	12.2%
Pakistan	2.3	0.8	-36.2%	0.1	0.1	17.7%
Russia	25.9	51.4	-6.7%	25.2	51.1	-23.6%
South Korea	7.5	9.9	-3.3%	11.5	33.0	13.7%
Thailand	6.7	8.6	10.6%	1.6	11.9	45.0%
United States	177.2	167.6	-26.1%	212.6	328.9	-17.1%
Vietnam	3.9	8.4	12.6%	0.4	1.2	26.3%
World	1,179.5	1,350.9	-18.2%	1,186.1	1,391.0	-17.1%

SOURCE: United Nations Conference on Trade and Development (UNCTAD), *World Investment Report*, 2004, 2005, 2007, and 2013.

Energy and the Environment

Asia's energy consumption continues to grow, with experts estimating that demand will increase annually by 2.7% on average over the next two decades. The United States, meanwhile, is reducing its reliance on energy sources outside North America. Asian nations that have free trade agreements with the United States could begin to import U.S. LNG by 2016.

- As gas, oil, and coal consumption has grown to fuel Asia's expanding economies, carbon emissions are on the rise, which could heighten the political impetus for multilateral cooperation to combat climate change.

- Nuclear power figures prominently in the future energy portfolios of many Asian nations, most notably South Korea, China, and Taiwan. Even Japan, despite the March 2011 disaster, has not abandoned nuclear power. In 2013, Prime Minister Abe pledged to reopen idled plants and signed nuclear technology deals with France and India.

- A majority of Asian states still struggle to provide their citizens with safe water, a problem that contributes to malnutrition and outbreaks of disease. This problem is particularly salient in India, where more than half of households lack access to basic plumbing.

TABLE 7 Primary energy consumption

	Primary energy consumption (million ton oil equivalent)				Rank	
	1990	2000	2012	2011–12 growth (%)	1990	2012
China	664.6	980.3	2,735.2	7.4%	3	1
United States	1,968.4	2,313.7	2,208.8	-2.8%	1	2
Russia	863.8	619.4	694.2	-0.6%	2	3
India	180.7	295.8	563.5	5.1%	5	4
Japan	434.1	518.2	478.2	-0.9%	4	5
South Korea	90	189.4	271.1	1.0%	6	6
Iran	72.9	123.9	234.2	2.9%	8	7
Indonesia	52.4	99.1	159.4	0.2%	9	8
Australia	87.5	107.1	125.7	-0.9%	7	9
Thailand	30.7	63.7	117.6	5.5%	11	10
Taiwan	49.7	87.1	109.4	-0.6%	10	11
Singapore	23.4	37.7	74	-0.2%	13	12
Pakistan	27.8	44.3	69.3	1.4%	12	13
Hong Kong	11.8	16.1	28.1	-2.0%	14	14
World	8,110.1	9,339.2	12,476.6	1.8%	N/A	N/A

SOURCE: BP plc, "BP Statistical Review of World Energy," June 2013, 41.

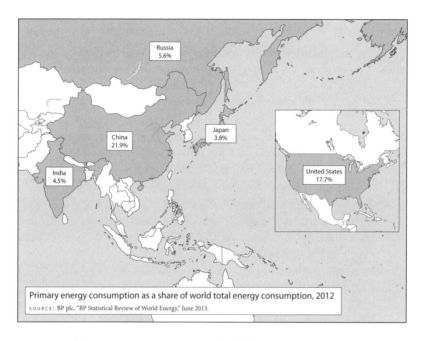

Primary energy consumption as a share of world total energy consumption, 2012
SOURCE: BP plc, "BP Statistical Review of World Energy," June 2013.

TABLE 8   Primary energy consumption by fuel type

	2012 energy consumption by fuel type (%)					
	Oil	Gas	Coal	Nuclear	Hydro	Renewables
China	17.7%	4.7%	68.5%	0.8%	7.1%	1.2%
Hong Kong	3.2%	0.4%	1.3%	–	–	1.9%
India	30.5%	8.7%	52.9%	1.3%	4.6%	1.9%
Indonesia	44.9%	20.2%	31.6%	–	1.8%	1.4%
Iran	38.3%	60.0%	0.4%	0.1%	1.2%	<
Japan	45.6%	22.0%	26.0%	0.9%	3.8%	1.7%
Kazakhstan	22.0%	14.6%	60.2%	–	3.1%	–
Malaysia	39.1%	39.3%	18.7%	–	2.4%	–
Pakistan	28.9%	53.8%	6.2%	1.9%	9.2%	<
Philippines	43.0%	10.3%	31.1%	–	8.3%	7.6%
Russia	21.2%	54.0%	13.5%	5.8%	5.4%	0.0%
Singapore	89.5%	10.1%	–	–	–	0.4%
South Korea	40.1%	16.6%	30.2%	12.5%	0.3%	0.3%
Taiwan	38.6%	13.4%	37.6%	8.3%	1.1%	1.0%
Thailand	44.6%	39.2%	13.6%	–	1.7%	1.0%
United States	37.1%	29.6%	19.8%	8.3%	2.9%	2.3%
Vietnam	31.9%	16.3%	28.7%	–	22.9%	<

SOURCE: BP plc, "BP Statistical Review of World Energy," June, 2013.
NOTE: Due to rounding, some totals may not add up to exactly 100%. Dash indicates that no data is available. Angle bracket indicates that value is less than 0.05%.

Security Challenges

Asia's nominal defense expenditures rose from $268.4 billion in 2011 to $287.4 billion in 2012, exceeding European defense spending for the second consecutive year. IHS Jane's anticipates that Asia's combined defense expenditures will outpace U.S. defense spending by 2021.

- U.S. forces increased cooperation with allies and partners. The Philippines agreed to reopen Subic Bay and Clark Air Force Base to U.S. rotational deployments, while Australia welcomed a second detachment of marines to Darwin. The first forward-deployed littoral combat ship, the USS *Freedom*, arrived in Singapore in April 2013.

- China announced a defense budget of $114 billion for 2013, a 10.7% nominal increase over 2012's figure. The U.S. Department of Defense estimates that China's actual military spending in 2012 was between $135 and $215 billion.

- Sequestration requires the U.S. Department of Defense to reduce FY2013 spending by $41 billion, or 6.5%. Over ten years, sequestration will cut about $500 billion from the defense budget, on top of the scheduled $487 billion in spending cuts over the next decade.

TABLE 9   Armed forces

	Armed forces (th)				Rank	
	1990	2000	2013	2012–13 change (th)	1990	2013
China	3,030	2,470	2,285	2,229	2	1
United States	2,118	1,366	1,520	-765	3	2
India	1,262	1,303	1,325	135	4	3
North Korea	1,111	1,082	1,190	888	5	4
Russia	3,988	1,004	845	322	1	5
South Korea	750	683	655	407	7	6
Pakistan	550	612	642	533	8	7
Iran	504	513	523	117	9	8
Vietnam	1,052	484	482	-677	6	9
Myanmar	230	344	406	-236	14	10
Indonesia	283	297	396	-561	11	11
Thailand	283	301	361	288	11	12
Taiwan	370	370	290	-365	10	13
Japan	249	237	247	-43	13	14
Singapore	55	60	73	-1,253	16	15
Australia	68	50	57	-425	15	16

SOURCE: International Institute of Strategic Studies, *The Military Balance*, various editions.
NOTE: Active duty and military personnel only. Data value for Russia in 1990 includes all territories of the Soviet Union.

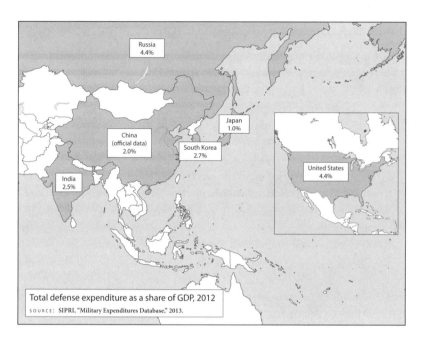

Total defense expenditure as a share of GDP, 2012

SOURCE: SIPRI, "Military Expenditures Database," 2013.

TABLE 10   Total defense expenditures

	Expenditure ($bn)				Rank	
	2000	2011	2012	2011–12 growth (%)	2000	2012
United States	394.2	711.4	668.8	-6.0%	1	1
China (official)	37.0	91.5	106.0	11.2%	3	2
China (DoD estimate)	–	120–80	135–215	12.9%–19.4%	–	2
Russia	32.5	78.3	90.6	15.7%	4	3
Japan	60.3	59.6	59.2	-0.6%	2	4
India	27.7	49.6	48.3	-2.8%	5	5
South Korea	20.0	30.9	31.5	1.9%	6	6
Australia	18.0	26.6	25.6	-4.0%	7	7
Taiwan	10.4	10	10.5	5.2%	8	8
Singapore	7.3	9.2	9.2	0.3%	9	9
Indonesia	–	5.7	7.0	23.5%	–	10
Pakistan	4.6	6.5	6.6	1.3%	10	11
Thailand	3.2	5.5	5.3	-3.4%	11	12
Malaysia	2.4	4.8	4.7	-3.0%	12	13
Vietnam	–	2.7	3.4	26.5%	–	14
Philippines	2.2	2.7	2.8	4.2%	13	15

SOURCE: Stockholm International Peace Research Institute (SIPRI), "Military Expenditures Database," and Office of the Secretary of Defense (OSD), *Annual Report to Congress: Military and Security Developments Involving the People's Republic of China*, various editions.

NOTE: Dash indicates that no data is available.

Nuclear Arms and Nonproliferation

In a June 2013 speech, President Obama reiterated his commitment to a nuclear-free future. However, Russia, China, India, Pakistan, and North Korea are all expanding or modernizing their nuclear capabilities.

- North Korea conducted its third nuclear weapons test in February 2013. The device's yield was estimated to be 6–7 kilotons—roughly twice that of its last tested device in 2009.

- According to the International Atomic Energy Agency, although Iran has boosted its uranium-production capabilities, it has not yet crossed Israeli prime minister Benjamin Netanyahu's 2012 "red line."

- In April 2013, within five days of each other, India and Pakistan successfully tested intermediate-range ballistic missiles capable of carrying nuclear or conventional warheads.

- Russia's first new Borei-class ballistic missile submarine (SSBN), the *Yury Dolgoruky*, was commissioned in January 2013. Russia intends to field ten Borei-class SSBNs by 2020, each capable of carrying sixteen to twenty nuclear missiles.

FIGURE 1   Nuclear warhead stockpiles by country and year

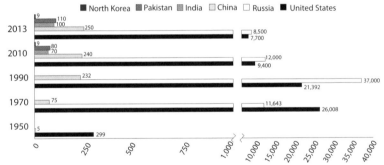

SOURCE: Robert S. Norris and Hans M. Kristensen, "Global Nuclear Weapons Inventories, 1945–2010," *Bulletin of the Atomic Scientists* 66, no. 4 (2010): 77–83; and Federation of American Scientists, "Status of World Nuclear Forces," 2013.

FIGURE 2   Nuclear weapons–capable platforms and delivery systems by country

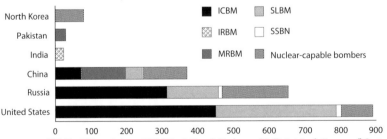

SOURCE: IISS, *The Military Balance*, 2013; "North Korea's Nuclear and Ballistic Missile Programs," Center for Arms Control and Non-Proliferation, July 2013; and OSD, *Annual Report to Congress* (2012).

NOTE: North Korea has working MRBMs but has not created a nuclear device capable of missile delivery. China's SLBMs are not thought to be operational. India and Pakistan are both testing IRBM-range missiles. All the countries in Figure 2 except India possess nuclear-capable cruise missiles.

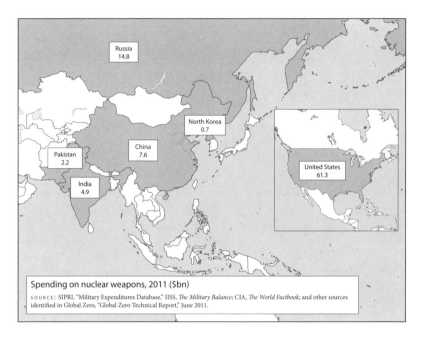

Spending on nuclear weapons, 2011 ($bn)

SOURCE: SIPRI, "Military Expenditures Database," IISS, *The Military Balance*; CIA, *The World Factbook*; and other sources identified in Global Zero, "Global Zero Technical Report," June 2011.

TABLE 11 Nonproliferation treaties

	NPT	Additional Protocol	CTBT	CWC	BTWC
Russia	Ratified	In force	Ratified	Ratified	Ratified
United States	Ratified	In force	Signatory	Ratified	Ratified
China	Acceded	In force	Signatory	Ratified	Acceded
India	–	Signatory	–	Ratified	Ratified
Pakistan	–	–	–	Ratified	Ratified
North Korea	Withdrew	–	–	–	Acceded

SOURCE: International Atomic Energy Agency; United Nations Office of Disarmament Affairs; Preparatory Commission for the Comprehensive Nuclear-Test-Ban Treaty Organization; and Organisation for the Prohibition of Chemical Weapons.

NOTE: NPT = Nuclear Non-Proliferation Treaty. Additional Protocol = IAEA Additional Protocol. CTBT = Comprehensive Nuclear-Test-Ban Treaty. CWC = Chemical Weapons Convention. BTWC = Biological and Toxic Weapons Convention. Dash indicates nonparticipation.

TABLE 12 WMD-export control regimes

	Nuclear Suppliers Group	Australia Group	Wassenaar Arrangement	Zangger Committee	MTCR
United States	Member	Member	Member	Member	Member
Russia	Member	–	Member	Member	Member
China	Member	–	–	Member	–
India	–	–	–	–	–
Pakistan	–	–	–	–	–
North Korea	–	–	–	–	–

SOURCE: Nuclear Threat Initiative; and Monterey Institute of International Studies.
NOTE: Dash indicates nonparticipation.

About the Contributors

Linton Brooks is an independent consultant on national security issues, a Senior Adviser at the Center for Strategic and International Studies (CSIS), a Distinguished Research Fellow at the National Defense University, a member of the National Academy of Sciences Committee on International Security and Arms Control, and an adviser to six of the U.S. Department of Energy's national laboratories. Ambassador Brooks has over five decades of experience in national security, much of it associated with nuclear weapons. He served from July 2002 to January 2007 as Administrator of the Department of Energy's National Nuclear Security Administration, where he was responsible for the U.S. nuclear weapons program and for international nuclear nonproliferation programs. His government career also includes service as Deputy Administrator for Nuclear Nonproliferation at the National Nuclear Security Administration, Assistant Director of the U.S. Arms Control and Disarmament Agency, chief U.S. negotiator for the Strategic Arms Reduction Treaty, and Director of Defense Programs and Arms Control on the National Security Council staff, as well as a number of assignments for the U.S. Navy and Defense Department as a 30-year career naval officer. Ambassador Brooks holds degrees in physics from Duke University and in government and politics from the University of Maryland and is a distinguished graduate of the U.S. Naval War College.

Christopher Clary is a PhD candidate in the Department of Political Science at the Massachusetts Institute of Technology and a Stanton Nuclear Security Predoctoral Fellow at the RAND Corporation in Washington, D.C. He was a Council on Foreign Relations International Affairs Fellow in India (2009), a country director for South Asian affairs in the Office of the Secretary of Defense (2006–9), a research associate at the Naval Postgraduate School (2003–5), and a research assistant at the Henry L. Stimson Center (2001–3). He regularly writes and speaks on South Asian security matters, and his work has appeared in *Survival, American Interest, Disarmament Diplomacy,* and *Disarmament Forum,* as well as several edited book volumes.

Abraham M. Denmark is Vice President for Political and Security Affairs at The National Bureau of Asian Research (NBR). Mr. Denmark has significant experience both inside and outside government. He previously worked as a Fellow at the Center for a New American Security and served in the Pentagon as Country Director for China Affairs in the Office of the Secretary of Defense. Mr. Denmark also is a Senior Advisor at the Center for Naval Analyses and serves on the Advisory Council of the Emerging Science and Technology Policy Centre. He is a member of the National Committee on United States–China Relations, the U.S. Naval Institute, and the International Institute for Strategic Studies, and was named a 21st Century Leader by the National Committee on American Foreign Policy. Mr. Denmark is widely published, having authored several book chapters and reports on U.S. strategy toward the Asia-Pacific region and the global commons. He has been featured in major media outlets in the United States and Asia, including the *Financial Times, Foreign Policy*, the *Global Times*, the *New York Times, Newsweek, Time*, and the *Washington Quarterly*. He holds an MA in International Security from the Josef Korbel School of International Studies at the University of Denver and a BA in History with Honors from the University of Northern Colorado, and studied at China's Foreign Affairs University and Peking University.

Richard J. Ellings is President and Co-founder of The National Bureau of Asian Research (NBR). Prior to serving with NBR, from 1986 to 1989 he was Assistant Director and on the faculty of the Jackson School of International Studies of the University of Washington, where he received the Distinguished Teaching Award. He served as Legislative Assistant in the U.S. Senate, office of Senator Slade Gorton, in 1984 and 1985. Dr. Ellings is the author of *Embargoes and World Power: Lessons from American Foreign Policy* (1985); co-author of *Private Property and National Security* (1991); co-editor (with Aaron Friedberg) of *Strategic Asia 2003–04: Fragility and Crisis* (2003), *Strategic Asia 2002–03: Asian Aftershocks* (2002), and *Strategic Asia 2001–02: Power and Purpose* (2001); co-editor of *Korea's Future and the Great Powers* (with Nicholas Eberstadt, 2001) and *Southeast Asian Security in the New Millennium* (with Sheldon Simon, 1996); founding editor of the *NBR Analysis* publication series; and co-chairman of the *Asia Policy* editorial board. He also established the Strategic Asia Program and AccessAsia, the national clearinghouse that tracks specialists and their research on Asia. Dr. Ellings earned his BA in Political Science from the University of California–Berkeley and his MA and PhD in Political Science from the University of Washington.

Gaurav Kampani is a Transatlantic Postdoctoral Fellow for International Relations and Security (2013–15) at the Norwegian Institute of Defence Studies in Oslo, the Center for Security Studies in Zurich, and the RAND Corporation in Washington, D.C. His research interests cover international security and focus on the relationship between domestic institutions and strategic policy, military strategy, operations planning, and weapons development. Dr. Kampani's dissertation project studied the lag in Indian nuclear decision-making from the 1980s until the present and examined how secrecy induced by the nonproliferation regime shapes proliferating states' learning practices. Between 1998 and 2005, Dr. Kampani was a Senior Research Associate at the James Martin Center for Nonproliferation Studies (CNS) at the Monterey Institute of International Studies. During 2010–11, he was a Stanton Nuclear Security Fellow at Stanford University's Center for International Security and Cooperation. He holds a PhD in International Relations from Cornell University.

Jacob W. Kipp is an Adjunct Professor at the University of Kansas and a columnist on Eurasian security for the Jamestown Foundation. From 1971 to 1985, he taught Russian and military history at Kansas State University. In 1986, he joined the newly founded Soviet Army Studies Office (SASO) at Ft. Leavenworth, Kansas, as a Senior Analyst. SASO later became the Foreign Military Studies Office (FMSO) in 1991, and Dr. Kipp became director of FMSO in 2003. He served in that capacity until October 2006, when he joined the School of Advanced Military Studies as Deputy Director. Dr. Kipp has published extensively on Russian and Soviet naval and military history. Topics have included Russian naval reform in the nineteenth century, Soviet naval history and analysis, operational art in theory and practice, and foresight and forecasting in Russian and Soviet military affairs. He has also written on Russian military doctrine, Sino-Russian relations, and the role of Russia's non-strategic nuclear forces. In addition, from 1992 to 2001, Dr. Kipp served as the U.S. editor of *European Security*. He received his PhD in Russian History from the Pennsylvania State University.

Jeffrey Lewis is an Adjunct Professor and the Director of the East Asia Nonproliferation Program at the James Martin Center for Nonproliferation Studies (CNS) at the Monterey Institute of International Studies. Before joining CNS, he was the Director of the Nuclear Strategy and Nonproliferation Initiative at the New America Foundation. Prior to that, Dr. Lewis was Executive Director of the Project on Managing the Atom at the Harvard Kennedy School's Belfer Center for Science and International Affairs, Executive Director of the Association of Professional

Schools of International Affairs, a Visiting Fellow at the Center for Strategic and International Studies, and a desk officer in the Office of the Undersecretary of Defense for Policy. He is also a Research Scholar at the Center for International and Security Studies at the University of Maryland's School of Public Policy (CISSM). Dr. Lewis is the author of *The Minimum Means of Reprisal: China's Search for Security in the Nuclear Age* (2007) and publishes ArmsControlWonk.com, the leading blog on disarmament, arms control, and nonproliferation. He received his PhD in Policy Studies (International Security and Economic Policy) from the University of Maryland and his BA in Philosophy and Political Science from Augustana College in Rock Island, Illinois.

John S. Park is an Associate with the Project on Managing the Atom at the Harvard Kennedy School's Belfer Center for Science and International Affairs. He was the 2012–13 Stanton Nuclear Security Junior Faculty Fellow at the Massachusetts Institute of Technology. His current research focuses on the North Korean regime's accumulated learning in evading counterproliferation-focused targeted sanctions. During 2007–12, he directed Track 1.5 projects involving Northeast Asia at the U.S. Institute of Peace (USIP). He advises officials focused on Northeast Asia at the U.S. Departments of Defense, State, and the Treasury; the National Security Council; and on Congressional committees. Dr. Park previously worked at Goldman Sachs, where he specialized in U.S. military privatization financing projects. His publications include "The Leap in North Korea's Ballistic Missile Program: The Iran Factor" (2012); "Assessing the Role of Security Assurances in Dealing with North Korea," in *Security Assurances and Nuclear Nonproliferation* (2012); "North Korea, Inc.: Gaining Insights into North Korean Regime Stability from Recent Commercial Activities" (2009); and "North Korea's Nuclear Policy Behavior: Deterrence and Leverage," in *The Long Shadow: Nuclear Weapons and Security in 21st Century Asia* (2008). Dr. Park received his MPhil and PhD from Cambridge University and completed his pre-doctoral and post-doctoral training at Harvard Kennedy School's Belfer Center.

Mira Rapp-Hooper is a PhD candidate in Political Science at Columbia University and 2013–14 Stanton Nuclear Security Fellow at the Council on Foreign Relations. She has worked on extended deterrence issues for the RAND Corporation. Ms. Rapp-Hooper's dissertation, entitled "Absolute Alliances: Signaling Security Guarantees in International Politics," analyzes the formation and management of nuclear security guarantees, with a particular focus on intra-alliance dynamics and allied assurance.

Her research interests include nuclear policy and strategy, nuclear nonproliferation, alliance politics, security in East Asia, U.S. foreign policy, and modern diplomatic history. Ms. Rapp-Hooper holds a BA in History from Stanford, an MA in Politics from New York University, and an MA and MPhil from Columbia University.

Robert Reardon is a Research Fellow with the Project on Managing the Atom and the International Security Program at the Harvard Kennedy School's Belfer Center for Science and International Affairs. He is an expert on nuclear security and nonproliferation policy and on the security and safety of dual-use technologies. Dr. Reardon was a Stanton Nuclear Security Fellow at the RAND Corporation, where he researched nuclear terrorism and developed U.S. strategies toward potential nuclear adversaries. His recent publications include *Containing Iran: Strategies for Addressing the Iranian Nuclear Challenge* (2012). Dr. Reardon holds a PhD in political science from the Massachusetts Institute of Technology.

Richard J. Samuels is Ford International Professor of Political Science and Director of the Center for International Studies at the Massachusetts Institute of Technology (MIT). He is also the Founding Director of the MIT Japan Program. In 2005, he was elected a member of the American Academy of Arts and Sciences. Dr. Samuels has served as Head of the MIT Department of Political Science, Vice Chairman of the Committee on Japan of the National Research Council, and Chairman of the Japan-U.S. Friendship Commission. He has spent more than a decade doing field research in Japan and Europe and is one of only three scholars (Japanese or foreign) to have produced more than one scholarly monograph recognized by the Nippon Foundation as among the top "one hundred books for understanding contemporary Japan." His most recent book is *3.11: Disaster and Change in Japan* (2013). His essays have appeared in *Foreign Affairs*, the *Washington Quarterly*, *Daedalus*, the *National Interest*, and other policy journals. Dr. Samuels received his PhD in political science from MIT.

James L. Schoff is a Senior Associate in the Asia Program at the Carnegie Endowment for International Peace. His research focuses on U.S.-Japan relations and regional engagement, Japanese politics, and regional security. He previously served as Senior Adviser for East Asia Policy at the U.S. Office of the Secretary of Defense and as Director of Asia-Pacific Studies at the Institute for Foreign Policy Analysis (IFPA). At the Department of Defense, Mr. Schoff was responsible for strategic planning and policy development for relations with Japan and the Republic of Korea. He also spearheaded bilateral deterrence dialogues and cooperation on regional security issues, including missile defense, disaster relief, and maritime security. From 2003 to 2010, Mr. Schoff directed Asia-Pacific Studies at IFPA in Cambridge, Massachusetts, where he specialized in security and deterrence issues in Northeast Asia, U.S. alliance relations, and nonproliferation measures focused on North Korea. Prior to joining IFPA, he served as a program officer in charge of policy studies at the United States–Japan Foundation in New York. Mr. Schoff's publications include a chapter on Japan in *Strategy in the Second Nuclear Age; Power, Ambition, and the Ultimate Weapon* (2012) and the report "Realigning Priorities: The U.S.-Japan Alliance & the Future of Extended Deterrence" (2009). He received an MA in International Relations from the Paul H. Nitze School of Advanced International Studies at Johns Hopkins University.

Travis Tanner is Senior Vice President and Chief Operating Officer of the 100,000 Strong Foundation, which is an independent, nonprofit organization born out of a presidential initiative to strengthen U.S.-China relations by expanding and diversifying the number of Americans studying Mandarin and studying abroad in China. Mr. Tanner previously served as Senior Project Director and Director of the Pyle Center for Northeast Asian Studies at The National Bureau for Asian Research (NBR). He is co-editor of *Strategic Asia 2012–13: China's Military Challenge, Strategic Asia 2011–12: Asia Responds to Its Rising Powers—China and India, Strategic Asia 2010–11: Asia's Rising Power and America's Continued Purpose*, and *Strategic Asia 2009–10: Economic Meltdown and Geopolitical Stability*. Prior to joining NBR, he was Deputy Director and Assistant Director of the Chinese Studies Program at the Nixon Center. He also worked as a Research Assistant at the Peterson Institute for International Economics in Washington, D.C. Mr. Tanner graduated from both the Paul H. Nitze School of Advanced International Studies at Johns Hopkins University and the Hopkins-Nanjing Center in Nanjing, China, where he earned an MA in International Relations. He received his BA from the University of Utah in Chinese Language and Literature.

Ashley J. Tellis is a Senior Associate at the Carnegie Endowment for International Peace, specializing in international security, defense, and Asian strategic issues. He is also Research Director of the Strategic Asia Program at The National Bureau of Asian Research (NBR) and co-editor of ten volumes in the annual series. While on assignment to the U.S. Department of State as Senior Adviser to the Undersecretary of State for Political Affairs (2005–8), Dr. Tellis was intimately involved in negotiating the civil nuclear agreement with India. Previously, he was commissioned into the Foreign Service and served as Senior Adviser to the Ambassador at the U.S. embassy in New Delhi. He also served on the National Security Council staff as Special Assistant to the President and Senior Director for Strategic Planning and Southwest Asia. Prior to his government service, Dr. Tellis was a Senior Policy Analyst at the RAND Corporation and Professor of Policy Analysis at the RAND Graduate School. He is the author of *India's Emerging Nuclear Posture* (2001) and co-author of *Interpreting China's Grand Strategy: Past, Present, and Future* (2000). His academic publications have also appeared in many edited volumes and journals. Dr. Tellis holds a PhD in Political Science from the University of Chicago.

About Strategic Asia

The **Strategic Asia Program** at The National Bureau of Asian Research (NBR) is a major ongoing research initiative that draws together top Asia studies specialists and international relations experts to assess the changing strategic environment in the Asia-Pacific. The program transcends traditional estimates of military balance by incorporating economic, political, and demographic data and by focusing on the strategies and perceptions that drive policy in the region. The program's integrated set of products and activities includes:

- an annual edited volume written by leading specialists
- an executive brief tailored for public- and private-sector decision-makers and strategic planners
- briefings and presentations for government, business, and academe that are designed to foster in-depth discussions revolving around major public-policy issues

Special briefings are held for key committees of Congress and the executive branch, other government agencies, and the intelligence community. The principal audiences for the program's research findings are the U.S. policymaking and research communities, the media, the business community, and academe.

To order a book, please visit the Strategic Asia website at http://www.nbr.org/strategicasia.

Previous Strategic Asia Volumes

Over the past thirteen years this series has addressed how Asia is increasingly functioning as a zone of strategic interaction and contending with an uncertain balance of power.

Strategic Asia 2001–02: Power and Purpose established a baseline assessment for understanding the strategies and interactions of the major states within the region.

Strategic Asia 2002–03: Asian Aftershocks drew upon this baseline to analyze changes in these states' grand strategies and relationships in the aftermath of the September 11 terrorist attacks.

Strategic Asia 2003–04: Fragility and Crisis examined the fragile balance of power in Asia, drawing out the key domestic political and economic trends in Asian states supporting or undermining this tenuous equilibrium.

Strategic Asia 2004–05: Confronting Terrorism in the Pursuit of Power explored the effect of the U.S.-led war on terrorism on the strategic transformations underway in Asia.

Strategic Asia 2005–06: Military Modernization in an Era of Uncertainty appraised the progress of Asian military modernization programs.

Strategic Asia 2006–07: Trade, Interdependence, and Security addressed how changing trade relationships affect the balance of power and security in the region.

Strategic Asia 2007–08: Domestic Political Change and Grand Strategy examined internal and external drivers of grand strategy on Asian foreign policymaking.

Strategic Asia 2008–09: Challenges and Choices examined the impact of geopolitical developments on Asia's transformation over the previous eight years and assessed the major strategic choices on Asia facing the new U.S. president.

Strategic Asia 2009–10: Economic Meltdown and Geopolitical Stability analyzed the impact of the global economic crisis on key Asian states and explored the strategic implications for the United States.

Strategic Asia 2010–11: Asia's Rising Power and America's Continued Purpose provided a continent-wide net assessment of the core trends and issues affecting the region by examining Asia's performance in nine key functional areas.

Strategic Asia 2011–12: Asia Responds to Its Rising Powers—China and India explored how key Asian states and regions have responded to the rise of China and India, drawing implications for U.S. interests and leadership in the Asia-Pacific.

Strategic Asia 2012–13: China's Military Challenge assessed China's growing military capabilities and explored their impact on the Asia-Pacific region.

Research and Management Team

The Strategic Asia research team consists of leading international relations and security specialists from universities and research institutions across the United States and around the world. A new research team is selected each year. The research team for 2013 is led by Ashley J. Tellis (Carnegie Endowment for International Peace). Aaron Friedberg (Princeton University, and Strategic Asia's founding research director) and Richard Ellings (The National Bureau of Asian Research, and Strategic Asia's founding program director) continue to serve as senior advisers.

The Strategic Asia Program has historically depended on a diverse base of funding from foundations, government, and corporations, supplemented by income from publication sales. Major support for the program in 2013 comes from the Lynde and Harry Bradley Foundation. In addition, the John D. and Catherine T. MacArthur Foundation provided support for several chapters in this year's volume.

Attribution

Readers of *Strategic Asia* and visitors to the Strategic Asia website may use data, charts, graphs, and quotes from these sources without requesting permission from NBR on the condition that they cite NBR and the appropriate primary source in any published work. No report, chapter, separate study, extensive text, or any other substantial part of the Strategic Asia Program's products may be reproduced without the written permission of NBR. To request permission, please write to:

NBR Publications
The National Bureau of Asian Research
1414 NE 42nd Street, Suite 300
Seattle, Washington 98105
publications@nbr.org

Index